Islamic Studies in European Higher Education

ISLAMIC STUDIES IN EUROPEAN HIGHER EDUCATION

Navigating Academic and Confessional Approaches

Edited by Jørgen S. Nielsen and Stephen H. Jones

EDINBURGH
University Press

Edinburgh University Press is one of the leading university presses in the UK. We publish academic books and journals in our selected subject areas across the humanities and social sciences, combining cutting-edge scholarship with high editorial and production values to produce academic works of lasting importance. For more information visit our website: edinburghuniversitypress.com

© editorial matter and organisation Jørgen S. Nielsen and Stephen H. Jones, 2023, 2024
© the chapters their several authors, 2023, 2024

Edinburgh University Press Ltd
13 Infirmary Street,
Edinburgh, EH1 1LT

First published in hardback by Edinburgh University Press 2023

Typeset in GoudyStd by Cheshire Typesetting Ltd, Cuddington, Cheshire

A CIP record for this book is available from the British Library

ISBN 978 1 3995 1085 1 (hardback)
ISBN 978 1 3995 1086 8 (paperback)
ISBN 978 1 3995 1087 5 (webready PDF)
ISBN 978 1 3995 1088 2 (epub)

The right of Jørgen S. Nielsen and Stephen H. Jones to be identified as editors of this work has been asserted in accordance with the Copyright, Designs and Patents Act 1988 and the Copyright and Related Rights Regulations 2003 (SI No. 2498).

Contents

Notes on the Contributors   vii
Preface   xii

1. Introduction: Incorporating Islam in European Higher Education   1
   Stephen H. Jones

2. Islamic Studies in University and Seminary: Contest or
   Constructive Mutuality?   14
   Jørgen S. Nielsen

3. (Re)habilitating the Insider: Negotiations of Epistemic Legitimacy
   in Islamic Theology and Newer Social Justice Mobilisation   32
   Birgitte Schepelern Johansen

4. What do the Terms 'Confessional' and 'Non-confessional' Mean,
   and are they Helpful? Some Social Scientific Musings   53
   Sophie Gilliat-Ray

5. A Decade of Islamic Theological Studies at German Universities:
   Expectations, Outcomes and Future Perspectives   69
   Bekim Agai and Jan Felix Engelhardt

6. Islamic Theology in a Muslim-minority Environment:
   Distinctions of Religion within a New Academic Discipline   92
   Lena Dreier

Contents

7. The *Taalib* as a Bricoleur: Transitioning from *Madrasah* to University in Modern Britain — 110
   Haroon Sidat

8. Why would Muslims Study Theology to Obtain an Academic Qualification? — 129
   Mohammad Mesbahi

9. Navigating alongside the Limits of Mutual Interdependence: Flemish Islamic Religious Education — 151
   Naïma Lafrarchi

10. The Need for Teaching against Islamophobia in a Culturally Homogeneous Context: The Case of Poland — 178
    Anna Piela, Katarzyna Górak-Sosnowska and Beata Abdallah-Krzepkowska

11. Theology Faculties in Turkey: Between State, Religion and Politics — 202
    Abdurrahman Hendek

12. Closing Reflections: Going Beyond Secular–Religious and Confessional–Academic Dichotomies in European Islamic Studies — 223
    Sariya Cheruvallil-Contractor

Index — 237

Notes on the Contributors

Beata Abdallah-Krzepkowska has an MA in Arabic Philology (Jagiellonian University, Kraków) and a PhD in linguistics (Silesian University). She is an Assistant Professor at Silesian University, and publishes widely on the topic of Qur'anic semantics, for example most recently she published a chapter on the Qur'anic concept of soul in the book *The Soul in the Axiosphere from an Intercultural Perspective* (2020). Her research interests focus on the language of the Qur'an, contemporary Islam and Islam in Europe. She participates in public education in relation to Islam and Arabic in Poland in her role as a research consultant for the Nahda Foundation, which promotes cultural collaboration between Poland and Arab countries.

Bekim Agai is director of the Academy for Islam in Research and Society. He studied Islamic studies, History and Psychology at the University of Bonn and completed his PhD at Bochum University. From 2010 to 2013, he headed the junior research group 'Europe as seen from the outside: Formations of Middle Eastern views on Europe from within Europe'. Since 2013, he has been Professor for Culture and Society of Islam. His research focuses on the history of ideas in the nineteenth century and constructions of identity and alterity with regard to Muslims in Europe.

Sariya Cheruvallil-Contractor is Associate Professor and Research Group Lead for Faith and Peaceful Relations at the Centre for Trust, Peace and Social Relations, Coventry University. She is Chair (2020–23) of the Muslims in Britain Research Network (MBRN) and is Series Editor of the *Review of Social and Scientific Study of Religion*. Her research emphasises collaborative methodologies that work with and for research participants. As a feminist sociologist of religion, she has a keen interest and appreciation of the power dynamics within knowledge production and the implications of the processes and systems of knowledge on society as a whole. Her portfolio of research aims to hear lesser-heard sections in society, including British Muslim communities, religious women and vulnerable children. She is the author of several books and numerous research articles, her most recent being *Islam on Campus: Contested Identities and the Cultures of Higher Education* (2020).

Lena Dreier is a PhD candidate at the Institute for the Study of Culture, Leipzig University, Germany, with a Fellowship granted by the Friedrich Ebert Stiftung. She is an associate member of the Centre for Advanced Studies in the Humanities and Social Sciences 'Multiple Secularities – Beyond the West, Beyond Modernities'. Her research focuses on the sociology of knowledge and religion, and qualitative research methods. Her dissertation deals with the construction of Islamic plurality in Islamic theology in Germany.

Jan Felix Engelhardt studied Islamic and Middle Eastern studies at the universities of Bonn, Istanbul and Leiden. In his PhD thesis at the university of Frankfurt, Germany, he analysed the establishment of Islamic Theological studies at German universities vis-à-vis academic, religious and political expectations. Until 2021 he was managing director of the Academy for Islam in Research and Society (AIWG) at the University of Frankfurt. His research interests include the academisation of Islamic knowledge in Western Europe and North America, transdisciplinary modes of theological knowledge production and the relation between theology, state and society.

Sophie Gilliat-Ray is Professor of Religious Studies at Cardiff University, and the Founding Director of the Islam-UK Centre. She has a longstanding interest in the sociology of religious professionals such as chaplains, imams and muftis, as well as the institutions associated with their training. She is the author of numerous books and journal articles on the subject of Islam and Muslims in Britain and has formerly served as the Chair of the Muslims in Britain Research Network. She is currently the Chair of the British Sociological Association Study Group for 'Religion'. In 2020 she was elected as a Fellow of the Learned Society of Wales.

Katarzyna Górak-Sosnowska is an Associate Professor and head of the Middle East and Central Asia Unit, SGH Warsaw School of Economics. She has a PhD in economics (SGH) and Habilitation in the study of religions (Jagiellonian University, Cracow). Her research focuses on Muslim communities in Poland

and Europe. She has published five monographs including *Deconstructing Islamophobia in Poland* (2014) and edited a book on *Muslims in Poland and Eastern Europe: Widening the European Discourse on Islam* (2011). Currently, she is leading two projects 'Managing spoiled identity: the case of Polish female converts to Islam' (funded by the National Science Centre, 2018–22) and 'EMPATHY: Let's Empower, Participate and Teach Each Other to Hype Empathy. Challenging Discourse about Islam and Muslims in Poland' (funded by the European Commission: Directorate General for Justice and Consumers, 2022–3).

Abdurrahman Hendek completed his PhD at the University of Oxford. His academic interests include religious education policy, home schooling, hifz and comparative religious education. He currently works as an Assistant Professor of Religious Education at the Faculty of Theology, Sakarya University, Sakarya, Turkey.

Birgitte Schepelern Johansen is Associate Professor at the Minority Studies Section, Faculty of Humanities, University of Copenhagen. She holds a PhD in the Sociology of Religion, and her research has mainly focused on the place and role of religion in secular societies, especially in the context of higher education, Muslim minorities in Europe as an object of governance, and the connections between secularity, politics and emotions. Among her publications are *Hate, Politics, Law* (co-edited with Thomas Brudholm, 2018); *Secular Bodies, Affect and Emotion: European Configurations* (co-edited with Monique Scheer and Nadia Fadil, 2019); and 'Secular Excitement and Academic Practice' in Christian von Scheve et al. (eds), *Affect and Emotion in Multi-Religious Secular Societies* (2019).

Stephen H. Jones is a sociologist of religion whose main areas of expertise are in Islam and Muslims in the United Kingdom, and religious and non-religious publics' perceptions of science. He is a lecturer in the Department of Theology and Religion, University of Birmingham, and author of *Islam and the Liberal State* (2021). He is presently Principal Investigator of a research project, 'Science and the Transmission of Islamic Knowledge in Britain', which examines views of Islam and science among students and teachers in Islamic educational institutions.

Naïma Lafrarchi is PhD researcher at the Department of History, Ghent University (Flanders/Belgium). Currently, she conducts research on didactics and pedagogy regarding controversial, sensitive issues and citizenship education in Flemish secondary education. Previously, she did research regarding Islamic religious education (IRE) in secondary education and IRE teacher training at the Department Conflict and Development Studies (MENARG, University of Ghent). She is a former lecturer in the Master's programme in Islamic Theology and Religious Studies at the Faculty of Theology and Religious Science of the Catholic University of Leuven. Her publications cover topics such as Islamic pedagogy and education, IRE teacher training and curriculum development, and currently controversial and sensitive topics and citizenship education. Her first book *Does Religion Make a Difference?* was launched in 2017 in the presence of the Minister of Education, Hilde Crevits, as well as national and international experts.

Mohammad Mesbahi's focus is Islamic education in the West, and its complexities have recently been central to his work. He is known for the development of several Islamic theology-related undergraduate and postgraduate degrees and diplomas within mainstream education through collaborative schemes. His most recent conference presentation was delivered at the World Muslim Communities' Council, titled 'Muslim Migration to Europe and the Challenges of Diversity and Education', and his most recent publication, 'The Role of Supplementary Schools Education in Shaping the Islamic Identity of Muslim Youths in Europe', appears in Ismail Hussein Amzat (ed.), *Supporting Modern Teaching in Islamic Schools* (2022).

Jørgen S. Nielsen is Emeritus Professor of Contemporary European Islam, University of Birmingham, and Affiliate Professor of Islamic Studies at the University of Copenhagen. He studied Arabic and Middle East studies at SOAS, London, and did his PhD in Arab history at the American University of Beirut. Since 1978, he has researched Islam in Europe at Selly Oak Colleges and the University of Birmingham. He was director of the Danish Institute in Damascus 2005–7 and then spent six years as Danish National Research Foundation professor at the Faculty of Theology, Copenhagen University. He is the author of *Muslims in Western Europe* (Edinburgh University Press, 1st edn 1993, 4th edn with Jonas Otterbeck 2016) and is involved in editing several book series as well as the *Journal of Muslims in Europe*.

Anna Piela is a visiting scholar at the Department of Religious Studies, Northwestern University, Evanston, Illinois. She has a PhD in Women's and Islamic studies (York, UK). Her monograph, titled *Muslim Women Online: Faith and Identity in Virtual World* (2011), focused on religious authority of Muslim women fostered in various online communities. Her second monograph is titled *Wearing the Niqab: Fashioning Identity among Muslim Women in the UK and the US* (2021). She has published articles in the *Journal of the American Academy of*

CONTRIBUTORS

Religion, New Media and Society and *Feminist Media Studies*. She is a member of the steering committee of the Islam, Gender and Women unit at the American Academy of Religion. Currently she is working on an American Academy of Religion-sponsored project exploring intersections of whiteness and Islam in Eastern Europe (2022–3).

Haroon Sidat is currently a Research Associate at the Centre for the Study of Islam at Cardiff University. He completed a PhD looking at the formation and training of British Muslim scholarship (*ulama*) with an ethnographic study of a *dar al-ulum*, or traditional Islamic seminary in modern Britain in 2019. He has a degree in Economics and Master's in education. He has authored an article 'Abode as Theological and Moral, and Territory as Legal: Competing Spaces of Religious Belonging: Deobandi Debates on Interest/Usury as Case Study', which is due to be published in summer 2022. Currently, he is working on an innovative and ground-breaking project looking at the lived experiences of imams in Britain. Haroon serves as an imam, and is the treasurer for British Association for Islamic Studies (BRAIS) alongside being a trustee for the Cambridge Muslim College (CMC).

Preface

The research that has been brought together in this volume was intended to be presented at the 4th Birmingham Spring Islam Conference in April 2020. Individually, we have both had a longstanding interest in the ways European Islamic studies is being reformed in response to demographic changes in European states, concerns over security and integration, higher education policy reforms, and social and political conflict over university curricula. We wanted to bring together experts from across Europe with the aim of creating a volume that can provide insight into the extent of these changes across Europe and the varied ways states have responded to a broadly similar set of issues.

In the event, this conference had to be held virtually due to the lockdowns brought about by the outbreak of the Covid-19 pandemic earlier in the year. This meant, of course, that it was not possible to have the in-depth discussions of the draft papers which can normally take place face to face. However, meeting on Zoom meant that we could have participants from further afield who would not have been able to take part in a conventional event – meaning that this collection has a wider range of contributions. Despite the unfavourable circumstances we held some good critical evaluations of the draft papers on Zoom in a meeting spread over two days. Responses to those discussions and further written comments from participants led to the present volume.

We are grateful to Emma House and Isobel Birks at Edinburgh University Press and to the two anonymous reviewers whose comments were very helpful to us in producing the final versions of the papers. We also want to thank colleagues at the Muslims in Britain Research Network for supporting and promoting the conference. We owe a particular debt of gratitude to Dr Sariya

Preface

Cheruvallil-Contractor for agreeing to provide a concluding chapter reflecting on the contents of the volume.

July 2022

Stephen H. Jones and Jørgen S. Nielsen
University of Birmingham

CHAPTER I

Introduction: Incorporating Islam in European Higher Education

STEPHEN H. JONES

MUSLIMS AND HIGHER EDUCATION IN EUROPE

Surveying the vast body of scholarship on Muslims in Europe published over the last two decades, a small group of interrelated questions reappears again and again. What steps, if any, should states take to incorporate Muslim minorities into European societies and public institutions (Vertovec 1996; Koenig 2007; Modood 2009)? How do such steps, when made in response to the emergence of public Muslim identities, challenge existing settlements between religious organisations and the state (Joppke 2000; Cesari and McLoughlin 2005; Meer 2010)? Who speaks for Muslim communities and for the Islamic tradition in Europe (Jones et al. 2015)? As a European Muslim presence becomes increasingly established across the continent, what forms of Islamic knowledge are being produced and popularised (Bruinessen and Allievi 2007)? Do European states need new centres of Islamic authority to address the distinctive challenges that European Muslims face and to counterbalance the influence of overseas patronage (Lewis 2007)? What space is there, if any, in centres of Islamic authority for the voices of Muslim women, and how should the availability of this space influence the way the state engages with Islamic institutions (Brown 2006; Scott-Baumann and Cheruvallil-Contractor, 2015; Rashid 2016)? How should European states address the challenge of Islamist extremism, and how have policies designed to prevent extremism impacted on social integration, public institutions and Muslim communities (Cesari 2009; Sunier 2014; O'Toole et al. 2016)? Have such policies contributed to Islamophobia in Europe, and how have Muslims resisted this and other forms of Islamophobia (Brown 2010; Pantazis and Pemberton 2013)? How has this resistance connected with other anti-racist and de- or post-colonial writers and movements (Sayyid and Vakil 2010; Rizvi 2020)?

There is, I want to suggest, no institutional setting that brings all these questions together in quite the way that Islamic studies in European higher education does. For this reason, discussion of contemporary Islamic studies in European states is of far greater significance than the modest numbers of students taking the subject might initially suggest. In a number of countries across Europe, governments have taken steps to expand and formalise Islamic studies at higher level, with these steps ranging from the full creation of Islamic theological faculties (Agai and Engelhardt, Chapter 5, this volume) to the facilitation of links between universities and private Islamic seminaries (Geaves 2012; Scott-Baumann and Cheruvallil-Contractor 2015; Nielsen, Chapter 2, this volume). Many governments have stressed the need to develop centres of Islamic knowledge production that can meet employment needs in sectors such as school-level religious education and chaplaincy. Often, they have pointed to the importance of fostering 'home-grown' (and implicitly, 'moderate') Muslim identities and sources of Islamic authority. Most controversially, almost all have, in one way or another, responded to the perceived threat of 'radicalisation', with many reforms to Islamic studies provision being implemented as a direct result of new counter-terrorism policies (Jones 2021; Lafrarchi, Chapter 9, this volume). These novel forms of state intervention have raised profound questions about the role the state plays in producing Islamic knowledge; and these questions have been debated with ferocity because of the apparent incursion of the logics of risk and control into an institutional setting that, in theory at least, is organised around the ideals of free enquiry and the pursuit of knowledge for its own sake.

These profound changes have, moreover, arrived in a sector that already features longstanding tensions over the proper place of confessional approaches in the study of theology and religion and the persistence of Orientalist and Islamophobic stereotypes in Islamic studies. As Jørgen S. Nielsen explains in Chapter 2 of this volume, Islamic studies in European universities – or at least, Western European universities – emerged out of the textual study of Arabic and the anthropological study of the Muslim world, with the field growing against a backdrop of imperial expansion. From the 1970s on, however, such 'traditional' approaches to Islamic studies were challenged on two fronts described in Chapter 3 (this volume) by Birgitte Schepelern Johansen. On the one side, Muslim settlement in Western European states and the subsequent founding of European Islamic institutions made traditional models of Islamic studies appear increasingly antiquated. Christian theologians have long maintained a space in universities to raise questions about religious truth and practice, and their Muslim counterparts rightly objected that the same space was not available to them (Siddiqui 2007; Mukadam and Scott-Baumann 2010). On the other side, Islamic studies found itself in the sights of social justice mobilisations, most notably post- and de-colonial movements whose spokespersons have – again, often with good reason – pointed to the biases of Islamic studies courses and the absence of ethnic and religious minority scholars. The coexistence of these varied perspectives has meant that very different worldviews and norms regularly collide with one another. For example, secular universities and Islamic educational institutions linked together by European states may follow sharply contrasting gender norms. Similarly, social justice movements and policymakers working in counter-extremism have both advocated for the increased presence of Muslim women in European universities, but they have done so for very different – indeed, incompatible – reasons (Rashid 2016).

Borders and Boundaries in European Islamic Studies

The purpose of this book is, first, to profile how these developments have played out in different European states and, secondly, to examine the impact they are having upon operational and epistemic distinctions utilised in religious studies – notably between 'confessional' and 'non-confessional', or between faith-based and secular teaching. What we seek to provide across the course of the volume is an overview of the varied ways in which the sometimes settled boundaries between religious and secular have been disturbed by innovations in the study of Islam – innovations which may have come about through bottom-up collaborations between universities and seminaries, the top-down creation of new qualifications, or counter-terror agencies intervening in courses and staff accreditation processes. These changes, we propose, necessitate a creative re-thinking of what the purpose and value of higher education is, and also raise broader questions about religion–state relations in contemporary European societies. To facilitate this creative re-thinking, the volume includes not only contributions from a range of national contexts but from varied author perspectives: some contributors are located in the social sciences, others in Islamic studies and still others (such as Chapters 7 and 8) draw from their experiences of straddling the boundary between seminary and university as students or teachers.

Conceptual and Social Changes

The collection begins by doing some groundwork to outline the history of the discipline and explain the origins – and limitations – of the concepts commonly used to separate out different types of enquiry in the field of Islamic studies. It starts with an overview, by Nielsen, of the history of, and recent changes to, Islamic studies in Europe. Concentrating mainly on the UK context, but with reference to Sweden, Belgium, Denmark and other states, Nielsen shows that a pattern has emerged across much of Europe, with states taking an interest in imam training and Muslim organisations becoming active stakeholders in higher education. In addition to drawing attention to what is at stake, socially and politically, in the recent reforming of Islamic studies, he examines how new innovations in the field raise profound questions about educational norms and standards – notably in relation to complex cases, such as when a student's research leads him or her to heterodox conclusions about the status of religious texts. Nielsen reminds us of the complexity and challenges of reforming the study of Islam by showing how certain types of student can suffer when academic boundaries are drawn in different ways.

The next two contributions then focus, in different ways, on the interaction between conceptual and social change. In Chapter 3, Schepelern Johansen examines the tensions between the three traditions of thought that currently influence, or aspire to influence, the norms governing European Islamic studies: the first rooted in naturalist universalism; the second in Islamic scripture and tradition; and the third in epistemic particularism. Each of these, she observes, mark the boundaries between 'insider' and 'outsider' in different ways. The first, which came to dominate European universities over the late nineteenth and twentieth centuries, sees authoritative knowledge as secular (and 'objective'), in contrast to a religious 'outsider'. The second, which seeks space on university campuses in response to demands from various government and civil society actors, is at least partially reliant on authoritative interpretations of religious texts, with the primary legitimating division in this case being between Muslim and non-Muslim. The third, which has gained prominence on university campuses since the late twentieth century, sees identity, knowledge production and social domination as inextricably bound up with one another, and marks its division not between secular and religious but between oppressor and oppressed. Tracing the influence of these traditions upon European Islamic studies, Schepelern Johansen focuses how the different forms of 'boundary work' (Gieryn 1983) undertaken by these competing intellectual communities together contribute to the reproduction of Islamic studies in Europe.

Without denying these points of epistemic and political tension, Sophie Gilliat-Ray, in Chapter 4, paints the same changes in a more hopeful light. She focuses her attention on the changes that have been engendered across Islamic studies by the settlement and institutional establishment of Muslim communities in Western Europe, and what these reveal about the (in)stability of the division between confessional and non-confessional teaching of religion. The term 'confessional', of course, emerged out of a Christian context, describing Christian communal organising and placing emphasis on credal statements of belief. Gilliat-Ray argues that the split between confessional and non-confessional has been complicated initially by Christian theological colleges working in collaborative partnership with university departments of theology and religious studies, and then, more recently, by collaborations (discussed further in Chapter 7) between secular universities and private Islamic seminaries in Britain. Close analysis of these instances of university–seminary collaboration, she suggests, reveal that the two methods of teaching can reflect back on one another in productive ways, despite their different starting points and epistemological assumptions. Looking at university–seminary collaboration, she concludes, offers hope for more imaginative varieties of intellectual inquiry.

Responses in Different European Nation-States

Chapters 5–11 allow the volume to compare and contrast how Islamic studies has been reformed in different European nation-states. Of course, across Europe there are significant historical, demographic and policy variations that mean the questions with which I opened this chapter do not apply equally across all contexts. (It makes little sense to talk, for example, about the 'recent settlement' of Muslims in Turkey, a country Abdurrahman Hendek covers in Chapter 11.) Nevertheless, what is striking, and what these seven chapters make clear, is how many different states across Europe are grappling with similar questions. Parallel state interventions in the field of Islamic studies can be found in the United Kingdom, Belgium and Germany; even in France, a state that is famously reluctant to recognise religious (especially Muslim) identity, the government has provided funding for one-year civic education programmes aimed primarily at imams (Zwilling 2021: 266; for analysis of the French state's engagement with Muslims, see Modood 2012). Across Europe there is hardly any country – from Catholic-dominated Poland to Muslim-majority Turkey – where *none* of this introduction's opening questions are relevant. Yet one can also see subtle and sometimes stark policy variations as one moves from one national context to the next. These variations, we want to suggest, allow one to helpfully unpick apparently binary distinctions between religion and state, confessional and non-confessional, and 'insiders' and 'outsiders'.

We begin, in Chapters 5 and 6, with the country where state intervention in Islamic studies has been arguably the most direct and far-reaching: Germany. Like many European countries, the German state has long actively supported higher-level Christian theological education, both Lutheran and Catholic (Carr 2007). It has also tended to take a 'top-down' approach to integration of its predominantly Turkish-origin Muslim minority (Casanova 2009). In keeping with these tendencies, in 2010 the German state founded a group of Islamic theological faculties, a development that responded, as in other countries covered in this volume, to a combination of population changes and security anxieties.

In Chapter 5, Bekim Agai and Jan Felix Engelhardt describe the context for the introduction of the new faculties and provide illustrations of how the incorporation of Islamic theological faculties in Germany unsettled established traditions and distinctions, both academic and religious. To take one striking example of this, they highlight how the founding of theological faculties in Germany involved the state, in effect, validating independent Islamic organisations, with such organisations being linked to universities and provided with ultimately state-backed authorisation to issue traditional teaching qualifications (*ijazah*) to professors. At the same time, this incorporation of Islam had the effect of transforming traditional Islamic processes of religious authorisation, with *ijazah* being altered from a teacher-to-student permission to an *institutional* accreditation. As Lena Dreier highlights in Chapter 6, these German theological faculties are popular – there were approximately 2,200 students at such institutions in 2019 – but they have reformed the nature of Islamic knowledge production, with a clearer distinction emerging between, in Dreier's terms, 'religion' as an external object of study and an Islamic theology student's own personal sense of 'religiosity'.

Chapters 7 and 8 all focus on the case of the United Kingdom, but here the contributions start not with public policy interventions, but the landscape of Islamic 'seminary' education. The United Kingdom has hosted Islamic seminaries – referred to variously as *hawzas*, *jamias* or *dar al-ulums*, depending on denomination – since the early 1970s, with the sector proliferating from the 1980s onwards. These institutions have their roots in educational traditions developed in south Asia and, to a lesser extent, the Middle East, with some originally taking shape against a backdrop of the consolidating British empire. The question of how qualifications earned within such institutions can be utilised in the United Kingdom has been asked with increasing urgency in recent years by students (who seek useful qualifications), teachers (who want to recruit new students) and the British state (which regards the integration of the sector as vital to counter-radicalisation efforts). In contrast to Germany, in the United Kingdom government interventions have tended to take the form of below-the-radar support to create what Sariya Cheruvallil-Contractor and Alison Scott-Baumann (2014) call 'bridges' and 'permeable membranes' between private seminaries and the publicly funded universities, notably via accreditation agreements between Islamic seminaries and secular institutions.

Bridging these religious and secular 'worlds' entails various challenges. These are vividly illustrated in Chapter 7 by Haroon Sidat, who shows from his own personal experience how the dominant Deobandi *dar al-ulums* emphasise personal nurturing of the religious 'seeker' (*taalib*), in marked contrast to British religious studies departments where, much like the German theological faculties, 'religion' and 'religiosity' are increasingly distinct. This, combined with differences in gender norms – Deobandi *dar al-ulums* are single sex, and women's provision is limited – has led to wariness on both sides of the divide and made linking private Islamic educational centres and universities a protracted process over many years. There are, however, signs of recent progress, with willingness being visible among government and university representatives and, as Sidat points out, signs emerging within seminary contexts of a new 'epistemic openness' (see also Gilliat-Ray 2018; Jones 2021). This is visible in British Shia contexts too, the focus of Mohammad Mesbahi in Chapter 8. British Shia institutions, although less numerous in Britain than their Sunni Deobandi counterparts, have had more success in linking with UK universities, and in his chapter Mesbahi explores how 'faith-based' and secular courses have operated together, with students mixing *hawza* accreditation with externally validated non-religious qualifications.

Importantly, such developments have started to challenge and reform the nature of Islamic studies in the UK as a whole. The landscape of Islamic seminary study has altered, with, for exaample, Muslim women's scholarship being more widely recognised. With training at women's Islamic schools and colleges becoming more limited, Muslim women's theological education was previously concentrated in informal study circles (*halaqahs*). In recent years, however, women-led campaigns have increased opportunities for women's Islamic education, extending to the creation of institutions such as the Women's Muslim College, founded in 2017 (Scott-Baumann and Cheruvallil-Contractor 2015; Jones 2021: 62). At the same time, the study of Islam in UK universities has changed, with the establishment of collaborative networks such as the British Association of Islamic Studies, which was set up via a combination of top-down and bottom-up pressure. The blurring of faith-based and secular education has begun to reorient university Islamic studies, with Muslims themselves, the erstwhile 'subjects' of Islamic studies, gradually becoming 'interlocutors' (Ebbiary 2021).

Chapters 9, 10 and 11 deal with three very different country contexts: Belgium, Poland and Turkey, respectively. These chapters illustrate very clearly both the promise and perils of enhancing the study of Islam within university contexts. Even despite the vastly different demographic and political settings represented, we can still see striking parallels between the country case studies. Chapter 9, by Naïma Lafrarchi, provides the volume's clearest account of how security and counter-terrorism policies have impacted on the sphere of Islamic studies. In Germany, the United Kingdom and, indeed, across almost all of Europe, the integration of Islamic studies has in large part been driven by the overarching goal of limiting 'radicalisation' in Muslim communities, but Larfrarchi's chapter goes furthest in showing the extent to which counter-terror policies (or in the Belgian context, 'Action Plans Radicalisation') have generated profound constitutional tensions and concerns about state interference in religious organisations. In common with many European states, the Belgian constitution was built on the principle of separation of church and state, but combined this with a strong system of state support for religious organisations. The state's recent support for Islamic education is in keeping with these overarching principles. As part of its drive to counter 'radicalisation', however, the Belgian federal and Flemish regional governments have ventured deeper and deeper into religious terrain. State bodies have empowered Muslim organisations, such as the Executive of Muslims of Belgium (EMB), to take a direct role in reform of Islamic studies, but the state, in turn, has taken a more overt role in influencing Muslim religious organisation, with, *inter alia*, the EMB being screened by the State Security Service. Counter-terror-driven Islamic education policies threaten, then, to unsettle centuries-old constitutional norms, with the religion–state divide being remade on the basis of a stereotyped understanding of 'Muslim radicalism'.

In Poland, as Anna Piela, Katarzyna Górak-Sosnowska and Beata Abdallah-Krzepkowska clearly show in Chapter 10, stereotypes about Islam are well-established too. Poland is an ethnically and culturally homogeneous society with a right-wing government and growing far-right movements. The Roman Catholic Church is *the* dominant religious institution, and religious instruction in schools is accordingly almost exclusively concerned with Catholic religious formation. Standing out in the countries covered in this volume, Polish higher education retains very little space for the discussion of Islam. Piela and her colleagues show, through a review of a dissertation database, that Polish higher education's inclusion of Islam is piecemeal, usually forming part of the study of society, politics and inter-community relations. Often, it is viewed through stereotypical lenses, with most dissertations looking into Islam as part of a broader enquiry into terrorism, women's oppression and the 'clash of civilisations'. The sharp rightward shift in Polish politics makes altering these norms a challenging task, but nevertheless the authors do point to some instances, and future possibilities, of using Islamic studies to counter Islamophobia, highlighting the potential function of higher education as a space to challenge prejudices.

The final country discussed in this collection is Turkey. Turkey has clear demographic differences from the other contexts included in this volume, as the only Muslim-majority state. Nevertheless, its history and recent political changes have raised parallel questions about the place of confessional and non-confessional teaching of religion. The Turkish republic abolished Islamic secondary and higher educational institutions in 1924, establishing Western-style theology faculties (*ilahiyat fakültesi*) in their place. Some of the older *madrasas* (*medrese* in Turkish) survived in unrecognised and unregulated form, but more recently, with the recent Islamisation of Turkish politics and society ushered in by President Erdoğan, there has been an opening of theology faculties to *madrasa* students through distance learning undergraduate programmes. As Hendek shows in Chapter 11, this has unsettled a previously clear divide, with questions of form and function arising that are not too distant from those asked, for different reasons, in Western European contexts. Much as in the UK case, there is uncertainty about what the relationship between the independent religious organisations and the theological faculties should be, and anxieties about the 'confessionalisation' of the more mainstream religious education institutions.

The Purpose of Islamic Higher Education: Competing or Collaborative Visions?

Looking across these various accounts of the reform of Islamic higher education in Europe, what is striking is the sheer range of views about what the study of Islam is *for*. In the chapters that follow, at different points one can see Islamic studies justified with reference to the state's 'soft power', national and civic coherence, security and wellbeing, vocational and institutional need, economic growth and personal moral reform. This is a long list even without mentioning the most prominent, and idealistic, reasons for making space in higher education institutions for the study of Islam – for instance, to increase the humanistic understanding of other worldviews or to ask penetrating questions about the nature of God. These last two, of course, are centuries old, but others have emerged only in the last two decades. Indeed, part of the reason the boundaries between religion and state, confessional and non-confessional, and 'insider' and 'outsider' have been jostled and reconfigured in recent years is that old visions of the function of higher education, while still widely discussed, have been joined by many new ones.

Yet despite the public presence of these new and competing arguments in favour of the higher study of Islam, it is worth mentioning that, even in countries where the discipline is comparatively well-established, its future is not always secure. In many European states, governments have found new arguments in favour of Islamic studies as old imperial justifications for the study of Islam and the Muslim world have waned, most of these being oriented around national security and integration. This, as we have already seen, has been accompanied by material support in many cases. One of the problems with this support, however, is that in many countries it stands in tension with the general thrust of higher education policies. An increasingly influential technocratic understanding of higher education – one that sees university degrees as a means of training productive, high-earning members of society and generating economic growth – has devalued the humanities, as has the rise of national populist governments in Europe and elsewhere (Graham 2005; Universities UK, 2017). We have already seen how scholars of Islam have argued for institutional space alongside their Christian and Jewish counterparts, but this is a much harder argument to make when – as is the case in the United Kingdom, to take just one example – a market-mimicking model of higher education has forced a sharp decline in student interest in theology and religious studies degrees (British Academy, 2019).

Islamic studies is in the paradoxical position of being, on the one hand, viewed by a range of actors as crucial to the realisation of important social goals but, on the other hand, placed in terrain that is frequently treacherous to navigate. When set against this backdrop, the range of competing arguments in favour of the study of Islam might be looked at not as a problem to be resolved, with one vision of Islamic studies being named victor over the others, but potentially as a productive interaction. Part of the reason for saying this is that, in practice, Islamic studies in Europe has been enhanced by separate agencies that have found a common cause despite maintaining incompatible visions of the discipline. There has been, at least at certain points, genuine synergy in European states between students of Islamic studies, universities, seminaries, Muslim civic organisations and governments, despite these different actors having very different reasons for wanting to build flourishing, well-connected centres of Islamic higher learning. When there is so little space in higher education institutions for the study of religion, maintaining a coalition of this kind is likely to be necessary for any reform or expansion of the discipline to happen.

Alongside this, however, there is also something to be said in favour of competition between these different views of why Islamic studies matters. Any student of the history of higher education in Europe will know that universities have *usually* been sites of fiercely competing educational visions, some religious and others secular (Rüegg 2004; Jacobsen and Jacobsen 2008). Indeed, some of the most important developments in the intellectual and religious life of higher education institutions have come *through* these points of tension. The growth of Muslim populations and Islamic institutions across Europe have created certain social tensions against the backdrop of a, for the most part, secularising context where higher education is increasingly dominated by an economistic justifications. Certainly, these tensions can be uncomfortable at times, especially because – as Sariya Cheruvallil-Contractor makes clear in her concluding discussion in Chapter 12 – they involve power dynamics that devalue scholars on the basis of their religious, ethnic and gender identity. But, as both Gilliat-Ray and Cheruvallil-Contractor hint, they could ultimately be productive, reshaping the sector and raising vital questions about the inclusiveness of higher education, the range of worldviews that are seriously considered within it, and, most fundamentally, the health of existing settlements between religious and secular domains. And these, as I observed at the start of this introduction, are not just questions that matter for higher education: higher education is merely the setting where they appear most vividly.

Introduction

References

British Academy, The (2019). *Theology and Religious Studies provision in UK Higher Education*, May. London: British Academy, available at: https://www.thebritishacademy.ac.uk/publications/theology-religious-studies-provision-uk-higher-education, last accessed 10 January 2020.

Brown, K. (2006). 'Realising Muslim Women's Rights: The Role of Islamic Identity among British Muslim Women', *Women's Studies International Forum* 29(4): 417–30. DOI: 10.1016/j.wsif.2006.05.002.

Brown, K. E. (2010). 'Contesting the Securitization of British Muslims', *Interventions* 12(2): 171–82.

Bruinessen, M. V. and S. Allievi (eds) (2007). *Producing Islamic Knowledge: Transmission and Dissemination in Western Europe*. London: Routledge.

Carr, D. (2007). 'Religious Education, Religious Literacy and Common Schooling: Philosophy and History of Skewed Reflection', *Journal of Philosophy of Education* 41(4): 659–73.

Casanova, J. (2009). 'Immigration and the New Religious Pluralism: A European Union–United States Comparison', in G. Brahm Levey and T. Modood (eds), *Secularism, Religion and Multicultural Citizenship*. Cambridge: Cambridge University Press, pp. 139–63.

Cesari, J. (2009). *The Securitisation of Islam in Europe*, 15, Research Paper. CEPS CHALLENGE Programme, EU Sixth Framework.

Cesari J. and S. McLoughlin (eds) (2005). *European Muslims and the Secular State*. Aldershot: Ashgate.

Cheruvallil-Contractor, S. and A. Scott-Baumann (2014). *Collaborative Partnerships between Universities and Muslim Institutions: Dismantling the Roadblocks*. Derby: University of Derby, available at: http://www.derby.ac.uk/media/derbyacuk/contentassets/documents/ehs/schoolofeducation/centreofsocietyreligionandbelief/Research-report.pdf, last accessed 4 September 2014.

Ebbiary, A. (2021). 'From Subjects to Interlocutors: Muslims in the Margins and the Academy', presented at Religious Diversity and the Secular University, Cambridge, 8 July.

Geaves, R. (2012). *An Exploration of the Viability of Partnership between Dar al-Ulum and Higher Education Institutions in North West England focusing upon Pedagogy and Relevance*, 30 July. Edinburgh: HEA, available at: https://www.heacademy.ac.uk/sites/default/files/geaves_daralulums_final_report_isn.pdf, last accessed 13 May 2016.

Gieryn, T. F. (1983). 'Boundary-Work and the Demarcation of Science from Non-Science: Strains and Interests in Professional Ideologies of Scientists', *American Sociological Review* 48(6): 781–95. DOI: 10.2307/2095325.

Gilliat-Ray, S. (2018). 'From "Closed Worlds" to "Open Doors": (Now) Accessing Deobandi darul uloom in Britain', *Fieldwork in Religion* 13(2): 127–50. DOI: doi.org/10.1558/firn.35029.

Graham, G. (2005). *The Institution of Intellectual Values: Realism and Idealism in Higher Education*. Exeter: Imprint Academic.

Jacobsen, D. and R. H. Jacobsen (eds) (2008). *The American University in a Postsecular Age*. Oxford: Oxford University Press.

Jones, S. H. (2021). *Islam and the Liberal State: National Identity and the Future of Muslim Britain*. London: Bloomsbury/I.B. Tauris.

Jones, S. H., T. O'Toole, D. N. DeHanas et al. (2015). 'A "System of Self-appointed Leaders"? Examining Modes of Muslim Representation in Governance in Britain', *British Journal of Politics and International Relations* 17(2): 207–23. DOI: 10.1111/1467-856X.12051.

Joppke, C. (2000). *Immigration and the Nation-State: The United States, Germany, and Great Britain*. New York: Oxford University Press.

Koenig, M. (2007). 'Europeanising the Governance of Religious Diversity: An Institutionalist Account of Muslim Struggles for Public Recognition', *Journal of Ethnic and Migration Studies* 33(6): 911–932. DOI: 10.1080/13691830701432756.

Lewis, P. (2007). *Young, British and Muslim*, annotated edn. London: Continuum.

Meer, N. (2010). *Citizenship, Identity and the Politics of Multiculturalism: The Rise of Muslim Consciousness*. London: Palgrave Macmillan.

Modood, T. (2009). 'The State and Ethno-Religious Mobilization in Britain, in J. L. Hochschild and J. H. Mollenkopf (eds), *Bringing Outsiders In: Transatlantic Perspectives on Immigrant Political Incorporation*. Ithaca, NY: Cornell University Press.

Modood, T. (2012). '2011 Paul Hanly Furfey Lecture: Is there a Crisis of Secularism in Western Europe?' *Sociology of Religion* 73(2): 130–49.

Mukadam, M. and A. Scott-Baumann (2010). *The Training and Development of Muslim Faith Leaders: Current Practice and Future Possibilities*, October. London: DCLG.

O'Toole, T., N. Meer, D. N. DeHanas et al. (2016). 'Governing through Prevent? Regulation and Contested Practice in State–Muslim Engagement', *Sociology* 50(1): 160–77. DOI: 10.1177/0038038514564437.

Pantazis, C. and S. Pemberton (2013). 'Resisting the Advance of the Security State: The Impact of Frameworks of Resistance on the UK's Securitisation Agenda', *International Journal of Law, Crime and Justice* 41(4): 358–74. DOI: doi:10.1016/j.ijlcj.2013.07.009.

Rashid, N. (2016). *Veiled Threats: Producing the Muslim Woman in Public Policy Discourses*. Bristol: Policy Press.

Rizvi, S. (2020). 'Reversing the Gaze? Or Decolonizing the Study of the Qur'an', *Method & Theory in the Study of Religion* 33(2): 122–38. DOI: 10.1163/15700682-12341511.

Rüegg, W. (2004). *A History of the University in Europe, Vol. 3: Universities in the Nineteenth and Early Twentieth Centuries (1800–1945)*. Cambridge: Cambridge University Press.

Sayyid, S. and A. Vakil (eds) (2010). *Thinking Through Islamophobia: Global Perspectives*. London: Hurst.

Scott-Baumann, A. and S. Cheruvallil-Contractor (2015). *Islamic Education in Britain: New Pluralist Paradigms*. London: Bloomsbury.

Siddiqui, A. (2007). *Islam at Universities in England: Meeting the Needs and Investing in the Future*. Leicester: Markfield Institute.

Sunier, T. (2014). 'Domesticating Islam: Exploring Academic Knowledge Production on Islam and Muslims in European Societies', *Ethnic and Racial Studies* 37(6): 1138–155.

Universities UK (2017). *Patterns and Trends 2016*. London: Universities UK, available at: http://public.tableau.com/views/PatternsAndTrends2016/Patterns2016?:embed=y&:showVizHome=no&:host_url=https%3A%2F%2Fpublic.tableau.com%2F&:tabs=yes&:toolbar=yes&:animate_transition=yes&:display_static_image=no&:disp

lay_spinner=yes&:display_overlay=yes&:display_count=yes&:loadOrderID=0, last accessed 28 July 2017.

Vertovec, S. (1996). 'Multiculturalism, Culturalism and Public Incorporation', *Ethnic and Racial Studies* 19(1): 49–69.

Zwilling, A-L. (2021). 'France', in E. Racius, S. Akgönül, A. Alibai et al. (eds), *Yearbook of Muslims in Europe*. Leiden: Brill, pp. 247–71.

CHAPTER 2

Islamic Studies in University and Seminary: Contest or Constructive Mutuality?[1]

JØRGEN S. NIELSEN

INTRODUCTION

Over a decade ago, the German Federal Ministry of Education and Research attracted headline attention when it announced that it was going to spend around €18 million over five years on the establishment of programmes of Islamic theology in five universities. Albrecht Fuess optimistically suggested that:

> The well-funded German institutions will certainly attract international attention and become an important meeting point for Muslim theologians throughout the world. The best educated, most professional and well paid Muslim theologians of Europe, and arguably the world, will come out of the German university system. This will not happen tomorrow as there are still obstacles in the way but in the long run it will be happening. (Fuess 2011).

The academic and research posts being funded in this manner have been filled (see Agai and Engelhardt and Dreier, Chapters 5 and 6, respectively, this volume), but it is still much too early to judge whether Prof. Fuess' dreams are likely to become anything approaching reality.

In this chapter I provide an overview of the development of Islamic studies in Europe till the end of the twentieth century, and then look at recent

---

[1] An earlier version of this chapter appeared as 'Islamic Studies: Scientific or Confessional? A Contested University Subject', in Abu Husayn, Abdul Rahim, Tarif Khalidi and Suleiman A. Mourad (eds), *In the House of Understanding: Histories in Memory of Kamal S. Salibi*. Beirut: American University of Beirut, 2017, pp. 423–46.

developments in the subject in universities and in interaction with Muslim students and organisations. First, I shall briefly indicate some of the heritage of the Islamic studies which have been opened to question in the latter half of the twentieth century. Britain was one of the countries where change first took place, so a closer look at the process in the field over recent decades follows. Given that a major driver of change has been the settlement of Muslim communities, a survey of responses to pressures for training imams and teachers comes next. Finally, I shall sketch some reflections on the implications of all this for Islamic studies as a European university subject.

It makes sense at this stage to briefly sketch where we have come from, in other words, how Islamic studies entered European universities and what it meant in practice. There is an extensive history of European intellectual responses to Islam virtually as old as Islam itself (Daniel 1960; Rodinson 1988; Irwin 2006; Thomas 2009–13). But the first sign of an institutionalisation of the subject can be attributed to the Collège de France where regular teaching of Arabic began in 1587.[2] In 1613 a chair in Arabic was established at Leiden University and soon after similar chairs appeared at Cambridge (1632) and Oxford (1634). At the end of the following century the École des langues orientales vivantes was founded in Paris, with the key figure of Silvestre de Sacy (1758–1838) becoming, in the words of Hourani, 'in some ways the founder of modern Islamic and Arabic studies' (Hourani 1991: 32).

For a long time Islamic studies was more an appendix to Arabic language studies than a subject in its own right, and Arabic language was often a subject supporting the study of Hebrew and thence of the Old Testament. It remained the situation well into the nineteenth century that much of the European research and publication on Islamic matters proper was conducted by travellers, missionaries and diplomats. Taken together, this meant that Islamic studies tended to develop in isolation from the major theoretical and methodological advances which took place especially in linguistics and history through the nineteenth and into the twentieth century. Starting in the late nineteenth century with individuals such as Ignaz Goldziher and Snouck Hourgronje, the realities of the Muslim world and Muslim societies began to impinge on the field, a process that accelerated with the development of social anthropology during the late nineteenth and early twentieth centuries – whose foundations were closely linked to the necessities of imperial administration.

Islamic studies, as an academic field, had traditionally been focused on what could be discovered from texts, which meant subject areas like philosophy, law and other forms of religious thought, literature, history and, to a small extent,

---

[2] The history of university teaching is outlined in Hourani 1991: 7–60. This source is a basic reference for much of the description of older Islamic studies in the present chapter.

the history of science, as well as art, crafts and architecture. In addition the subject had been constricted by the limits on access: not many people in Western academe could read the manuscripts (access to which were often limited in any case), and not very many manuscripts had been edited and only very few translated. The growth of interest in the Muslim world among social scientists tended to remain marginal to Islamic studies in this sense until, in some institutions, well after the Second World War: Islamic studies and the study of the Muslim world only very slowly began to interact.

Edward Said's critique of 'Orientalism' at the end of the 1970s (Said 1978) quickly became the iconic attack on traditional approaches, although they had started before. But his at times well-targeted and at other times rather more diffuse criticism of 'Orientalism' was not alone in motivating the changes we have seen in the last several decades. Other, possibly just as significant, drivers of change have been:

– the growth in the direct involvement – some sceptics might be tempted to say infiltration – of diplomatic and funding interests from the Muslim world, especially by oil-producing states, since the 1970s;
– a continuing movement against eurocentrism in the humanities and social sciences;
– developments in university approaches to teaching in a more participatory direction since the student protests of the late 1960s;
– perhaps most significantly, the settlement of large Muslim communities in Europe (mostly in the west) and the appearance of their children in our lecture theatres;
– and, finally, the sharp growth in security concerns since the 1990s.

As these various dimensions are difficult, if not impossible, to disentangle I shall in the following look at experiences in selected countries.

The Experience of the UK

The United Kingdom has one of the oldest European university traditions of Islamic studies with the establishment of chairs in Arabic at Cambridge and Oxford universities in 1632 and 1634, respectively. The nineteenth century saw a major expansion of interest in the broad field driven by the needs of running an empire with major Muslim subject populations and a related growth in plain curiosity. From the early twentieth century, as university policy became increasingly centrally managed, a number of working groups and commissions considered the role and nature of Islamic studies. In 1909, the Reay Report expressed concern that Britain was falling behind universities in mainland

Europe, with Cambridge and Oxford still being the only providers in England and they focused primarily on classical languages and literature. Reay pointed to the need for the training of people who could work in the Muslim world in a variety of government and private capacities. The foundation of the School of Oriental Studies in London, later to become the School of Oriental and African Studies (SOAS), was one result. Reay was, of course, written in an imperial context, but its major contribution has also been to insert an area studies dimension into Islamic studies pointing towards the involvement of a multitude of disciplines (Hourani 1991; Bernasek n.d.). After the Second World War the interdisciplinary and area studies dimension was strengthened by the 1946 Scarborough Report, which looked beyond empire but still with a focus on training resources for national policy. In the meantime, the War Office and the Foreign Office had in 1944 founded the Middle East Centre for Arab Studies (MECAS) specifically to meet their needs for Arabic speakers (Tempest 2006). Several other universities were now teaching Arabic and other Middle Eastern languages (especially Persian and Turkish) as well as Middle East area studies, most notably Durham, Manchester and Edinburgh (where Arabic had been taught since the late eighteenth century). In 1961, the Hayter Report confirmed the areas studies approach, recommending the establishment of six to eight area studies centres to meet the broader needs of society as a whole, including now explicitly commerce.

With increasingly centralised management of government funding for higher education and research, smaller subjects – smaller in the sense of small numbers of students in any one undergraduate programme – were finding themselves in danger of being squeezed out. There followed a number of enquiries driven by concerns expressed both by industry and commerce and by the Foreign and Commonwealth Office (FCO) that the pool from which they could recruit competent staff was diminishing. The most notable of these enquiries led to the 1986 Parker Report, in reaction to which the then University Grants Committee (UGC) allocated seed-funding for a number of new junior posts in the languages of African and Asia (Latham 1986). Less than two decades later the same problem returned, with the FCO again particularly worried. In the meantime, there had been a rapid growth in the number of postgraduate students from outside Europe entering Middle East and Islamic studies at various British universities while the number of home students was falling, exacerbating the FCO's problem.

By this time the environment had changed, with increases in security concerns relating to Islam starting in the 1990s and made critical by the terrorist attacks in New York in September 2001, in Madrid in March 2003, and in London in July 2005. Renewed British military and political engagement in key parts of the Muslim world had only served to increase the demand for expertise.

Equally important was the growing number of young people of immigrant Muslim background entering universities across the disciplines (McLoughlin 2012). Universities found themselves having to make decisions on practical matters arising from this Muslim recruitment (access to places of worship, how to deal with women's headscarves and face veils, and then political radicalism on some campuses), and those universities which taught Islamic and relevant area studies were faced with challenges to syllabus construction and teaching methods.[3] This came on top of a longer history of recruitment of graduate students from the Muslim world, including many doing various forms of Islamic studies. In 2005–6, there were 281 graduate students in Islamic studies (by a narrow definition which did not include areas studies) in Britain and 188 undergraduates, reflecting a steady rise of over 10 per cent over the previous three years. They were spread over more than a dozen universities (HEFCE 2008: 6–9).

In April 2007, a report on Islam at universities in England was published. It had been requested by the minister for higher education and written by the late Dr Ataullah Siddiqui of the Islamic Foundation near Leicester (Siddiqui 2007). Siddiqui pointed out the disagreements over what constitutes Islamic studies and whether it can even be called a 'discipline'. One of his significant interests was the growing community-based sector of university-level teaching. While a number of independent and privately financed Muslim colleges had come into existence – Siddiqui listed twenty-five, although that may be an underestimate – only few of them had acquired some form of university accreditation – a later report from the Higher Education Funding Council for England listed four (Bernasek and Bunt 2010: 10–11). The report took note of some of the cooperation between universities and local Islamic institutions and the community, as well as of the interest of local young Muslims to study Islam at university, although there was a common wish that the 'theological' aspects of Islam be taught by Muslim scholars.

The very small number of Islamic institutions that had established links with universities, only four or five, illustrated a central challenge in this context to both sectors, the public and the Islamic. Many universities have been reluctant to extend their academic validation to the programmes taught at such colleges, even though many more, including a number of the older universities, have a long tradition of validating the teaching programmes of the numerous and varied church-related seminaries. This reflects in part a lack of confidence in the colleges' ability (or preparedness) to deliver the degree of critical analysis that they identify with a university education. In some cases it probably also reflects

---

[3] When I studied Arabic at SOAS in the late 1960s we were four students in the year. Three decades later there were 50–60 students, a significant proportion of them young people of Muslim background.

a lack of confidence in their own ability to monitor and assess satisfactorily what goes on in these colleges' teaching. But it also reflects a wish on the part of many of the Islamic institutions to remain independent of public university scrutiny. After all, their religious legitimacy and authority rests overwhelmingly in their standing in the communities, which they see themselves as serving – and if they want an enhanced Islamic standing in that environment, they are more likely to get it through an association with a respected Islamic institution such as Al-Azhar in Cairo or, in the case of many of them, from their being part of the Deobandi *dar al-ulum* system. This reluctance to cooperate also reflects the widespread assumption that only Muslim scholars can legitimately teach Islam.

The recommendations of the Siddiqui report (2007: 62–4) covered a range of concerns, some of them to do with the pastoral care of Muslim students at universities. Regarding the way Islamic studies is taught, Siddiqui called for investment in 'the establishment of intensive language courses, research studentships, postgraduate awards, collaboration with universities abroad, and the appointment of suitable qualified staff'. He also looks to the funding of one or more inter-university centres to strengthen the subject. He wanted new courses to be developed 'keeping in mind the religious and specific cultural needs of the [Muslim] community'. Courses should have a greater focus on 'theological and civilizational aspects of Islam', and students 'should be given the opportunity to study under competent scholars of Islam who have been trained via traditional Islamic routes and in subject areas which are of particular relevance to Muslims'. In other words, said Siddiqui, not only should Islamic studies, as traditionally conceived of, be strengthened, especially by encouraging an influx of domestic students, but the subject area should be rebalanced to, in a sense, give equal time (my term) to those aspects of Islam which are a priority for Muslim students.

Less than three months after the publication of the Siddiqui report the government announced, in connection with a lecture in London by Prime Minister Tony Blair commending the Siddiqui report, that it was allocating £1 million to support the development of Islamic studies in Britain.[4] Much of this funding went into supporting existing departments in staff and curriculum development. Separately, some of the research councils combined to establish a Centre for the Advanced Study of the Arab World (CASAW). This investment was boosted a couple of years later, when the Saudi Prince Walid bin Talal decided to support the formation of two new centres in Edinburgh and Cambridge with a particular

---

[4] See at: http://news.bbc.co.uk/2/hi/uk_news/politics/6718235.stm, last accessed 18 January 2013, which includes a link to the full text of the speech. Apparently, the funding announcement came as something of a surprise to a number of the key institutions, in particular the university funding councils, as there was no new money involved and they had to find this sum out of their existing budgets.

focus on contemporary Islam and outreach to the broader community.[5] These centres extended a network of centres previously funded by the prince at Harvard and Georgetown in the United States and at the American universities in Cairo and Beirut. This was a continuation of substantial funding initiatives from the Arab and Muslim world, including to the universities of Durham, Exeter and SOAS, as well as the Oxford Centre for Islamic Studies, independent but with staff relations to various Oxford colleges.

The Training of Imams and Teachers

Siddiqui did briefly touch on the training of Islamic religious scholars, a matter which in the general debate over recent years has tended to be focused on 'imam' training. In some ways this theme has been simmering in various European countries for some decades (Drees and van Koningsveld, 2008: pt 2). In 1993, one well-known British Muslim leader, Muhammad Raza, published a small study in which he bemoaned the low level of qualifications among imams and mosque leaders in Britain and called for the systematic development of training for Muslim community leadership, including the possibility of government support (Raza 1993). In late 2010, a study which had been commissioned by then previous Labour government was published on the training of 'Muslim faith leaders'.[6] In essence, it concluded that much was already going on, and that these various developments should be encouraged and supported.

Public funding for the training of Islamic scholars in Europe had until this point otherwise been focused on the training of schoolteachers of Islamic religious education primarily in Belgium and Austria, where Islam had joined the small list of formally recognised religious communities in 1974 and 1979, respectively (Janssens 2016; Potz 2021). In both countries the recognition entailed the right to publicly funded provision of Islamic religious instruction (RI) for Muslim children and for the training of the necessary teachers.

For various reasons, including especially difficulties involved in persuading the main Moroccan and Turkish Muslim community institutions in Belgium to cooperate, and the regular changes in the Belgian constitution governing the identities and powers of the regions, the process of instituting university-level training of Islamic teachers has progressed only slowly (see Lafrarchi, Chapter 9, this volume). For the first many years after recognition, teachers were authorised by the relevant Islamic authority, but there was no system of quality assurance either in terms of the nature of their Islamic knowledge or of their ability

---

[5] See at: http://www.ed.ac.uk/schools-departments/literatures-languages-cultures/alwaleed and http://www.cis.cam.ac.uk, both last accessed 13 April 2021.
[6] See at: https://www.gov.uk/government/uploads/system/uploads/attachment_data/file/6155/1734121.pdf.

to teach. Only in 2003 did the government education authorities appoint a small team of inspectors to check on the teaching. As in many other European countries, voices were raised in official and media circles after the events of 9/11 demanding government-sponsored imam training, on the unproven assumption that 'home-grown' imams would be a bulwark against the 'radicalisation' of young European Muslims. In 2007, the Université Catholique de Louvain started a programme on Islam with a social science approach aimed at a Belgian market. Two years later, the University of Antwerp started a programme to train teachers of Islam (Manço and Kanmaz 2009: 35–47).

In Austria, the development followed a similar course, although the officially recognised Islamic community organisation kept closer control over the authorisation of teachers and, from 1998/9, the publicly subsidised first-degree programme of its Religious-Pedagogical Academy (IRPA). In 2006, the University of Vienna's Faculty of Philosophy and Educational Sciences started a two-year Master's programme in Islamic religious pedagogy which is intended to become the main teacher qualification for the subject (Aslan and Heinrich 2009).

In May 2008, the Swedish government commissioned a small report on the situation of imams there (SOU 2009). In Sweden, official recognition of religious communities is extended primarily through the financial support administered by the Commission for Government Support to Religious Communities.[7] Part of the enquiry involved a questionnaire sent to 181 representatives of local Muslim organisations which at some time had been in receipt of public funding; there were 121 responses. Of these, only five stated that they had had their training in Sweden. Three had been trained in Germany, three in Britain, four in France, one in Belgium and ten in Bosnia. The rest had their training from Turkey (47), Saudi Arabia (9) and the remainder from fifteen different countries in Africa and Asia. But when they were asked whether they liked the idea of establishing an imam training in Sweden 94 out of 116 were strongly in favour. But what they are looking for in such training, and what the commission has chosen to emphasise, is the need for imams to have a grounding in aspects of Swedish society and public institutions which can enable them to play the role of counsellor and adviser to members of their community, roles which are familiar from the functions of priests and ministers of the churches.

In Denmark, the question of the training of imams has briefly been up for public debate but for a variety of reasons did not progress any further. Over the winter of 2004–5, the University of Copenhagen Research Priority Area 'Religion in the 21st Century' commissioned a study on the training of imams in Europe as part of the preparation for a one-day conference on the subject, which was held in November 2005 (Johansen 2005). By the time the conference

---

[7] See at: www.sst.a.se.

took place the 'cartoons crisis' had started, and the subject had become publicly sensitive. If any of the organisers had hoped that the project might lead to the beginnings of some form of Islamic theological training at the university, it was not only this sensitivity which prevented it, it was also quite fundamental opposition from some academics in the Faculty of Humanities – in Islamic and Middle Eastern studies and in Religious studies. On the one hand, it was said, Theology need not innovate in this field, as Islamic studies was already being taught in Humanities. On the other hand, it was argued, in a secular university, such as Copenhagen, that there could be no room for a confessional academic programme. From the Muslim side, there were occasional arguments that the university should be involved in imam training, just as it was in the training of Lutheran ministers, but more often a reluctance to involve what was ultimately a state institution in internal Muslim matters. The subject reappeared briefly at the sixth annual meeting of Muslim and Christian leaders held in November 2011, where the additional point was made that in a country the size of Denmark there simply was not sufficient demand to sustain an academic programme (Folkekirke og Religionsmøde 2011).

As part of a major project on 'Religious communities, state and society', the Swiss national research council in June 2010 published a report on imam training.[8] This appeared under the shadow of the November 2009 federal referendum which had voted to ban minarets on new mosque construction. A majority of the Muslim officials approached were in favour of publicly supported imam training, primarily because the general experience had been of imams being badly qualified both in terms of religious competence and familiarity with the Swiss institutional and cultural environment.

The experience in the Netherlands has been rather more developed (Boender 2021). Despite the separation of church and state implemented in the 1983 constitution, the government continues to fund the training of clergy at both public and private universities. Following a decision of parliament in the 2003/4 session, it was agreed that such funding should also be available for Islamic theological training. Initially arrangements were made for new programmes and staff appointments at the (Protestant) Free University of Amsterdam, where a Centre for Islamic Theology was established in 2005 in the Faculty of Theology, in the Institute for Religious Studies at Leiden University, and in 2006 at the INHOLLAND University of Applied Sciences in Amsterdam (this is explicitly a teacher training programme) (Ferreiro 2011: 294–8). In 2008, before it really got going, Leiden decided to withdraw from the project in the context of an internal reorganisation with a major Faculty of Humanities, which finally put an end to a centuries-long tradition of teaching theology. But not before two new

---

[8] Website not available.

academic staff in the field of Islamic studies had been appointed. In effect, therefore, the situation today is that the Free University of Amsterdam trains Islamic 'theologians', while the INHOLLAND training teachers for Islamic RI closed in 2013 (Szumigalska 2015: 72–6). Separately, there are two privately funded Islamic universities, both in Rotterdam, one of which, the Islamic University of Rotterdam, has achieved public recognition and a degree of public funding (de Koning 2022: 463).

As indicated at the start of this chapter, probably the most interesting development has been what is going on in Germany. Politically it is remarkable for representing the culmination of a major shift in the attitude of the German state towards the Muslim communities. At the beginning of the 1980s it came to be recognised in some of the states that this situation was increasingly untenable, including in North-Rhine Westphalia where a project for Islamic religious instruction for Turkish children was developed under the heading *religöse Unterweisung* instead of the legal term of *Religionsunterricht*. By the end of the 1990s, the authorities had concluded that there was, in fact, nothing in the legislation which necessarily made Islamic religious instruction conditional on formal recognition (Rosenow-Williams 2011: 104–11). It was only required that a community be recognised under the individual state's laws on education. This took place in a context where the federal republic at long last dropped its insistence that it was not a country of immigration. Various states began to look more creatively at possibilities, including an initiative at the University of Münster, North-Rhine Westphalia, which in 2004 established the first chair in Islamic theology with a view to training teachers in the subject. The subsequent developments are discussed in detail by Agai and Engelhardt, Chapter 5, and Dreier, Chapter 6, this volume.

An indication of how politically sensitive the topic of imam training has been in Europe has been the way in which the media has on several occasions jumped to the conclusion that a new university research initiative on Islam has had the objective of instituting some form of imam training. This was the case when the Dutch Institute for the Study of Islam in the Modern World (ISIM) was established in the late 1990s (it closed in 2009), and it was the case again when the establishment of my own Centre for European Islamic Thought, University of Copenhagen, was announced in early 2007, although in neither case had any involved party made any such suggestion.

More fascinating, however, in the context of the present investigation, is what these developments imply about the changing functions of an imam in the European setting (Hashas, de Ruiter and Vinding 2018). Basically, of course, the imam is the person who leads congregational prayers, and this remains the case. But from an early stage in the immigration and settlement of Muslims in western Europe, we have witnessed growing expectations that an 'imam' should somehow be equivalent to a parish priest or the pastor of a congregation. Such expectations were encouraged by both churches and by local governments seeking some representative interlocutor, as they attempted to engage with local Muslim communities. Occasionally, the expectations were confirmed, as was often the case with Turkish congregations in Germany, Belgium, Austria and the Netherlands, where the Turkish government's official religious institution, the *Diyanet İşleri Başkanlığı* (commonly *Diyanet*), was quick to set root. However, the imams sent by the Diyanet, usually for three-year periods, although religiously qualified had little preparation for functioning in a European setting – that has only come slowly since the 1990s. In other instances, many people playing the role of imams in local mosques had either no or very little preparation beyond what was required to lead prayers and possibly to teach children bits of Qur'anic text in phonetic Arabic. In such situations, it has often been a family or clan leader, or a prominent businessman who has been selected (or self-appointed) to speak for the community – often politically effective but theologically amateur.

This situation has become increasingly unsatisfactory for Muslim congregations themselves. The children and grandchildren of the immigrants are often well-educated, also in Islamic matters, although they are often self-taught. As mosques and community organisations have become established and seek to engage with the social, cultural, political and institutional environments, also at a national level, the need for qualified leadership has become ever more apparent, thus creating a demand, uneven to be sure, for institutions where such leadership can find the necessary qualifications.

The 'Market' Factor

The various European developments sketched above raise a number of questions of an institutional political nature as well as to the concept of Islamic studies as a university-taught subject. One way of approaching this could be in terms of stake holders, namely, those people and institutions which in one way or another have an interest in the development and provision of Islamic studies in the broadest sense.

Funding

Since the nineteenth century, the growing involvement of state-funding in universities has been a major driver in how the subject has developed. First, it was a small esoteric niche subject, in many ways somewhat like a medieval guild with a few senior professors acting as, often, very restrictive gatekeepers, in which theology and the churches had the main interest, even if some of the scholars involved were not necessarily all that sympathetic to the church. From the late eighteenth century and with increasing strength through the nineteenth century, the needs of empire became dominant while remaining in competition with the Enlightenment ideas of a search for 'factual' knowledge. This led to an expansion of the subject area in the direction of social sciences, especially ethnology and anthropology, and more regionally focused work: Britain in south Asia (where interests also included the other south Asian religious cultures), the Netherlands in the East Indies, and France in North Africa. By the middle of the twentieth century, it is increasingly difficult to speak of Islamic studies without also making more than passing reference to the variety of disciplines which were being included in the movement towards area studies. It made more sense to talk of the study of Islam, Muslims and the Muslim world, but language-based focuses – Arabic, Turkish, Persian and Urdu especially – continued with varying fortunes, and especially Middle Eastern studies had acquired a life of its own. Increasingly it is clear that it was governments' perceptions of what was important which determined, primarily through the funding instrument, where the focus of the general area of teaching should be placed and whether parts of the subject, or the subject as a whole, should advance or retrench – and since the 1960s retrenchment has been a prospect more often than advance.

It was in Britain that relevant university departments first almost systematically sought independent funding from the Muslim world to ensure the survival of their interests. This was focused mainly on chairs and research activities, which could be expected to be more attractive to potential funders, but additional academic staff also meant that undergraduate activities could be maintained. This way forward became a serious option only after the jump in oil prices of 1972–4 filled the treasuries of a number of Muslim states and their leading businesses. Private Iraqi funding ensured the continuation of the chair in Islamic Studies at Edinburgh after Prof. W. M. Watt retired in 1979. Subsequently, other universities have found substantial funding sources in Saudi Arabia, Brunei, Shajar, Kuwait and Turkey among others, in some cases from governments, in others from wealthy private individuals. There has been much less such funding activity in mainland Europe: the funding from the Sultanate of Oman for a chair in the study of Islam in the West at Leiden is unusual.

There have been recurring questions about the degree of influence which funders expect over the activities of the recipients. Influence is very difficult to prove, although often one is entitled to assume that at least there is a coincidence of interests when a university department approaches a specific funder for support (only occasionally does the initiative come from the funder). In the early 1980s, there was a common view that a lecturer at one British university had to be released because his interest in esoteric forms of Islam displeased the donor. Often the question of funders' influence on teaching and research policy has been discussed in a partial fashion. The focus has been on the alleged impact of a foreign funder, in our field usually from one of the wealthy oil states that have tended to be identified with conservative forms of Islam. In my view, the British experience does not permit any clear-cut conclusion. But it is commonly the case that complaints about the dangers of the influence of conservative Islam via such funding are blind to the fact of the profound influence of the domestic national governments on teaching and research priorities. The focus on research relating to security, radicalisation of young Muslims, and related fields over the last fifteen years should be sufficient reminder, especially if one were to take into consideration the enormous expansion of such activity in the United States during the last two decades.

Students as Users

In the first instance the users, the 'consumers' of Islamic studies, are the students, undergraduate and graduate. Before the middle of the twentieth century not only were there few students, but those who did exist had little say in the content and approach of the courses they followed. The professor knew best and had almost dictatorial powers in the determination of course content and, often, on the graduate student's choice of research topic. Two parallel developments have taken place in the last half-century to change that. On the one hand, was the expectation that arose out of the student revolts of the late 1960s, namely, that students should have a say in what was taught, a demand that often brought with it the demand for 'relevance'. On the other hand, was the gradual shift of higher education from being confined to an academic elite to becoming a forum for mass education. From a situation where less than 5 per cent of the year cohort entered higher education in the 1960s, in some European countries today we are approaching 50 per cent. With the distribution of public funding being increasingly tied to the distribution and movement of students, universities have had to learn how to function in a quasi-market environment, where supply cannot afford to distance itself too far from the patterns of demand. At the graduate level, the degree to which British universities since the 1990s have seen overseas students' tuition fees as a significant source of income has probably had an impact on decisions as to which specialisms to seek when filling academic posts.

Communities as Users

In some specific environments, it is in one way or another the Muslim community that is the stakeholder rather than the individual student. This is the case in countries where Islamic religious instruction is a publicly funded provision for Muslim children, usually because such a provision is already available for the main Christian communities. The German case discussed elsewhere in this volume is a case in point, as is Austria. There is in such instances the possibility of tensions between the academic criteria of the university that is hosting the teacher training and the expectations of the community sponsoring the programme, where the latter is likely to have an influence both on appointments and on course content. An example of such tensions coming to a head was the withdrawal of church teaching authorisation from the Roman Catholic theologian Hans Küng at the University of Tübingen in 1979 following his criticism of the doctrine of papal infallibility. However, as he had been appointed to the university under its regulations, he continued to teach though no longer in the Catholic theological programme. More recently in 2008–9, Dr Muhammad Sven Kalisch, teaching Islamic theology at the University of Münster on the first training programme in the country for Islamic RI teachers, found himself in a similar situation when he announced that he had concluded that the Prophet Muhammad had probably not existed. The university had to keep him on the academic staff under its own regulations while the sponsoring Muslim committee withdrew its cooperation from the university, obliging it to move him out of the Islamic teacher training programme. The university then appointed a new person to teach on the teacher training programme.

This experience will have coloured the appointment processes in the five universities which have been looking for qualified people to fill their new chairs. But equally interesting will be the expansion of this system to the training of teachers of the Alevi religion, especially since the Austrian constitutional court in December 2010 decided that the government had to accept an Alevi application for recognition separate from that already granted to 'Sunnis of the Hanafite rite' (Schmiedinger 2011: 32–43). This is likely to require not only that Alevi religious instruction is made available, including teacher training, but that Alevis will need to develop a degree of consensus on what Alevism is in terms of theology and ritual, likely a cause for internal rifts in the future with consequences for relations with schools and the university teacher training department.

Approaches to Teaching

In this environment the teaching of Islam has been challenged by the growth of Muslim students in first degree programmes.[9] A substantial proportion of

---

[9] In many European countries, where the 'Bologna model' of a three-year bachelor programme, followed by a two-year masters and then a three-year PhD is being implemented, the first degree remains in practice the five-year masters.

these students have not chosen to study the subject with a view to relevant employment but as part of their personal search for forms of Islamic faith and practice which makes sense to them in their European urban environment in a way which the Islam of their parents and mosque imams often fails to do. Many of these students, in some universities a majority, are women, but while this will clearly have major impact on the professionalisation of Islamic religious professionals (arguably this is already happening) the impact on teaching is not (yet) discernible.

On the face of it, most European university theology departments have long since adopted the critical scientific principles of learning, whereby particularly historical critical methods reign supreme. So it is possible for certain Christian theologians to present historical analyses which completely contradict traditional beliefs. Of course, in recent years we have seen, especially in the United States, a reaction against this academic tradition. In some universities, and certainly in seminaries, dogma has again begun to set the limits for academic research. In most Islamic faculties in the Muslim world, essential dogmas never stopped setting the limits. Not only is it difficult, if not impossible, to challenge received core truths, it is often difficult to challenge teachings which were widespread in the third/ninth century but subsequently fell out of favour – Muʿtazilism is a case in point. It is certainly very difficult to follow through research which looks like leading to serious revisions in the understanding of the Prophet or the interpretation of the Qur'anic text, as a number of scholars have discovered to their cost.

In a European university, which is usually governed by rules of religious neutrality if not explicitly secular, if a student's research leads to the conclusion that the Prophet Muhammad never existed, then so be it. This is an extreme case and very unlikely, but in my own experience I have regularly been faced with the problem relating to, for example, the study of hadith. Some of my academic colleagues would insist that no study of a topic based on hadith can be legitimate without engaging in the question of their authenticity. I would argue that the fact that, for the vast majority of Muslims, the hadith, certainly those conventionally accepted as *saḥīḥ*, are regarded as authentic must be the starting point for a study which might be looking, for example, at developments in the contemporary Islamic law of tort. Some of our academic colleagues would agree, but many would not. This is not just a theoretical discussion, because a university system like the British one insists on the supremacy of the external examiner, and the external examiner might very well be someone who disagrees with our starting point. And it is the student who suffers.

This brings me to a related and, to my mind, equally important issue. Muslim students often come from quite different academic traditions from those of Britain and many other European countries. This is obviously the case in areas like the emphasis on rote learning in many regions and communities, as it is in some cultures where the teacher is regarded as an authority who should not be challenged. But it goes deeper. The debate on 'orientalism' was interesting while it lasted, and it has had some effect in terms of political stances of institutions and individuals. But I am not sure that it has gone much beyond that. We still have an institutionalised consensus which says that the way our universities teach and conduct research is the right and the best one in terms of both teaching methods and objectives. But we are working with students and institutions who have other ideas. Do we simply ignore them and assume that they have to meet our requirements? Or do we take advantage of this situation and explore the interaction and, perhaps, the possibilities of creative interaction between different traditions of learning which this situation offers us? And how might we do this without being accused of being seduced by the flexible vagueness of post-modernism or, worst of all, of lowering standards?

Given these kind of considerations it is not surprising that many Muslim organisations prefer to develop their own religious teaching institutions. They exist in more or less formal ways – and are more or less well-funded – in many European countries, in especially large numbers, several dozen, in Britain. Some have sought or are seeking formal recognition either, as in the Netherlands, directly by the relevant government body or, as in Britain, indirectly through accreditation by a public university. This process, still at a very early stage, could be pointing in the direction of the solution which many churches have arrived at. Church seminaries, Protestant and Catholic, have existed for decades and centuries to train the clergy. At a time when universities were still overwhelmingly of a religious foundation this was not a problem, but as universities became secular institutions various models were devised to ensure that space could be preserved for confessional theological training and research. In some cases, as in Germany, this meant a reserved space within the universities. In other cases, the relationship was more distanced. And there were always smaller tendencies, either within the major churches or smaller independent churches, which insisted on remaining completely independent of the public higher education sector. Muslim organisations in Europe are beginning to experiment in a similar direction characterised by an acceptance of the distinctiveness of 'seminary' from the secular university, which in some cases may mean a complete rejection of cooperation and in others, and more usually, a degree of mutuality.

References

Aslan, Ednan and Petra Heinrich (2009). 'Austria', in Jørgen S. Nielsen, Samim Akgönül, Ahmet Alibašić, Brigitte Maréchal and Christian Moe (eds), *Yearbook of Muslims in Europe*, vol. 1. Leiden: Brill, pp. 25–34.

Bernasek, Lisa, n.d. 'Middle Eastern Studies in the United Kingdom', available at: http://www.llas.ac.uk/resources/gpg/3192, last accessed 13 April 2021.

Bernasek, Lisa and Gary Bunt (2010). *Islamic Studies Provision in the UK: Report to HEFCE by the Higher Education Academy*. Bristol: HEFCE.

Boender, Welmoet (2021). 'Professionalizing the Imam in Europe: Imam Training Programs as Sites of Deliberative Engagement', *Religions*, 12:308. DOI: 10.3390/rel2050308.

Daniel, Norman (1960). *Islam and the West: The Making of an Image*. Edinburgh: Edinburgh University Press.

de Koning, Martijn (2022). 'The Netherlands', in Stephanie Müssig, Egdūnas Račius et al. (eds), *Yearbook of Muslims in Europe*, vol. 13. Leiden: Brill, pp. 452–68.

Drees, Willem B. and Pieter Sjoerd van Kongsveld (eds) (2008). *The Study of Religion and the Training of Muslim Clergy in Europe: Academic and Religious Freedom in the 21st Century*. Leiden: Leiden University Press.

Ferreiro, Juan (2011). *Islam and the State in the EU*. Frankfurt am Main: Peter Lang.

Folkekirke og Religionsmøde (2011). *Rapport fra den sjette konference i Kristent-Muslimsk Samtaleforum, 18–19 November 2011*. Copenhagen: Folkekirke og Religionsmøde.

Fuess, Albrecht (2011). 'Introducing Islamic Theology and German Universities, Aims and Procedures', *Copenhagen University Islam Lecture Series*, 13 April 2011, available at: http://islam.ku.dk/lectures/Fuess.pdf, p. 1, last accessed 13 April 2021.

Hashas, Mohammed, Jan Jaap de Ruiter and Niels Valdemar Vinding (eds) (2018). *Imams in Western Europe: Developments, Transformations and Institutional Challenges*. Amsterdam: Amsterdam University Press, 2018.

HEFCE (2008). *Islamic Studies: Trends and Profiles*. Bristol: Higher Education Funding Council for England.

Hourani, Albert (1991). *Islam in European Thought*. Cambridge: Cambridge University Press.

Irwin, Robert (2006). *For Lust of Knowing: The Orientalists and their Enemies*. London: Allen Lane.

Janssens, Yaiza (2016). *Annotated Legal Documents on Islam in Europe: Belgium*. Leiden: Brill.

Johansen, Birgitte Scheperlern (2005). *Imamuddannelse i Europa: udfordringer og perspektiver*. Copenhagen: University of Copenhagen.

Latham, J. Derek (1986). 'The Parker Report'. *Bulletin: British Society of Middle East Studies* 13(1): 3–14.

McLoughlin, Sean (2012). 'United Kingdom', in Jørgen S. Nielsen et al. (eds), *Yearbook of Muslims in Europe*, vol. 4. Leiden: Brill, 2012, pp. 619–41.

Manço, Ural and Meryem Kanmaz (2009). 'Belgium', in Jørgen S. Nielsen, Samim Akgönül, Ahmet Alibašić, Brigitte Maréchal and Christian Moe (eds), *Yearbook of Muslims in Europe*, vol. 1. Leiden: Brill, 2009, pp. 35–47.

Nielsen, Jørgen S. (2017). 'Islamic Studies: Scientific or Confessional? A Contested University Subject', in Abu Husayn, Abdul Rahim, Tarif Khalidi and Suleiman A. Mourad (eds), *In the House of Understanding: Histories in Memory of Kamal S. Salibi*. Beirut: American University of Beirut, pp. 423–46.

Potz, Richard (2021). *Annotated Legal Documents on Islam in Europe: Austria*. Leiden: Brill.

Raza, M. S. (1993). *Islam in Britain: Past, Present and Future*, 2nd edn. Leicester: Islamic Foundation.
Rodinson, Maxime (1988). *Europe and the Mystique of Islam*. London: I. B. Tauris.
Rosenow-Williams, Kerstin (2012). *Organizing Muslims and Integrating Islam in Germany: New Developments in the 21st Century*. Leiden: Brill.
Said, Edward (1978). *Orientalism*. London: Routledge & Kegan Paul.
Schmiedinger, Thomas (2011). 'Austria', in Jørgen S. Nielsen, Samim Akgönül, Ahmet Alibašić, Hugh Goddard and Brigitte Maréchal (eds), *Yearbook of Muslims in Europe*, vol. 3. Leiden: Brill, pp. 33–43.
Siddiqui, A. (2007). *Islam at Universities in England: Meeting the Needs and Investing in the Future*. London: Department for Innovation, Universities and Skills.
SOU (2009). *Staten och imamerne: Religion, integration, autonomi*, SOU 2009:52. Stockholm: Statens Offentliga Utretninger.
Szumigalska, Agnieszka (2015). *Annotated Legal Documents on Islam in Europe: The Netherlands*. Leiden: Brill.
Tempest, Paul (ed.) (2006). *The Arabists of Shemlan: MECAS Memoirs 1944–78*. London: Stacey International.
Thomas, David (ed.) (2009–13). *Christian–Muslim Relations: A Bibliographical History*, 5 vols. Leiden: Brill.

CHAPTER 3

(Re)habilitating the Insider: Negotiations of Epistemic Legitimacy in Islamic Theology and Newer Social Justice Mobilisation

BIRGITTE SCHEPELERN JOHANSEN

One of the challenges facing the attempts at establishing public higher education in Islamic theology in Europe has been the forging of Islamic religious authority. Creating viable cooperation between universities and Muslim stakeholders (including potential students as well as subsequent employers for graduates) and finding the right teachers who can meet the requirements for academic positions at a European public university as well as present a convincing religious habitus, have not always been easy. One of the available frameworks for understanding and debating these challenges has been the insider–outsider distinction. In the context of Islamic theology this distinction seems to indicate both a distinction between confessional and non-confessional teaching, between Islamic and non-Islamic, and between inside and outside the epistemic domain of the public university. Across the board, insider–outsider discussions here largely draw upon what we could call a secular discursive repertoire, for example, assumptions about the category religion and its position vis-à-vis domains of publicly sanctioned knowledge. In neighbouring areas of European academia, a different conversation has intensified during the last decade, legitimising certain forms of insider positionality as more insightful, knowing and authentic. This conversation has been launched mainly by students in the humanities and the social sciences, it focuses on the role of power in knowledge production, and it is driven by a critique of claims to universality and the exclusion of non-Western knowledge traditions from university curricula. In many respects, this mobilisation continues debates from the 1970–90s about black history, feminist epistemology, post-colonialism and Eurocentrism, and it is articulated not through a distinction between confessional and non-confessional, but rather through the binary of oppressor–oppressed, lodging the discussion within a struggle for justice and equality.

Both Islamic theology and what I in the remainder of this chapter will call newer social justice mobilisation in the academy represent attempts to open up the public European universities to new and potentially challenging forms of knowledge. As such, they elicit various forms of boundary work (Gieryn 1983; McCutcheon 2003; Johansen 2006; also Dreier, Chapter 6, this volume) that in different ways contribute to the conflictual reproduction of a European academic field. My aim in this chapter is to unpack and compare these two forms of boundary work in order to discuss their different ramifications and consider what they tell us about the epistemic underpinnings of European (secular) universities.

Insider–Outsider Debates as Epistemic Boundary Work

Discussions about insider–outsider positionalities can be found across most of the social sciences and the humanities. As generic discussions, they often index the difference between embedded ways of knowing that connote lived experience, habituation and familiarity – something that you are part of and (able to) do yourself – and then more detached and systematic forms of knowledge production (e.g., McCutcheon 2003). As such, they are also, at least in principle, flexible and moving lines of demarcation: one may attempt to 'step outside' and objectify one's own familiarities, just as one may familiarise oneself with new domains of practice, thereby changing one's embodied knowledge in ways that make it possible – at least partly or momentarily – to 'step inside' the life worlds of others. Thus, at this generic level the distinction between insider and outsider can be seen as an attempt to make sense, through the use of spatial metaphors, of different styles and modes of knowing, which could also be addressed and discussed through concepts like habitus, embodiment and capital (Engelhardt 2016). We are in the domain of the ongoing processes of and movements between different types of understanding, different degrees of engagement and different modes of objectifications, and as such the difference between inside and outside should be thought of as a gradient, not a rift (Sinding Jensen 2011: 42). By implication, we are all – at any given time – insiders to some aspects of the processing of knowledge in the sense that knowledge activities always imply an embodied, habituated doing.

In practice, however, such movement between different styles of knowing will obviously depend upon the sanctioning from specific others, who might or might not accept one's claim to know. In other words, the question of where and with whom the 'true' inside resides is inevitably cast within a domain of power and claims to ownership. This might, for example, be the case when such claims are attached to specific social identity markers, such as gender or religious orientation, as preconditions for knowing the right things in the right way. At stake in these debates are continuous variations as well as contestations of two basic arguments. One that emphasises the privileged nature of the insider position as a source of authentic and authoritative knowledge (inside = insight), and one that problematises the insider position as a source of bias, distortion and potential diverted interests. Obviously, the two types of argumentation imply the reverse problematisation and appraisal of the outsider position. Or in the words of Robert K. Merton in his seminal essay on insider–outsider positions, what emerge are: 'Insider truths that counter Outsider untruths and Outsider truths that counter Insider untruths' (Merton 1972: 4).

Thus, while insider–outsider positions do have some purchase as concepts that can grasp different ways of knowing, here I will rather approach them as signposts of what Thomas Gieryn (1983) calls academic boundary work. Academic boundary work is the ongoing negotiation of what forms of knowledge should be included in and excluded from the realm of academic knowledge. Here, the very act of invoking insider or outsider positions installs a line, which in complex ways becomes implicated in crafting the boundaries of the domain of academic knowledge. First, we may notice how insider positionality is virtually always associated with the *topic* to be studied rather than the academic tools and habitus of the researcher.[1] In the study of religion, considerations typically evolve around the scholar's relationship with a particular religious tradition (McCutcheon 1999); in migration studies they typically evolve around the scholars' ethnic identifications and place of origin (Carling et al. 2014); in critical race studies and feminist studies, they evolve – not surprisingly – around the scholars' racial or gendered identities (Powers 1996). And so on. Rarely is someone considered an insider qua sociologist or historian, or by coming from a family with longstanding traditions for being educated in the Humanities. Rather, insider positionality tends to be associated with traits that connects the scholar with domains or qualities typically considered external to the academic endeavour. In short, being 'inside' is often made relevant regarding characteristics that from a certain point of view (or the point of view of certain scholars) belong 'outside' the university. The curious reversal at stake in the insider–outsider categorisations is interesting because it points towards the ambivalent, precarious but also potent status of the knowledge associated with the 'inside', which lies at the heart of the attempts to problematise as well as promote it. Continuing this line of thinking, I believe that Russell McCutcheon (2003) is quite right in suggesting that insider–outsider references are likely to emerge when there is a disturbance in epistemic legitimacy in a given field.

---

[1] One important exception from this observation could be Thomas Kuhn's work on paradigms and scientific revolutions, where he distinguishes between those who work inside the paradigm, conducting what he calls normal science, and those who work outside the paradigm.

The disturbance of interest for McCutcheon is the situation where a scholar is challenged on her or his (religious) convictions by an academic investigation of the traditions upon which she/he feels obliged. In such situations, the appeal to insider positions as something to be respected or valued emerges as a defence mechanism: it serves to fence off and protect particular forms of knowledge that might otherwise be undermined by the academic endeavour. However, the same goes for the appeal to outsider positions, which may serve to fence off and keep out certain forms of knowledge from the academic realm by deeming them to be suspicious or biased. So insider–outsider debates are – whatever else they might be – signals that a negotiation of the legitimacy of knowledge is taking place, and as such they are likely to emerge when changes in the institutionalised frameworks of universities are being sought. This is exactly the situation in the two cases to be discussed here.

Methodological Imaginations

What I embark upon in this chapter is a comparative investigation. The aim is to reconstruct the basic logics at work in two different cases in order to unpack the nature of the disturbance in epistemic legitimacy that they indicate. In this reconstruction, I draw upon existing research into Islamic theology at European universities and my current occupation with newer social justice mobilisation in the academy.[2] The material at hand has some obvious limitations regarding scope and comparability. References to and discussions about insider positionality may occur among many actors: students and teachers, researchers working with the topic, institutions promoting their educations, and non-academic actors with stakes in the maintenance and dissemination of certain forms of knowledge (organisations, politicians). It varies quite a lot whose voices on the topic are available in the existing research. As Göran Larsson (2018) has rightly pointed out, research into student life and student choices is quite limited concerning Islamic theology (some exceptions being Boender 2013; Wagner 2019; Dreier and Wagner 2020; Dreier, Chapter 6, this volume). The well-documented voices are mainly the institutions offering courses, researchers working with the field, politicians and Muslim stakeholders. This is different from the social justice mobilisation, where student voices are prominent (such as the 'Why is my curriculum white'-project at UCL, the 'Rhodes must fall'-movement at Cape Town and Oxford University or the student organisations 'Front' and 'Critical

---

[2] I hesitate to call the latter *research* in any strict sense, that is, a systematic empirical investigation driven by a theoretically informed research question. Rather, I have during the last four years followed debates and events especially at UK, US and Danish campuses regarding curriculum issues, decolonisation and anti-racism/anti-sexism, as part of a broader interest in the university as a site for negotiating social justice issues (Brudholm and Johansen 2019; Johansen 2019, 2021).

anthropologist' at the University of Copenhagen). These student voices draw – among other things – upon and re-articulate arguments found in certain strands of post-colonial studies, critical race studies and feminist studies from the 1960s and onwards. So there is a certain degree of intertextual and inter-discursive overlap or exchange between student voices and this strand of research. Finally, there is a small but growing, largely US-focused and rather critical research *on* such student activism (see, e.g., Furedi 2016; Zimmerman 2016; Campbell and Manning 2018).

These differences in available material partly reflect different social dynamics in terms of who are in fact the central actors engaged in the conversations. Still, to the extent that the availability of material also reflects gaps in the existing research, there are, of course, limitations to the reconstructions I make. However, it should be emphasised that my aim is not a systematic or encompassing empirical elaboration of the different, locally shaped institutional negotiations of epistemic legitimacy. Rather, I aim to put forth what appear to me to be two different grammars that I have encountered in quite different settings. In doing this, I allow myself to read across and connect a range of empirical examples and scholarly reflections, mainly related to the Scandinavian and German experiences with Islamic theology, and Danish and UK examples of social justice mobilisation. In the latter case, I will also make a few references to US examples and scholarship, since there is a high degree of discursive flows between a US and European context on these matters. Such reading across examples inevitably implies crafting bridges and making rifts, possibly making distinct or separate what in some other empirical context might be connected or even indistinguishable. My claim, then, is not that the reconstructions of inside–outside discussions presented below never overlap or intersect in practice. They may very well do so, just as some of the same signifiers (say, religion, Islam, justice or equality) may occur across the board. However, what I do claim is that there is a certain systemic quality – hence, the reference to grammar – in the way these signifiers work (e.g., Islam as revealed truth versus Islam as object of recognition), just as there are different institutional origins and locations, which makes it intelligible to speak of two different types of boundary work. Thus, what I do can best be seen as forging suggestive typologies for the sake of comparison and discussion – typologies which can and should be nuanced by other empirical examples, other readings. Let us now turn our attention towards the appeals to insider positionality in these two different sites.

Islamic Theology

The creation of institutions for Islamic higher education in Europe has a long, varied and by now rather well described history (e.g., Fuess 2007, 2011;

Aslan and Windisch 2012; Larsson 2018; Groeninck and Boender 2020). The specific trajectories of such institutionalisation differ between countries and depends among other things on historical contacts with Muslim regimes, colonial and migratory histories and – not least – the structures of the national educational system. Where attempts have been made at incorporating Islamic higher education into public institutions for higher education, Islamic *theology* has been a favourite terminology, even though also contested for its Christian heritage (Fuess 2011: 4). This choice of terminology is not surprising, and it testifies to an ordinary form of incorporation, where the new is made familiar by identifying it through already well-known systems of classification. In this case, the already known is, of course, theology as a broad and flexible term for the academic, university-based explorations of the Christian tradition, which in many European countries have structural connections with the churches and with other parts of the educational system. In Denmark, the Social Democratic Party has on two occasions (in 2004 and 2006) voiced a call for Islamic theology, and the way this has been done quite accurately expresses this equation between Islam and the already known structures for cooperation between the theological faculty and the Danish national church. Hence, the suggestion has been to establish:

> a specific higher theological education in Islam with the aim of creating an academic foundation for the occupation of specific religious functions in the Muslim faith community. (BSF 90, made to the Danish parliament, 14 March 2006)

Processes of translation are obviously productive: things get lost and new things are added, and they may be more or less characterised by domestication of the new (Bassnet 1998). This also goes for the choice of 'Islamic theology' as an umbrella term for the various aspects of Islam as knowledge tradition. As argued by Thomas Hoffmann (2016), this choice of the term theology is intelligible, but potentially misleading. While there are somewhat equivalent Arabic concepts (such as *kalam* or *usul ad-din*), the prime Islamic discipline of higher learning has rather been *fiqh*: 'the study to determine God's shari'a and His intentions in the form of a dynamic and all-encompassing legal framework for the state and its people' (Hoffmann 2016: 146). So another possible translation could perhaps have been that of 'Islamic law' or 'Islamic legal studies', which would have implied its own losses and gains, and which would have pointed towards an incorporation into quite different institutional structures for education and quite different domains of subsequent social practices.[3] For our purpose here,

---

[3] For a discussion of European attempts to 'read' Islam through distinctions between religion and law, see, for example, Asad 2003; Shah 2010; Ahmed 2015; Johansen and Spielhaus 2019.

the relevant point is to notice the interpretative framework that activates a distinction between law and religion and emphasises the latter, because this shapes the kind of insider–outsider discussions that have emerged as Islam has entered the public university systems in this new way.

As mentioned, some of the prime actors involved in establishing Islamic theology in public universities have been staff at departments for exactly theology and religious teachers training (Larsson 2018). Here university staff and departments have all along been working with an awareness of the overarching political interests in Islamic theology as a tool for integration and anti-radicalisation, which have lodged the initiatives in a difficult tension between recognition and control (Birt 2006; Johansen 2008; Boender 2013; Groeninck and Boender 2020). Thus, the process has to some extent been one of opening doors and making invitations in a way that would make such educational offers appealing to potential students and other Muslim stakeholders. In this context, appeals to insider perspectives may work as a reassurance that the interests that attach to the 'Islamic' part of the equation will be catered for in appropriate ways. For example, a couple of years ago, the theological faculty at the University of Copenhagen offered a series of flexible electives under the headline Islamic theology, and the courses were introduced in the following way:

> Islam will be studied both from an inside and an outside perspective: Islamic theology and practices will be investigated with reference to the context in which it has developed, but at the same time the study will address the current interpretations and expressions of Islam to be found among Muslims in Europe today.[4]

This reference to a 'double approach' is not unique to presentations of Islamic theology. It is also evoked as a means of describing Christian theology. In an answer to a young man who wonders whether he, as a Muslim, can study theology in Copenhagen, professor and theologian Niels Henrik Gregersen describes theology as the study of Christianity from an inside as well as an outside perspective.[5] The inside in Gregersen's answer is described as 'the self-reflection of a Christian tradition', while the outside is connected to a more historical approach. As Lena Dreier points out in her chapter in this volume (Chapter 6), every kind of theology has to challenge neat boundaries between faith, religious and theological knowledge. Regarding the theological study in Denmark, the mobilisation of the inside–outside distinction seems connected

---

[4] See at: http://teol.ku.dk/uddannelser/efter_og_videreuddannelser/islamisk_teologi_og_-praksisformer, my translation.
[5] See 'Kan jeg læse teologi, selvom jeg er muslim?', religion.dk, 13 December 2013.

to the fact that even though the study is non-confessional, many (but not all) students at the faculty identify as Christians and many (but not all) students want to pursue a career as priests in the Danish Lutheran state church. The 'self' in the self-reflective inside, then, seems to create a space for this Christian self-identification of the students, as well as an openness towards the interests of the religious organisation that will become the work place of many of its candidates, even though the faculty is declared non-confessional.

With regard to the presentation of Islamic theology, we notice the (re)use of the idea of a double approach, which might be intended to work somewhat in the same way, that is: it signals some unspecified openness for the religious self-identification of students and the interests of Muslim stakeholders outside the university. Yet the distinction is here added a spatio-temporal dimension. It is connected with a distinction between the context in which Islam has emerged and then the 'here and now' for European Muslims. In this case, the invocation of the inside–outside perspective probably testifies to an awareness of the limited scope of the epistemic authority that a Danish university carries regarding this tradition – and for good reasons. One of the practical challenges for the successful realisation of Islamic theology has been to convince students and Muslim stakeholders that an education offered by a European public university can indeed be Islamic in 'the right way' (Fuess 2011; Boender 2013; Engelhardt 2021). Such considerations about the different nature and quality of knowledge provided by different institutions are also expressed in the previously mentioned response to the young Muslim man, who considered studying theology. The other adviser, Safia Aoude, gave the following answer:

> As a Muslim, you should not expect theology or the study of religion to be the same as classical, traditional Islamic education. Both disciplines are characterised by a theory of science approach, so if you want to learn more about such approaches of religion, studying theology and/or the study of religion will be a good point of departure. The benefit of studying these topics at a university level is that you get an all-round introduction to the ways the academic elite in the West approaches among other things Islam . . . However, if you want to study Islamic jurisprudence and/or other classical Islamic disciplines, theology and the study of religion are not the right places to start. Then it would be better to go to al-Azhar in Egypt or to Leiden University in the Netherlands, who offers a two-year Islam education as a sort of mixture of the study of religion and classical Islam studies.[6]

---

[6] See at: https://www.religion.dk/sp%C3%B8rg-om-religion/kan-jeg-l%C3%A6se-teologi-selvom-jeg-er-muslim, my translation.

This exchange took place in 2013, before the theological faculty at the University of Copenhagen began offering electives in Islamic theology, so it is quite possible that Safia Aoude would have recommended these courses as a 'sort of mixture', along with the one in Leiden (which, by the way, was merely planned but not realised). However, the relevant point here is the way the knowledge offered by the University of Copenhagen is particularised as the thinking of a Western elite, which points towards the difficult task of expanding the epistemic authority regarding Islam in a way that can pass as 'classical', while this authority lies unproblematically elsewhere (al-Azhar, for example).

Not surprisingly then, the hiring of teachers/professors who can inhabit what Felix Engelhardt calls socio-cultural insiderism has been an important aspect of the project of bridging the divide between 'here' and 'there'. Socio-cultural insiderism is described by Engelhardt as grounded in the:

> social and cultural capital of the scholar, which proves beneficial for his or her research and may materialise in form of a range of advantages an insider scholar in the study of Islam might possess: language skills, an early education at Islamic institutions that provides a deep knowledge of classical sources, or the belonging to a religious or ethnic group which allows knowledge about 'real-life' Islam. (Engelhardt 2016: 742)

This kind of insiderism is, according to Engelhardt, the least challenging for the traditional Western paradigms for engaging Islam, because it can co-exist with ideals of faith neutrality and disinterestedness in theological questions (Engelhardt: 2016: 741). However, the more disturbing aspect associated with Islamic theology emerges when explicitly confessional demands on teachers and curriculum are to be negotiated (Fuess 2011; Hoffmann 2016; Larsson 2018). By confessional, I mean an obligation by teachers and students upon a faith in or submission to something (truth, dogmas, God) that is prior to and beyond the critical scope of the academic enterprise. This is the potent and problematic 'something' that universities can hardly disregard, if they want to be relevant as part of a transmission of a living religious tradition, yet they cannot include it straightforwardly either and still claim to be (largely) secular institutions. For one thing, because any kind of confession holds the potential to set limits to the scholarly investigation by marking certain questions as off limits. But also because the confessional – from a secular point of view – is considered exclusive and particular, in the sense that the knowledge processed is mainly or only relevant for those who already confess (Berglund 2015: 9ff.). And this clashes with ideals of openness and public relevance of academic knowledge.

Thus, the confessional elicits different kinds of boundary work. In the Danish context, such obligations or attachments are formally beyond the boundaries of what can legitimately be included in the academic sphere. As stated by Thomas Hoffmann, professor in Islamic studies at the Theological Faculty, a couple of years before the launch of the electives: the piety of the students and teachers are irrelevant to the academic enterprise, and this might be a stumbling block for some Muslims.[7] Also, in a feature article in the daily *Politiken* by five of the initiators and teachers behind the electives it is emphasised that the courses do not contain any teaching in confessional Islamic practices.[8] In this situation, evoking the inside–outside distinction seems to indicate an ambivalent possibility for exchange or contact with the idea of an Islamic truth. Also in a German context, where cooperation with religious organisations is part of the institutional set-up for theology, and where the Muslim faith of students as well as staff is mobilised as a resource to guarantee an 'inner' perspective (Dreier, Chapter 6, this volume,), the confessional still seems to elicit boundary work in teaching. In an article on al-Quantara from May 2017, Harry Harun Behr and Mouhanad Khorchide, professors in Islamic religious pedagogics at Goethe University and Münster University, respectively, were interviewed on the current status of Islamic theology in Germany. They both draw on an explicitly secular vocabulary, stating that many students 'are keen to deepen their faith rather than pursue academic study', and that it can be a challenge to make it clear to the students what it means to study theology at a secular university, since the students 'want to have their faith confirmed, yet the university is a place at which to reflect upon one's faith' (see also Dreier and Wagner 2020). Of particular interest here is the distinction between confirming and reflecting upon one's faith, and the inclusion of the latter (an inclusion that resonates with the insider perspective as self-reflection promoted in the Danish context). So while faith may be a more legitimate starting point for the theological endeavour in a German than in a Danish university context, this inclusion is still ambivalent, and distinctions still need to be drawn between appropriate ways of engaging faith (as an object of (self-)reflection) and problematic ones (ones that confirms what is already believed).[9]

Summing up, one way to interpret the appeal to insides mobilised by the universities upon introducing Islamic theology is then to understand their function as a kind of sluice. This sluice makes it possible to imagine a partial or sequential opening of the doors of the university towards something, which might otherwise constitute a disturbance or be difficult for the university to own, namely, an explicitly confessional engagement with Islam, which again is associated

---

[7] 'På universitetet skal Islam kunne tåle et syrebad', *Kristeligt Dagblad*, 21 October 2013.
[8] 'En islamisk teologisk uddannelse i Danmark', *Politiken*, 27 August 2015.
[9] Distinctions between faith and knowledge and debates about their roles and relationship are, of course, not foreign to Islamic discourses. The point here is to highlight the specific boundary work that emerges regarding the appropriate relationship between the student and her/his faith.

with knowledge traditions that comes from outside Europe. The sluice seems to suggest 'this is (partly) done your way' (which is by implication not entirely 'our way'), and this can be done without compromising either the academic standards of the university or the epistemic authority of the potentially disturbing other. Let us now turn to the student-driven social justice mobilisation where the appeals to insiders seems to work slightly different.

Social Justice Mobilisation

White men should not speak about what it is like to be a brown woman, but they are of course welcome to try and educate themselves and learn what it means to be a brown woman. A white man might teach a brown woman's writings, but I would trust a brown woman teaching it more. His gaze would not be neutral, but very specifically defined by being a white, European man. (Tara Skadesgaard Thosen, *Kristeligt Dagblad* (12 December 2018, my translation))

Twenty years ago, I found nothing wrong with my teaching an entire course on African American literature, because there wasn't anyone else on our campus who might do it. Now, however, I wouldn't think of teaching such a course, even if there were no minority faculty available, and I'm astounded by my own arrogance in once thinking that I could. The scenario has changed: now there are well-trained African American faculty who represent their culture as Insiders, and who may resent the idea of an Outsider speaking for them. (Janet M. Powers, 'The Outsider's Gaze' (1996))

Let us now turn the attention towards a different field, where appeals to insider perspectives have recently regained force. I say regain because some of the central tropes and arguments of this mobilisation reiterate discussions about representation and power in the academy that since the 1960s have emerged in different domains, focusing on the relation between social identity and the right to speak.[10] At stake is a claim, raised by students and university staff, that Western universities are implicated in a larger history of global relations of oppression, slavery and colonialisation; that they embody and sustain unjust racialised and gendered structures of inequality; and that changes therefore need to be made to, among other things, the composition of curricula, the

---

[10] For example, the 1972 essay by Robert Merton on insider–outsider discussions was written as a response to ongoing US discussions in the 1960s on 'black history'. The introductory quote to this section by Janet M. Powers is from a mid-1990s debate on teaching multiculturalism – the title of the book quite tellingly being *Teaching What You're Not*.

composition of staff, and the composition of language.[11] The aim here is also to make space for new or not previously included forms of knowledge within the public universities, just as the kind of knowledge to be included emerges from sites outside the European mainstream. However, in this case the mainstream is configured as white, male and Eurocentric rather than Christian or secular. Further, the aim is not to expand the educational infrastructures to include new educations but to alter the existing epistemic framework by provincialising claims to universality. According to the introductory sections of a report from Goldsmith University, *Insider–Outsider: The Role of Race in Shaping the Experiences of Black and Ethnic Minority Students* the project is to strengthen decolonisation, which is described in the following way as:

> an expression of the changing geopolitics of knowledge whereby the modern epistemological framework for knowing and understanding the world is no longer interpreted as universal and unbound by geo-historical and biographical contexts.[12] (Akel 2019: 17)

Institutionally, this field has quite a different origin and shape than the field of Islamic theology. First and foremost, it does not exist as distinct educations or courses, but as a largely student-driven mobilisation that emerges in class room discussion, in student evaluations, in student organisations and in student complaints about injustices endured through the kind of knowledge being presented to them in class. It also exists in institutional initiatives like codes of conduct, in alterations made to curricula, in heightened sensitivities of teachers when dealing with issues such as race, gender, sexuality and – to a lesser extent – religion. And then it exists amongst staff and in particular scholarly discourses, which are often used by students in their mobilisation. The institutional bedrock is not theology departments but rather arts and humanities (e.g., literary studies, cultural studies, pedagogy and anthropology), and while Islam may figure in this discourse, it seems mainly to do so as an object of prejudice associated with the racialisation of Muslims (e.g., Akel 2019: 27). Consequently, the dynamics of this discourse are not that of an institutional invitation in a context of potential suspicion and political control, but rather that of protest, entitlement and defence. The appeals to insider–outsider positions therefore seem to evolve

---

[11] For example, the 'Rhodes must fall' movement at Cape Town and Oxford University, 'Why is my curriculum white' which started at the UCL, the student movements 'Front' and 'Critical Anthropologists' at University of Copenhagen, and a range of reports on student life and wellbeing, such as *Insider–Outsider* (2019) from Goldsmiths, or *Race for Equality* (2015) from the UK National Union of Students.

[12] Illustrative of the intellectual flows between a US and European context, the quote is from a paper given by Michael Baker, 'Decolonial Education: Meanings, Contexts, and Possibilities', at the Annual Conference of the American Educational Studies Association in 2012.

around (a lack of) ownership and (lack of) representation in public institutional spaces that *ought* to cater for the needs of all students, and this issue of representation is variously connected with the quality of knowledge as well as with issues of social discrimination and recognition.

To give an example: a couple of years ago, discussions about the 'white curriculum' emerged in a Danish context, among other things propagated by the student organisation Front and the student organisation Critical Anthropologists. Especially, the spokesperson from Front, Tara Skadesgaard Thorsen was active in the public debate, at a time when the media were already occupied by the first wave of #MeToo. Thorsen, amongst other things, pointed towards the need for a revision of curricula, because of the connection between social identity and epistemic capacities. So reading only white men would limit the scope of what can be known, because their thinking would be limited by their embodied experiences (an argument found in different versions among feminists and critical race scholars, such as Sara Ahmed, Shannon Sullivan or George Yancy). But more so, the revision of curricula also pertains to credibility. Asked about whether a white man can teach about a brown woman's writing, Thorsen in an interview with Danish daily *Kristeligt Dagblad* in 2018 gave the answer quoted above, that white men are welcome to educate themselves in order to understand better what it is like to be a brown woman, but she would rather trust the teaching of a brown woman's authorship done by a brown woman.

Explicit attempts to provincialise the knowledge of a white majority, and the strong sense that social identity, qua assumed experience, gives superior credibility, I have also increasingly encountered in student assignments and classroom discussions. At stake is not merely a methodological awareness of the situated character of knowledge, the related potential clashes between different epistemic horizons, and the ethical questions about power and ownership that emerges during research. At stake is an insistence on an unquestioned respect for and acceptance of the authoritative character of the voice of the other regarding topics considered 'theirs' (along the lines of the initial quote from Janet M. Powers). So, for example, students insisting that they would never question or problematise statements made by their interlocutor, because they as insiders know better. Or students stating that ideally, their interlocutors should have written the academic assignment, because then we would have gained the most accurate knowledge about the topic at hand. Or a student questioning whether a colleague could teach about hate crime, given that he or she (as far as the student knew) did not inhabit a minority identity and therefore did not know 'what it was like'. Such statements go hand in hand with an increased student occupation with *experience* as the object of inquiry as well as the ultimate authoritative source of knowledge. And conversations with colleagues reveal that sometimes such appeals to insider authority elicit reverse boundary work from more senior faculty, who are trained to be suspicious of any notion of authenticity, or who feel that the independence of academic work is on the line.

In a UK context, where the discussions about social justice and the academy were (re)ignited in 2010 by the UCL campaign 'Why is my curriculum white?', the question of having people 'speak for themselves' is more explicitly connected with the colonial experience than in the Danish context. At stake is the quality of public knowledge, for example, about British colonial history, and the hope that a recognition of different voices and perspectives may contribute to a broader and more nuanced knowledge about the topic at hand.[13] And the question of power, ownership and exploitation is at the heart of the discussion. Thus, to the question 'Why is my curriculum white', one of the answers provided is (and reiterating the importance of experience):

> The curriculum is white because it reflects the underlying logic of colonialism, which believes the colonised do not own anything – not even their own experiences . . . the white curriculum reinforces the fallacy that Europe's current pre-eminence is the result of 'enlightenment' and not 'expropriation'. The manichean [sic] world of colonialism determined that while 'the natives' may be able to run, fight and dance, what they could never do is think. That was the sole preserve of, at worst, the European mind, and at best, anyone else who could adequately mimic it. ('8 Reasons the curriculum is white', 23 March 2015)

A central object of critique, then, is the idea that universities are carriers of a knowledge that is superior because it is true or enlightened. Rather, epistemic superiority emerges from geopolitical dominance, whose implicit aim has been to delegitimise 'the natives' as knowledge subjects (while they might have been well suited as knowledge objects). Consequently, the result of dominance is not better knowledge, but the contrary: an exclusion of thinking that could have made valuable contributions to the academic enterprise. The call for diversification of knowledge – or inclusivity, which seems to be another favourite spatial metaphor in this field – is then aimed at improving the shared knowledge, not least about past injustices. But more so, because the knowledge of the white curriculum is not merely limited but also to some extent flawed by its unjust pretext of dominance, there is a revolutionary potential in the critiques that makes some scholars react quite defensively, fearing that the 'best knowledge' should be replaced by something of lesser quality. As one of the harsh critics

---

[13] Listen, for example, to the critical and sarcastic reflections from students of South Asian background about the teaching they received in school on British colonial history, where the British empire was largely depicted as a 'benign Elizabethan NGO', see at: https://www.youtube.com/watch/Dscx4h2l-Pk.

of the 'Why is my curriculum white' movement, Joanna Williams formulated the ethos that should guide the content of curricula: it is not about 'different but equal', but about 'true hence better' (Williams 2017). More elaborate, the curriculum movement:

> assumes that all curricular knowledge is equally valid, that it doesn't really matter whether you read literature by Dickens or Achebe; study the sociology of WEB Du Bois or Émile Durkheim; or the philosophy of Alain Locke or John Locke. When all knowledge is of equal worth, its merit is entirely dependent on the cultural identity of the theorist. According to this reasoning, all knowledge propounded by white males is reduced simply to a reflection of dominant power structures and is therefore tainted. It becomes morally better to study work that gives a voice to underrepresented groups. (*Spiked*, 22 October 2014)

Thus, the worry is that knowledge is reduced to power, and – so I interpret the concerns expressed by people like Williams – other coordinates of quality and excellence are lost (such as truthfulness or beauty). In any case, the boundary work is here more confrontational, because it to some extent seems to imply a zero-sum game: that the inclusion of new forms of knowledge will be at the expense of something else (e.g., excellence and academic freedom). My impression is that this is quite different from the way the discussions about Islamic theology have played out. The project here has all along been about carving out new space, rather than fighting over existing grounds. Further, it has all along been particularistic since a main aim is to cater for the educational needs of Muslims in Europe. While this aim is not uncontroversial (which is why most universities flag that their courses are open to anyone interested in Islam) and while there are some indications that Islamic theology might eventually seek to become an intellectual resource of broader public relevance (see, e.g., Leirvik 2016), the conversation has not been driven by a demand for space in a context of misrecognised (epistemic) entitlement.

But the picture is more muddled than this, and traversing the UK discussion, it is also striking how the social justice discourses sometimes shift to a language that is more aligned with special interests and particularity. This is done under the headline of representation. Especially in a UK (and for that matter US) context, the appeal to insides and inclusivity does not pertain only to the quality of publicly shared knowledge, but also to the recognition and wellbeing of the students. The composition of the curriculum is, alongside a host of other marginalising aspects of the university, linked to a general experience of exclusion, which is seen as a key factor in the attainment gap between non-white and white student (e.g., NUS 2011; Akel 2019). At stake is the experience of exclusion that emerges from a teaching that does not sufficiently provide points of identification for non-white students, either in case of the identity of authors or in the content of the texts read. As explained by a black British student in the 2011 NUS report *Race for Equality*:

> When it comes to education, different people approach it in different ways. Things have to be taught in a way that suits the learners' needs. They [the university] could try teaching ethnic groups about their history and personalise their education. They could bring in successful ethnic figures to demonstrate that any goal is achievable. (NUS 2011: 22)

The issue here is not so much epistemic credibility or an expansion of the shared knowledge about, say, history, but a longing for recognition of one's life experiences and aspirations in the institution of higher education. And just as the idea of equality and the idea of an unquestioned respect for peoples' experiences elicit boundary work, so does the idea of fair or just representation. As Alka Sehgal Cuthbert argues in a critique of the British 'decolonise the university' movement:

> the metaphor of education as a mirror in which you expect to see your racial group's experience reflected back to you, common in decolonising discourses, fundamentally confuses education with more therapeutic practices. (*Spiked*, 29 June 2020)

Again, we notice how boundary work emerges in a way that problematises continuity/confirmation (the mirror) and aligns adequate education with the ability to detach oneself and expand one's horizons. Only in this case, the problematic confirmation is not of faith but of racial identity and social experience. However, implicit in both Cuthbert and Williams' defence is a denial of the claim raised in social justice discourses that the existing university structures in fact already work as a mirror – only it is a mirror for the white, majority students, and its power resides exactly in its capacity to deny this. In that sense, the debates rehearse some classical political positions about equality: whether equality emerges from shared maybe even universal norms, or whether equality implies equal access to shape the norms or having different norms recognised. And this leads me to the closing remarks for this section: that across the board, the disturbing and potent substance that elicits the inside–outside discussion in this field seems to be the political rather than the confessional. More specifically, a particular political project, namely, one that seeks justice through equality and does so through a specifically democratic vocabulary of fair representation as an unquestionable good. So continuing the metaphors from the prior section, the insider–outsider scheme seems here not so much to function as a sluice that allows gradual exchange and cohabitation, but rather as a battering ram intended to crush (invisible) barriers of unjust exclusion and discrimination.

Concluding Remarks

In this chapter, I have sought to reconstruct and compare the appeals to insider–outsider positions in two different fields where changes to the academic landscape are currently sought and partly realised. In both cases, the appeals indicate the presence of something potentially disturbing, which elicits different kinds of boundary work. In the case of Islamic theology, the boundary work seems to emerge both from the threat of political interference and from the predicament of including certain forms of religious confessionality. At stake is a concern that the university will become a site for the exercise of political control and a concern about the submission to an unquestionable religious truth. In the case of the social justice mobilisation, the boundary work seems to be elicited more explicitly by the political, understood as the pursuit of a better, more just life for marginalised subjects. At stake is a concern that knowledge is reduced to power and that the university will become a site for the pursuit of justice and identity politics rather than a site for the pursuit of universally valid expert knowledge. Related to this, we see the contours of two different kinds of boundary work. One that mainly seeks to expand the already existing structures of the university to include Islam as an instance of something already known: a religion with an intellectual tradition that can find a home in the modern, research university. And one that seeks to challenge the existing structures of knowledge production by pointing towards their foundational injustices, and thus potentially aiming at a more revolutionary project. I say potentially, because, of course, the degree of revolution in the social justice movement can be discussed, since the protests are largely articulated within scholarly discourses that already have an established position within the European universities. But still, the decolonising moment in this discourse – that other ways of knowing and other ways of institutionalising knowledge than those that govern the modern European research universities, are equally valid and should be recognised as such – potentially opens the doors for more radical change. To illustrate by way of a thought experiment: the decolonising moment could, for example, logically imply a claim that institutional formats and styles of learning known from various Muslim majority contexts should be accepted into the university as equally valid and valuable, rather than the translated versions of Islamic theology that are currently being realised.

Leaving thought experiments aside, what we do see across the differences is a struggle with or negotiation of the idea of *independence* of the academic sphere. The condensed version expressed in the boundary work goes something like this: that the university should be independent from political agendas and religious truth claims, and while it may legitimately produce knowledge of relevance for particular functions in society, it should not merely cater for the needs of particular identity groups. That the religious and the political emerge as two sites for negotiating independence is not surprising. The ideal of academic independence from political or state interference goes back at least to Humboldt's idea of academic self-governance (Humboldt 1810). A later landmark in this discussion could be Weber's programme statement about the social sciences as value-free, which has had an enormous influence on the scientific study of religion (Weber 1904). And not least during the post-war period, the consequences of scholarly engagements in dubious political projects (evolutionist, racist and eugenicist) spurred decades of critical self-reflection regarding the ethos and responsibilities of scholars vis-à-vis political interests (Merton's CUDOS from 1942 being one famous attempt to articulate this ideal of independence through the concept of disinterestedness). Likewise, the idea of a necessary independence of the academic endeavour from religious interference has a long and complex genealogy (e.g., Symoens 2003; Asad 2003; Brook and McLean 2005; Taylor 2007); a genealogy that crystalised during the late nineteenth century into more or less confrontational secular narratives of separation, emphasising either conflict or a more peaceful division of labour (Drees 2008; McMullin 2008). My limited analysis of academic boundary work in this chapter testifies to the persistence and stability of these deeper, modern currents, which emerge more or less defensively as new domains of knowledge seek incorporation into the public European universities.

References

Agai, Bekim and Jan Felix Engelhardt (forthcoming). "One decade of Islamic theological studies at German universities: Expectations, outcomes and future perspectives," in Jørgen S. Nielsen and Stephen H. Jones (eds), *Islamic Studies in European Higher Education*. Edinburgh: Edinburgh University Press.

Ahmed, Shahab (2015). *What is Islam?: The Importance of Being Islamic*. Princeton, NJ: Princeton University Press.

Akel, Sofia (2019). *Insider–Outsider. The Role of Race in Shaping the Experiences of Black and Minority Ethnic Students*, report from Goldsmiths University of London, Attainment Gap Project.

Asad, Talal (2003). *Formations of the Secular: Christianity, Islam, Modernity*. Stanford, CA: Stanford University Press.

Aslan, Ednan and Zsófia Windisch (eds) (2012). *The Training of Imams and Teachers for Islamic Education in Europe*, Wiener Islamstudien. Frankfurt am Main: Lang.

Bassnett, S. (1998). 'The Translation Turn in Cultural Studies', in S. Bassnett and A. Lefevere (eds), *Constructing Cultures: Essays on Literary Translation*. Bristol: Multilingual Matters, pp. 13–23.

Berglund, Jenny (2015). *Publicly Funded Islamic Education in Europe and the US*, Brookings Project on US Relations with the Islamic World, Analysis Paper No. 21, 2 April.
Birt, Yahya (2006). 'Good Imam, Bad Imam: Civic Religion and National Integration in Britain Post-9/11', *Muslim World* 96: 687–705.
Boender, Welmoet (2013). 'Embedding Islam in the Moral Covenants of European States: The Case of a State-Funded Imam Training in The Netherlands', *Journal of Muslims in Europe* 2: 227–47.
Brook, John and Ian McLean (2005). *Heterodoxy in Early Modern Science and Religion*. Oxford: Oxford University Press.
Brudholm, T. and B. Johansen (2018). 'Fighting Hate on Campus', roundtable at the INHS conference, Oshawa/Toronto, 30 May.
Campbell, Bradley and Jason Manning (2018). *The Rise of Victimhood Culture*. London: Palgrave Macmillan.
Carling, Jørgen, Marta Bivand Erdal and Rojan Tordhol Ezzati (2014), 'Beyond the Insider–Outsider Divide in Migration Research', *Migration Studies* 2(1): 36–54.
Cuthbert, Alka Sehgal (2020). 'The Danger of "Decolonising" Education', *Spiked*, 29 June.
Drees, W. B. (2008). 'Academic Freedom and the Symbolic Significance of Evolution', in W. B. Drees and S. v. Koningsveld (eds), *The Study of Religion and the Training of Muslim Clergy in Europe: Academic and Religious Freedom in the 21st Century*. Leiden: Leiden University Press, pp. 59–90.
Dreier, Lena and Constantin Wagner (2020). *Wer studiert Islamische Theologie. Ein Überblick über das Fach und seine Studierenden*, report from AIWG, Goethe Universität, Frankfurt am Main.
Dreier, Lena (forthcoming). 'Islamic Theology in a Muslim-minority environment: Distinctions of Religion within a New Academic Discipline', in Jørgen S. Nielsen and Stephen H. Jones (eds), *Islamic Studies in European Higher Education*. Edinburgh: Edinburgh University Press.
Engelhardt, Jan Felix (2016). 'On Insiderism and Muslim Epistemic Communities in the German and US Study of Islam', *Muslim World* 106: 740–58.
Engelhardt, Jan Felix (2021). 'Beyond the Confessional/Non-Confessional Divide: The Case of German Islamic Theological Studies', *Religions* 12(2): 2–12.
Fuess, Albrecht (2007). 'Islamic Religious Education in Western Europe: Models of Integration and the German Approach', *Journal of Muslim Minority Affairs* 27(2): 215–39.
Fuess, Albrecht (2011). 'Introducing Islamic Theology at German Universities, Aims and Procedures', Copenhagen University Islam Lecture Series, 13 April, available at: https://islam.ku.dk/lectures/Fuess.pdf, last accessed 15 May 2021.
Furedi, Frank (2016). *What's Happened to the Universities? A Sociological Exploration of its Infantilisation*. London: Routledge.
Gieryn, Thomas F. (1983). 'Boundary-Work and the Demarcation of Science from Non-Science: Strains and Interests in Professional Ideologies of Scientists'. *American Sociological Review* 48(6): 781–95.
Groeninck, Mieke and Welmoet Boender (2020). 'Introduction to Special Issue on "Exploring New Assemblages of Islamic Expert Education in Western Europe"', *Religions* 11(6). DOI: 10.3390/rel11060285.

Hoffmann, Thomas (2016). 'Islamic Theology and Theological Engineering in the Nordic Setting: Critical Perspectives from the Danish Experience', *Nordic Journal of Theology* 70(2): 145–59.

Humboldt, W. v. (1810). 'Über die innere und aussere Organisation der hoeheren wissenschaftlichen Anstalten in Berlin', in Leitzmann et al. (eds), *Wilhelm von Humboldts Gesammelte Schriften*, Band X. Berlin 1903–35.

Johansen, Birgitte S. (2006). 'Islamic Theology at the European Universities: Secularisation, Boundaries and the Role of Religion', *Nordic Journal of Religion and Society* 19(2): 93–106.

Johansen, Birgitte S. (2008). 'Legitimizing Islamic Theology at the European Universities', in W. B. Drees and P. S. van Koningsveld (eds), *The Study of Religion and the Training of Muslim Clergy in Europe*. Leiden: Leiden University Press, pp. 445–67.

Johansen, Birgitte S (2019). 'On the White Curriculum', paper presented at the conference 'Tracing Social Problems and Racialization in Europe', Roskilde University, 5 November.

Johansen, Birgitte (2021). 'Democratizing Scholarship: Reflections on the Current Curriculum Debates', paper presented at the Nordic Migration Research conference, Helsinki University, 11 January.

Johansen, B. S. and R. Spielhaus (2019). 'Quantitative Knowledge Production on Muslims in Europe as a Practice of Secular Suspicion', in M. Scheer, N. Fadil and B. S. Johansen (eds), *Secular Bodies, Affects and Emotions: European Configurations*. London: Bloomsbury.

Larsson, Görran (2018). 'Studying Islamic Theology at European Universities', in Mohammad Hashas, Jan Jaap de Ruiter and Niels Valdemar Vinding (eds), *Imams in Western Europe*. Amsterdam: Amsterdam University Press, pp. 121–42.

Leirvik, Oddbjørn (2016). 'Islamic University Theology', *Nordic Journal of Theology* 70(2): 127–44.

McCutcheon, Russell T. (ed.) (1999). *The Insider/Outsider Problem in the Study of Religion: A Reader*. London: Cassell.

McCutcheon, Russell T. (2003). 'The Ideology of Closure and the Problem with the Insider/ Outsider Problem in the Study of Religion', *Studies in Religion/Science Religieuse* 32(3): 337–52.

McMullin, Ernan (2008). 'Academic Freedom and Competing Authorities: Historical Reflections', in Willem B. Drees and Peter Sjoerd van Koningsveld (eds), *The Study of Religion and the Training of Muslim Clergy in Europe: Academic and Religious Freedom in the 21st Century*. Leiden: Leiden University Press, pp. 31–46.

Merton, Robert K. (1972). 'Insiders and Outsiders: A Chapter in the Sociology of Knowledge', *American Journal of Sociology* 78(1): 9–47.

National Union of Students (NUS) (2011). *Race for Equality: A Report on the Experiences of Black Students in Further and Higher Education*. London: NUS.

Powers, J. M. (1996). 'The Outsider's Gaze', in K. J. Mayberry (ed.), *Teaching What You're Not: Identity Politics in Higher Education*. New York: New York University Press, pp. 70–84.

Shah, Prakash (2010). 'A Reflection on the Shari'a Debate in Britain', *Studia z Prawa Wyznaniowego (Studies in Ecclesiastical Law)* 13: 71–98.

Sinding Jensen, Jeppe (2011). 'Revisiting the Insider–Outsider Debate: Dismantling a Pseudo-problem in the Study of Religion', *Method & Theory in the Study of Religion* 23(1): 29–47.

Symoens, Hilde de Ridder (ed.) (1994). *A History of the University in Europe*, vol. 1. Cambridge: Cambridge University Press.

Taylor, Charles (2007). *A Secular Age*. Cambridge, MA: Belknap Press of Harvard University Press.

Wagner, C. (2019). 'Islamische Theologie an deutschen Hochschulen studieren? Zu den Erfahrungen Studierender einer jungen Disziplin', in D. Heitzmann and K. Houda (eds), *Rassismus an Hochschulen: Analyse – Kritik – Intervention*. Weinheim: Beltz Verlagsgruppe, pp. 90–112.

Weber, Max (1904). 'Die "Objektivität" sozialwissenschaftlicher und sozialpolitischer Erkenntnis', *Archive für Sozialwissenschaft und Sozialpolitik* XIX. Band, 1. Heft, pp. 22–87.

Williams, Joanna (2014). 'In Defence of "the White Curriculum"', *Spiked*, 22 October 2014.

Williams, Joanna (2017). 'The "Decolonise the Curriculum" Re-racialises Knowledge', *Open Democracy*, 1 March.

Zimmerman, Jonathan (2016). *Campus Politics: What Everyone Needs to Know*. Oxford: Oxford University Press.

CHAPTER 4

What Do the Terms 'Confessional' and 'Non-confessional' Mean, and are they Helpful? Some Social Scientific Musings

SOPHIE GILLIAT-RAY

INTRODUCTION

Debates about the relationship between Islamic seminaries and institutions of higher education often distinguish these two sectors by reference to their pedagogical and epistemological approaches as being either 'confessional' or 'non-confessional'. This is likely to reflect a discourse and vocabulary that has shaped the world of religious education in schools for many years (Thompson 2004), and to some extent the respective approaches of 'theology' and 'religious studies' in the academy. Over the last decade or so, this vocabulary seems to have grafted itself onto discussions about the relationship between Islamic seminaries and universities as well, but often with little critique.

Given the changed landscape of advanced teaching and learning about Islam and Muslims in Britain over the last twenty-five years (Scott-Baumann and Cheruvallil-Contractor 2015), this chapter questions whether the terminology 'confessional' and 'non-confessional' remains helpful (at all – to anyone). Influenced by the way in which the binaries of 'insider' and 'outsider' have come to be regarded as problematic in relation to ethnographic social scientific fieldwork (for an example in British Muslim studies, see Abbas 2010), I propose that the assumed binary of confessional/non-confessional presents similar difficulties, and is arguably outdated. Influenced by social scientific perspectives which argue that identities and positionalities (in relation to more or less anything) are contextually dependent, negotiated, socially constructed and performed, I suggest that it may be helpful to move beyond the assumptions that seem to be inherent in the terms 'confessional' and 'non-confessional'.

But this exploration is necessarily interdisciplinary, as well as being informed by social scientific perspectives. It will involve reference to developments in religious studies, philosophy of religion and religious education. Traversing through these various disciplines, I hope to argue that concepts and vocabulary, and people and institutions, are far more complex, untidy and confused than any simplistic notions of 'confessional' and 'non-confessional' seem to suggest. In the last part of this chapter, I want to present some ideas about enabling criteria and opportunities for supporting partnership between Islamic seminaries and universities in the teaching of the Islamic tradition.

A Brief Literature Review

Notwithstanding some excellent research of recent years, the terms 'confessional' or 'non-confessional' are rarely problematised in publications concerned with teaching and learning about Islam. In their report on a project funded by the Economic and Social Research Council (ESRC), which explored the means by which the 'roadblocks' of collaborative partnership between universities and Muslim institutions could be dismantled, Scott-Baumann and Cheruvallil-Contractor record that there are 'Muslim institutions – seminaries and colleges – that take a more *confessional* approach' to the study of Islam (Scott-Baumann and Cheruvallil-Contractor 2013: 7, emphasis added). In the introduction to their seminal volume on Islamic education in Britain, they note the range of dichotomies at work in this field: 'sacred and profane, religious and secular, *confessional* and critical . . .' (Scott-Baumann and Cheruvallil-Contractor 2015: 1, emphasis added), though, of course, I do not assume they accept the reality, necessity or acceptance of these dichotomies. They add that Islamic education reflecting these dichotomies currently 'occupy separate and perceptually insular spaces' (ibid.: 1) while, of course, noting important signs of change via a small number of partnership arrangements that have emerged in Britain over the last decade. Similarly, in his study exploring the potential for partnership between UK higher education institutions and *darul uloom*, Ron Geaves notes that when it comes to religious education, 'a fully *confessional* approach to RE is far more relevant to its intended purposes' (Geaves 2015: 78, emphasis added). The very influential Siddiqui Report (2007) makes reference to the disconnect between 'insider' and 'outsider' approaches to the study of Islam and Muslims in Britain (Siddiqui 2007), grounded on the radically different origins, histories and curricula of so-called 'traditional' centres of (confessional) learning and academic institutions such as universities. The construction of these binaries poses significant problems, linguistically and conceptually, not least due to developments over the last decade.

What do 'Confessional' and 'Non-confessional' Mean?

Religious Education Perspectives

Before examining this conundrum in more depth, it is worth noting that the debate about bridging the gap between Islamic seminaries and universities is in fact a new chapter in a discussion that began in Britain just over fifty years ago. The work of the pioneering religious studies scholar, Prof. Ninian Smart, was critical in transforming the study of religion in Britain. His work enabled the phenomenological study of so-called 'world religions' to find its place within academic departments that had hitherto focused upon Christian theology dominated by confessional perspectives (Flood 1999: 233). This kind of confessional stance implied that Christian belief and the cultural identity in which it was grounded needed to be passed on with integrity from generation to generation, and, as such, the university (or indeed the school room) should be a space which 'should teach for belief, and not only a sphere in which beliefs are merely taught' (Diez de Velasco 2007: 79). This confessional approach placed the emphasis upon the individual and the consolidation of personal faith, albeit with the rigour of academic scholarship in theology and biblical studies. This left the non-confessional approach to deal with the social and collective heritage of faith communities, and the study of non-Christian religious texts, rituals and sacred languages, albeit empathically. Writing about Smart's contribution in bringing non-confessional religious studies into the world of confessional Christian theological studies, the religious education specialist Prof. Denise Cush wrote in 2011: 'Smart's approach appealed because it combined an attempt to study religions "objectively" (academically) with the realisation that the subject matter dealt with the deepest convictions, cherished values, ancestral traditions and very identity of fellow human beings, requiring an attitude of respect and empathy' (Cush 2011: 71).

Alongside his role as a professor of religious studies, Smart was deeply engaged in debates about religious education in schools. As such, he was instrumental in bringing about the development of multifaith religious education in schools that mirrored the incorporation of the emergent discipline of religious studies into departments of theology in British universities in the 1970s onwards. Cush's paper helpfully identifies the criteria for this so-called 'non-confessional' study of religion in schools. They included the idea that rather than teaching children to 'be religious' (or more specifically, Christian) they should be taught to understand the phenomenon of religion; religious education was viewed as an academic subject and an integral part of the school curriculum rather than something set apart; religious education was for all pupils, irrespective of their personal beliefs or family background; and, teachers were educated qualified professionals, rather than approved agents of religious organisations (Cush 2011).

Of course, with the benefit of time and hindsight, the kind of phenomenological approach advocated by Smart has been subject to intense critique, and to cite the title of the book by religious studies scholar Prof. Gavin Flood, we have now moved 'Beyond Phenomenology' (Flood 1999). Few would today accept the idea that religion can be studied 'objectively', and the various 'dimensions' of religion identified by Smart (the ethical, material, doctrinal, and so on) (Smart 1996) are arguably regarded as orientalist constructs that are ill-suited to a world shaped by religious diversity.

However, despite these criticisms, a respectful attitude to the study of the religious beliefs of others remains a valuable and enduring endeavour in the discipline of religious studies, and Smart can be credited with successfully bringing the non-confessional study of religion into an academic world that had been dominated by confessional study of Christian theology. The legacy of Smart's contribution to this 'bridging of the gap' is the creation of academic departments and professional associations up and down the country that accommodate 'theology and religious studies' as mutually reinforcing and usually harmonious academic companions. For example, at Cardiff University, our Department of Religious and Theological Studies benefits from the teaching contribution of colleagues based in South Wales Baptist College. They teach our students, we teach theirs, and there is a mutual respect for the different positions that colleagues occupy. In other words, the scope to bring Muslim institutions into partnership with universities in a similar way could build on the kind of agreements that have existed in the past between universities and Christian theological colleges. This would take us beyond a situation which characterises some of the arrangements in place today, where degree schemes offered by Muslim institutions are given mere 'validation' by a largely disinterested university administration. While 'stamp of approval' agreements of this kind have been useful to both parties in many ways, they do not reflect what is perhaps most needed, namely, the creation of new approaches to scholarship and intellectual endeavour that render any confessional/non-confessional binary obsolete.

Looking back to the 1980s and 1990s, the incorporation of so-called non-confessional approaches to the study of religion and school-based education was perhaps an inevitable development at a time when the Christian churches were in decline, and religious diversity was becoming more apparent in Britain. But there was little critical interrogation of what the terms 'confessional' or 'non-confessional' might imply, and to some extent, that remains the case. A notable exception comes from Penny Thompson, writing from the perspective of religious education in schools. She writes: 'non-confessionalism is founded on a contradiction: that education can proceed without "confessing" anything . . . [whereas] In fact, many different types of "confession" operate in religious education' (Thompson 2004: 61). She goes on to say 'a teacher declares something, even if that something is that religion is a matter in which the truth may not be known' (Thompson 2004: 64). We all have a worldview that inevitably shapes the way in which we learn, teach and understand the world – and this worldview is an ingredient in our social relations with others.

> The atheist has his or her own view about religion, just as the believer does. To begin to construct a syllabus requires that a view is taken, even on so basic an issue as to what constitutes a religion. (Thompson 2004: 64)

This useful critique provides a helpful introduction to other ways in which we might think in more depth about the vocabulary and assumptions that often shape debates about the relationship between Muslim/confessional institutions, and non-Muslim/non-confessional universities. A brief examination of religious language from a philosophical perspective comes as a prelude to some considerations shaped by the social sciences.

Religious Language

Most dictionaries define 'confession' or 'confessional' as indicating a statement of some kind, such as the admission of a criminal misdemeanour, or a pronouncement of a religious doctrine. But influenced by philosophers and linguists, religious studies scholars have critically interrogated the nature of religious language and the statements upon which 'confessional' positions rest. For example, the philosopher of religion, Peter Donovan, argues that doctrinal statements about religious faith are inherently problematic (Donovan 1976). When a religious believer recites a creed or says a prayer, we might legitimately ask them in what sense they are making a particular religious claim. Do their claims mean they think something is literally true, or not? He gives a good example, derived from the Lord's Prayer, of how confusing religious language can be when we try to understand, in day-to-day terms, exactly what is meant (Donovan 1976: 7):

> 'Our Father' (though not our parent)
> 'Who art in Heaven' (though not among the stars)
> 'Give us our daily bread' (which we will have to buy)
> 'Deliver us from evil' (does that mean accidents and illness too?)

'The words are clear enough, but what do they really tell us', he asks (Donovan 1976: 7). I do not mean for this to become an exploration in the philosophy of religious language, but I hope that I have made the point that when a religious believer recites a creed or doctrinal statement – thus adopting a position we might call 'confessional' – there are significant problems in relation to what their words actually mean, and, of course, what they themselves understand them to mean. Religious utterances do not 'express truth-claims in the same sense as scientific or empirical utterances' (Franck 2015: 227). Even the most devout religious believer is unlikely to proclaim their beliefs about the Divine with a view to empirical or scientific testing of their claim in order to establish undisputed proof. Rather, they are declaring that they have a reliance and confidence in something that requires faith (Franck 2015) and that by its very nature cannot be proven or falsified, or even subjected to the same kind of tests that might be applied to other spheres of knowledge. As Franck writes, confessional statements of faith 'have the character of being "eternal truths", unaffected by any empirical evidence presented to prove or disprove the claims' (Franck 2015: 227).

Social Science Perspectives

In recent years, social scientists have similarly queried the idea of 'neutrality' when it comes to sociological theory, data collection or data analysis: 'it is impossible for academics to refrain from rendering judgement, whether implicit or explicit, about the beliefs of the subjects they study' (Yong 2012: 18). Everything we do is filtered through our biographies and embodied selves, thus ruling out any possibility of being 'objective'. What we are therefore required to do is bring a self-critical and reflexive awareness of our positionality, in order to consider how it might be affecting our fieldwork practice and our interpretation of data. This emphasis on reflexivity (Coffey 1999) has led to a breakdown of all sorts of binaries and boundaries, and a critique of concepts akin to 'confessional' and 'non-confessional'. For example, relatively hard borders were once placed around those who were deemed to be 'insiders' or 'outsiders' to (religious) communities. It was relatively easy to assume that 'insiders' undertaking fieldwork in their own communities were those who assented, at least to some degree, to orthodox religious teachings, while 'outsiders' to a religious community were those who did not.

The insider–outsider problem in the study of religion, perhaps influenced by methodological and theoretical discussions in sociology and anthropology, has been carefully examined by scholars of religion alive to these debates. One of the clearest expositions is given by Prof. Kim Knott in her chapter in John Hinnells' edited collection on the study of religion, in which she uses a diagram to 'portray insider and outsider positions based on a model of participant/observer roles in the social sciences' (Knott 2005: 246, influenced by Gold 1958) (Figure 4.1). This continuum is self-explanatory in the way it depicts the scholarly activities of those who undertake participatory research within their

What do 'Confessional' and 'Non-confessional' Mean?

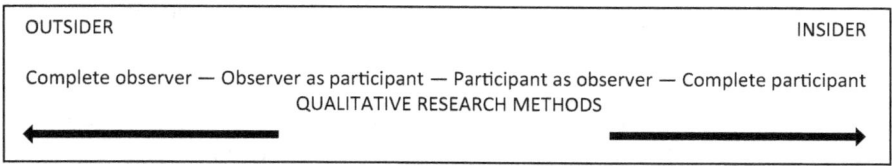

Figure 4.1 Insider and outsider positions

Source: K. Knott, 'Insider/Outsider Perspectives', in J. Hinnells (ed.), *The Routledge Companion to the Study of Religion*. London: Routledge, 2005, pp. 243–58.

own faith communities as 'insiders', while more detached, purely observational roles are taken up by those who are 'outsiders' to a faith community.

Via a range of excellent examples, Knott explores the way in which these simplistic theoretical and methodological categorisations can completely break down when we factor in the socially constructed, negotiated and contextually dependent circumstances in which empirical research actually happens, and the real-life world of individuals. As a result of her arguments, we come to realise that:

> ... perhaps religion is always the product of a creative symbiosis of insiders and outsiders, populated by individuals who cannot simply be placed into the rigid categories of believer and unbeliever, just as the scholarly community contains theories and individuals who cannot be so easily placed into an either/or schema in terms of religious thinking. (Salomon and Walton 2012: 408)

Taking inspiration from the way that Knott has examined the issue through a range of fine examples, I want to suggest that we can and should equally deconstruct the 'confessional' and 'non-confessional' binary in relation to teaching and learning about Islam and Muslims in Britain today.

For example, a confessional approach to the study of Islam may assume an uncritical and sympathetic insider, while the non-confessional approach is adopted by the critical outsider. Neither of these assumptions may be true. So-called 'insiders' to faith communities can be as critical and questioning as anybody and may pose searching and difficult questions about their traditions, their heritage, their history and, yes, even their theology. Conversely, a sympathetic 'outsider' may be so awed and emotionally bound-up in their engagement with a faith community that they lose the capacity for real critical questioning. Arguably, it is educationally unhelpful to students (regardless of institution) to assume that 'confessional' teaching delivered by an 'insider' to a faith community is somehow more 'authentic' or correct compared with the teaching offered by the non-confessional but knowledgeable 'outsider', that is, if education also involves helping students with the skill of 'how to think'.

Secondly, the simplistic use of the terms confessional and non-confessional seems to imply the holding of positions that place individuals at opposite ends of a spectrum, thus not allowing for the fact that one may adopt stronger or weaker positions in relation to all manner of doctrines or practices. One may hold orthodox 'confessional' positions in some aspects of belief and theology, but not others. Characterising a group of Muslim scholars as holding 'confessional' positions assumes a homogeneity that is not likely to be reflected in reality. Thirdly, the confessional position seems to imply a relationship to religious practice that may or may not be evident in reality. Do all 'practice what they preach?'. Fourthly, recent empirical evidence demonstrates that the assumption that confessional and non-confessional study of Islam are somehow oppositional is incorrect.

The evidence for this comes via the recent work of Jenny Berglund and Bill Gent where they have demonstrated the way in which young school-aged Muslims are able to find a degree of symbiosis between the two (Berglund and Gent 2019). The skills of critical thinking acquired in the religious education classroom had helped one of the Muslim pupils in their study in relation to his (confessional) Islamic studies: 'source criticism/evaluation of sources, you find it in Islam as well I now know, but I have learned to look critically: "Who said this? Is there evidence?" . . .' (Berglund and Gent 2019: 329). They go on to note that:

> for this student, learning about evaluation of sources in secular RE not only meant that he looked at different sources in Islamic education critically, but also eventually made him realise that critical thinking has also been an inherent part of the Islamic tradition, as seen in the classical and ongoing study of *hadith*, for example. (Berglund and Gent 2019: 329)

Once again, research derived from the field of religious education provides a useful lens through which to examine the rich potential for dismantling the supposed binary between confessional and non-confessional advanced Islamic studies. The timing could not be more opportune. The emphasis in contemporary university-based Islamic studies on texts, history and language arguably presents the Islamic tradition in a way that has lost touch with the way in which Islam is practised by ordinary believers. 'Bridging the gap' would help to re-shape the Islamic studies field in a way that more closely reflects the meanings of Islam to Muslims themselves, not least because:

> the Study of Islam and Muslims is as much about Muslims (people, in society and in history) as its about 'understanding Islam'. And indeed, it is

often about both, since Muslim people are so often in the business of trying to live according to particular understandings of Islam. (El-Awaisi and Nye 2006: 26)

Arguably, there is an ethical responsibility to open up teaching and learning about Islam in British universities to make it more hospitable to confessional perspectives. Universities are spaces in which knowledge about Islam and Muslims is being produced and they should therefore become spaces that allow for the study of both conventional academic discourses, but also the discourses and worldviews that come from the world of Islamic seminaries, without placing harsh limits on what counts as an 'acceptable' or 'unacceptable' confessional perspective. But on the flip side:

the agenda must challenge the more 'traditionally' focused styles and approaches to 'understanding Islam', which are often deeply faith based. As the proliferation of Muslim institutions of learning has shown, teaching on Islam is often structured on the assumption that it is only for Muslims, that non-Muslims are to be left out (or brought in on the hope of convincing). (El-Awaisi and Nye 2006: 25)

There is much to gain from a meeting on middle ground, not least because bridging the gap between Islamic seminaries and universities is more than just the combining of educational institutions – it involves a broader dialogue about the place of Islam and Muslims in society and academia.

Compounding the philosophical and linguistic problems bound up with the vocabulary surrounding the 'confessional' and 'non-confessional' study of Islam, social science perspectives indicate that the criteria for determining what counts as 'confessional' or 'non-confessional' (and, of course, who is qualified to arbitrate the answer) are so complex and socially constructed that we seem to reach a complete impasse. The either/or dichotomy that is assumed in the binary 'confessional' and 'non-confessional' creates a gulf between 'us' and 'them' which is unhelpful, unnecessary and does not seem to reflect the complicated, situated and contingent positions that individuals often take in relation to particular circumstances and negotiations. Ethnographic studies of contemporary Muslim communities depict the reality that individuals on their religious journey often move through 'moments of conviction, scepticism, and believing; their roaming through different denominations; their elated successes or discouraging failures and struggles to accomplish religiosity . . . their renewal of commitments, engagement in healings, and so on' (Oustinova-Stjepanovic 2015: 118). So, behind even an apparently confessional or non-confessional position is likely to be an individual who is continually shifting and developing with the acquisition of new knowledge and experience. Within this state of flux, any rigid categorisation, label, stereotype or assumption becomes problematic.

Beyond Binaries

Having tried to inject some shades of grey into a debate about seminary and university partnerships that have sometimes been characterised by assumptions resting on frequently unquestioned use of the terms 'confessional' or 'non-confessional', we can move on to think about what, or rather who, are the critical ingredients for successfully navigating the relationship between them when it comes to teaching and learning about Islam. Excellent prior research has been done about the challenges and the importance of seeking to build a partnership between seminary and university (Scott-Baumann and Cheruvallil-Contractor 2013; Geaves 2015). There is nothing more I can add to some of the insights they have reached about issues to do with pedagogy, assessment, infrastructures, validation of learning and so on. But some of the work we have done at the Islam-UK Centre at Cardiff University may have something useful to bring to the debate.

Before proceeding, I should be transparent about my interest in this matter. Early in my career, I needed to recruit researchers who could work on projects that demanded an in-depth and to some extent embodied knowledge of Islamic sources, law and texts in Arabic and south Asian languages, alongside a capacity to undertake qualitative social scientific research. I use the word 'embodied' here deliberately, because, for example, my AHRC/ESRC project on the work of Muslim chaplains required a fieldworker whom our research participants would recognise as being capable of understanding how a complex pastoral situation could be managed in accordance with the finer points of Islamic law (Ali and Gilliat-Ray 2012; Gilliat-Ray et al. 2013). During their interviews, and in order to explain their practice, Muslim chaplains would often recite verses from the Qur'an in Arabic or allude to particular *du'as* they would use as part of their work with Muslim prisoners or hospital patients. I needed a fieldworker who could understand and interpret as far as possible what they were saying in these languages. Finding researchers with all the skillsets needed was nigh on impossible. While there were some excellent Muslim social scientists to be recruited, not all of them had an accompanying in-depth understanding of the Islamic tradition and its languages. Conversely, there seemed to be a large pool of classically trained Islamic scholars who could be appointed to research assistant roles, but often they lacked any familiarity with the social sciences and the processes of qualitative data collection. Faced with this situation, two remedies seemed prudent. One was the appointment of colleagues who had already 'bridged the gap' in their own educational journeys, combining seminary-based studies with doctoral-level research in the academy. They seemed most likely to be responsive to a rapid introduction to the social sciences! Secondly, we developed a Masters degree that offered students a thorough grounding in 'British Muslim Studies' with a strong emphasis on social science method and theory. Via the Jameel Scholarship Programme, we have welcomed a number of students to both MA- and PhD-level study who have similarly 'bridged the gap' between the seminary and university in their prior education. In this way, we have slowly been shaping a hospitable environment where classically trained Islamic scholars are equipped to undertake ethnographic social scientific projects. Some of these projects are externally funded, others are shaped by an understanding of what students themselves regard as research priorities for Muslim communities. These colleagues are equipped to situate their Islamic belief and heritage within the frameworks of contemporary academic theories and discourses, and, in so doing, they have acquired an ability to:

> to view and interpret the world along two sight lines: that of a fieldworker and that of a ritual participant ... the simultaneity of these perspectives prevents radical relativism and the hierarchical (de)valuation of religious and non-religious experiences, regardless of whether a researchers is an atheist, agnostic, or 'believer'. (Oustinova-Stjepanovic 2015: 121)

The career development of those with capacity to see 'along two sight lines' is arguably critical for the future relationship between seminaries and universities. This is because colleagues with these skills and biographies can act as inter-institutional 'brokers' in unique ways. Trained in social sciences, they have the capability to undertake what Gavin Flood describes as a position of 'dialogical reflexivity' (Flood 1999: 226) which can expose and question positionality, motivations, agendas and the different vocabularies upon which we draw. Such colleagues can ask: how much thought has been given to the underlying power dynamics in the conversations that underpin efforts to bridge the gap between seminaries and universities? To what extent is there an implicit assumption that the former are required to adapt what they do in order to become acceptable in the sphere of the latter? Colleagues who traverse between the seminary and university are uniquely placed to question and critique the power of the university sector to shape 'what counts' as a meaningful programme of study, assessment or validation of learning. They are equally well-placed to articulate to seminaries the potential benefits of engagement with universities, such as the opportunities for development of employability skills.

The intellectual development of a new generation of Islamic scholars who can traverse the world of the seminary and academy may find the theory of Islamic critical realism a useful way to bridge an epistemological gap that can exist between the two spheres (Wilkinson 2015). Social scientific theories that assume knowledge about humanity and our place in the world to be socially constructed, negotiated and contextually-dependent do not sit well alongside orthodox Muslim views about knowledge as divinely revealed and non-negotiable. The recent work of Matthew Wilkinson takes the social theory of critical realism developed by Roy Bhaskar and brings it into conversation with the Islamic tradition. The outcome is an approach to research and teaching about Islam that has value in both the seminary and academy by virtue of the fact that it allows for 'ontological realism, epistemological relativism and judgemental rationality' (Wilkinson 2015: 50). The profundity of Wilkinson's work is poorly reflected in the brief discussion here. But, in essence, the idea of ontological realism gives space to the notion that 'being exists independently of our knowledge of it, and in particular, our ability to describe it, so that it cannot be reduced to discourse, nor is it contained or constructed in the semiotics of our speech' (Wilkinson 2015: 51). This theoretical stance makes it possible to hold a position whereby God/Allah can be said to exist (or not exist) 'independently of our knowledge of or belief in Him, or lack of knowledge or belief in Him' (Wilkinson 2015: 54). In other words, a Muslim and non-Muslim scholar can 'agree to differ' with integrity and without diminishing the perspective of either party. Epistemological relativism – the idea that the world can be experienced, understood and interpreted by different people in different ways – creates a theoretical space for intellectual hospitality and a recognition that in matters of belief, there is room for diversity. Judgemental rationality provides the toolkit for making assessments about 'the accuracy and validity of competing accounts of phenomena according to sets of religious, scientific and experiential criteria' (Wilkinson 2015: 59). Intellectual conversation and exploration can be conducted with reference to 'processes of logic, discourse and debate that pertain to any particular field or discipline, the operation of effective and coherent research methods and design, and personal self-scrutiny and reflexivity' (Wilkinson 2015: 60). Wilkinson's work provides a valuable and much needed theoretical underpinning to the emergent field of 'British Muslim studies' by offering both Muslim and non-Muslim scholars a shared intellectual environment characterised by academic and religious (or non-religious) integrity. By way of a conclusion to this section, and reflecting on some twenty-five years or so of research in the field of British Muslim studies, it has sometimes seemed to me as though Muslim communities and organisations are being asked to develop themselves and generate capacity at a rate that is simply not possible within the confines of natural, organic, inter-generational change and the socio-economic situation of Muslim communities more broadly. Some of the policy interventions of recent years that have underpinned discussions about the relationship between seminaries and universities have been driven by concerns about 'radicalisation' on university campuses, or the capacity of imams to manage extremism in their communities. While these are legitimate concerns, any truly successful effort to tackle these 'problems', or, more positively, to create new forms of flourishing engagement between seminaries and universities, is likely to arise from the imagination and energy of individuals who can spearhead change within both institutions, simultaneously, and with integrity vis-à-vis their histories and approaches. The career of such individuals needs to be nurtured and supported, and I would like to think that Cardiff University has been one of the institutions that has helped to play a small role in this process. But it will take time, and generational change cannot happen overnight. We are still on the cusp of having a sufficient critical mass of individuals who can enable enduring and sustainable future collaboration.

Thinking Outside the Walls

Many of the actual or exploratory partnerships that have evolved between seminaries and universities in the United Kingdom over the last decade or so have often been pitching their potential collaboration efforts at postgraduate or undergraduate degree level and have often been premised on face-to-face teaching within a classroom. There is a lot at stake in terms of human and financial resources when degree programmes lasting a year, or more, are involved. In view of this, and the entirely new teaching and learning context arising from the Covid-19 pandemic of 2020–21, there is an opportunity to re-think the development of partnerships between Muslim seminaries and universities from new angles.

Many universities have units devoted to adult learning and continuing professional development (CPD) programmes which deliver courses via blended learning approaches, online-only platforms such as Blackboard and in the classroom. These can be both credit and non-credit bearing. Similarly, since around 2014, many universities have developed Massive Open Online Courses ('MOOCs') hosted on platforms such as FutureLearn which offer free short online courses to the general public (Gilliat-Ray 2020). Outward-facing opportunities of this kind are delivering what the then Labour Party leader, Jeremy Corbyn, advocated in his 2019 Labour Party conference speech when he said that education should be 'like an escalator running alongside you throughout life, that you can get on and off whenever you want' (Coughlan 2019). Thus far, it would appear that the Muslim seminary sector in the United Kingdom relies on fairly conventional classroom-based, textually orientated learning that is geared towards young Muslims up to their early twenties. And yet, early findings from a current research project at the Islam-UK Centre at Cardiff University provides clear evidence that many seminary graduates (some of whom go on to become imams) feel that they lack opportunities (and time) for learning and CPD, once they leave the seminary. The 'before' and 'after' of seminary education seems ripe for growth and presents universities and Muslim educational institutions with a different kind of opportunity for collaboration and partnership.

This scenario presents a chance to explore ways to unlock the potential and infrastructures of both the university and seminary sectors that 'blends' the knowledge and capacities of both. The development of short courses, jointly hosted seminars or visiting staff exchanges – as a means of relationship-building and bridging the gap – is less risky and expensive than the validation of full-time degree programmes, which, despite the best efforts of those involved, seem to be some way from being realised on any significant scale. Over the years, initiatives of various kinds seem to have been blown hither and thither by changing political winds, amongst other things.

By force of circumstances, universities are currently being pushed towards blended learning, with far greater emphasis on the use of virtual learning environments than ever before. The rapid acceleration of technology and expertise in online pedagogy, while challenging, is nonetheless an opportunity for an expansion in distance-learning provision. Those who are committed to the project of enabling partnerships between universities and seminaries will hopefully find that they are pushing at an open door, were they to consider the development of collaborative short courses – or even a MOOC – with a seminary. The gulf between the two sectors is only likely to widen if seminaries are 'left behind' by the rapid expansion of university-based online learning, frustrating even further the eventual goal of validating the post-18 education provided in seminaries. By virtue of their relationships across institutions, those *darul uloom* graduates with the capacity to 'see along two sight-lines' are well-placed to broker exploration of new opportunities for 'life-long learning' that involves the seminary sector, but in entirely new ways.

Conclusion

Under closer inspection, the binary 'confessional' and 'non-confessional' learning about Islam seems problematic, and arguably breaks down entirely when examined through the disciplinary lenses of the social sciences. The binary falters even more in light of the kind of pragmatic arrangements that have enabled Christian theological colleges to work in collaborative partnership with university departments of Theology and Religious studies for decades. This is compounded by recent research evidence suggesting that many devout young Muslims appear able to navigate seminary studies with conventional RE school work seamlessly and unproblematically (Berglund and Gent 2019). With a more fluid and flexible vocabulary, it may be easier to find a 'middle way' that might see seminaries and universities moving closer, in mutually beneficial ways.

In the short term, their collaboration may not necessarily be driven by the expensive and demanding project of finding ways to validate the post-18 seminary curriculum – also known as the *darsi-i nizami* (Sidat 2018; Sidat 2019). Instead, the challenges and opportunities posed by coronavirus and the dramatic shift towards online and blended education, presents those with capacity to 'see along to two sight lines' scope to explore new avenues for collaboration on projects that may be of smaller scale, but of no less importance if the idea of formal, structured 'life-long learning' is to become more firmly embedded into the world of Muslim education and continuous professional development. Likewise, driven by necessity and pragmatism, the sector-wide adoption of 'blended learning' approaches to university education in 2020 is a felicitous opportunity for academics to re-think how and why they teach what they do. But such a challenging pedagogical shake-up may in the fullness of time inadvertently create a new and more hospitable environment for conversation between seminaries and universities, and a willingness to 'think outside the walls'.

References

Abbas, T. (2010). 'Muslim-on-Muslim Social Research: Knowledge, Power and Religio-cultural Identities', *Social Epistemology* 24(2): 123–36.

Ali, M. and S. Gilliat-Ray (2012). 'Muslim Chaplains: Working at the Interface of "Public" and "Private"', in W. Ahmad and Z. Sardar (eds), *Muslims in Britain: Making Social and Political Space*. London: Routledge, pp. 84–100.

Berglund, J. and B. Gent (2019). 'Qur'anic Education and Non-confessional RE: An Intercultural Perspective', *Intercultural Education* 30(3): 323–34.

Coffey, A. (1999). *The Ethnographic Self: Fieldwork and the Representation of Identity*. London: Sage.

Coughlan, S. (2019). 'Labour Promises Free Jobs Retraining for Adults', available at: https://www.bbc.co.uk/news/education-50378666, last accessed 21 September 2020.

Cush, D. (2011). 'Without Fear or Favour: Forty Years of Non-confessional and Multifaith Religious Education in Scandinavia and the UK', in L. Franken and P. Loobuyck (eds), *Religious Education in a Plural, Secularised Society: A Paradigm Shift*. Münster: Waxmann Verlag, pp. 69–84.

Diez de Velasco, F. (2007). 'Religion, Identity and Education for Peace: Beyond the Dichotomies: Confessional/Non-confessional and Global/Local', *British Journal of Religious Education* 29(1): 77–87.

Donovan, P. (1976). *Religious Language*. London: Sheldon Press.

El-Awaisi, A. a-F. and M. Nye (2006). *Time for Change: Report on the Future of the Study of Islam and Muslims in Universities and Colleges in Multicultural Britain*. Dundee: Al-Maktoum Institute Academic Press.

Flood, G. (1999). *Beyond Phenomenology: Rethinking the Study of Religion*. London: Cassell.

Franck, O. (2015). 'Critical Religious Education: Highlighting Religious Truth-Claims in Non-confessional Educational Contexts', *British Journal of Religious Education* 37(3): 225–39.

Geaves, R. (2015). 'An Exploration of the Viability of Partnership between dar al-ulum and Higher Education Institutions in North West England Focusing upon Pedagogy and Relevance', *British Journal of Religious Education* 37(1): 64–82.

Gilliat-Ray, S. (2020). 'Learning about Islam and Muslims Online: Reflections on the Design and Delivery of a Massive Open Online Course (MOOC) 2014–2019', *Teaching Theology & Religion* 32(1): 1–13.

Gilliat-Ray, S., M. M. Ali and S. Pattison (2013). *Understanding Muslim Chaplaincy*. Aldershot: Ashgate.

Gold, R. (1958). 'Roles in Sociological Field Observations', *Social Forces* 36: 217–23.

Knott, K. (2005). 'Insider/Outsider Perspectives', in J. Hinnells (ed.), *The Routledge Companion to the Study of Religion*. London: Routledge, pp. 243–58.

Oustinova-Stjepanovic, G. (2015). 'Confessional Anthropology', *Social Analysis* 59: 114–34.

Salomon, N. and J. Walton (2012). 'Religious Criticism, Secular Critique, and the "Critical Study of Religion": Lessons from the Study of Islam', in R. Orsi (ed.), *The Cambridge Companion to Religious Studies*. Cambridge: Cambridge University Press, pp. 403–20.

Scott-Baumann, A. and S. Cheruvallil-Contractor (2013). *Collaborative Partnerships between Universities and Muslim Institutions: Dismantling the Roadblocks*. Derby: University of Derby.

Scott-Baumann, A. and S. Cheruvallil-Contractor (2015). *Islamic Education in Britain: New Pluralist Paradigms*, London: Bloomsbury.

Sidat, H. (2018). 'Between Tradition and Transition: An Islamic Seminary, or Dar al-Uloom in Modern Britain', *Religions* 9(10): 1–14.

Sidat, H. (2019). 'Shedding Light on the Modalities of Authority in a Dar al-Uloom, or Religious Seminary, in Britain', *Religions* 10(12): 653.

Siddiqui, A. (2007). *Islam at Universities in England: Meeting the Needs and Investing in the Future*. London: Department for Innovation, Universities and Skills.

Smart, N. (1996). *Dimensions of the Sacred*. London: HarperCollins.

Thompson, P. (2004). 'Whose Confession? Which Tradition?', *British Journal of Religious Education* 26: 61–72.

Wilkinson, M. (2015). *A Fresh Look at Islam in a Multi-Faith World*. London: Routledge.

Yong, A. (2012). 'Observation–Participation–Subjunctivation: Methodological Play and Meaning-making in Tte Study of Religion and Theology', *Religious Studies and Theology* 31: 17–40.

CHAPTER 5

A Decade of Islamic Theological Studies at German Universities: Expectations, Outcomes and Future Perspectives

BEKIM AGAI AND JAN FELIX ENGELHARDT

INTRODUCTION

Just over ten years ago in 2010, the first institutes for Islamic theological studies at public German universities opened their doors to students. In the background, a whole society was awaiting something between complete failure and absolute fulfilment of prevailing high expectations. Scholars of Oriental and Islamic studies both welcomed the establishment of a theological neighbouring discipline and warned against a confessionalisation of research on Islam. The state had high expectations of successfully integrating migrant Muslims into German society, and addressing complex issues such as de-radicalisation. Muslim organisations saw the emerging academic field as an opportunity to make progress on their way to official recognition by the state, on the one hand, while fearing state influence on their religion, on the other. Muslim students had vast expectations and projections about a new academic discipline that teaches their religion. Ten years on, where do Islamic theological studies in Germany stand against these expectations? How did it establish itself as an academic discipline, and what future challenges and prospects await it?

In this chapter, we will first present the backdrop of the establishment and the ideas that led to the science policy decision to introduce departments of Islamic theological studies at public universities. We will argue that this process did not take place in a linear form, but was determined by different actors, different expectations and fears. We will give an insight into the first decade of experience and we will present discussions around and within the discipline, its academic staff, the students, the impact of and on the Muslim community and the relationship to Islamic studies. We will also sketch out how the departments are integrated within the larger university setting vis-à-vis other disciplines that take Islam as an object of study, and how far the assumption of a confessional perspective on Islam is valid in this context. Here, we will argue that a closer look at the practices of knowledge-production at universities shows that boundaries between confessional and non-confessional studies are clearer to define in theory than to find in practice. It is worth looking at the epistemic challenges the canon of an Islamic theological tradition receives from being engaged with an interdisciplinary setting and practical demands. We will conclude with future perspectives on challenging fields like the involvement in practical issues such as imam education, pastoral and spiritual care that need a reconfiguration between university, Islamic communities and the state.

Backdrop of the Establishment

Without a doubt, the science policy decision to establish Islamic theology marks the beginning not only of an academic discipline, but also of an experiment at the crossroads of society and academia. Yet this move marks only one milestone in societal processes that began decades earlier and that produced both the necessity and the capacity to establish Islamic theological studies: an Islamisation of migrants and integration discourses; a securitisation of Islam and Muslims; and the emergence of Muslim organisations and individual actors. In contrast to many other scientific disciplines, Islamic theological studies therefore did not primarily come into being due to differentiation and overspill of communication processes within existing disciplines (Stichweh 2003), but because of societal processes and political decisions. More so, it was cast into an existing mould of theology at the university, which shaped central aspects of Islamic academic knowledge production. This backdrop makes the discipline special and explains academic discussions with regard to self-understanding, political expectations and suspicions of it being a political project rather than an academic discipline that have since accompanied Islamic theological studies.

Islamisation of Integration

What were the societal processes that preceded the introduction of Islamic theology at German universities? First, the migration from predominantly Muslim countries – Turkey, southeastern Europe and the Middle East/North Africa – mainly since the 1960s, which has subsequently added up to a significant number of people with (some kind of) Muslim belief, primarily in West Germany. As a result, Muslims became a demographic and social reality in Germany (Agai and Omerika 2017: 330). However, speaking of a 'Muslim minority' at that point would, in our view, not yet have been appropriate, as this term implies the existence of a distinct, in this case religious group that stands in a subaltern relation to a dominant majority. While today the idea of a 'Muslim minority' has become omnipresent in both research and public and political perception (Amir-Moazami 2018), for the first decades migrants in Germany were primarily perceived as foreigners, categorised according to the nation-states they came from, not as Muslims. Until the 1990s, a dominant political assumption was that these migrants and their families would one day 'return' to their home countries (Rosenow-Williams 2012: 113–15). It was only in 1999 that a new citizenship law facilitated the naturalisation of foreigners and their children, as a result of which about 45 percent of people of Muslim belief/heritage became German citizens (Haug et al. 2009: 80). Official statistics now estimate the number of Muslims in Germany at between 4.4 and 4.7 million or approximately 5.5–5.7 percent (BMI 2022). If one considers Muslims as a group that is homogeneous enough to qualify as a religious community, it is the largest non-Christian community in Germany. We are cautious of speaking of a Muslim group, community or minority here, since the creation of 'Muslims' as a category of social differentiation is heavily based on perceptions of Muslims as a homogeneous group, the 'other' and, ultimately, a threat. The identification as Muslims increased after the terror attacks in the United States and Europe between 2001 and 2005. Hence, at a time where many migrants with Turkish, Arabic, Bosnian or other backgrounds became German nationals, they were also labelled as 'Muslims',[1] regardless of their actual religious belief or practice. An 'Islamisation of the integration debate' took place (Spielhaus 2011; Hierl 2012; Tezcan 2012).

For decades, German politics considered the religious needs of Muslims in Germany as matters concerning their countries of origin, a foreign affair (Rosenow-Williams 2012: 145). The religious demands of Muslims in Germany were not perceived as an issue for German domestic policies. Most Islamic organisations in Germany were closely linked to governments or movements in countries their members or their members' ancestors migrated from. This had the convenient effect that mosques, religious education and other religious needs did not need to be governed by the German state, which long clung to the idea that (Muslim) migrants would one day return to their home countries. Yet it also meant that these states retained a grip on 'their citizens' at a time where integration was fostered by new laws on citizenship and fear of 'foreign influence' for safety reasons. There was, and still is, a fear that religious and political ideologies in other countries have effects on the landscape of Islam in Germany

---

[1] It is important to note that 'Muslim' in this sense is not identical with belief or practice or membership in organisations (like in the Christian context), but according to proportions of Muslims in the country a person or a family comes from, making it a racial attribution rather than a religious category (Ramm 2010: 188–92).

and on German citizens categorised as Muslims. Especially the development of a Salafi movement in Germany (Thielmann 2014), sometimes directly connected to foreign influence, gave rise to the securitisation of Islam in Germany and other European countries.

Securitisation: Islam as a Problem

Public attention to religion has increased over the last two decades in Germany, and discourses as well as political decisions on religious affairs have been inextricably linked with discourses on Islam and Muslims in Germany, which in turn focus on security and integration issues. In this respect, Germany is no different from other European countries (Cesari 2012: 433–4; Rosenow-Williams 2012: 127–9). The securitisation of discourses on Muslims, as well as the Islamisation of people with a migrant background from majority Muslim countries, led to a series of governmental practices that critically re-evaluated the idea of Muslims in the German diaspora as being nurtured and influenced by foreign states and transnational movements. Instead, Muslims in Germany were increasingly considered as a community that ought to be integrated into German society by implementing a body of regulation and acknowledgement practices (Tezcan 2012) that connect integration and control.

Key to these practices has been the German Islam Conference. Established in 2006 as a forum for exchange between the state and Islamic organisations and Muslim individuals, it has been heavily burdened with security issues and questions of integration (see Amir-Moazami 2011: 8–9; Rosenow-Williams 2012: 119–20; Tezcan 2012). Here, one key area of acknowledgement and regulation became the educational sector. Islamic religious education at public schools, parallel to the existing classes in Catholic or Protestant religion, now obtained a central significance. Islamic organisations had been calling for it since as early as the late 1970s (Søvik 2006: 333). Educating Muslims in Germany within schools and universities in the political context was not presented as a question of equality, but as a question of security and a tool for integration. As teachers for religious education have to be trained at universities, Islamic theology at public universities came into play as a necessary precondition.

Muslims as Central Actors

The state's interest, governing practice and domesticising policies that foster an Islam suitable to interact with have been described and criticised in multiple ways, for example, as a political project for disciplining the Muslim subject and part of a framework of governmentality (Tezcan 2012; Aguilar and Ahmad 2020). Yet in our view, these critiques too often neglect the central role Muslims played in these processes, their motives for seeking interaction with the state (in order to obtain recognition, security, influence and access to resources) or interpret them as proof of either opportunistic manoeuvres or internalisation of domestic quasi-colonialisation of religious actors (Engelhardt 2019: 112–17). These critiques miss that Islam is organised in civil society organisations which need the state to address matters that are located at the intersection of religion and politics: education, anti-discrimination, spiritual care at public institutions, needs of religious personnel, etc. All of these issues are vital for the community and, to different degrees, need consultation and cooperation between the state and religious organisations.

It is important here to take into consideration that the top-down approach of establishing Islamic theological studies had been preceded by two important developments within the Muslim communities and the academic study of Islam in Germany from bottom-up. One is the social formation of 'Muslims', which not only takes place via external discursive forces, but is also advanced by the creation of Islamic organisations and their formulation of Islamic positions. It took years for Muslims as religious individuals in Germany to form organisations beyond specific groups and identify common goals that they pursued *as Muslims* despite their ethnic, linguistic, cultural and inner-Islamic heterogeneity, such as religious education at public schools and official recognition (Rosenow-Williams 2012: 17). Among Muslims and their organisations, the quest for systematic equal treatment translated, among others, into the demand for Islamic religious education at public schools. While for the majority of Christian pupils religious education was provided in cooperation between church and state, supervised and paid for by the state, Muslim (and other non-Christian) schoolchildren could only visit an alternative, ranging from supervised school break to ethics classes. Islamic religious education was expected to treat Muslim pupils on the same level as Christian pupils, teach Islam in German language (not the case in most mosques) and reach all pupils, not only those connected to mosque community teaching. German would become their religious lingua franca and Islam a part of the normality of Germany starting with the school.[2] Having religious education in schools with a backbone of theology in universities became not only a question of a specific need but also a question of equality of Muslims as citizens.

The other bottom-up development took place in German academia, mainly within Islamic studies and in the field of pedagogy. Here, a number of Muslim scholars had emerged and formed a small epistemic community (Haas 1997),

---

[2] In 2002, the Central Council of Muslims in Germany (Zentralrat der Muslime in Deutschland, ZMD) demanded German-language religious instruction at schools, as well as the establishment of academic professorships for the university education of teachers of Islam and imams as under the headline 'Dignified life in the midst of society' (Central Council of Muslims in Germany, 2002).

based on shared epistemic and normative convictions that provided a common framework for knowledge production. They combined scientific expertise with the personal interest to make their knowledge relevant for Muslims in Germany. This Muslim epistemic community started to produce academic knowledge under a religiously informed epistemic-normative framework, focusing on religious pedagogy, Qur'anic studies, inter-theological topics, and other fields of research that were considered relevant to contextualise and create Islamic knowledge in its German setting (Engelhardt 2017: 101–21). These topics and their advocates came together at the German Islam Conference, in 2008, where Islam at schools and universities was on the agenda.

The Model of Theology at Public Universities in Germany

To understand the place of Islamic theology at German universities one has to understand how Christian theology is embedded into the university. As a result of the antagonistic relation between the state and the Catholic Church, the 1919 Weimar Constitution introduced a number of common matters (*res mixtae*) of both the state and religious communities which were then adopted by the 1949 German Basic Law. Besides church taxes collected by the state and distributed to the churches, spiritual care in public institutions such as prisons and the military, as well as religious education at public schools, one of these *res mixtae* is theology at public universities. These *res mixtae* work as a trade-off between state and religious communities. While the state grants these communities privileges and autonomy within its own areas of authority (education, tax collection), the religious communities not only subscribe to following the Basic Law, but also agree to specific regulations such as educational standards for priests and teachers for religious education, or to observe the Basic Law's liberal democratic basic order in the curricula for religious education. While this system allows for many privileges that religious communities in other European countries do not enjoy, it also creates a great dependence on the state.

With regard to the German university system, these *res mixtae* include theology in the system of academic disciplines, including some unique features. Since a university degree is required for teachers of religious education at schools, as well as for priests of the main Christian churches (the Catholic Church and the several recognised Protestant churches of the states/*Länder*), theology and religious pedagogy have to be offered for their specific denominations at the university. Thus the existence of a Catholic and a Protestant theology. As a *res mixta*, theology, on the one hand, enjoys academic autonomy granted by the Basic Law, while, on the other hand, its curricula and, to a repeatedly debated extent, its research falls under the approval of its respective religious community. Theology professors are employed as civil servants who need a permission to teach, issued by the religious community (*nihil obstat* by the Catholic Church, see Schüller 2017). The category of confessionality comes into play here, as it is expected that academic staff adhere to the religious tradition they research and teach, and can, if they contradict basic tenets of belief, be removed from their position. At the same time, a professor has the right of freedom of research, which is protected by the state. In that case, professors can be transferred to a non-confessional position (such as comparative religious studies) and excluded from teaching theological studies at their university. This framework creates a tension for theological knowledge production between academic approaches, which should be able to criticise and deconstruct every aspect of knowledge about religion, and a discipline that trains students in their religious tradition.

Historically, this model of university theology had only been realised for Catholic and Protestant theology. Jewish scholar and rabbi Abraham Geiger's and others' requests to establish seminaries for Jewish theology at German universities in the last third of the nineteenth century had been rejected (Homolka 2013: 56–7; Reich 2020: 88), and the first Jewish academic institution in Germany to be associated with a public university is the Jüdische Hochschule in Heidelberg, established in 1979.[3]

This was the historical and structural situation in which the decision to establish Islamic theological studies was made in 2010.

INTO THE FIRST DECADE

In light of this context, we argue that the introduction of Islamic theological studies can be understood only as a project with multifactorial explanations. Without the migration from Muslim countries to Germany, changes in citizen laws and the perception of migrants as Muslims, the subsequent formation of a Muslim minority, the Islamisation of integration discourses and the securitisation of Islam, Islamic theological studies would probably not have come into being. In retrospect of its first ten years, the discipline faced several challenges and open questions that we will sketch in the following framework provided by science policy, including the integration of Islamic organisations in advisory boards, the recruitment of Muslim scholars and the quest for a canon in research and teaching.

---

[3] Jewish academic institutions that were established in nineteenth- and twentieth-century Germany, such as the Hochschule für die Wissenschaft des Judentums in Berlin (Higher Institute for Jewish Studies, 1872–1942), the Jewish Theological Seminary in Breslau (1854–1938) and the Akademie für die Wissenschaft des Judentums (Academy for Jewish Studies, 1919–34) were not part of or associated with public universities, but independent private institutions for research and training. For a short overview of the connection between Jewish and Oriental studies in nineteenth-century Germany, see Rohde (2020: 267–73).

Science Policy Framework and Establishment of Centres

In 2010, the recommendation to introduce Islamic theological studies by the German Council of Science and Humanities (*Wissenschaftsrat*), the country's most important advisory institution for the science sector, was included in the 'recommendations on the advancement of theologies and sciences concerned with religions at German universities' (Wissenschaftsrat 2010). This was surely the decisive moment that enabled theological Islamic knowledge production at universities.[4] The general recommendations on university theologies, including Islamic theological studies, argue that 'modern, constitutional democracies have a vital interest in utilizing religious orientations of their citizens towards the stability and development of the community' (Wissenschaftsrat 2010: 54). According to the recommendations:

> [t]he higher education portfolio in Islamic [Theological] Studies or Islamic religious education, respectively, aims to (1) prepare future teachers of religious education for their role in religious instruction, (2) meet the demand for Islamic religious scholars at mosque communities, (3) train qualified Islamic social workers, (4) and produce Islamic theologians for university-level teaching and research. (Wissenschaftsrat 2010: 78)

This describes the discourses by which Islamic theological studies is framed quite well. Religion is being considered as a potential source of social cohesion, and with regard to Islam concrete practical needs are addressed. Those trained in Islamic theological studies are expected to facilitate cohesion in the educational sector, religious communities and in the social sector. To encompass this scope, an Islamic knowledge production has to be established that develops into an academic discipline grounded both in research and in practical training. This is easier said than done. Training teachers for a newly introduced school subject, social workers in a post-secular migration society, or religious community professionals are all projects that do not have any blueprints at hand. In all of these areas, Islamic theological studies have to manage a balancing act between adapting to a scholarly tradition that academically re-evaluates the 'Islamic knowledge archive' (Schulze 2019) and its social relevance that made the discipline possible and requires concrete educational output.

---

[4] The council used the term 'Islamische Studien' (Islamic studies) in order to avoid speaking of 'theology', a term from a Christian tradition. However, due to possible confusion with *Islamwissenschaft* (Islamic studies) and since the discipline was clearly modelled after the existing theologies, this denotation did not prevail but was replaced by 'Islamic theology', 'Islamic theological studies' or 'Islamic religious studies'.

Islamic Theological Studies at German Universities

The following will give an overview of the current status quo of Islamic theological studies at German universities. In 2010–11, the German Ministry of Education and Research selected from among several applicants five centres for Islamic theological studies at the universities of Erlangen-Nuremberg, Department for Islamic Religious Studies, along with the Interdisciplinary Centre for Islamic Religious Education; Frankfurt am Main/Gießen, Centre for Islamic Studies; Münster, Centre for Islamic Theology; Osnabrück, Institute for Islamic Theology; and Tübingen, Centre for Islamic Theology. Additionally, Humboldt University in Berlin, Institute for Islamic Theology, and the University of Paderborn, Seminar for Islamic Theology, were selected as centres in a second tier of appointments in 2019. With these centres, as well as a handful of chairs at other universities (Hamburg, Karlsruhe, Ludwigsburg), by 2020 the discipline included around forty professorships and eighty postdoctoral scholars and PhD students (Engelhardt 2021: 3). About 2,500 students were enrolled.

Mission Im-possible: the Integration of Islamic Organisations into the Secular University

German Basic Law separates state and religion. However, it does not keep apart these fields as strongly as other European countries, such as France. It calls for a number of areas of cooperation between them (Korioth and Augsberg 2010: 322–3). As mentioned above, theology at the university is one of them, and in that legal sense an academic discipline can be identified as theology only when its object of teaching and research is considered by a religious community as belonging to their religion. In light of this argument, the Wissenschaftsrat had called for a 'regulated relationship to the Muslim communities' (2010: 73). Both science policy and universities faced the question of how to extend the existing model of cooperation between state, university and churches to Islamic academic knowledge-production. What should a Muslim equivalent to a church commission that is entitled to testify that the teaching is actually considered to be part of its own tradition look like? The solution was to integrate Islamic organisations in the form of advisory boards, where they, together with Muslim individuals, were assigned to give teaching permission (*ijazah*) to professors that had been appointed by university commissions (Wissenschaftsrat 2010: 75–7).[5] The *ijazah* traditionally denotes a teacher-to-student permission to pass on certain texts or subjects. In the context of German Islamic theology, it has been altered into an organisational body's permission to train students and therefore

---

[5] Another assignment is the approval of curricula.

does not resemble the traditional definition of *ijazah* (Kellner 2017: 150). Such a testimonial by a third party about one's own belonging to the Islamic tradition and permit to teach is uncommon in the Islamic tradition, but is the logical consequence of the implementation of a state-religion model that was formed according to state–church relations in Germany.[6] Being part of advisory boards, organisations which had developed as migrant self-associations for the pursuit of specific practical demands of Muslims in the diaspora, suddenly were expected to cooperate and decide whether or not an appointed professor was, from an Islamic perspective, eligible to teach and research Islam at the university. While this certainly met the demand to be accepted as institutional representation of Muslims in Germany, it did oftentimes overstrain the theological and academic capacity of these organisations. One reason is that most of these organisations centre around a specific tradition within Islam (a distinct version of a Turkish Sunni Islam, for example) and do not organise and represent 'Islam' as such. Another reason is that inter-organisational cooperation was and still is mostly based on political issues, not religious-theological ones. And many organisations draw their theological competences (and staff) from abroad, so that the advisory boards have been filled with laymen representatives that are not theologically trained. Talks between appointed professors and advisory boards therefore have often remained at a superficial level and could not bridge the gaps between an academic understanding of theological studies and one that caters to the needs of these organisations.

While, so far, all appointed professors have in fact received an *ijazah* (in some cases after heavy discussions within the advisory boards and between boards and universities), there was one outstanding example. In the case of the professor for Islamic religious education, Mouhanad Khorchide at Münster University, those Islamic organisations who were members of the advisory board of the centre for Islamic theology publicly withdrew their *ijazah* in 2013 and demanded that he be removed from his chair. They presented an account of Khorchide's theological reasoning in his book *Islam is Mercy* (Khorchide 2014), which to their understanding breached his obligation to confessionality (Koordinationsrat der Muslime 2013: 5–6). Some of Khorchide's arguments indeed follow a reformist agenda, not unheard of in contemporary Muslim discourses, and some of them can be traced back in the Islamic tradition to minority opinions (for example, a non-physical, but metaphorical perception of hell fire). The authors of the account on Khorchide argued that he had put himself outside their 'classical doctrine' (Koordinationsrat der Muslime 2013: 23), and therefore could no longer be considered eligible to teach students in Islamic theological studies. However, besides these disputes

---

[6] It emulates the *missio canonica* of the Catholic Church.

over theological arguments, other reasons can be identified that motivated this pushback: Khorchide, like other professors, has been quite critical about Islamic organisations and gained much public and political attention for his standpoints, which put pressure on established Islamic organisations. Yet the university saw Khorchide's writings as being within his freedom of research and supported him. Since the published account itself did not convincingly lay out where Khorchide contradicted the very basic creeds of Islam, and the case added to the public's perception of anti-liberal organisations, the withdrawal of the *ijazah* was not pursued to an end, and Khorchide remained at the theological centre. Paradoxically, the account published against Khorchide was the first theological document that Islamic organisations published together. To some extent, it therefore marks the beginning of an academisation of Islamic discourse in Germany. With the presence of an academic Islam at universities, it has become more and more important for Islamic organisations to express their concerns in German and on an academically sound level. For this they either have to build up their own theological expertise (possibly by employing graduates of the universities) or build on the expertise of the universities and include it in their own arguments.

In this view, Islamic theological studies also respond to developments within the wider Muslim civil society in Germany, where a series of new initiatives has emerged besides Islamic organisations. These focus on specific issues, such as spiritual care, youth work, general education on Islam, interreligious dialogue, violence prevention or environment protection, and can be considered as secondary religious actors (Chbib 2017: 393–5). They, too, ask for academic theological knowledge for their respective fields and seek cooperation with the university institutes. Hence, Islamic organisations are not the only Muslim stakeholders for Islamic theological studies.

After the discussions around Khorchide, the idea (and fear) that organised Islam would gain control over an academic discipline appeared to be unrealistic. On the whole, the university does act as an autonomous system in which academic merits count and academic freedom prevails. The structural systemic integration of Islamic organisations on various levels increased the potential damage and costs of pushing one's rights to the limits. Instead, one can detect that both Islamic theological studies and Muslim civil society organisations approach each other functionally, with one side contributing academic theological expertise and the other side providing relevant topics and a transmission of academic knowledge into society. This, of course, does not work without conflicts, as many issues are located at the interchange of the scientific and the religious fields, and it remains a matter of negotiation and competition where these issues are addressed appropriately. The question of imam training may serve as an example for this, as we will discuss later.

The Muslim Scholars

One challenge has been the recruitment of qualified, theologically trained Muslim scholars that pass the test of not only the confessional Islamic boards at the respective institute, but also of the scientific communities surrounding Islamic theological studies (Islamic studies, educational sciences, Christian theologies, etc.). Several times, the appointment procedure for chairs had to be repeated since no candidate was considered qualified enough, often because they lacked the necessary academic qualification or did not know (or subscribe to) the German model of theology. The Wissenschaftsrat had expected that 'it will be necessary to draw on qualified personnel from abroad, because it will be several years before the first generation of home-grown scholars can be available in Germany' (Wissenschaftsrat 2010: 80). As it turned out, however the societal relevance of Islamic theology, as well as the high expectations of Muslim communities, universities and the general public towards Muslim university theologians made applications by scholars without any experience in this specific German setting unsuccessful. Knowledge about what this new discipline means within a secular science system and for young Muslim students in Germany emerged as a crucial factor in many appointment processes.

The new discipline was staffed with 'home-grown scholars' indeed, but in a different way. Most of the first generation of scholars that were appointed to chairs had been working in Islamic studies departments in Germany before switching to Islamic theological studies (yet none of them had actually been professor in Islamic studies). The interest in theological topics and research questions relevant for a Muslim audience had already been central for many of them while in Islamic studies. Changing disciplines enabled those scholars to openly work theologically, yet they did not depart from the knowledge, theories and methods they had acquired in Islamic studies. Instead, they continued to use them in Islamic theological studies (Engelhardt 2017: 176–89). Only recently have young scholars trained in Islamic theological studies filled professorships. In this sense, the first professors were successful in educating a future second generation in the discipline.

A Canon in the Making

The first decade has been characterised by a twofold disciplinary differentiation. Firstly, areas for research and teaching had to be identified and brought into an epistemological structure. There existed an array of possible blueprints for establishing an academic knowledge system, ranging from models of higher Islamic education in relevant countries such as, for example, Turkey, Morocco, Bosnia or Egypt, on the one hand, to paradigmatic orders of knowledge from historical episodes of the Islamic tradition on the other (Bakker 2012). Secondly, this structure had to be filled with adequate subjects, theories and methods.

The Wissenschaftsrat suggested organising Islamic theological studies along similar differentiations as in Christian theologies. It promoted the establishment of research areas such as: 'Exegesis (incl. Sunnah), Systematic Theology (Fundamental Theology, Dogmatics, Morals/Ethics, Islamic Ecumenism), Historical Theology (incl. Sunnah, Kalam, Mysticism, Philosophy), Islamic Law and Jurisprudence, Practical "Theology" and Religious Education Studies' (Wissenschaftsrat 2010: 79). However, this suggestion has not been put into practice. Both the denomination of chairs at the centres as well as the course programmes show that following the path of the traditional canon of Islamic knowledge systems, with some variations and add-ons, has been the overall goal. Several centres cover Qur'anic studies, Islamic law, Arabic (as well as Turkish and Farsi), history of Islam, Kalām, Sufism, as well as Islamic philosophy. Hadith studies are also offered in teaching, but so far it has been a research area that has not been covered by more than one or two chairs. Until now, however, a cross-university canon with regard to authors, scholars, texts, bodies of knowledge, and theories and methods that each student has to learn is, if it exists at all, only in the making.

During this process of identifying a canon – which is still running – non-canonical requests are being directed at Islamic theological studies, too. They come either from neighbouring disciplines such as Islamic studies, Christian theologies, educational studies, migration studies or religious studies, or from students and non-academic actors, aiming at concrete occupational fields (which has led to the introduction of master's degrees in Islam and media studies, social work and spiritual care), as well as questions such as the contextualisation of Islam in Europe, (de-)radicalisation, gender equality, sexual diversity, etc., which have been burning issues for students. Considering this background, it comes as no surprise that the context of Islam in Germany, and in a university setting, heavily shapes the study programmes. Major additional features of the programmes are Islamic religious education, courses on non-Islamic theologies, and courses as well as master's degrees at the interchange of theology and practical fields.

Interdisciplinary Exchange: Crossing Imaginary Boundaries

A strong exchange between Islamic theological studies and its neighbouring disciplines comes as no surprise, given the socialisation of many scholars in Islamic studies, the high and sometimes not uncritical interest of other scholars in this new discipline and its setting as a small discipline at the university. And since scholars of other disciplines often constitute a majority in the appointment committees, an interdisciplinary outlook is a feature without which it is hard to convince in application processes.

On a university level, Islamic theological studies do not constitute an independent faculty but are usually part of philosophical departments. At some universities, they form joint clusters or study courses with Islamic studies, such as in Münster and Berlin, or a shared campus with Christian theologies is planned (such as at Münster and Tübingen). The institutes and their staff are part of various collaborations across disciplinary boundaries. While this prevents the theoretical and methodical isolation of Islamic theological studies, it also makes the concentration on genuine theological research more difficult. This leads to a situation whereby Muslim theologians often try to be on par with theoretical discussions in other disciplines. But they rarely have sufficient resources (particularly in times of high demand from other disciplines, public and politics) for significant deep research on their own or to enable them to have a significant impact on interdisciplinary questions emanating from Islamic theology into other subjects.

Some scholars within Islamic studies initially voiced concerns about confessional limitations, the establishment of confessional advisory boards and a theological shift in the general study of Islam at German universities. Yet after ten years a normalisation has set in, and in some research areas scholars from Islamic theological studies and Islamic studies complement each other, for example, in classical fields such as Qur'anic studies, Arabic philology, philosophy, kalām and law, which are widely considered relevant for theological research.

Open Questions and Future Challenges

Ten years are only an artificial milestone over which to look back. In the light of differentiation processes of academic disciplines, this is a rather short time span. Hence, all abovementioned processes and challenges will continue to be present in the years to come. Yet we want to focus on three aspects that we consider central to the further development of Islamic theological studies in Germany: questions of confessionality, future research areas and student expectations.

Confessionality in Islamic Theology

What turns a scientific study on religion within a university into theology? Is it the way to do things, the purpose, one's own standpoint, the public, the applied methods and theories? Confessionality in theological studies is usually understood as the adherence of scholars to the religious tradition they research and teach (Engelhardt 2021: 4). Catholic theological studies are being conducted by Catholic scholars, Protestant by Protestants, and Islamic by Muslim scholars.

In our view, confessionality in Islamic theological studies comes into play in an institutional, functional and scholarly way.

In the institutional dimension of confessionality, professors in some form have to attest to Islamic advisory boards that they belong to the respective religion and will subscribe to its basic tenets and traditions. As mentioned above, this is supposed to guarantee a link between Islamic theology and Islamic communities. Yet this institutional approach poses some serious pitfalls: does this apply to both teaching *and* research? Which theological findings, conclusions or statements fall within the realm of these religious tenets, and which do not, and who defines that? Might private behaviour of theological scholars affect their eligibility to teach Islam? And whose Islam? Islamic theology at German universities has not been further differentiated into Sunni and Shia theology, and no professor is obliged to stick to a distinct denomination, school of law (*madhhab*) or specific theological tradition.

Closely linked with its institutional dimension, confessionality is key to the social function that is being ascribed to Islamic theological scholars: they act as representatives of an academic *and* religiously informed knowledge-production, as interpreters of Muslim communities and their traditions, and as academic ambassadors of Islam (Engelhardt 2021: 5). The establishment of Islamic theological studies thus advanced a 'first-person authority' (Godlove 2005) of Muslim scholars in academic and societal discourse on Islam, formed by a combination of scholarly knowledge and credibility *and* religious belonging. The high interest in personal biography and religious identity of German Muslim scholars speaks to that. Yet the question remains: who is actually a theologian? What makes academic knowledge theological? To what degree is it a question of a scholar's personal religious affiliation and her/his (attributed) identity markers? And to what degree is it a question of the relevance that academic knowledge has for its non-academic audience?

Closely related to the functional dimension of confessionality in Islamic theological studies here is the idea of authenticity. This is a term used by representatives of Islamic organisations, theologians and even politicians, but with different understandings. Two concepts of authenticity compete with each other. On the one hand, proponents of a collective authenticity demand that theological conclusions and statements in research and teaching comply to a considerable degree with religious convictions of specific Muslim communities. Hence, theology is authentic when it sticks to the teachings of defined Islamic traditions without taking too much into question. The theological authority would be based on the acceptance by Muslim stakeholders outside academia. On the other hand, scholars criticise the institutional argument behind this definition and advance the understanding of authenticity as accordance between theological work and individual convictions. In a joint declaration, professors of almost all institutes for Islamic theological studies in Germany, Austria and Switzerland underlined that upholding the Islamic discursive tradition in the form of theological studies is not bound to particular interests, but based upon the intention of the individual scholar to continue, update and interpret this tradition (FachvertreterInnen 2019).

In light of academic knowledge-production, confessionality poses even more difficulties. Given the academic socialisation of many professors in Islamic studies, and the close interdisciplinary connections Islamic theological studies have with Islamic studies, the field is far from resembling religious seminaries (to the frustration and irritation of some students, see Wagner and Dreier 2020: 38–9). Some scholars in fact reject the idea that their academic work could be identified as confessional and see this category as a disregard of their scientific qualities (Engelhardt 2021). They rely on an Islamic tradition that gave reasoning a high place in theology, never had a church-like regulating body and that was composed of different traditions and very reluctant to label someone or a position as outside Islam. Scholars of Islamic theological studies at the University of Frankfurt published a joint statement making the point that Islamic theology cannot be *bound* to a belief (bekenntnis*gebunden*), but its questions and findings are *oriented* to a creed of the researcher and the audience (bekenntnis*orientiert*) (Agai et al. 2014: 13–15).

While using theories and methods from other disciplines (such as social sciences, linguistics, history, educational sciences or digital humanities) and relying to a great extent on literature from Islamic studies, Islamic theological studies are closest to confessional when it comes to research premises – the Qur'an as God's revelation, Muhammed being the Prophet – as well as research interests that are often conceptualised from a religiously informed starting point. How can we understand the Qur'an adequately as Muslims? How can we transform Islamic principles into a secular Western European context? How can we develop an understanding of secularism, religious diversity, gender equality, sexual pluralism on the basis of the tradition? How can we contribute to a good Islamic religious education at school?

Future Research Areas

As mentioned, one initial aim whilst establishing Islamic theological studies was to cover a range of subjects and subdisciplines of the 'Islamic knowledge archive' (Schulze 2019). At the same time, this structural order followed subdisciplinary traditions (in establishing chairs for Qur'anic studies, Islamic law, Arabic, hadith), merged several study areas (e.g., in chairs covering Islamic mysticism, philosophy and kalām at once), created new, cross-disciplinary perspectives (with chairs for practical theology or text studies) and introduced areas highly influenced by the German context (chairs for religious education, for comparative theology). Gradually, this structure is being filled with research content that is increasingly inspired by practical questions and problems: the theological foundation of Islamic spiritual care and social work; questions of gender justice; or the search for sexual ethics are examples for that. Instead of merely transferring Islamic archival knowledge from Muslim times and places, Islamic theological studies exhibit a strong will to contextualise. The field of *fiqh* (usually translated as Islamic law) illustrates this very well. The designations of the chairs and the discipline vary considerably, from Islamic law to doctrine of Islamic norms. This takes into consideration that the object of research in a secular context is not law, but is related to the private norms of Muslims. However, this directly raises another question. What normative relevance can Islamic law uphold and develop in a Western European setting in which secular law organises society? How can one translate jurisprudence into normativity (see on this also Rohe 2015: 453–5)?

Other questions relate to the constitution of hadith studies, which are an integral part of traditional orders of knowledge but have not found adequate entry into Islamic theological studies in terms of chairs and research projects. Do hadith studies merely provide knowledge for other areas, such as law and exegesis, or might they constitute a research field in its own right? What should they teach? Should they transmit hadiths, which is not really scientific? Should they talk about ways to critically analyse the material with students memorising it? And what happens if the findings with regard to authenticity of established material of the tradition are doubtful? Is this a scientific opinion or a statement against the fundamentals of Islam as an established tradition?

These are only some examples of fundamental research questions that will have an effect on the outlook of specific research areas and their further development in a secular setting in both university and society. In contrast to Christian theologies, Islamic theological studies do not have the bonus of historical tradition at the university. And ten years after their top-down establishment, their *raison d'être* cannot be a science policy decision anymore. At the university, they will be judged primarily by their ability to contribute valid perspectives and knowledge to academic research.

Islamic Theological Studies and Training for the Job Market

One of the central assignments of Islamic theological studies is to train teachers for Islamic religious education at public schools. This will be the most important field of employment for graduates, if religious education is further implemented in most of the German *Länder*. Most students are enrolled in one of the pedagogically oriented programmes that are offered at every theological institute. However, the implementation of Islamic religious education at schools does not keep up in all of the German *Länder*. Since education policy in Germany is a matter for the sixteen states, the effect to which Islamic religious education is being offered at schools varies greatly. In 2020, only seven states provided Muslim school children with an Islamic religious education that is comparable to its Christian counterparts, although in some of these states only a handful of schools actually offer this subject. In other states, Islamic religious education is either not offered at all because of a lack of a significant number of Muslim schoolchildren or because these states offer one religious education course for all religions. A third group of states offers an Islamic education that non-confessionally informs about Islam, but does not provide confessional education on Islam. Here, Islamic organisations are not involved, and these models do not follow the existing religious basic law. All in all, approximately only one in ten Muslim schoolchildren in Germany participates in one of these courses (Engelhardt et al. 2021: 2, 14). This, of course, has implications for Islamic theological studies: training teachers alone will probably not be a sufficient rationale for this discipline.

And training Imams will not be either. So far, none of the university institutes offers an imam training programme, and it is very unlikely that imam training will ever be at the core of Islamic theological programmes,[7] as the occupation of the imam requires practical knowledge in rituals, liturgy and a memorisation of Qur'anic passages and important hadiths. Such forms of practical knowledge cannot be part of an academic university curriculum.

On the one hand, some Islamic institutions have built and are building up their own training institutions in Germany, and some of them do not have plans for academic training (Ceylan 2019) as the education should be vocational and directed to the transmission of practical knowledge for their respective community. The biggest Islamic organisation in Germany, the Diyanet İşleri Türk-İslam Birliği (DITIB, or Turkish-Islamic Union for Religious Affairs), on the other hand, reaches out for German graduates of international theology (a university programme taking place in Turkey) as well as for graduates from Islamic theology in Germany. Only the Institute for Islamic Theology at the University of Osnabrück has partnered with some Islamic organisations and the German Ministry of the Interior to establish an 'Islamkolleg' that offers graduates of Islamic theological studies an imam training (Islamkolleg 2021). The future will show the demand for university expertise on a broader level here. For most students, becoming an imam is not an option, be it for reasons of gender exclusion, poor payment or lack of open positions. Therefore, besides training teachers Islamic theological studies will have to develop other options

---

[7] At the Institute for Islamic Theology at the University of Osnabrück, a training programme for foreign imams working in Germany was offered between 2010 and 2018 (IIT 2021).

of employability for their graduates, such as social work and spiritual care. These sectors, however, will become attractive employment options only when Islamic organisations, state institutions and universities join forces and reconfigure their cooperation.

Islamic theological studies here have a duty to provide for academically sound training. Yet, although theology is traditionally a discipline in which the education of experts for religious contexts has been key, training students for practical needs may oftentimes be considered the less attractive aspect of the duality of research and teaching by many scholars, especially when trained in disciplines that have no direct connection to the field of practice. Recently collected data shows that one of the leading motivations for enrolling for Islamic religious education is to bring about societal change (Wagner and Dreier 2020: 21–5). It is up to the academic staff to meet this motivation within the scope of their teaching.

With regard to the students, Islamic theological studies stand out against other study programmes in terms of social and educational background. A great majority of them are young women who are the first in their families to pursue an academic education, who do not speak German as their first language in the family and who possess less educational capital than the average students. For many students, the university programmes are the first context in which they openly reflect upon their religious identity in the German language within a pluralistic Islamic setting that goes beyond their own community, and in which they have to accept that religious questions can be answered quite differently within Islam and from other perspectives as well. While the overwhelming majority of students consider their religious identity to be very important (Wagner and Dreier 2020: 20), they do come from very different religious and ethnic backgrounds, and theological, cultural, political or sexual plurality is as common as in other university settings. In order to conduct, represent and integrate religion into society, both religious communities and non-religious institutions in Germany need academically trained experts. This public Islam will most probably be staffed with these graduates of Islamic theological studies.

Conclusion

Islamic theological studies came into being as the result of societal, political and academic processes. It now faces the challenge to become more than this result, namely an academic discipline in its own right. Being aware of its assigned function as an integration device in a socio-political setting that Islamised integration and securitised discourses on Islam is key to its further development. Islamic theological scholars have to constantly critically examine their position as members of an academic discipline vis-à-vis the political and the religious field.

Ten years into its development, Islamic theological studies have established a strong exchange with its neighbouring disciplines, and exhibit a variety of research areas and questions. Scholars of Islamic theological studies now have to define, at least very broadly, the discipline's purpose at the university, its subjects, research and teaching areas, and they have to develop concepts about appropriate methods and theories. In terms of confessionality, drawing a clear line between the confessional and the non-confessional will remain hard to do, as the discipline's research will have to stand the test of interdisciplinary inquiries and provide orientation knowledge for Muslim audiences outside academia.

The integration of Islamic organisations in advisory boards will remain a mode of cooperation, but it will not substantially improve the linkage between communities and theology. This linkage is put into practice on a micro-level with the students who combine community affiliation with academic education. Their commitment and curiosity in Islamic theological subjects also speak against the idea that Islamic theological studies is a mere political project to domesticate Islam in Germany, as they oftentimes critically examine both religious traditions and public perceptions of Islam. A major challenge will be the necessary reconfiguration of fields of work for these graduates, for which Islamic actors, state institutions and universities will have to come together.

References

Agai, Bekim et al. (2014). 'Islamische Theologie in Deutschland. Herausforderungen im Spannungsfeld divergierender Erwartungen', *Frankfurter Zeitschrift für Islamisch-Theologische Studien* 1(1): 7–28.

Agai, Bekim and Armina Omerika (2017). 'Islamic Theology in Germany: A Discipline in the Making', in M. Kemper and R. Elger (eds), *Islamic Piety and Learning: Islamic Studies in Honor of Stefan Reichmuth*. Leiden: Brill, pp. 330–57.

Aguilar, Luis Manuel Hernández and Zubair Ahmad (2020). 'A Dangerous Text: Disciplining Deficient Readers and the Policing of the Qur'an in the German Islam Conference', *ReOrient* 6(1): 86–107.

Amir-Moazami, Schirin (2011). 'Pitfalls of Consensus-Orientated Dialogue: The German Islam Conference (Deutsche Islam Konferenz)', *Approaching Religion* 1(1): 2–15.

Amir-Moazami, Schirin (2018). 'Epistemologien der muslimischen Frage in Europa', in S. Amir-Moazami (ed.), *Der inspizierte Muslim. Zur Politisierung der Islamforschung in Europa*. Bielefeld: transcript, pp. 91–124.

Bakker, Jens (2012). *Normative Grundstrukturen der Theologie des sunnitischen Islam im 12./18. Jahrhundert*. Berlin: EB-Verlag.

Bundesministerium des Innern und für Bau und Heimat (BMI) (2022). *Islam in Deutschland*, available at: https://www.bmi.bund.de/DE/themen/heimat-integration/staat-und-religion/islam-in-deutschland/islam-in-deutschland-node.html, last accessed 6 December 2022.

Central Council of Muslims in Germany (Zentralrat der Muslime in Deutschland) (2002). 'Islamic Charta', available at: http://zentralrat.de/3037.php, last accessed 1 February 2021.

Cesari, Jocelyne (2012). 'Securitization of Islam in Europe', *Die Welt des Islams* 52(3–4): 430–49.

Ceylan, Rauf (2019). *Imamausbildung in Deutschland. Perspektiven aus Gemeinden und Theologie.* Frankfurt am Main: Akademie für Islam in Wissenschaft und Gesellschaft.

Chbib, Raida (2017). *Organisation des Islams in Deutschland. Diversität, Dynamiken und Sozialformen im Religionsfeld der Muslime.* Würzburg: Ergon-Verlag.

Engelhardt, Jan Felix (2017). *Islamische Theologie im deutschen Wissenschaftssystem. Ausdifferenzierung und Selbstkonzeption einer neuen Wissenschaftsdisziplin.* Wiesbaden: Springer.

Engelhardt, Jan Felix (2019). 'The Illusion of Agency? Domestication, Academic Autonomy and Self-Reflection in Islamic Knowledge Production in Germany', in J. F. Engelhardt and H. Schmid (eds), *Islam in Knowledge–Power Relations: A Challenge for Muslim Theologies?* Special Issue Frankfurter Zeitschrift für Islamisch-Theologische Studien, Berlin: EB-Verlag, pp. 105–20.

Engelhardt, Jan Felix (2021). 'Beyond the Confessional/Non-Confessional Divide: The Case of German Islamic Theological Studies', *Religions* 12(2): 1–12.

Engelhardt, Jan Felix, Fahimah Ulfat and Esra Yavuz (2021). *Islamischer Religionsunterricht in Deutschland. Qualität, Rahmenbedingungen und Umsetzung.* Frankfurt am Main: Academy for Islam in Research and Society, available at: https://aiwg.de/wp-content/uploads/2020/12/AIWG-Expertise-Isamischer-Religionsunterricht-in-Deutschland_Onlinepublikation.pdf, last accessed 1 February 2021.

FachvertreterInnen der Islamisch-Theologischen Studien (2019). *Erklärung der FachvertreterInnen der Islamisch-Theologischen Studien (Islamische Theologie, Islamische Studien, Islamisch-Religiöse Studien, Islamische Religionspädagogik) an europäischen Universitäten und Hochschulen zur aktuellen Lage ihrer Fächer, Institute und Zentren,* Wien, available at: https://aiwg.de/wp-content/uploads/2019/02/Erkla%CC%88rung-FachvertreterInnen-Islamisch-Theologische-Studien.pdf, last accessed 29 January 2021.

Godlove, Terry F. Jr (2005). 'Religious Discourse and First Person Authority', in R. T. McCutcheon (ed.), *The Insider/Outsider Problem in the Study of Religion: A Reader.* London: Continuum, pp. 164–78.

Haas, Peter M. (ed.) (1997). *Knowledge, Power, and International Policy Coordination.* Columbia: University of South Carolina Press.

Haug, Sonja, Stephanie Müssig and Anja Stichs (2009). *Muslimisches Leben in Deutschland im Auftrag der Deutschen Islam Konferenz.* Nürnberg: Bundesamt für Migration und Flüchtlinge.

Homolka, Walter (2013). 'Der lange Weg zur Errichtung des Fachs Jüdische Theologie an einer deutschen Universität', in W. Homolka and H.-G. Pöttering (eds), *Theologie(n) an der Universität. Akademische Herausforderung im säkularen Umfeld.* Berlin: de Gruyter, pp. 53–78.

Hierl, Katharina (2012). *Die Islamisierung der deutschen Integrationsdebatte. Zur Konstruktion kultureller Identitäten, Differenzen und Grenzziehungen im postkolonialen Diskurs.* Berlin: LIT Verlag.

Institut für Islamische Theologie Osnabrück (IIT) (2021). 'Imamweiterbildung', available at: https://www.islamische-theologie.uni-osnabrueck.de/studium/imamweiterbildung.html?no_cache=1, last accessed 5 February 2021.

Islamkolleg Deutschland e.V. (n.d.). 'Islamkolleg', available at: https://www.islamkolleg.de, last accessed 5 February 2021.

Kellner, Martin (2017). 'Iğāza. Autorisierung und Sozialisation in islamischen Wissenstraditionen', in R. Ceylan and C. P. Sajak (eds), *Freiheit der Forschung und Lehre? Das wissenschaftsorganisatorische Verhältnis der Theologie zu den Religionsgemeinschaften.* Wiesbaden: Springer, pp. 141–52.

Khorchide, Mouhanad (2014). *Islam is Mercy: Essential Features of a Modern Religion.* Freiburg: Herder-Verlag.

Koordinationsrat der Muslime in Deutschland (2013). *Gutachten zur 'Theologie der Barmherzigkeit' von Mouhanad Khorchide, dem Leiter des Zentrums für Islamische Theologie Münster.* Köln.

Korioth, Stefan and Ino Augsberg (2010). 'Religion and the Secular State in Germany', in J. Martínez-Torrón and W. C. Durham Jr (eds), *Religion and the Secular State/La religion et l'État laïque: Interim National Reports/Rapports Nationaux Intermédiaires, issued for the occasion of the XVIIIth International Congress of Comparative Law, Washington, D.C., July 2010.* Provo, Utah: International Center for Law and Religious Studies, Brigham Young University, pp. 320–30.

Ramm, Christoph (2010). 'The Muslim Makers: How Germany "Islamizes" Turkish Immigrants', *Interventions* 1(2): 183–97.

Reich, Eli (2020). 'The Return of Liberal Rabbinic Education to Berlin: Abraham Geiger College, Zacharias Frankel College and the School of Jewish Theology', *Nordisk judaistik. Scandinavian Jewish Studies* 31(1): 87–92.

Rohde, Achim (2020). 'Rekonfiguration einer Matrix: Islamisch-Theologische Studien, Islamwissenschaft und die "Anderen" der deutschen und europäischen Geschichte', *Jahrbuch für Antisemitismusforschung*, vol. 29. Berlin: Metropol-Verlag, pp. 258–84.

Rohe, Mathias (2015). *Islamic Law in Past and Present.* Leiden: Brill.

Rosenow-Williams, Kerstin (2012). *Organizing Muslims and Integrating Islam in Germany: New Developments in the 21st Century.* Leiden: Brill.

Schüller, Thomas (2017). 'Lehrerlaubnis für katholische Theologinnen und Theologen an Hochschulen und Schulen. Eine kirchenrechtliche Bestandsaufnahme', in R. Ceylan and C. P. Sajak (eds), *Freiheit der Forschung und Lehre? Das wissenschaftsorganisatorische Verhältnis der Theologie zu den Religionsgemeinschaften.* Wiesbaden: Springer, pp. 93–124.

Schulze, Reinhard (2019). 'Islam, Islamic Knowledge and the Modern Order of Authority', in J. F. Engelhardt and H. Schmid (eds), *Islam in Knowledge–Power Relations: A Challenge for Muslim Theologies?* Special Issue Frankfurter Zeitschrift für Islamisch-Theologische Studien, Berlin: EB-Verlag, pp. 15–38.

Søvik, Magrete (2006). 'Islamic Religious Instruction in North-Rhine-Westphalia (1979–1999): Constructing a German Muslim Identity between Authenticity and Responsibility', in S. G. Ellis (ed.), *Citizenship in Historical Perspective.* Pisa: Pisa University Press, pp. 317–32.

Spielhaus, Riem (2011). *'Wer ist hier Muslim?' Die Entwicklung eines islamischen Bewusstseins in Deutschland zwischen Selbstidentifikation und Fremdzuschreibung*. Würzburg: Ergon Verlag.

Stichweh, Rudolf (2003). 'Differentiation of Scientific Disciplines: Causes and Consequences', in *Encyclopedia of Life Support Systems (EOLSS)*. Paris: UNESCO.

Tezcan, Levent (2012). *Das muslimische Subjekt. Verfangen im Dialog der Deutschen Islam Konferenz*. Paderborn: Konstanz University Press.

Thielmann, Jörn (2014). 'Salafism in Germany', in F. Peter and R. Ortega (eds), *Islamic Movements of Europe: Public Religion and Islamophobia in the Modern World*. New York: I. B. Tauris, pp. 165–8.

Wagner, Constantin and Lena Dreier (2020). *Wer studiert Islamische Theologie? Ein Überblick über das Fach und seine Studierenden*. Frankfurt am Main: Academy for Islam in Research and Society, available at: https://aiwg.de/wp-content/uploads/2020/03/Wer-studiert-islamische-Theologie_Expertise.pdf, last accessed 8 January 2021.

Wissenschaftsrat (German Council of Science and Humanities) (2010). *Recommendations on the Advancement of Theologies and Sciences Concerned with Religions at German Universities*. Berlin.

CHAPTER 6

Islamic Theology in a Muslim-minority Environment: Distinctions of Religion within a New Academic Discipline

LENA DREIER

INTRODUCTION

In many European countries, forms of knowledge related to Islam from an 'inside' perspective are currently being incorporated into educational systems (cf. Johansen 2006; Ferreiro Galguera 2011; Aslan and Windisch 2012; Vinding 2013). In higher education, various efforts are being made to introduce courses in Islamic theology or Islamic studies, imam and clergy training, and Muslim welfare work. Higher education programmes also seek to meet the need for religious education in schools, mosques, hospitals, prisons and the military (Pattison et al. 2013). In Muslim-minority countries in Europe, this development started about forty years ago (Aslan 2012: 59).[1] The specific forms of Islamic studies or Islamic theology courses[2] vary according to the national or regional educational

---

[1] Bosnia and Herzegovina, which has a much denser Muslim population (about 50 per cent of the total population) than other European countries, has long had a renowned Islamic theology department in Sarajevo. In research on Islam in Europe it is often not visible that therefore Muslim education has a long history in Europe. Outside Bosnia, the Cambridge Muslim College in the United Kingdom, established in 2008, is pioneering and renowned for developing Muslim scholarship in Europe (Sinclair 2016).

[2] The name attributed to the discipline varies throughout Europe and indeed globally, reflecting distinct epistemological approaches, religion–state relations and educational traditions (see Nielsen 2012). The subject is only called 'Islamic theology' in Germany, Austria, the Netherlands and Turkey. In other countries, it is called 'Islamic studies', or 'Islamology', or professional qualifications are offered, such as 'Islamic social worker' or 'Islamitisch Geestelijk Werker' in the Dutch case (for the Netherlands, cf. Meuleman 2012). Meuleman (2012: 229) describes a general trend in Europe of calling the subject 'religious studies' instead of 'theology'. Writing about Denmark, the Netherlands and Germany, Johansen states: 'The institutions mainly use the term "theology" as an equivalent to the concept in a Christian context, covering a wide range of disciplines, as opposed to the narrower concept of *kalām*' (Johansen 2006: 94).

system. In France, for example, imam training is offered at a private Islamic university, although there was one short-lived effort to teach Islamic theology at a public university in Strasbourg. This differs from the situation in Austria and Germany, where Islamic theology courses are offered at state universities (cf. Ferreiro Galguera 2011; Aslan 2012; Nielsen 2012). European countries also have differing state–religion conceptions (cf. Fetzer and Soper 2005; Nielsen 2012), and differing conceptions of the secular–religious distinction. In the countries that have established some form of Islamic higher education (e.g., the United Kingdom, Germany, the Netherlands, Spain, Italy and Bulgaria), this has mostly been done through cooperation with religious representatives or organisations, in what are clearly top-down state initiatives. This is also true of the renowned Islamic theology programme in Bosnia (cf. Karić 2012). None of these countries have established Islamic higher education solely at the initiative of religious communities, in the sense of formally recognising private initiatives. Many do, however, have bottom-up initiatives in the form of private, traditional seminaries (cf. Haroon Sidat, Chapter 7, this volume). In France for example, degrees from the Institut Européen des Sciences Humaines (IESH), a private Muslim teaching institution, are not recognised within the state's educational system. Overall, there are many private initiatives and schools in Europe, while public and state initiatives are rare (cf. Aslan 2012: 59). Various models (e.g., private or public) of institutionalising Islamic knowledge in European countries are developing in juxtaposition (Bochinger 2010: 90). Despite the growing incorporation of institutions referring to Islam in education or Muslim education, in some of them it remains uncertain whether they are representing 'Islam', whether they will persist, and whether their graduates will be employed by Muslim organisations. We also do not know enough about practices and knowledge production *within* new Muslim scholarship in Europe.

The establishment of higher education institutions relating to Islam was accompanied by debates on promoting a so-called democratic version of Islam, and on politics of security and prevention, in nearly all European countries (Johansen 2007; Nielsen 2012; Rosenow-Williams 2013; Vinding 2013; Schönfeld 2014; Engelhardt 2017; Hashas et al. 2018; Peter 2018).[3] Nielsen (2012) and Peter (2018) argue that discourses of prevention and security were the political motivation behind efforts to foster Muslim education and imam training in Europe. Rosenow-Williams (2013), applying organisational theory, argues that Muslims are treated as security concerns in these discourses. Although these studies take diverse approaches (discourse, organisational analyses), they

---

[3] Nielsen dates the discussion to the aftermath of 9/11: 'After the events of 11 September 2001, many governments suddenly developed an interest in encouraging "Imam training" within their own countries in the belief that this would counter the processes of "radicalization" and "home-grown" terrorism at the core of the security-led agendas after 9/11' (Nielsen 2012: 92).

point to the same processes of homogenising and governing Muslims for the sake of security and control in European countries (cf. Salvatore 2005). This is also the case in the disciplines of Islamic theology (Engelhardt 2016, 2017) and imam training in Germany (Schönfeld 2014; Peter 2018). In addition to Muslim education, studies on interreligious dialogue (Malik 2013) and political projects of dialogues with 'Islam' in Germany (Tezcan 2006), show that 'the dialogue is intermingled with disciplining endeavours and securitization' (Malik 2013) and 'governmental rationality' (Tezcan 2006), and that imam training is intermingled with the aim of 'domesticating' religion (Schönfeld 2014).

State control of religion through theology or, more broadly, through establishing academic disciplines or universities for political purposes, is not a new idea. The strategy of establishing political control over religion by promoting theology can be found in late thirteenth-century Europe (Verger 1996), in the period of Prussian state-building with regard to Protestant theology (Howard 2006), as well as in examples outside Europe, such as Atatürk and Reza Schah, who both promoted theology courses (Engelhardt 2017: 63). In this sense, state recognition is understood as a technique to bring social and cultural differences under governmental control (Schönfeld 2014: 414). While public discourse in Europe after 9/11 was quite homogeneous, with widespread calls for European imams, what happened in practice was quite diverse (Koningsveld and Drees 2007: 18). One product of these broader developments was the new discipline of Islamic theology in Germany, a confessional theology, claiming to study Islam from an inside perspective, which was intended to meet the state's aim of training imams. Although there is not yet an imam training programme in Germany,[4] the discipline of Islamic theology was established at five state universities in Germany, as Bachelor's and Master's programmes, and expanded to two more universities in 2019 (Dreier and Wagner 2020).[5]

Although we know a lot about the discourses on Muslim education in European countries, we know very little about the forms of institutionalisation and practices *within* the institutions. Generally, there are two kinds of studies on this subject. One group of studies evaluates projects of Islamic studies/theology/imam training, describing the field from an internal or legal perspective, in some cases to legitimate it (Özdil 2011; Agai et al. 2014). The other group

---

[4] A main expectation when Islamic theology courses were first established was that they would provide training for imams (Ceylan 2014). It was thought that imams trained in Germany would be more 'democratic' than those trained abroad. However, to this day, it is not clear whether mosques will employ new German Islamic theologians as imams, social workers or other professionals. Further research is needed to understand what happened to the graduates of these courses. In 2020, the University of Osnabrück started another academic imam-training project.

[5] Indeed, Islamic theology is taught at a total of ten universities in Germany. In addition to those already mentioned, three more universities offer Islamic theology programmes, though these are not part of an associated department of Islamic theology.

of studies investigates the new discipline's practices from an analytical perspective (Johansen 2006, 2007, 2011; Nielsen 2012; Engelhardt 2016, 2017; Wagner, 2019; Dreier and Wagner 2020), or analyses the practices of comparable institutions (Schönfeld 2014; Sinclair 2016; Bano 2018). For Germany, Anne Schönfeld's (2014) discourse analysis suggests that Islamic educational organisations train 'European' imams for 'domesticating' purposes. Schönfeld argues that, with the establishment of Islamic theology at German universities, recognition was tied to the condition of modifying the Muslim self, such that secular, liberal principles were not called into question (Schönfeld 2014: 414). Also, Kirstine Sinclair (2016, 2019) argues that specific forms of subjectivity are produced by the establishment of new Muslim institutions. She shows that at the Cambridge Muslim College in the United Kingdom and the Zaytuna College in Berkeley, California, 'students look … for guidance in their development as both working and moral subjects' (Sinclair 2016: 46). Although (moral or Muslim) subjectivity is an important factor in new Muslim education teaching institutions, it remains unclear if forming a specific subjectivity is important only in the education institutions or also from the student's perspective.

Comparing different forms of new Islamic scholarship in three countries (the Netherlands, Denmark and Germany), Birgitte Schepelern Johansen (2006) argues that the way in which Islam is brought into academia reflects the religious–secular boundaries in the countries in question. The states use theology to draw boundaries between religion and the secular. At the same time, the disciplines also establish epistemic positions. Johansen categorises the religious–secular boundary within Islamic theology in the Netherlands and Germany as 'conceptual osmosis' (Johansen 2006: 103–4): religious concepts from insiders diffuse into the educational system, and religion is understood as one position among other positions. Science is then seen as 'positioned knowledge' (Johansen 2006: 103). In Denmark, by contrast, religion is understood as a disposition which must be separated from academic work, and science is constructed as being independent from religion. The two models reflect different inside–outside relationships, because '[w]hen science is constructed as sharply separated from religion, an inside perspective must inevitably contaminate academic standards; when science is constructed as a tool to obtain an understanding of a confessional way of life, the inside perspective becomes indispensable' (Johansen 2006: 104). The analysis shows not only that Islamic institutions in higher education vary with regard to legitimating religion as part of university, but also that this legitimation depends on how religion is constructed (Johansen 2006: 103). Following this line of thought, the discussion surrounding Islamic theology, as well as the debate on imams and Islamic higher education, can be understood as a debate on religion within European countries (Johansen 2006: 93). As such, discourses as well as practices of governing and institutionalised forms of Islam could be taken as negotiations on religion and boundaries of religion. While discourse on Islamic theology clearly involves religion–secular boundaries, investigation is needed to establish whether these boundaries are present in Islamic theology in practice.

This chapter contributes to the mentioned debate about the kind of boundaries produced by educational projects and disciplines (Nökel and Tezcan 2005; Sinclair 2016, 2019) focusing on Islamic studies from an 'inner' perspective. Concentrating on Islamic theology in Germany, it investigates how religion is constructed and distinguished *within* these institutions. It will also highlight the wider process of how boundaries between religion and its others are drawn in Islamic theology. My research is driven by a more general question regarding constructions of religion within the process of incorporating Islam into educational systems. Taking the broader development in Europe into account, Islamic theology could be taken as an example of more general relationships between religion and non-religion. It shows how dimensions of religion are integrated into and excluded from educational institutions such as universities. From a socio-constructivist approach (Schütz and Luckmann 1973; Berger and Luckmann 1979) to Islamic theology, I will argue that while religion is clearly distinguished from academic knowledge in Islamic theology (i.e., institutionalised), the distinction between religion and religiosity is negotiated within the field, and is less institutionalised.

In this chapter, I will explore findings from my fieldwork on Islamic theology in German universities. The interactions I observed at various universities contained references as well as boundaries to *subjective* religion. Connecting the discourse of control and 'domestication' of Islam with this, distinctions between religion and religiosity seem to indicate the negotiation of subjective dimensions of religion when constructing knowledge. By contrast, where institutional forms of Islam were integrated into the discipline (if at all), they were not negotiated. The negotiations within the discipline point therefore to a specific form of religion: to religion as subjective and individualistic entity – that is to say, to religiosity.

Methods and Description of the Research Field

In Germany, Islamic theology was established in 2010, and Jewish theology in 2012. Despite uncertain post-university employment prospects, many students have attended these courses. In 2019, there were approximately 2,200 students on Islamic theology university courses in Germany, a minority in teacher education, the majority on Islamic theology or Islamic pedagogy (BA or MA) study programmes without specified vocational goals (Dreier and Wagner 2020).[6]

---

[6] My own data based on interviews with teachers and on numerical data from university websites.

A large proportion of graduates see their future in the field of education (Dreier and Wagner 2020: 7). One can only speculate that this is also related to the fact that most of the students are female, and that in education generally women are over-represented. While Islamic theology departments are funded by a special state programme, the discipline has become well-established in universities both in Germany and abroad in recent years, with its own journals, associations, networks and an academy. The question of which organisations could represent Islam as the state's partner when establishing Islamic theology as a university discipline is challenging for universities, because it entails legitimising actors to speak for Islam. In line with the German cooperation rule, which provides for state–church cooperation for theology and religious education in state institutions, nearly all universities have chosen to convene advisory boards. Some have chosen an advisory board that comprises members of different Islamic organisations, some involve important Muslim intellectuals. The advisory boards are expected to provide their opinion on matters of curriculum and on the appointment of professors.[7] Currently, the most represented organisations on these advisory boards are the largest Sunni Islamic organisations,[8] although Shia and Alevi organisations are represented on the boards at some universities as well. The selection of organisations on these boards has been criticised by the Liberal-Islamic Association (LIB), as well as in public debates.

My fieldwork was carried out between 2017 and 2019, at three of the first five universities to introduce Islamic theology courses. In order to gain multiple perspectives, three different methods were used to collect empirical data: participatory observation in classes and within the departments; biographical narrative interviews with students; and narrative interviews with teachers. The participatory observations in classes and workshops were used to enter the field and speak to potential interviewees, as well as to investigate interactions in teaching. The twenty-nine biographical narrative interviews were conducted mostly in the departments, and in some cases in the students' apartments. Additionally, I interviewed thirteen lecturers, research assistants and professors to find out more about the new discipline's development, and their perspective on teaching and the students. In terms of theoretical sampling (Glaser and Strauss 1999), minimal and maximal contrasts were taken into account in the student interviews, and a wide range of social backgrounds, religious positions, as well as reasons for studying the subject were considered. By combining the

---

[7] By law in Germany, the state is neutral on matters of ideology and religion (cf. Fetzer and Soper 2005), and it is thus illegal for the state to employ someone on the basis of their religion. As academics in German Islamic theology are generally expected to be religious, the advisory boards square this circle by advising on the suitability of the candidates.
[8] The Turkish-Islamic Union for Religious Affairs (DİTİB), Millî Görüş and the Association of Islamic Cultural Centers (VIKZ e.V.).

wide range of the students' positions and biographies, the teachers' perspectives, and interactions within classes, a multi-sided perspective on Islamic theology was established. This multi-sided approach to the research field was combined with interpretative analysis of the empirical data within the study. The various materials were analysed by sequence analysis, an in-depth interpretative method proposed by Ulrich Oevermann (cf. Flick 2005; Knoblauch et al. 2005). It is a text-based method pointing to social structures and meanings, documented by texts (cf. Reichartz 2004), and it was connected to the concept of theoretical sampling in grounded theory methodology (cf. Glaser and Strauss 1999). The following section provides insight into the results regarding distinctions between, and references to religion and faith based on this qualitative data.

References to Faith, and Boundaries between Religion and Religiosity

All forms of theology challenge the boundaries, differentiations and intersections between faith, religious and theological knowledge.[9] Discussions regarding Islamic theology have revived broader discussions on faith-based disciplines in universities, as well as on the relationship between science and religion. These discussions were part of the historical development of theology. Thomas A. Howard's study (2006), for example, shows that while Protestant theology in Germany was challenged and redefined by both the Prussian nation-building process and positivistic criticism of theological explanations, it was ultimately retained as a 'normal' discipline within the modern university system (Howard 2006: 409). In the discipline's history, the relevance of Catholic and Protestant theology was relativised and negotiated not only by the state, but also by other disciplines that developed in the field of studying religion (Krech 2002; Howard 2006). The central controversy and object of distinctions in the study of religion and the different disciplines was an epistemological one: the question of enlightenment (cf. Schelsky 1959), that is, whether religion and faith or belief are part of an academic position or not. Islamic theology was built upon the presumption of studying Islam from an 'inner perspective'. This claim to an inner perspective indicates that belonging and believing have an influence on epistemological and scholarly positions.

---

[9] In Germany, the educational system was historically strongly influenced by Protestantism and Catholicism (Koenig and Willaime 2008: 14). By law (and concordats), theology in Germany and other European countries is defined as confessional theology (Munsonius 2017). In the German case, theology is part of the *res mixtae* – areas where the state and religious organisations have a common interest (see Agai and Engelhardt, Chapter 5, this volume). The state is thus required to provide theology in cooperation with religious organisations, and it is prohibited from providing the subject theology *without* the involvement of religious communities or representatives.

In this section, I will illustrate the constructions of religion referred to within the discipline, and how these constructions are considered in the negotiating process within Islamic theology.[10] I will first consider a course description, which provides insight into the relevance of students' faith when studying Islamic theology. I will then analyse interactions between teachers and their students and establish which constructions of religion are involved in these interactions. Finally, I will consider the way one student talks about the distinction between personal conviction and established opinions in Islamic theology.

Involving Religion: A Course Description

Whether faith is a requirement for admission to Islamic theology programmes is a central question for students of Islamic theology themselves, as well as when comparing Islamic theology courses in Germany to Islamic studies courses elsewhere. While faith is not a formal requirement for students of Islamic theology in Germany, it is an important reference for the students and institutions. We can see this, for example, in the course information sheet from one of the universities. The course description is preceded by the Basmala (the Qur'an's opening), written in Arabic calligraphy: 'in the name of God, the most gracious, the most merciful'. The Islamic theology course is then described as follows:

> For the first time, the programme of Islamic theology at [university] allows Muslims in Germany to explore and reflect on their own religion academically. It enables graduates to contribute to giving Islamic theological discourse a home in Germany – in academia/science [Wissenschaft], religious communities and society. (Brochure B.A. Islamische Theologie, June 2017)

This description makes it clear that students' faith is the starting point for scholarly reflection within the discipline. However, the institutes' websites underline that students are not formally required to be of a particular faith in order to study Islamic theology. As such, the relationship between subjective dimensions of religion and Islamic theology is not clearly defined.[11] But in this information

---

[10] The category religion has been critically discussed (especially as a generalising term) in religious studies for some long time (see, e.g., Smith 1991). Also, with regard to Islam, is has been discussed whether the term religion could be analytically used, and especially independently from its Western, academic and so-called protestant history, as well as discourse of 'othering' (cf. Masuzawa 2005: 20). For a critical view on this invention-thesis, see Krämer (2021: 14). I am referring here to religion as a constructed category in the research field as well as in research. According to Dreßler it is a social reality and a 'product of continuous negotiation and objectification' (Dreßler 2019: 10).

[11] The definition of theology in German Islamic theology is structurally connected to theologies that were established earlier, and therefore to a concept of church membership comparable wih these theologies. In Islamic theology, the relation between church and university is transferred to the new discipline.

sheet it becomes a starting point of academic reflection and exploration, and important for the subject as such. Simultaneously, faith is and is *not* part of the subject. While it has long been recognised that the relationship between religion and theology is one main feature of theology (cf. Schelsky 1959; Beyer 2003), the course descriptions make clear that religion is involved in a specific way to university: as a starting point of intellectual reflection and as 'their own religion'. Religion is involved as a personal condition for the study programme. In the next section, I will explore the question of how this subjective dimension is challenging the interactions withing the discipline using ethnographic data.

Double-reference: An Ethnographic Note

When considering this configuration of involvement, it is crucial to consider whether, and how, religion is negotiated in interactions between students and teachers. My ethnographic observations from a seminar should answer this question: during my fieldwork, I visited a class for students of theology and teacher training at one of the institutions of Islamic theology. The room was very crowded when I came in. Four female students were sitting at the front to one side, while the teacher was sitting in line with the other students. After the teacher allowed me to join the class, he warned me that the lessons were like a 'circus' when controversial topics arose. The unit's topic was women in the Qur'an. At the beginning, one of the students outlined the task, which was to discuss whether 'women and men are equal from a Muslim perspective'. After a lively debate between the four female students who had the task of discussing the topic, one of the students opened a dialogue with the professor:

> One of the presenters turned to the professor now. She asked him: what happens if a woman decides that she wants to work even if it was prohibited by the Nikah [Islamic marriage]? The professor asked whether her question referred to former times or to all times. The student answered: 'To today'. The professor explained that marriage is a contract in Islam. It is explicitly not a sacrament as it is in Christianity. Due to this fact, the contract contains obligations. But a contract could be cancelled. (Extract from field notes)

The student's question refers to the unit's topic of women in the Qur'an, and to questions of theological relevance as defined by the topic and class. The professor provides an opportunity for the student to decide whether she is interested in a historical answer ('former times') or a normative answer ('all times'). The question seems to be relevant to the student's lifeworld, so she answers that she is interested in the answer pertaining to 'today'. Although we learn from sociology of knowledge that every kind of knowledge entails normative references, it is not by chance that the professor draws a timeline between former times and all times. He connects the topic to both: to the history of religion and to the field of norms. By framing the topic in a contemporary context, the answer is potentially more than just a theological or historical one. It is also an explicitly normative answer that could *directly* legitimate action. Therefore, the answer could be used by the student in another context without transformation and is ambiguous. It could be understood as a theological question referring to what we know about the Qur'an, and as a normative question referring to gender norms and religious or moral rules that are of relevance within her lifeworld. The student asks about women's rights within marriage. She wants these rights to be secured by theological justifications.

Generally, the actors (students, professors, etc.) are referring to institutionalised codes of scholarship when they talk about historical or theological knowledge. By connecting this knowledge with questions pertaining to their lifeworld (how to manage Islamic marriage today) they are connecting theological knowledge with life-worldly knowledge,[12] and transforming practical, gender-related questions into more theological knowledge. The subjective dimension is included without a distinction being made between the historical and normative level of the question. Ambiguities and double references facilitate connections to the lifeworld and to theological knowledge. Tracing this back to the question on the role of religion in Islamic theology, one can conclude that religion is involved in a specific dimension within the field. It is involved when *religiosity*, namely, *religious questions with explicitly subjective references*, is connected to theology. The religious dimension is potentially the *direct transmission* of knowledge into a religiously legitimated action. The analysed interaction indicates a double reference of knowledge produced in Islamic theology: to faith and religious rules, on the one hand, and to academically institutionalised knowledge, on the other.

Distinguishing from Personal Conviction: An Interview Piece

A third insight into constructions of religion in Islamic theology is provided by the following excerpt from an interview with one of the students. When I asked him whether the faith of teachers and professors is of relevance to him, he told me:

> ... if individual lecturers have a specific personal conviction that is not the consensus view, that is contentious. There are points where not everyone agrees, and that's to be expected in religion. If such issues are brought into

---

[12] The connection could be compared with the connection between religion and world, *dīn wa-dunya*, see, for comparison and differences to the concept of religion Dreßler et al. (2019: 25) and Krämer (2021: 29).

the classroom on the basis of personal inclination, I have a problem with that. (interview with Ian)

Ian talks about the boundaries between personal convictions and commonly accepted knowledge. If personal convictions are contrary to the consensus view, he finds it problematic to talk about these in class. Thus, he distinguishes sharply between accepted and negotiated knowledge and opinions in religion. He wants the teacher to teach common, not personal opinions on religion. Established knowledge and opinions are acceptable to teach; personal, subjective opinions and convictions are not.

Coming back to the question of how religion is constructed within the discipline, it should be noted that Ian gives an example of how distinctions between personal, subjective understandings of religion and collective, objectified standpoints are made. He distinguishes between a personal 'conviction' and the consensus views. Negotiated issues must be part of subjective, personal opinions and not part of teaching. Ian points to a construction of religion as official, accepted knowledge, to a common ground between different Islamic law schools and denominations that is acceptable to teach in Islamic theology. The other part – personal conviction on negotiated issues – is not, although it is part of religion, too. In contrast to the second example from the lesson, where religiosity is connected to the lesson's topics, Ian distinguishes sharply between objectified, collectively accepted knowledge, and personal, subjective knowledge.

Summarising the three examples, one can see that diverse references to religion are made within the discipline of Islamic theology. One of the students refers to questions of faith and the lifeworld, another wants personal conviction to be excluded from the discipline. In the course description, religion as faith plays a role in Islamic theology, but it is defined as a starting point, not as the subject of the discipline. What all three examples have in common are negotiations over whether religion should be part of the practices. Dimensions of religion are negotiated through talking (example 3), interacting (example 2) and defining (example 1), exclusion and inclusion of religion. Boundaries between the official, objectified meaning of religion, on the one hand, and personal convictions, the life-worldly (and gender-related) dimension of religion and faith, on the other, seem to be especially controversial.

Conclusion: Subjective Dimensions of Religion as Part of Islamic Theology

The empirical findings explored in this chapter indicate a central thesis in answer to the research question regarding constructions of religion within the discipline, and how these distinctions relate to the 'domestication' of Muslims through Islamic theology. The boundary-work within the discipline shows that subjective dimensions of religion (faith, religiosity, experiences with religion) are much more negotiated than dimensions pertaining to institutionalised and objectified forms of religion, for example, religious knowledge. The discipline's practices seem to be based on a specific concept of religion: on the presumption that religion could be divided into objective, collectively accepted religion, and subjective religion. It seems that negotiations on religion focus on topics relating to subjectivity. In this sense, institutionalised forms of religion are not getting part of functionalised Islam here. It is not religion in general that is domesticated and controlled by Islamic theology, because only subjective dimensions of religion are negotiated in knowledge-production within the analysed practices. Domestication would mean, that these subjective dimensions become a specific form in Islamic theology – a Protestant form or 'secular' form, for example. The empirical insights show that not *one* but diverse references are possible in Islamic theology: this understanding of religion could be related to Protestant understandings of religion as a personal feeling (see Schulze 2010), and also to specific Islamic concepts, for example, an individualistic understanding of Islam. In this sense, the references on subjective religion are much more open to different understandings of religion than performing domestication would be.

If Islamic theology reflects a religion-faith[13] boundary, one must ask whether this distinction relates to secular ideas and expectations of Islam, as the domestication thesis emphasises. Is the boundary between religion and faith in Islamic theology specifically secular? My results suggest that in Islamic theology in Germany, references are made to the individual dimension of religion, and thus to a conception of religion that is suited to a secular university as well as to individualistic understandings of Islam.[14] The constructions of non-religion in Islamic theology in Germany are less explicit and less negotiated because they refer to an established structure, namely, academia. Arguably, on this level the distinction could be a sign of the domestication of Islam in Germany, for the sake of secularity, if we understand domestication as functionalisation religion by theology.[15] The negotiation on subjective religion also points to an emphasis on subjective dimensions of religion as a general trend in the relationship between

---

[13] Faith is here understood as *one* possible form of subjective religion. On faith and belief in Islam see Schulze (2010); Krämer (2021). Schulze describes the semantic shifts in Islamic understandings of this subjective dimension and how, for example, Wilfried Cantwell Smith semantically contributes to a shift of *iman* as belief to *iman* as faith (Schulze 2010: 147). Semantic references also to subjective dimensions are historically and culturally altered.
[14] On individualistic forms of lived Islam in Germany, see Jeldtoft (2011).
[15] As I have shown at the beginning of this chapter, theology has always been a way to control religion in history.

state and religion. If we think of Islamic theology and new Muslim scholarship this way, it is possible to think of it not just as a project established unilaterally by the state, but also as a project of collective knowledge-production. It is not about a state producing a domesticated Islam by theology, it is a project of different actors with different agencies. From the students' perspective it seems to be a place that relates to their faith, which distinguishes it from knowledge and institutionalised religion.

Dualism between religion, that is to say, objectified dimensions of religion, and religiosity or faith is therefore a central boundary-marker in Islamic theology in Germany. Within the discipline, religion and faith are distinguished, first through the involvement and exclusion of different dimensions of religion in the new academic discipline, and, secondly, in ambiguous references to faith and religious rules, and to academically institutionalised knowledge. In interpreting these findings, it must be remembered that analyses of constructions of religion focus on the *meaning* produced in interactions within the field of study. In these interactions, the concepts of subjective religion are used to refer to the individual as the counterpart to a collective and objectified religion. Religion is addressed as subjective religion, as well as knowledge-production in Islamic theology being based on a specific subjective position. The relationship between subjective dimensions (as a counterpart to objectivity) and religion might be particularly highlighted in Islamic theology or theologies in general; but one could guess that references to the question of what kind of references to subjective dimensions are accepted as part of the discipline might come up in other forms in other disciplines. Further research is necessary to understand whether this development could be generalised, and to compare it with the involvement of subjectivity in other disciplines, educational institutions, to other Muslim-minority as well as Muslim-majority countries.

Furthermore, the empirical findings lend support to the argument that Islamic theology is a boundary-marker between religion and the secular. It indicates not only how religion is constructed, but also which role it should play in academic work (Johansen 2006). My results potentially add nuance to Johansen's findings. While Islamic theology was intended as a means for the state to control religion, at an organisational level, the empirical insights show that the boundaries of religion are drawn by mobilising subjective dimensions through faith. The distinction between religion as an organisation and religiosity as faith is a dominant configuration in this field. Even in the German case, the dualism between religion and academia is taken for granted in interactions. The empirical insights tell us little about the state functionalisation of Islam, though they do tell us a lot about the transmission and relevance of political agendas within the study programmes and interactions. The political purpose of domesticating Islam through academic knowledge-production is transmitted in practices of functionalising and distinguishing between objective and subjective religion. Initially, political agendas of integration and control of Islam were a driving force behind new Muslim scholarship in Germany. Today, work on differentiating dimensions of religion is more central. Coming back to the question of religion and the secular, Islamic theology could be understood as a secularising institution, in that dimensions of religion are distinguished by students, teacher and the study programme.[16] The students' part here is not to involve a secular religion in this process, but to work on their own faith, as it is conceptualised in the study description as 'reflexion'.

As mentioned in the introduction, the discussion surrounding Islamic theology and negotiations around Islam could be taken as part of a more general negotiation of religion in European countries (Johansen 2006; Schulze 2013). If this is the case, Islamic theology shows that the 'domestication' of religion is an important agenda within the discourse on Islam, but other agendas, namely, the distinction of religion and the importance of subjective religion are becoming important with the establishment of the discipline. It can therefore be concluded that religion could be part of this official and non-religious field, if it is limited to subjectivity. The political project of Islamic theology is a project of producing connections between subjective Muslim religion and knowledge. It remains to be seen whether the distinction between religion and religiosity also applies in other contexts where Islam is integrated into educational systems, and whether this is indicative of a more general trend of legitimating only subjective dimensions of religion in academia and beyond.

References

Agai, Bekim, Mahmoud Bassiouni, Ayşe Başol, Jamel B. Abdeljelil, Mark C. Bodenstein, Naime Çakır, Serdar Güneş, Armina Omerika, Fateme Rahmati, Ömer Özsoy, Ertuğrul Şahin and Udo Simon (2014). 'Islamische Theologie in Deutschland: Herausforderungen im Spannungsfeld divergierender Erwartungen'. *Frankfurter Zeitschrift für islamisch-theologische Studien* 1(1): 7–28.

Aslan, Ednan (2012). 'Training of Imams and Teachers in Europe', in Ednan Aslan and Zsófia Windisch (eds), *The Training of Imams and Teachers for Islamic Education in Europe*. Frankfurt am Main: Lang, pp. 19–70.

Aslan, Ednan and Zsófia Windisch (eds) (2012). *The Training of Imams and Teachers for Islamic Education in Europe*. Frankfurt am Main: Lang.

Bano, Masooda (ed.) (2018). *Modern Islamic Authority and Social Change, Vol. 2: Evolving Debates in the West*. Edinburgh: Edinburgh University Press.

---

[16] It is an institution referring to secularity in the sense of 'culturally and symbolically as well as institutionally anchored forms and arrangements of differentiation between religion and other social spheres' (Wohlrab-Sahr and Burchardt 2012: 881).

Berger, Peter L. and Thomas Luckmann (1979). *The Social Construction of Reality: A Treatise in the Sociology of Knowledge*. Harmondsworth: Penguin.

Beyer, Peter (2003). 'Conceptions of Religion. On Distinguishing Scientific, Theological, and "Official" Meanings', *Social Compass* 50(2): 141–60.

Bochinger, Christoph (2010). 'Imamausbildung in Deutschland? Gründe, Chancen und Probleme der Verankerung im deutschen Wissenschaftssystem', in Bülent Uçar, Martina Blasberg-Kuhnke, Rauf Ceylan, Arnulf von Scheliha and Michael Bommes (eds), *Imamausbildung in Deutschland: Islamische Theologie im europäischen Kontext*. Göttingen: V & R Unipress, pp. 87–95.

Ceylan, Rauf (2014). *Cultural Time Lag: Moscheekatechese und islamischer Religionsunterricht im Kontext von Säkularisierung*. Wiesbaden: Springer.

Dreier, Lena and Constantin Wagner (2020). 'Wer studiert Islamische Theologie? Ein Überblick über das Fach und seine Studierenden', *AIWG Expertisen*, available at: https://aiwg.de/wp-content/uploads/2020/03/Wer-studiert-islamische-Theologie_Expertise.pdf, last accessed 2 April 2020.

Dreßler, Markus (2019). 'Modes of Religionization: A Constructivist Approach to Secularity', *Working Paper Series of the HCAS*, 'Multiple Secularities: Beyond the West, Beyond Modernities', no. 7, Leipzig, February 2019, available at: https://www.multiple-secularities.de/media/wps7_dressler_religionization.pdf, last accessed 31 May 2021.

Dreßler, Markus, Armando Salvatore and Monika Wohlrab-Sahr (2019). 'Islamicate Secularities: New Perspectives on a Contested Concept', in Markus Dreßler, Armando Salvatore and Monika Wohlrab-Sahr (eds), 'Islamicate Secularities in Past and Present: Mixed Issue', special issue, *Historical Social Research* 44(3/169): pp. 7–34.

Engelhardt, Jan F. (2016). 'On Insiderism and Muslim Epistemic Communities in the German and US Study of Islam', *Muslim World* 106(4): 740–58.

Engelhardt, Jan F. (2017). *Islamische Theologie im deutschen Wissenschaftssystem: Ausdifferenzierung und Selbstkonzeption einer neuen Wissenschaftsdisziplin*. Wiesbaden: Springer.

Ferreiro Galguera, Juan (2011). *Islam and State in the EU: Church–State Relationships, Reality of Islam, Imams Training Centres*. Frankfurt am Main: Peter Lang.

Fetzer, Joel S. and J. C. Soper (2005). *Muslims and the State in Britain, France, and Germany*. Cambridge: Cambridge University Press.

Flick, Uwe (2005). 'Qualitative Research in Sociology in Germany and the US: State of the Art, Differences and Developments', *Forum Qualitative Sozialforschung/Forum: Qualitative Social Research* 6(3).

Glaser, Barney G. and Anselm L. Strauss ([c. 1967] 1999). *The Discovery of Grounded Theory: Strategies for Qualitative Research*. New Brunswick, NJ: Aldine.

Hashas, Mohammed, Jan Jaap de Ruiter and Niels Valdemar Vinding (eds) (2018). *Imams in Western Europe: Developments, Transformations, and Institutional Challenges*. Amsterdam: Amsterdam University Press.

Howard, Thomas A. (2006). *Protestant Theology and the Making of the Modern German University*. Oxford: Oxford University Press.

Jeldtoft, Nadia (2011). 'Lived Islam: Religious Identity with "Non-organized" Muslim Minorities', *Ethnic and Racial Studies* 34(7): 1134–51.

Johansen, Birgitte S. (2006). 'Islamic Theology at the European Universities: Secularisation, Boundaries and the Role of Religion', *Nordic Journal of Religion and Society* 19(2): 93–106.

Johansen, Birgitte S. (2007). 'Legitimizing Islamic Theology at European Universities', in Pieter S. Koningsveld, and Willem Drees (eds), *The Study of Religion and the Training of Muslim Clergy in Europe: Academic and Religious Freedom in the 21st Century*. Leiden: Leiden University Press, pp. 445–68.

Johansen, Birgitte S. (2011). '"Doing the Secular": Academic Practices in the Study of Religion at Two Danish Universities', *Arts and Humanities in Higher Education* 10(3): 279–94.

Karić, Enes (2012). 'Higher Educational Institutions in the Balkans which Educate Imams and Religious Teachers: Overview from 1990–Present', in Ednan Aslan and Zsófia Windisch (eds), *The Training of Imams and Teachers for Islamic Education in Europe*. Frankfurt am Main: Lang, pp. 71–90.

Knoblauch, Hubert, Uwe Flick and Christoph Maeder (2005). 'Qualitative Methods in Europe: The Variety of Social Research', *Forum Qualitative Sozialforschung/Forum: Qualitative Social Research* 6(3): art. 34.

Koenig, Matthias and Jean-Paul Willaime (2008). 'Religion und die Grenzen des Politischen. Frankreich und Deutschland in religionssoziologischer Perspektive', in Matthias Koenig and Jean-Paul Willaime (eds), *Religionskontroversen in Frankreich und Deutschland*. Hamburg: Hamburger Edition, pp. 7–35.

Koningsveld, Pieter S. and Willem Drees (2007). 'Academic and Religious Freedom: An Introduction', in Pieter S. Koningsveld and Willem Drees (eds), *The Study of Religion and the Training of Muslim Clergy in Europe: Academic and Religious Freedom in the 21st Century*. Leiden: Leiden University Press, pp. 13–28.

Krämer, Gudrun (2021). 'Religion, Culture, and the Secular: The Case of Islam', *Working Paper Series of the HCAS 'Multiple Secularities: Beyond the West, Beyond Modernitites'*, no. 23, pp. 1–88, available at: https://www.multiple-secularities.de/media/wps_kraemer_web_1.pdf, last accessed 1 June 2021.

Krech, Volkhard (2002). *Wissenschaft und Religion. Studien zur Geschichte der Religionsforschung in Deutschland 1871 bis 1933: Ernst Cassirer und die Theologie*. Tübingen: Mohr Siebeck.

Malik, Jamal (2013). 'Integration of Muslim Migrants and the Politics of Dialogue: The Case of Modern Germany', *Journal of Muslim Minority Affairs* 33(4): 495–506.

Masuzawa, Tomoko (2005). *The Invention of World Religions: Or How European Universalism was Preserved in the Language of Pluralism*. Chicago: University of Chicago Press.

Meuleman, Johan (2012). 'Educations for an Old Profession in a New Context: The Imam Training Programme of Inholland University, the Netherlands', in Ednan Aslan and Zsófia Windisch (eds), *The Training of Imams and Teachers for Islamic Education in Europe*. Frankfurt am Main: Lang, pp. 223–39.

Munsonius, Hendrik (2017). *Institutionalisierung Islamischer Theologie. Religionsrechtliche Rahmenbedingungen und Modelle der Beteiligung Islamischer Verbände*. Göttingen: Staats- und Universitätsbibliothek Göttingen.

Nielsen, Jørgen S. (2012). 'Reflections on the Role and Training of Imams and Islamic Teachers for Europe', in Ednan Aslan and Zsófia Windisch (eds), *The Training*

of Imams and Teachers for Islamic Education in Europe. Frankfurt am Main: Lang, pp. 91–101.
Nökel, Sigrid and Levent Tezcan (eds) (2005). 'Islam and the New Europe: Continuities, Changes, Confrontations', special issue, Yearbook of the Sociology of Islam, vol. 6.
Özdil, Ali Ö. (2011). Islamische Theologie und Religionspädagogik in Europa. Stuttgart: Kohlhammer.
Pattison, Stephen, Sophie Gilliat-Ray and Mansur Ali (2013). Understanding Muslim Chaplaincy. Farnham: Ashgate.
Peter, Frank (2018). 'Training of Imams and the Fight against Radicalization', IEMed Mediterranean Yearbook, pp. 342–5.
Reichartz, Jo (2004). 'Objective Hermeneutics and Hermeneutic Sociology of Knowledge', in Uwe Flick, Ernst v. Kardorff and Ines Steinke (eds), A Companion to Qualitative Research. London: Sage, pp. 570–82.
Rosenow-Williams, Kerstin (2013). Organizing Muslims and Integrating Islam in Germany: New Developments in the 21st Century. Leiden: Brill.
Salvatore, Armando (2005). 'Muslims in the New Europe: Between Religious Traditions, Multiple Identities, and the Conflicted Emergence of New Secular Spaces', in Sigrid Nökel and Levent Tezcan (eds), 'Islam and the New Europe: Continuities, Changes, Confrontations', special issue, Continuities, Changes, Confrontations, Yearbook of the Sociology of Islam, 6: 94–113.
Schelsky, Helmut (1959). 'Religionssoziologie und Theologie', Zeitschrift für Evangelische Ethik, pp. 129–45.
Schönfeld, Anne (2014). 'Regulierung durch Wissensproduktion: Staatliche Versuche einer Institutionalisierung der Ausbildung von Imamen in Deutschland', in Ahmet Cavuldak, Oliver Hidalgo, Philipp W. Hildmann and Holger Zapf (eds), Demokratie und Islam: theoretische und empirische Studien. Wiesbaden: Springer, pp. 399–423.
Schulze, Reinhard (2010). 'Islam und Judentum im Angesicht der Protestantisierung der Religionen im 19. Jahrhundert', in Lothar Gall and Dietmar Willoweit (eds), Judaism, Christianity, and Islam in the Course of History. Berlin: Walter de Gruyter, pp. 139–66.
Schulze, Reinhard (2013). 'On Relating Religion to Society and Society to Religion', in, Samuel M. Behloul, Susanne Leuenberger and Andreas Tunger-Zanetti (eds), Debating Islam: Negotiating Religion, Europe, and the Self. Bielefeld: Transcript, pp. 333–56.
Schütz, Alfred and Thomas Luckmann (1973). The Structures of the Life-world. Evanston, IL: Northwestern University Press.
Sinclair, Kirstine (2016). '"Liberal Arts are an Islamic Idea": Subjectivity Formation at Islamic Universities in the West', Review of Middle East Studies 50(1): 38–47.
Sinclair, Kirstine (2019). 'An Islamic University in the West and the Question of Modern Authenticity', Numen 66(4): 403–21.
Smith, Wilfred C. (1991). The Meaning and End of Religion. Minneapolis, MH: Fortress Press.
Tezcan, Levent (2006). 'Interreligiöser Dialog und politische Religionen', Aus Politik und Zeitgeschichte: APuZ 56(28/29): 26–32.
Verger, J. (1996). 'Entstehung der Universitäten', in Walter Rüegg and Asa Briggs (eds), Geschichte der Universität in Europa. Munich: C. H. Beck, pp. 58–65.

Vinding, Niels V. (2013). *Muslim Positions in the Religio-organisational Fields of Denmark, Germany and England*. Copenhagen: Centre for European Islamic Thought, Faculty of Theology, University of Copenhagen.

Wagner, Constantin (2019). 'Islamische Theologie an deutschen Hochschulen studieren? Zu den Erfahrungen Studierender einer jungen Disziplin', in Daniela Heitzmann and Kathrin Houda (eds), *Rassismus an Hochschulen: Analyse–Kritik–Intervention*. Weinheim: Beltz Verlagsgruppe, pp. 90–112.

Wohlrab-Sahr, Monika and Marian Burchardt (2012). 'Multiple Secularities: Toward a Cultural Sociology of Secular Modernities', *Comparative Sociology* 11(6): 875–909.

CHAPTER 7

The Taalib as a Bricoleur: Transitioning from Madrasah to University in Modern Britain

HAROON SIDAT

> Our Majnun, by contrast, is seeking a narrative with claims to transcendent truth and soteriological promise.
>
> Murad (2020: 217)

> University education is about getting you a job, so that you earn money, pay tax and then spend it. Because you've spent money you need more. So, you go back to work and repeat the whole process. We're all slaves but slaves of different things. But is this why Allah really sent us here?
>
> Interview with a seminary student[1]

INTRODUCTION

After completing the *darsi-i nizami*, a classical form of Islamic education at a *dar al-ulum* in modern Britain, I enrolled at a university to complete a BA in Economics and Social studies. A few years later, an opportunity arose to pioneer a partnership with a university in offering the first two years of a BA in Islamic studies at the *dar al-ulum*. At the time, I saw the partnership as the beginning of a broader project to address the educational needs of future Muslim scholars, or the *ulama*, in Britain. I wanted to be part of the discourse that improved the understanding of *dar al-ulums*, and Islam more generally. As a young British-born

---

[1] This taken from my doctoral thesis completed in 2019. I am currently in the slow process of carving the thesis into a monograph.

Muslim, I was a student, or *taalib*,[2] when 9/11 happened. I went on to complete a doctoral thesis, which was the first-ever ethnographic account of a Deobandi *dar al-ulum* in Britain.[3]

As we will see, the *ulama* were not only 'religious' but were open to and engaged with various epistemologies. With colonial modernity, this horizon became narrow. Deoband, as it emerged in 1866, was in response to and with modernity (Ingram 2018: 33). However, what we are observing in modern Britain is the early signs of an epistemic openness. This presents an opportunity for *dar al-ulums* and some of their *taalibs* to work with(in) British universities. The universities can also benefit from this rich tradition, though the challenge will be whether they are open to such overtures in advancing the quest of providing a public good and exploring alternative paradigms of knowledge-production. In sum, my experience of seeking accreditation between a university and a *dar al-ulum*, alongside ethnographic research, and my role of as a *taalib* working in academia will be deployed to reflect on possibilities and challenges for such developments. There is much promise with *taalibs* forging their own path in acquiring the 'best of both worlds'. Such a grounded *taalib* has much to offer to and benefit from the academy.

Tracing the Broad Contours

The *dar al-ulum* traces its genealogy through the *madrasah*. The *madrasah* is a conjugate of the triliteral Arabic root verb *d-r-s* which means to study very closely. It also means to wipe away and efface, implying an active learning process that wipes away ignorance. The word *madrasah* is a noun of place (*ism makān, nomen loci*) and here refers to a place of instruction (Makdisi 1981; Petry 1981; Metcalf 1982; Berkey 1992; Messick 1993; Chamberlain 1994; Ephrat 2000; Zaman 2002, 2012; Sikand 2005; Moosa 2015; Ingram 2018). The archetypal teacher (*mudarris*) is the Prophet who focused on the progressive nurturing of his community (*tarbiyyah*) which was largely undertaken informally.[4]

---

[2] Throughout the chapter I will use the word '*taalib*' instead of student to remain close to the native use of the noun. This is taken from the phrase *ṭālib al-'ilm* in Arabic, or *ṭālib-i 'ilm* in Urdu, which is often translated as 'seeker of knowledge'. I will use the Urdu spelling because it is the one used in the Dar al Uloom setting. Secondly, my use of this word seeks to reflect authentically what learning is: a form of seeking truth. Thirdly, it is inspired by John Butt's (2020) excellent account of being the first westerner to graduate from the religious seminary of Deoband in northern India.

[3] Throughout this chapter the name of the *dar al-ulum* and my research participants have been anonymised.

[4] Some would argue that a more apt description may be that it was unstructured. I have chosen the distinction between formal and informal rather than structured and unstructured primarily because this is the way most authors have described it. For an excellent example of the *tarbiyyah* of the Prophetic period, see *Lamḥāt min at-Tarbiyyah al-Fiqhiyyah fī Khayr al-Qurūn Zamāni ar-Risālah wa aṣr as-Ṣaḥābah wa at-Tābi 'īn*, Abdul-Haleem Nomani (n.d.).

Significantly, it mattered less where one studied than with whom one studied. This form of education could be characterised as being personal, intensive in terms of content, with the centrality of the interaction of a *taalib* with the teacher.

The *madrasah* as it developed was a more specialised place for 'shariah-minded religious studies' (Hodgson 1974: 441). They were broadly reflective of a conservative spirit of the revealed religion where the aim was the faithful transmission of knowledge from one generation to the next. Over time, what constituted knowledge (*'ilm*) became broadly defined. One reason for this was the decentralised nature of Islam itself and the presence of the scholarly consensus (*ijmā*) that left the borders of legitimate knowledge broadly defined (Berkey 2007: 47). In fact, contrary to the popular perception of 'nomocentric boundary-loving ulama',[5] we find that many of them were indeed polymaths and exhibited a certain 'epistemic openness'.[6] Such pre-modern *ulama* were comfortable living with ambiguity while frowning upon exclusivity (Bauer 2021).[7] As a result, theirs was a world that exhibited 'diversity, hybridity, polyphony and agglomeration' (Murad 2020: 218).[8] Underpinned by Islamic spirituality, such a capaciousness in interpretation was guided by Prophetic statements like 'if a judge makes a ruling, striving to apply his reasoning and if he is correct, he will have two rewards. If a judge makes a ruling, striving to apply his reasoning and he is mistaken, he will have one reward' (Bukhārī 6919, Muslim 1716).[9] While there was always agreement on forms of evidence that were epistemically decisive (*qaṭ'ī*), in other areas plurality led to the emergence of a group referred to as the *musawwiba*, where the ruling of God agrees in some sense with every qualified scholars' opinion.[10]

Within this 'discursive tradition' (Asad 2009) the sciences were generally divided between two complementary fields: the revealed, transmitted or religious sciences (*'ulūm naqliyyah*); and the rational or intellectual sciences (*'ulūm*

---

[5] Murad (2020: 218). In fact, this is how Shahab Ahmed (2016) characterises them in his book.

[6] Moosa (2005: 26), whereas Pickett defines this as a 'unity in eclecticism' (2020: 245).

[7] I mention this example because it is often portrayed that the *ulama* were moribund legal conformists who had little interest in what we would now call the humanities. See also Khaldun (2005: 367–98); Ahmed (2016: 36–46).

[8] For more, see Binbaş (2016); Hirschler (2016); Bora (2019). Shams al-Din Muhammad Hafiz of Shiraz (d. c. 1390) whose poems on love, the 'Divan of Hafiz', were widespread was also a renowned student of a complex commentary of the Qur'an, the *Kaṣḥāf* of al-Zamakhsharī (d. 1144).

[9] This can be seen in the development of the genre of 'ethics of disagreement' (*adab al-ikhtilāf*). For a recent treatise on this, see *Athar al-Ḥadīth as-Sharīf fī Ikhtilāf al-a'immat al-Fuqahā Wayālīhi Adab al-Ikhtilāf fī Masā 'il al-'Ilm wa al-Dīn*, Muhammad Awwamah (2013).

[10] '... the truth of the legal question or the correct answer is present within the mind of God, but it remains unknown to the jurists', see Sohaira Siddiqui, available at: https://www.oasiscenter.eu/en/sunni-islam-many-authorities. Truth, however, is one. Yet 'doctrinal exclusion entailed by objective truth does not preclude sociopolitical harmony ...' (Khan 2020: 2).

'aqliyyah) (Makdisi 1981: 77–80).[11] The former were central to the position of the *madrasah* in its role of preservation of revelation. This is because reason remains, even without preservation, but revelation does not.[12] The *ulama* entertained multiple interpretations, as is obvious to someone trained within the Muslim intellectual tradition. Being confessional did not imply being uncritical.[13]

Developments in India

This tradition travelled to India with the establishment of the Delhi sultanate in the thirteenth century. Under the rule of Muhammad ibn Tughluq (d. 1351) and Sikander Lodi (d. 1517), scholars from all over the Muslim world continued to arrive.[14] Many *madrasahs* were established, such as the Mu'izziyah, Nasriyyah and Firoz Shahi in Delhi.[15] The rational sciences continued to play an important role in scholarship (Robinson 2001).[16] For example, towards the end of the fifteenth century under the reign of the Mughal emperor Akbar, rationalist trends of the Persian world were given wide berth by his educational minister, Fathullah Shirazi (d. 1589) who fled Persia, followed by an influx of scholars from Central Asia. Subjects such as logic, philosophy and theology (*kalām*) gained prominence (Ahmad 1969: 54; Anooshahr 2014; Moosa 2015: 130). This was interwoven into spirituality with the existence of various Sufi orders (sing. *ṭarīqah*; pl. *ṭuruq*)

---

[11] It is worth noting that the religious–secular binary was not a central concern for pre-modern Muslims '. . . the medieval *dīn–dunyawī* binary represented a conceptual separation of the world into distinct religious and non-religious spheres analogous to the modern religious–secular, with things like worship, prayer, and divine law on one side and all worldly matters on the other . . . In this sense, the categories are in a mutually defining relationship, but not necessarily one of opposition, as will be shown. The *dunyawī* was also viewed as a more universal and neutral space, whereas the *dīn*; was seen as particular and limited in scope and thus in more need of explication' (Abbasi 2020: 7–8). Makdisi also states that three fields had emerged by the middle of the ninth/third century: Islamic sciences, the philosophical sciences and the literary arts. The last one largely disappeared, however (Makdisi 1981: 75–7). See also Pedersen and Makdisi (2009).

[12] Bernard Weiss refers to this as a textualist and intentionalist approach where Muslims sought to understand what God 'intended' in the text. For them, reason was a tool that was essential though not independent and certainly circumscribed by revelation (Weiss 2006).

[13] For excellent recent examples of this in *fiqh*, see Sohail Hanif's thesis, *A Theory of Early Classical Ḥanafism: Authority, Rationality and Tradition in the Hidāyah of Burhān al-Dīn 'Alī ibn Abī Bakr al-Marghīnānī* (d. 593/1197), and in Islamic theology, see the recent translation of Imam Nur al Din al Sabuni's *al Bidāyah fī uṣūl al-dīn* by Khan (2020).

[14] Under Sikander Lodi, Persian came to replace Hindi as the language of the lower administration, with the result that Hindu communities began to learn Persian. He also placed a greater emphasis on the rational sciences (Law 1916: pp. 75–6; Jaffar 1936: 49–58; Nadwi 1936: 35–6; Ahmad 1969: 53–4). The Mughals who emerged later, remained Hanafi, and continued with the patronage of important scholarly works such as the *Fataawa-i Alamgiri*, under Aurangzeb (d. 1707). On the *Fatawayi Alamgiri*, see Guenther (2003).

[15] For more details on *madrasahs* being established, see Nadwi (1936). For more details on *madrasahs* in early India, see Pedersen and Makdisi (2009); on Muslim India, Law (1916); Keay (1918: 114–44); Jaffar (1936); Ahmad (1969).

[16] Despite this, there was a large overlap of texts and commentaries being taught in other parts of the Muslim world.

such as the Qadiriyyah, Chistiyyah and Naqhsbandiyyah. The impact of the Chishti Sufi and scholar of Delhi Nizam al-Din Awliya (d. 1325), for example, was significant (Nizami 2012; Moosa 2015: 85). This world continued with heterogeneity and the productive synthesis of many sciences.

The formalisation of teaching occurred under Mulla Nizam al-Din (d. 1748), referred to as the 'Ustadh al-Hind', the teacher of Hindustan. It is claimed that he developed the *dars-i nizami* syllabus which at the that time inherited a large composition of both the rational and revealed sciences.[17] Over time, this syllabus gained wide currency, allowing *taalibs* to become highly skilled scholars, bureaucrats and intellectuals.[18] The texts, though chosen carefully, were secondary to the primary aim of gradually developing the *taalibs*' intellectual ability to become independent *ulama* upon graduation. The texts, some dating back to the ninth century, were often archaic and terse, yet their mastery by unlocking linguistic puzzles prepared the *taalib* for life as a scholar. The *taalib* acquired the essential repertoire of disciplines such as philosophy, logic and theology by the time they graduated to specialise. The *dars-i nizami* provided stability in an otherwise uncertain political climate since by the end of the eighteenth century the Mughal Empire was effectively run by the British East India Company. Colonialism, with its distinction between the religious and the secular realm was being exported to a civilisation which knew no clear distinction, at least how it was conceived in the western sense.[19] As a consequence, a narrowing of the horizon of learning occurred where concerns around maintaining Sunni normativity under such conditions became central.

The turning point came because of the failed joint rebellion of Muslims and Hindus in 1857. One response was the founding of the Madrasa Islamiyyah in the city of Deoband in north India on Thursday, 30 May 1866.[20] The 'reformist

---

[17] I emphasise 'claimed' because there are debates around its authenticity. This requires further research. The formalisation of teaching came after the murder of a member of the scholarly elite, Mulla Qutb al-Din Sihali in 1692, which led to the Mughal emperor Aurungzeb (d. 1707) offering a vacated property that belonged to a European merchant, the Farangi Mahall in Lucknow to one of his sons, Mulla Nizam al-Din (d. 1748). See Muhammad Riza Ansari (1973); Muhammad Raza Ansari (1975).

[18] For books that made up the syllabus, see Mujeeb (1967: 406–8). Others have argued against its 'integrational potential' and that it was indeed intended to remain as a faith-based curriculum and was highly confessional. See Hartung (2013), where the so-called division between religious and rational sciences and the focus on the latter by the Farangi Mahall *ulama* is challenged.

[19] As we have seen, both the revealed and transmitted sciences complemented each other. This distinction, however, was referred to as '*asrī*' or '*jadīd*' *ilm* (Sikand 2005: 67). For how the British sought to refashion 'religion' as the private domain in colonial India, see Chatterjee (2011); Ingram (2018: 48–52).

[20] It was initiated by Maulana Muhammad Qasim Nanotwi (d. 1880), Maulana Rashid Ahmad Gangohi (d. 1905) and Haji Abid Husayn (d. 1912). Maulana Yakub Nanotwi (d. 1886) was appointed as the headteacher (see Sherkoti 1974). They were disciples of the Sufi master of the Sabri-Chishti order, Haji Imdadullah (d. 1899). Nanotwi, Gangohi and Imdadullah were all educated at the Delhi college which housed the scholar Mamluk Ali (d. 1851). See Ingram (2018: 35–8, and fn. 33 which summarises some discrepancies over the actual founding year). See also Khan (2001). In 1879, the name was changed to Dar al-Uloom Deoband (Rizvi 1977: 187–8). On Nanotwi, see Naeem (2015); Gilani

ulama' (Metcalf 1982: 12)[21] sought to revive Islam by educating Muslims in attaining salvation while being steered away from incorrect beliefs and practices. The 'modern religious' *madrasah* and its curriculum became increasingly distanced from its pre-colonial tradition.[22] The founders were familiar with the British educational and governmental system (Moosa 2015: 101–5; Ingram 2018: 11–16).[23] This 'school of thought' (Rizvi 1977: 1–11) emphasised the teaching of hadith as a method of moral reform, and fiqh for correct performance of ritual duties. Their focus on reform led them to introduce the six canonical collections of hadith (*siḥaḥ sittah*) to the *dars-i nizami* (Metcalf 1982: 101).[24] Fiqh as a prime discipline in the *madrasah* required a strong background in logic and legal reasoning.[25] The *taalibs*, in other words, were expected to sharpen their intellectual skills alongside its ethical embodiment.

In many ways Deoband neatly evaded the distinction between the modern and traditional. Breaking from traditional modes of finance, Deoband reduced its reliance on pious endowments (*waqf*) and patronage related to kindship ties with funds instead coming from public donations.[26] With the enunciation of eight principles, the founders emulated the bureaucratic style of the British; it was a distinct institution that was not attached to the *masjid*; it had a formal structure and a 'extra-local character'; it was formed with professional staff and

---

(n.d.). It is worth noting that Nanotwi had a strong interest in logic and philosophy. See Mirathi (1977); Metcalf (1982: 76–8). Muhammad Qasim did not teach in the *madrasah* and only witnessed the first fourteen years of its establishment. Also see Zaman (2002). For Gangohi, see Mirathi (1977); Metcalf (1982: 78–9). See also Gilani (n.d.: 231–2, vol. 2). The key sources on Deoband are the following: Metcalf (1982); Zaman (2002, 2012); Moosa (2015); Ingram (2018). Nanotwi discussed the idea of setting up a *darul uloom* with Imdadullah in Mecca in 1861. See Mian (2015: 27–38) for footnotes providing a list of primary sources for Haji Imdadullah. See also Zaidi (1978); Nizami (2017: 197–204). For a study of the Chisti order, see Nizami (1980); Ernst and Lawrence (2002); Kugle (2007: 221–64); Pernau (2013: 30–8).

[21] For a criticism of Metcalf's assertion that the Deoband founders constituted in an 'inward turn' being symptomatic of imposing secular liberal binaries, see Tareen (2020: 241). For an alternative conceptualisation that moves away from accounts that are 'global and deracinated, rational and individualist, disenchanted and "Protestant", and "tradition" and "reform"', see Green (2011: 8).

[22] This is not to suggest that there did not exist any attempt to bring both streams together. The establishment of the Mohammedan Anglo-Oriental High School in Aligarh, which was later upgraded to a college by Sir Sayyed Ahmad Khan is an example. Khan has studied under Mamluk Ali, who, as we will see below, was a teacher of the founders of Deoband. The *madrasah*, Dar al-Nadwa in Lucknow is another example of seeking rapprochement (Sikand 2005: 77–83).

[23] Sufism will be discussed later. For Mamluk Ali, see Sherkoti (1974). On the Delhi College, see Metcalf (1982: 71–5); Pernau (2006, 2013: 106–15).

[24] As Zaman (2021) points out the reading of the six books was already in vogue in India, particularly in Shāh Walī Allāh's (d. 1762) circles of teaching. It is worth mentioning there existed extensive debate around which books should form the canon. Ibn Mājah's Sunan, for instance, had initially contended with more reliable texts like Mālik's Muwaṭṭa' and al-Dārimī's Musnad; ultimately, utility trumped authenticity (Zaman 2021).

[25] Therefore, the study of *fiqh* is not 'mere legalism' (Hartung 2013: 137).

[26] As Kozlowski notes, 'The endowments clearly focused on the community of faith formed by the neighbourhood or town in which the founders lived (Kozlowski 1985: 61). See Metcalf (1982: 94–100); Kozlowski (1985: 60–80).

had a defined curriculum (Metcalf 1982: 94–116). In other ways, in seeking to refashion the public, the railway allowed them to reach a wider audience (Goswami 2004; Aguiar 2011; Metcalf and Metcalf 2012: 95–7). Furthermore, in response to the decline of state judges (*qadis*), they started issuing fatwas directly to the public.[27] The technology of print became an important tool for mass reform (Metcalf 1982: 146; Agrama 2010; Ingram 2018: 105–15).

The medieval *madrasah*, as we have seen, did not have exams, and mastery of texts was certified by way of granting a licence (*ijāzah*). Crucially, it was largely informal. This has led some to argue that such institutions 'jettisoned' this medieval tradition (Berkey 2007: 49). The question was less 'who is your teacher?' but rather 'where did you study?'. While scholarly prestige was still present, the attraction for *taalibs* was the institution of Deoband. It became replicable with Mazahir al-Uloom in nearby Saharanpur being established within six months of Deoband (Kandhlavi 1972: 5; Metcalf 1982: 128). Though it followed Deoband in many ways, it was seen to be relatively less inclined to academic pursuits and more Sufi in its orientation (Metcalf 1982: 132–3). It was this strand of Deoband that migrated to Britain.

Dar al-ulum in Britain

The *dar al-ulum* in Bury, Greater Manchester, Dar al-Uloom Al-Arabiyyah Al-Islamiyyah, was the first to be established in Europe in 1973.[28] It was established by a Gujarati Indian scholar, Yusuf Motala (d. 2019). The second *dar al-ulum* to be established was in the town of Dewsbury, in West Yorkshire, in 1982.[29] It is part of larger mosque complex and has been referred to by various names, such as the Markazi Masjid, Dewsbury Markaz or just as Dewsbury Dar al-Uloom. It was to become the headquarters for the Tablighi Jama'at movement in Europe (Timol 2019). According to one statistic, Deobandi-affiliated *masjids* make up 42 per cent of the total number of *masjids* in the United Kingdom.[30] Unlike Christian theological seminaries, the syllabus of the *dar al-ulums* in Britain has not been accredited by mainstream higher education, though there have been recent attempts to bridge the gap (Gilliat-Ray 2005; Mukadam

---

[27] Though fatwas are not binding, their demand and mastery with which the *ulama* responded informs us of a religious consciousness, a 'care of the self' and respect for the Islamic tradition in the public domain, not to mention how fatwas allow the *ulama* to respond creatively to changing circumstances, see Agrama (2010: 13). The establishment of a fatwa department, a Dar al-Ifta, occurred in 1892 (Metcalf 1982: 199–206).

[28] Various academics have provided different dates for when the *dar al-ulum* was established. Reetz (2007), citing a website linked to the *dar al-ulum* (http://www.inter-islam.org/Pastevents/Historical.html), quotes 1974, while Lewis (2004) mentions both 1974 and 1975; Bowen (2016) states 1973.

[29] Bowen (2016: 36) has the year as 1989. For an MA thesis looking at this *dar al-ulum*, see Mahmood (2012).

[30] See at: http://muslimsinbritain.org/statistics/statistics01.php.

et al. 2010; Geaves 2012, 2015). No less significant, and this obvious point seems to have been missed by many writers, is that just as Christian theological seminaries and universities exhibit diversity in their values and engagement, so it is the case with *dar al-ulum*s in Britain.[31] Due to the central role *ulama* and imams play in the lives of Muslims, a report by the Citizens UK Commission on Islam, Participation and Public Life, titled 'The Missing Muslims: Unlocking British Muslim Potential for the Benefit of All' (2017), recommended that universities consider pairing with seminaries so that educational schemes for imams become accredited, allowing them to receive both an educational qualification along with a religious qualification.[32] My research found that few *taalib*s go on to become imams in the traditional sense and, unlike Christian seminaries, they are not primarily focused on producing imams.

Pre-modern *madrasah*s and the *ulama* acted as moral stewards of society in their roles as 'Heirs of the Prophets'.[33] It is only in the modern era that the established scholarly freedom and diversity has been inverted and brought under the remit of the modern state.[34] The breadth, richness, and vitality that characterised most of the Islamic scholarly tradition over its long history has been swamped with fundamentalist and narrow upstarts.

However, it is here in the West, unlike certain parts of the Muslim world, where greater diversity and openness is likely to ferment and show promise.[35] Islamic studies departments now study Muslim societies in addition to their staple diet of textual studies. However, vestiges of Orientalism remain with old commitments to suspicion of insider perspectives (Said 1985; Hussain 2005: 253). Yet, as I have argued in my thesis, alongside the Bourdieusian reflexive sociology, insiders often bring enriching perspectives that are difficult for so-called positivist 'outsiders' to appreciate.[36] For example, my familiarity with the languages of Gujarati, Urdu and Arabic allowed me to appreciate the nuances of culturally specific use of words and phrases. This 'socio-cultural insiderism' (Engelhardt 2016: 742) is also borne out of the fact that I studied at a *dar al-ulum*

---

[31] Therefore, my experiences and research should reflect that of one *dar al-ulum* among many. Though, the general observations could be applied across all of them. My intentional use of language should help in differentiating between the general and specific.

[32] See at: https://www.citizensuk.org/missing_muslims, last accessed 30 September 2020.

[33] This is the famous narration of the Companion of the Prophet, Abū Dardā, wherein the Prophet is reported to have said: 'the scholars are the successors of the prophets. Verily, the prophets do not pass on gold and silver coins, but rather they only impart knowledge'. For more, see the translation by Zaid Shakir in 2002 of a treatise by Ibn Rajab al-Hanbali titled 'The Heirs of the Prophet'.

[34] Murad has furnished examples in the Muslim world of states 'often clutching to the fig leaf of counter radicalisation' (2020: 225) that impose a narrow and intolerant version of the *madrasah* syllabus alongside the production of state-sponsored of fatwas.

[35] Indeed, this is a question that Bano (2018) attends to and argues that intellectual inquiry in Islam flourishes in societies that are politically and economically vibrant.

[36] Bourdieu et al. (1992), see at: https://bsabourdieu.wordpress.com/2012/11/08/bourdieusien-or-bourdieuien.

and was able to ground myself in the classic Islamic intellectual tradition. As for some Muslims, based on their experience with and of Orientalism, guarded suspicions remain.[37] Yet perhaps this is exactly where the solution lies wherein partnerships and dialogue can flourish and expand the horizon of knowledge of the study of Islam, alongside developing innovative methods and theories.[38]

Beyond concerns over Orientalism, there is the related question of epistemology. This concerns reconciling a post-modern culture, combined with the monetisation of education, where knowledge-production is highly specialised with a world of both truth and ambiguity (see Higton 2013: 111; Scott-Baumann and Cheruvallil-Contractor 2015: 135). The question is whether this episteme can flourish within a positivist secular academy that has largely given up asking some of the big metaphysical questions on life. The experience of Germany and the study of Islam is perhaps useful. The emergence of a Muslim epistemic-normative framework as an autonomous discipline within academia was supported by the state which would allow for an Islam that is contextually relevant to flourish.[39] In the United Kingdom, a study published in July 2020, titled 'Islam and Muslims on UK University Campuses: Perceptions and Challenges' found, for example, that the government's counter-terrorism strategy, Prevent, actually deepened negative stereotypes of Muslims leading to a toxic culture of suspicion and surveillance.[40] If anything, according to the report, it has limited free speech. This raises the question of the sustainability of a university that historically encouraged intellectual freedom, openness and debate.

The Western Academy

The truth, however, is that work is already underway. The growth of Islamic studies departments and engagement with the Islamic tradition might revive universities 'that were once thought to pursue truth in order to train students in virtuous service to society' (Murad 2020: 238). Despite a shift towards studies that look at Islam and Muslims through the lens of securitisation, the more pressing need is for a more careful, considered and nuanced understanding of Islam, its traditions and the way it is lived in order to contribute to fulfilling the

---

[37] This is not unfounded. A report published in 2020, cited below, stated that while Islamic studies approaches is diverse, essentialisation of Islam and Muslims still exists.
[38] Andrew Rippin (2012) has spoken of the potential benefits of research partnerships when it comes to Qur'an translation, for example. There are others, for example, see Martin (2012).
[39] Engelhardt (2016). It is worth pointing out that '. . . while epistemic insiderism may constitute a key feature of Islamic Theology, it does not materialize in a monopolistic form that excludes outsiders from its systems of knowledge' (p. 750).
[40] See at: https://www.soas.ac.uk/representingislamoncampus/publications/file148310.pdf, pp. 50–2, last accessed 4 October 2020.

universities' role in providing a public good.⁴¹ It is in the West, as Abdal Hakim Murad recently argued, that:

> A specifically Muslim style of intellectuality in the Western academy is starting to grow into a salient and influential fact which is exercising a reach in the less free 'Islamic world' as well, and its access to contemporary examinations of Muslim texts and proof-claims and an awareness of the 'culture of ambiguity' equips it to offer an alternative to local, homogenised, nationalised or fundamentalist interpretations. (Murad 2020: 241)

The *dar al-ulums* can provide universities with a deep-rooted and rich engagement with key disciplines in the Islamic sciences, alongside an understanding of their unique cultural perspectives. The universities, increasingly open to alternative paradigms, can and should benefit the *dar al-ulums* with their study of the contemporary world, history, philology and comparative religion. Moreover, by working with universities this can act as a bridge for the *taalibs* to contextualise their studies to modern Britain and benefit from the social sciences (Scott-Baumann and Cheruvallil-Contractor 2015: 142; Scott-Baumann et al. 2019; for an earlier discussion on this, see Lewis 2006). Arabic, a core language of *dar al-ulum* education specifically and for Muslims generally, is neglected in Islamic studies courses. This is an odd omission. Then there are *taalibs* who have become Muslim chaplains and are an excellent example of positive influence (Gilliat-Ray et al. 2013). Therefore, combined expertise will only bring more depth to a pluralist Britain (Scott-Baumann and Cheruvallil-Contractor 2015: 104). Highly gendered Islamic studies provision can benefit from the pool of *dar al-ulum* graduates who are split equally between both genders.⁴² Research commissioned by the Department for Communities and Local Government in 2008, titled 'The Training and Development of Muslim Faith Leaders: Current Practice and Future Possibilities', provided cases of successful collaborative efforts between so-called 'confessional and academic approaches' (Scott-Baumann and Cheruvallil-Contractor 2015: 32, 136–9). It recommended pathways to overcome 'roadblocks' to be created for accreditation and validation.⁴³ Yet progress has been slow. This recommendation in 2008 was repeated, as we have seen, in

---

[41] 'Many staff involved in Islamic Studies covering textual, historical and cultural approaches to Islam took a view against securitisation, suggesting a deeper, richer account of Islam can combat societal misperceptions as well as extremist ideas', p. 58, available at: https://www.soas.ac.uk/representingislamoncampus/publications/file148310.pdf.

[42] '. . . our research revealed a clearly gendered aspect at the heart of Islamic Studies provision: many teaching staff are white, non-Muslim males', p. 59, see at: https://www.soas.ac.uk/representingislamoncampus/publications/file148310.pdf.

[43] See also Scott-Baumann and Cheruvallil-Contractor (2015: 141–6).

2017; it was repeated again in 2020.[44] Where attempts have succeeded, universities have exhibited reluctance to benefit from Islamic colleges.

One experience of working with the university is instructive in this regard. This occurred before I undertook my postdoctoral research at the same *dar al-ulum*. The *dar al-ulum* was provided with a course handbook and was then left to deliver the course without much help from the university. Engagement was minimal and contact was made when fees needed to be paid. Like the discourse on integration, it was one-directional: fees were paid, and they provided the credits. At no time was there any attempt to learn from the *dar al-ulum*. It reflected less of a partnership and more of a rubber-stamping exercise. After a few years the contract was ended by the university, and the *dar al-ulum* was disappointed because *taalibs* were really benefiting from the course. The reason given for the termination of the agreement by the university was that the course was no longer on their offerings. However, the *dar al-ulum* remains determined to seek out alternative meaningful partners. Over the years, spurred by teachers at the *dar al-ulum*, I have been involved in dialogue with other universities to bring them closer in more meaningful relationships with the *dar al-ulum*. Yet, while the *dar al-ulum* I researched remained enthusiastic and was willing to alter its timetable, the universities, after promising meetings and dialogue, proffered several reasons for a lack of engagement.[45] For some, increasing partnerships was not a priority unless an economic case could be made. They could not see that such partnerships are more than likely to increase their income streams with the sheer number of students that study across the *dar al-ulums*. We were told this by well-intentioned academics who were keen to foster relationships. For other universities, it was the perceived challenges of matching Islamic studies modules with the *dars-i nizami* even though we had provided a detailed mapping and course module handbook. Others have noted caution due to Islamophobia in the media and this seems most plausible in a polite society (Scott-Baumann and Cheruvallil-Contractor 2015: 148). Such disinterest and apathy will only lead to further misinformation and misrepresentation at universities and of Muslims more generally. One could argue that, given that Muslims are over-represented

---

[44] See at: https://www.soas.ac.uk/representingislamoncampus/publications/file148310.pdf, p. 7. At the time of writing, there is an ongoing project, titled 'The Universities and Muslim Seminaries Project (UMSEP)', that emerged in response to the British government's 2018 Integrated Communities and Strategies Green Paper. The project seeks to provide a model through which the seminaries five-year project that will lead to a template and model through which the UK's traditional Muslim seminaries can work towards accreditation of their courses alongside developing relationships with universities (Scott-Baumann et al. 2019).

[45] Scott-Baumann and Cheruvallil-Contractor (2015) note that 'from 1998 to 2015, we have evidence of this, where university staff have spent months working with staff from Muslim colleges and, despite developing a good working relationship, the university has ultimately refused partnership' (p. 147).

in universities, there is a moral and civic duty for them to understand their students and in providing the public good of reducing Islamophobia in society.[46]

Given that the model of collaboration appears sluggish with universities showing a lack of interest (Scott-Baumann and Cheruvallil-Contractor 2015: 157–8), what are the options for someone wanting to experience the 'best of both worlds'? Hybridised places that seek to merge such intellectual steams are already in existence. In the United Kingdom, the Cambridge Muslim College has achieved accreditation, and there are places for *taalibs* at the University of Warwick[47] and the Markfield Institute of Higher Education in Leicester. The latter has recently paired with As-Suffa Institute in Birmingham to offer a BA in Islamic studies. Places such as the WhiteThread Institute and Ebrahim College, for example, offer courses that reflect current realities. In the United States, there are places like Zaytuna College and Darul Qasim (Scott-Baumann and Cheruvallil-Contractor 2015: 45–9; Bano 2018). More research is required of the less well-known yet informal ways of bricolage among young Muslim *taalibs*.

My own research and experiences at the *dar al-ulum* provide further insights. The *taalibs* did not see the secular–religious divide as pronounced.[48] *Taalibs* pursue their *dars-i niẓami* alongside completing GCSEs and A levels at the *dar al-ulum*. They are excelling in their studies with inspections consistently noting excellent outcomes. This success extends to Muslim faith state schools, many of which are leading the UK's league table of secondary schools.[49] This reflects a broader ethos of the 'best of worlds' or '*dīn aur dunyā*' where *taalibs* are encouraged to excel in both fields.[50] Importantly, this vision stems from the principal of the *dar al-ulum* itself:

> Prophets before Noah, and after them, they generally came with this kind of knowledge (both worldly and religious). They used to teach the human being how to do farming, how to make clothes, how to do this, how to do that.

---

[46] Muslim students constitute 8–9 per cent of the Muslim population, though the Muslim population in Britain is around 5 per cent. See at: https://www.soas.ac.uk/representingislamoncampus/publications/file148310.pdf, p. 8. Of course, there is also a low-level of religious literacy in society at a time when it is perhaps most needed.
[47] See at: https://warwick.ac.uk/fac/soc/ces/prospective/postgraduate/taught/islamicpga.
[48] This confirms the observation of others who note that while there may be some form of dichotomy it was less pronounced than expected (Scott-Baumann & Cheruvallil-Contractor 2015: 24).
[49] See at: https://www.compare-school-performance.service.gov.uk/schools-by-type?step=default&table=schools&region=all-england&for=secondary.
[50] For a discussion on the word *dīn*, see Karamustafa (2017). As for my understanding, the word for this world, *dunyā*, as that which is immediate and is more suited to be situated on a spectrum with the other world, the *ākhirah*, for it is something that follows. As for *dīn*, it functions at both the level of the public and private, individual and collective. In this way, it appears to be a much more capacious form of monotheism, and it evades any simple translation to 'religion'. My reason for deploying the religious–secular binary here is because it appears to be the closest (not exact) approximation of *dīn* and *dunyā*. For more, see Abbasi (2020) for whom they are analogous and he demonstrates the *dīn–dunyā* binary as a conceptual separation into distinct spheres.

In other words, whatever was beneficial. So, if the worldly knowledge is done for the hereafter (ākhirah), then that is counted as knowledge. (Fieldnotes, October 2017)

This passage echoes with Ghazali, cited earlier, who states that:

> the purposes of creation are comprised in the [domain] of dīn and dunya. There can be no organising of dīn without the organising of dunya. This is because the dunya is the cultivating field for the akhirah, and it is a means of reaching God, the Exalted, for the one who takes it as a means and temporal abode, and does not take it as a permanent abode and home . . . (Ghazali 2013: 49)[51]

This was further confirmed when we partnered with the university course cited above. We found that it was oversubscribed as taalibs sought to acquire the 'best of both worlds' (Scott-Baumann and Cheruvallil-Contractor 2015: 42). This is reflective of the fact that Muslim faith leadership as embodied in the taalib is very diverse. Taalibs recognise that their tradition and its compass of knowledge is as wide as the roles they take on in society. In response, they viewed engagement with the university course as supplementing and enhancing their roles as active ulama in society. This was not unique to dar al-ulums. The report cited above, noted that despite a level of anxiety among students for their faith in being at a university, 70 per cent felt it was a place to develop their faith in novel and critical ways, alongside being an enriching experience.[52] Chaplaincy remains one of many career pathways for the taalib, where recent research has shown that further and higher education is a popular option, both for men and women (Gilliat-Ray et al. 2013; Scott-Baumann et al. 2019: 7, 12). A graduate of the Bury dar al-ulum, and a PhD holder, Dr Mufti Abdur-Rahman Mangera, summarises the trajectories of graduates:

> As a result, many 'ālimiyya graduates of his institutes are trained in law, mainstream medicine, natural medicine and homeopathy, mental health, child protection, finance, IT, education, chaplaincy, psychology, philosophy, pharmacy, physics, journalism, engineering, architecture, calligraphy, typography, graphic design, optometry, social services, public health, even British Sign Language. His students also include several who have completed PhDs and lecture at universities. His vision was to train British-born (or other) Muslim scholars who would be well versed in contemporary thought and

---

[51] For a more thorough engagement with Ghazali on this topic, see Abbasi (2020: 207–13).
[52] See at: https://www.soas.ac.uk/representingislamoncampus/publications/file148310.pdf, p. 23.

discipline along with their advanced Islamic learning, equipping them to better contribute to society.[53]

Bricolage

Our journey brings us to a promising plateau. The historical nature of informal learning in Islam, while in some ways altered by modernity and colonialism, may end up being its greatest strength. My thesis confirmed that the inherited tradition I depicted is engaged in the act of bricolage, led by young creative *taalibs* in a dialogical relationship with a cherished past of venerated teachers and texts that hail from a different time, both geographically and culturally (Sidat 2019). Yet this difference should not disguise its creative potential. Ghazali, who we referred to above, is and remains central to the Muslim religious imagination. He was a bricoleur par excellence 'who creatively managed to put to work different ideas in a coherent framework for himself, for his society, and for the community that he served' (Moosa 2005: 27). It is worth noting that some *dar al-ulum*s may venture out to seek external validation and accreditation with universities. Others, seeking to maintain a focus on their *raison d'être* of providing a strong foundation in the Islamic sciences, may not. Uniformity is alien to Islam here. However, a *taalib* that graduates from a *dar al-ulum*, if taught well, will have enough of a base to specialise in other fields should they wish to do so. They will have learned the process through which learning in Islam is acquired. With this, they can engage in a specialism (*takhaṣṣuṣ*) as many do in hadith or in fiqh, in training to become a mufti. Others, should they wish, enrol in Islamic studies departments. For example, having mastered Arabic, the *taalib* may choose to study Middle Eastern literature or focus on the oeuvre of a certain historical figure. Such a *taalib*, trained in the Islamic sciences and with a broad view of and inter-relationship within the sciences will become the antidote to the often atomistic and highly specialised nature that plagues university departments (Kronman 2007: 93). Our *taalib*-turned-budding-bricoleur can take advantage of a tradition to adapt and fit it within their new environment. As Ebrahim Moosa, a *taalib*-turned-professor, puts it:

> 'Your Lord inspired [*awha*] the bee', a delightful parable in the Qur'an begins [16:68] ... As a matter of habit, this insect draws from a diverse variety of sources – pollen and nectars – in order to produce a synthetic product that reflects all the colors and fruits of its immediate habitat. While the honey produced is in some way the aggregate of many diverse types of nectar, it is simultaneously something very new and unparalleled. In the end, the bee not

---

[53] See at: https://www.themuslim500.com/wp-content/uploads/2019/10/TheMuslim500-2020-low.pdf.

only produces a delectable substance but also furthers reproduction through cross-pollination that in turn generates new flowers and restarts the cycle for the future production of honey. (Moosa 2005: 37)

This is the third path, which seems more viable, realistic, and authentic for the *taalib*, for now. Many are undertaking this journey. The author of this chapter is one. During my research *taalib*s were applying for university courses to enrol on to Master's programmes and have proven themselves to be exemplary *taalib*s. In the long run, it is my belief that such *taalib*s, having proven themselves in academia, hold the key to unlocking the doors to help universities and *dar al-ulum*s to see the mutual benefit of coming together.[54] In the meantime, the *taalib*-academic will bring much unique, nuanced and rich perspectives in our collective endeavour to contribute to the production of knowledge. In return they will benefit from historical, philological and social scientific perspectives in the academy where 'the Muslim theologian not just as *object* but also as *subject* in investigations' can play a role.[55] This is what the business of education ought to be about.

References

Abbasi, R. (2020). 'Did Premodern Muslims Distinguish the Religious and Secular? The Dīn–Dunyā Binary in Medieval Islamic Thought', *Journal of Islamic Studies* 31(2): 185–225. DOI:10.1093/jis/etz048.

Agrama, H. A. (2010). 'Ethics, Tradition, Authority: Toward an Anthropology of the Fatwa', *American Ethnologist* 37(1): 2–18.

Aguiar, M. (2011). *Tracking Modernity: India's Railway and the Culture of Mobility*. Minneapolis: University of Minnesota Press.

Ahmad, A. (1969). *Intellectual History of Islam in India*. Edinburgh: Edinburgh University Press.

Ahmed, S. (2016). *What is Islam? The Importance of Being Islamic*. Princeton, NJ: Princeton University Press.

Anooshahr, A. (2014). 'Shirazi Scholars and the Political Culture of the Sixteenth-Century Indo-Persian World', *Indian Economic & Social History Review* 51(3): 331–52.

Ansari, M. R. (1973). *Bani-i Dars-i Nizami: Ustaad al-Hind Mulla Nizamuddin al-Din Muhammad (Farangi Mahalli)*. Lucknow: Farangi Mahall Kitabgarh.

Ansari, M. R. (1975). 'A very Early Farman of Akbar', *Proceedings of the Indian History Congress* 36: 353–7, available at: http://www.jstor.org/stable/44138861.

---

[54] Bano (2018) in her work on Muslim diaspora communities in the West has argued that 'affluent' Muslim scholars educated in the West hold promise of an indigenisation of Islam from below. See also Bano (2020).

[55] Martin (2012: 380). The same author quotes Josef Van Ess of Tübingen where he concludes that 'Islamic studies scholars who want to have conversations with Muslims will have to know a great deal about Islamic textual and intellectual history' (p. 381).

Asad, T. (2009). 'The Idea of an Anthropology of Islam', *Qui Parle* 17(2): 1–30.
Awwamah, M. (2013). *Athar al-Hadith al-Sharif fi Ikhtilaf al-a'immat al-Fuqaha Wayalihi Adab al-Ikhtilaf fi Masa'il al-'Ilm wal Din*. Beirut: Dar al-Minhaaj & Dar al-Yusr.
Bano, M. (2018). *Modern Islamic Authority and Social Change: Evolving Debates in the West*, vol. 2. Edinburgh: Edinburgh University Press.
Bano, M. (2020). *The Revival of Islamic Rationalism: Logic, Metaphysics and Mysticism in Modern Muslim Societies*. Cambridge: Cambridge University Press.
Bauer, T. (2021). *A Culture of Ambiguity: An Alternative History of Islam*, trans. H. Biesterfeldt and T. Tunstall. New York: Columbia University Press.
Berkey, J. B. (1992). *The Transmission of Knowledge in Medieval Cairo: A Social History of Islamic Education*. Princeton, NJ: Princeton University Press.
Berkey, J. P. (2007). 'Madrasas Medieval and Modern: Politics, Education, and the Problem of Muslim Identity', in R. W. Hefner and M. Q. Zaman (eds), *Schooling Islam: The Culture and Politics of Modern Muslim Education*. Princeton, NJ: Princeton University Press.
Binbas, İ. E. (2016). *Intellectual Networks in Timurid Iran: Sharaf al-Dīn 'Alī Yazdī and the Islamicate Republic of Letters*. Cambridge: Cambridge University Press.
Bora, F. (2019). *Writing History in the Medieval Islamic World: The Value of Chronicles as Archives*. London: I. B. Tauris.
Bowen, J. (2016). *On British Islam: Religion, Law and Everyday Practice in Shari'a Councils*. Princeton, NJ: Princeton University Press.
Butt, J. (2020). *A Talib's Tale: The Life and Times of a Pashtoon Englishman*. Delhi: Penguin.
Chamberlain, M. (1994). *Knowledge and Social Practice in Medieval Damascus, 1190–1350*. Cambridge: Cambridge University Press.
Chatterjee, N. (2011). *The Making of Indian Secularism: Empire, Law and Christianity, 1830–1960*. Basingstoke: Palgrave Macmillan.
Engelhardt, J. F. (2016). 'On Insiderism and Muslim Epistemic Communities in the German and US Study of Islam', *Muslim World* 106(4): 740–58. DOI:10.1111/muwo.12168.
Ephrat, D. (2000). *A Learned Society in a Period of Transition: The Sunni 'Ulama' of Eleventh-Century Baghdad*. Albany: State University New York.
Ernst, C. W. and B. B. Lawrence (2002). *Sufi Martyrs of Love: The Chishti Order in South Asia and Beyond*. New York: Palgrave Macmillan.
Geaves, R. (2012). 'The Symbolic Construction of the Walls of Deoband', *Islam and Christian–Muslim Relations* 23: 315–28.
Geaves, R. (2015). 'An Exploration of the Viability of Partnership between "Dar Al-Ulum" and Higher Education Institutions in North West England Focusing upon Pedagogy and Relevance', *British Journal of Religious Education* 37: 64–82.
Ghazali, A. H. (2013). *Ihya Uloom al-Din (The Revival of the Religious Sciences)*. Jeddah: Dar al-Minhaj.
Gilani, M. A. (n.d.). *Savanih Qasimi, ya'ni sirat-i shams al-Islam*, vol. 3. Lahore: Maktaba-yi Rahmaniyya.
Gilliat-Ray, S. (2005). 'Closed Worlds: (Not) Accessing Deobandi Dar al-uloom in Britain'. *Fieldwork in Religion* 1: 7–33.
Gilliat-Ray, S., M. Ali and S. Pattison (2013). *Understanding Muslim Chaplaincy*. Burlington, VT: Ashgate.

Goswami, M. (2004). *Producing India: From Colonial Economy to National Space*. Chicago: University of Chicago Press.
Green, N. (2011). *Bombay Islam: The Religious Economy of the West Indian Ocean, 1840–1915*. Cambridge: Cambridge University Press.
Guenther, A. M. (2003). 'Hanafi Fiqh in Mughal India: The Fatawai Alamgiri', in R. M. Eaton (ed.), *India's Islamic Traditions: 711–1150*. New Delhi: Oxford University Press.
Hanif, S. (2017). 'A Theory of Early Classical Ḥanafism: Authority, Rationality and Tradition in the Hidāyah of Burhān al-Dīn 'Alī ibn Abī Bakr al-Marghīnānī (d. 593/1197)', unpublished PhD dissertation, University of Oxford.
Hartung, J-P. (2013). 'Abused Rationality? On the Role of Ma'quli Scholars in the Events of 1857/1858', in C. Bates (ed.), *Mutiny at the Margins*. London: Sage.
Higton, M. (2013). *A Theology of Higher Education*. Oxford: Oxford University Press.
Hirschler, K. (2016). *Medieval Damascus: Plurality and Diversity in an Arabic Library: The Ashrafīya Library Catalogue*. Edinburgh: Edinburgh University Press.
Hodgson, M. G. S. (1974). *The Venture of Islam: The Expansion of Islam in the Middle Periods*, vol. 2. Chicago: University of Chicago Press.
Hussain, A. (2005). 'Teaching Inside-Out: On Teaching Islam', *Method & Theory in the Study of Religion* 17(3): 248–63.
Ingram, B. (2018). *Revival from Below: The Deoband Movement and Global Islam*. Oakland: University of California Press.
Jaffar, S. M. (1936). *Education in Muslim India, Being an Inquiry into the State of Education During the Muslim Period of Indian History, 1000–1800*. Delhi: Idarah-i Adabiyat-i Delhi.
Kandhlavi, M. Z. (1972). *Tarikh-i Mazaahir*, vol. 1. Saharanpur: Kutub Khana-i Isha'at al-'Ulum.
Karamustafa, A. T. (2017). 'Religion, Theory, Critique', in K. Richard (ed.), *Islamic Dīn as an Alternative to Western Models of 'Religion'*. New York: Columbia University Press, pp. 163–72.
Keay, F. E. (1918). *Ancient Indian Education: An Inquiry into Its Origin, Development and Ideals*. London: Oxford University Press.
Khaldun, I. (2005). *The Muqaddimah: An Introduction to History*, ed. N. J. Dawood, trans. F. Rosenthal. Princeton, NJ: Princeton University Press.
Khan, F. A. (2020). *An Introduction to Islamic Theology: Imam Nūr al-Dīn al-Ṣābūnī's Al-Bidāyah fī uṣūl al-dīn*. Berkeley, CA: Zaytuna College.
Khan, S. (2001). *Bani-yi Dar al-'Ulum Deoband*. Gujranwala: Maktaba-yi Safdariyya.
Kozlowski, G. C. (1985). *Muslim Endowments and Society in British India*. Cambridge: Cambridge University Press.
Kronman, A. (2007). *Education's End: Why Our Colleges and Universities Have Given Up on the Meaning of Life*. New Haven, CT: Yale University Press.
Kugle, S. A. (2007). *Sufis and Saints' Bodies: Mysticism, Corporeality, and Sacred Power in Islam*: Chapel Hill: University of North Carolina Press.
Law, N. N. (1916). *Promotion of Learning in India During Muhammadan Rule (by Muhammadans)*. London: Sagwan Press.
Lewis, P. (2004). 'New Social Roles and Changing Patterns of Authority amongst British 'Ulama', *Archives de sciences sociales des religions* 49(125): 169–87.

Lewis, P. (2006). 'Only Connect: Can the Ulema Address the Crisis in the Transmission of Islam to a New Generation of South Asians in Britain?' *Contemporary South Asia* 15: 165–80.

Mahmood, H. (2012). 'The Dars-e-Niẓāmī and the Transnational Traditionalist Madāris in Britain', Masters thesis, Queen Mary London.

Makdisi, G. (1981). *The Rise of Colleges: Institutions of Learning in Islam and the West.* Edinburgh: Edinburgh University Press.

Martin, R. C. (2012). 'The Uses and Abuses of Criticism in the Study of Islam: A Response to Aaron Hughes', *Method & Theory in the Study of Religion* 24(4/5): 371–88.

Messick, B. (1993). *The Calligraphic State: Textual Domination and History in a Muslim Society.* Berkeley: University of California Press.

Metcalf, B. D. (1982). *Islamic Revival in British India: Deoband, 1860–1920.* Princeton, NJ: Princeton University Press.

Metcalf, B. D. and T. R. Metcalf (2012). *A Concise History of Modern India*, 3rd edn. Cambridge: Cambridge University Press.

Mian, A. A. (2015). 'Surviving Modernity: Ashraf 'Ali Thanvi (1863–1943) and the Making of Muslim Orthodoxy in Colonial India', PhD dissertation, Duke University, North Carolina.

Mirathi, A. I. (1977). *Tazkirat al-Rashid.* Saharanpur: Kutub Khana-yi Isha'at al-'Ulum.

Moosa, E. (2005). *Ghazali and the Poetics of Imagination.* Chapel Hill: University of North Carolina Press.

Moosa, E. (2015). *What is Madrasa?* Chapel Hill: University of North Carolina Press.

Mujeeb, M. (1967). *Indian Muslims.* London: McGill University Press.

Mukadam, M., Alison Scott-Baumann, A. Chowdhary and S. Contractor (2010). *The Training and Development of Muslim Faith Leaders: Current Practice and Future Possibilities.* London: Department of Communities and Local Government.

Murad, A. H. (2020). *Travelling Home: Essays on Islam in Europe.* London: Quilliam Press.

Nadwi, A. a.-H. (1936). *Hindustan ki Qadeem Islami Darsgahaien.* Azamgarh.

Naeem, F. S. (2015). 'Interreligious Debates, Rational Theology, and the 'Ulama' in the Public Sphere: Muhammad Qasim Nanautivi and the Making of Modern Islam in South Asia', PhD dissertation. Georgetown University, Washington DC.

Nizami, K. A. (1980). *Tarikh-i masha'ikh-i Chisht.* Delhi: Idarah-i Adabiyat-i Delhi.

Nizami, K. A. (2012). *The Life and Times of Shaikh Nizam-ud-din Auliya.* New Delhi: Oxford University Press.

Nizami, M. A. (2017). *Reform and Renewal in South Asian Islam: The Chishti-Sabris in 18th–19th Century North India.* Oxford: Oxford University Press.

Nomani, M. A. H. (n.d.). *Lamhaat min al-Tarbiyyah al-Fiqhiyyah fi Khayr al-Quroon Zamani al-Risaalah wa Asr al-Sahaabah wa al-Tabieen.* Dar al Fath.

Pedersen, J. and G. Makdisi (2009). *Madrasa*, vol. 2. Brown University: Brill online.

Pernau, M. (2006). 'The Delhi College: Traditional Elites, the Colonial State, and Education before 1857', in M. Pernau (ed.), *Entangled Translations: The History of the Delhi College.* New Delhi: Oxford University Press.

Pernau, M. (2013). *Ashraf into Middle Classes: Muslims in Nineteenth-Century Delhi.* New Delhi: Oxford University Press.

Petry, C. F. (1981). *The Civilian Elite of Cairo in the Later Middle Ages*. Princeton, NJ: Princeton University Press.

Pickett, J. (2020). *Polymaths of Islam: Power and Networks of Knowledge in Central Asia*. New York: Cornell University Press.

Reetz, D. (2007). 'The Deoband Universe: What Makes a Transcultural and Transnational Educational Movement of Islam?.' *Comparative Studies of South Asia, Africa and the Middle East* 27(1): 139–59. DOI:10.1215/1089201x-2006-049.

Rippin, A. (2012). 'The Reception of Euro-American Scholarship on the Qur'an and tafsīr: An Overview', *Journal of Qur'anic Studies* 14(1): 1–8.

Rizvi, S. M. (1977). *Tarikh-i Dar al-'Ulum Deoband*. Deoband: Idarah-yi Ihtimam-i Dar al-'Ulum Deoband.

Robinson, F. (2001). *The Ulama of Farangi Mahall and Islamic Culture in South Asia*. Delhi: Hurst.

Said, E. W. (1985). 'Orientalism Reconsidered', *Cultural Critique* 1: 89–107. DOI:10.2307/1354282.

Scott-Baumann, A. and S. Cheruvallil-Contractor (2015). *Islamic Education in Britain New Pluralist Paradigms*. London: Bloomsbury.

Scott-Baumann, A., A. Ebbiary, S. A. D. Mohammad, S. Dhorat, S. Begum, H. Pandor and J. Stolyar (2019). 'Towards Contextualized Islamic Leadership: Paraguiding and the Universities and Muslim Seminaries Project (UMSEP)', *Religions* 10(662).

Sherkoti, A. H. (1974). *Sirat-i Ya'qub o Mamluk*. Karachi: Maktaba-yi Dar al-'Ulum Karachi.

Sidat, H. (2019). 'Formation and training of British Muslim scholars (Ulama): An ethnography of a Dar al-Uloom in Britain', PhD dissertation, Cardiff University.

Sikand, Y. S. (2005). *Bastions of the Believers: Madrasas and Islamic Education in India*. Delhi: Penguin.

Tareen, S. (2020). *Defending Muhammad in Modernity*. Notre Dame, IN: University of Notre Dame Press.

Timol, R. (2019). 'Structures of Organisation and Loci of Authority in a Glocal Islamic Movement: The Tablighi Jama'at in Britain', *Religions* 10(10): 573.

Weiss, B. (2006). *The Spirit of Islamic Law*. Atlanta: Georgia University Press.

Zaidi, S. N. (1978). *Hajji Imdad Allah Muhajir Makki: Sirat o savanih*. Gujarat: Maktaba-yi Zafar.

Zaman, M. Q. (2002). *The Ulama in Contemporary Islam: Custodians of Change*. Princeton, NJ: Princeton University Press.

Zaman, M. Q. (2012). *Modern Islamic Thought in a Radical Age: Religious Authority and Internal Criticism*. New York: Cambridge University Press.

Zaman, M. Q. (2021). *Hadith Scholarship in the Indian Subcontinent: Aḥmad 'Alī Sahāranpūrī and the Canonical Hadith Literature*. Leicester: Qurtuba Books.

CHAPTER 8

Why would Muslims Study Theology to Obtain an Academic Qualification?

MOHAMMAD MESBAHI

INTRODUCTION

Islam is not limited to one particular region or centre, grounded by its 'intrinsic universality' which Islam shares with Judaism and Christianity (Hirschkind 2001: 3). Consequently, there is an acceptance that it can be 'entirely re-territorialised' (Kahani-Hopkins and Hopkins 2002: 288), and thus the practice of faith becomes fundamentally imperative to discussions around Muslim identities in Europe. Over the last seven decades or so Europe has experienced a significant influx of migrants and refugees, huge numbers of whom are predominately from the Middle East and Africa who identify themselves as Muslims. In fact, according to the PEW Research Center, the Muslim share of the European Unions' total population as of mid-2016, was estimated at 25.8 million (4.9 per cent of the total population), up from 19.5 million (3.8 per cent) in 2010. With the high migration rates continuing, this figure is expected to increase to 14 per cent of Europe's population by 2050 (PEW Forum 2010, 2017). Changes in religious profiling and the recording and analysis of their religious behavioural characteristics are different across various countries in Europe, and the levels of religious commitment or religiousness among the Muslim population also differ. Other factors such as differences in fertility rates, the size of youth populations and people changing their faith also need to be taken into account (PEW Forum 2015). Nonetheless, there is a growing body of research noting an increase in the prominence of religion as a key marker of identity, particularly when religious groups are positioning themselves within a secular environment (Hashemi 2009: 2). Although this sense of religious identity can influence Muslims both 'positively and negatively', it has raised anxiety in Europe. There is now an increase in discourse around the 'Muslim question' (Norton 2020: ix), and the term 'Muslimness' is often used in research literature. This comprises three categories: a person's own understanding of their Muslim identity; their association with the larger Muslim community – *ummah*; and the 'visible display' or 'practice of commitments' to their faith within society (Shah 2019: 344).

Despite religious identity profoundly shaping the daily lives of some Muslims residing in Europe, for whom it is a crucial link to their 'sense of belonging and self-worth' (Modood 2005: 31), for other Muslims regarded as 'secular Muslims' (Panjwani 2017: 601), it may not be so salient. Additionally, today's Europe consists of Muslims that 'include people of many nations and colours, who speak many languages' (Meer and Modood 2009: 483), with differences in 'social class, ethnicity, gender, sexuality, country of origin, educational attainment, language proficiency, occupation and many other factors' (Merry 2018: 168). 'Since the ethnic or the religious affiliations of Muslims are not fixed, nor internally homogeneous, and not necessarily an easily identifiable entity', their ability to negotiate circumstances being encountered would also be different (Mesbahi 2020: 32). For example, religious identity is regarded as more salient for the second- and third-generation Muslims, regarded as 'European Muslims', rather than other ethnic or regional affiliations. For them, 'multiple identifications' are present, and 'different identifications would be prioritised within different situations' (McLoughlin 1996: 227). However, for many Muslims the crucial test is to see whether the commitment to Islamic beliefs and practices is 'maintained in a non-Muslim environment' particularly by the youth (Ryan 2014: 446). Thus, the issue of Muslimness within the educational context has emerged as a subject of intense suspicion and debate, often constructed as the 'complex problem' in Europe (Shah 2015: 175). The growing significance of the issue has brought a 'religious turn' to educational debates in Europe, in recognition of Islam's role in shaping 'discourses, social change, and practices' within a 'variety of cultural contexts' (Panjwani and Moulin-Stożek 2017: 519). In the midst of such tensions, countries such as France with a large Muslim minority population are contemplating radical steps in defence of secularism. Proposals include the 'allocation of identification numbers' to Muslim children to ensure their attendance at secular schools, and restrictions to their home-schooling (BBC 2020). The capacity of schools run by the public sector to support the needs of Muslim pupils, and the extent to which secular education can attend to their identity needs is debatable. In light of the youthful demographic of Muslim communities, the educational discussion can become 'a proxy' for the 'wider tensions' between Islam and European societies (Shah 2015: 175).

In the European context, Britain is recognised as a multi-faith country, with Muslims accounting for the second largest religious group after Christianity (Census 2011). The Muslim presence in Britain, which is 'inevitably linked with the British Empire' (Samad 2004: 2), has accommodated an easier settlement process for this significant minority religious group than in other places in Europe. The most recent census of 2011 indicated that there were 2.7 million Muslims living in England and Wales, which equated to 4.8 per cent of the total. That percentage was expected to increase in the 2021 census. Some areas in London such as Brent or Newham had the most diverse regions in the country, and Tower Hamlets recorded over 38 per cent of residents to be Muslim (Census 2011), The projection according to the PEW Research Center was that the overall population had increased to 6.3 per cent of the total population in 2016, and would reach 9.7 per cent by 2050, in a zero-migration scenario (PEW Forum 2017). Additionally, the 2011 Census has shown approximately half of the Muslims to be under the age of 25 and a third under the age of 15 (Census 2011). For British Muslims, there is an increased interest not only merely to succeed in secular academic subjects, but also to hold onto their religious and cultural roots. For them, the educational discourse about Muslims needs to move beyond 'the binary of Muslims as religious and the West as secular' (Panjwani 2017: 596) to a system that caters for all. Hence, it is pointed out that the 'Muslim question within the educational context', which is often flagged for the growing tensions over Muslim integration into the British society (Modood 2006: 37), should be viewed as an opportunity for providing an educational space in the sharing of common values and challenging the ideology of othering (Ameli et al. 2006: 32). Muslim leaders in Britain have highlighted that if the aim is to create 'autonomous and critical individuals', a 'secular perspective' is not sufficient, because it fails to approach 'the divine' and excludes 'religious principles and priorities' (Nielsen 2004: 58). Consequently, an approach that scrutinises Muslim identities, denies Muslims the capacity to incorporate Muslimness within the educational context. The late Dr Ataullah Siddiqui in his report on Islam in universities in England[1] indicated that 'teaching and research programmes need to be re-oriented' and stated that 'Britain could give the lead to Europe in such a re-orientation' (Siddiqui 2007: 6). He wrote: '. . . of special interest to policy makers and community leaders, are (a) how far Islam can be integrated within the secular/humanist ethos; and (b) how future leadership of Muslims can be formalised at higher educational levels so as then to provide a controlled position for Islam' (Siddiqui 2007: 8).

---

[1] Universities in the United Kingdom do not have a particular faith context, in contrast, programmes at theological colleges are grounded in committed faith positions. Although there are some theological colleges that have awarding powers, most are accredited or validated by a university. Recently this provision has become available to Muslim theological colleges. This research is the culmination of extensive study carried out at one such institution, the Islamic College, that dates back to 2008 with work by Saida Nasser on the further education provision. The study on higher education degree programmes was proposed in 2012 to the 'Collaborative partnerships between UK universities and Muslim colleges: dismantling the road blocks', but carried out recently prior to the Covid-19 pandemic.

Dr Siddiqui also stated that 'there is a need for the community and the universities to find ways to cooperate and collaborate in order to widen the influence of higher education among Muslims' (Siddiqui 2007: 35). In support of this idea, there are suggestions that 'government has a key role to play in supporting the developments and improvements' within provisions 'facilitating closer partnerships and relationships between Muslim institutions and publicly funded institutions' (Mukadam and Scott-Baumann 2010: 13).

This forms the basis for this research focusing on teaching delivered at an Islamic educational institution that has both a collaborative partnership to a British higher education provider as well as a traditional theological Islamic learning provision. The use of the term seminary is avoided in this study as it is 'borrowed from the Christian lexicon' and is 'emblematic of the perpetual urge to force Western Christian terms on to Islamic cognates' (Gilliat-Ray and Timol 2020: 5). Since the Islamic concept of 'the learned' is one that incorporates both knowledge and action, it should be noted that the true scholar is not simply someone who 'knows', but someone whose actions are an embodiment of the teachings of the Qur'an and the traditions of the Holy Prophet and the guidance of his progeny and companions. As such, this work will assess the reasons behind why Muslims would study theology to obtain a secular academic qualification. It will explore various aspects of the question, such as the programme objectives, offering new knowledge to the students that they may not already know, moving beyond the monologue style of teaching and consequently not focused on indoctrination of beliefs, increasing the level of spiritual understanding behind acts of worship, helping to internalise Islamic values, allowing students to link to their Muslim identities, and evolving in the face contemporary realities. It will then question if those who embark on this study do so not only to gain Islamic knowledge from a qualified academic perspective or as a route to obtaining an increase in spirituality and religiousness, but also to help adherents to develop their identity within the British Muslim context. In doing so this research will reflect on the possibilities of attaining such religiousness without the traditional programme or developing the British Muslim identities perspective without the access to the secular standards within the validated programmes, as well as the necessity for an exemplar role and, thus, identify the importance of collaborative programmes that are well-constructed and viable, playing a strategic role in promoting mutual respect and understanding in a multi-faith society.

The Islamic Educational Provision

Islamic education is a generic term and the ambiguity in its use quite often revolves around the type of educational activity involved and its objective. These can be summarised in three educational categories that are readily available in Britain, although a fourth strand is also distinguishable. First, education of Muslims in their Islamic faith, referring to the Muslim community's efforts to educate the next generation by passing along the heritage of Islamic knowledge in educational settings where emphasis is placed on religious instruction. Secondly, education for Muslims which includes the religious and secular disciplines, referring to a mainstream faith-based school or college setting that embraces a much broader curriculum of both secular academic and religious instruction. Thirdly, education about Islam within a set curriculum, referring to education about Islam in a mainstream secular school, college or university settings often delivered as part of the religious studies or Islamic studies subject using resources that serve as the medium for educating students about Islam. The fourth type, education in an Islamic spirit and tradition, refers to the traditional concepts of Islamic education, where knowledge is sought without making a distinction between religious and secular knowledge (Douglass and Shaikh 2004: 7). Although some see the educational institutions in which religious instruction traditionally takes place as *madrasa* or colleges of law (Makdisi 1981: 1) or in the Shi'i context as *hawza* (Elmi 2012: ii), references to such terms need clarity. Their use by Muslims in Britain can be summarised into three educational categories: the faith-based Muslim schools and colleges; the *darul uloom* or *hawza 'ilmiyya* (Islamic theological institutions); and the *madrasa* (Muslim supplementary religious schooling for children). Additionally, within literature, reference is made to such religious schools as Islamic or Muslim, but the terms are used interchangeably. In practice, Islamic schools and colleges are those aiming to define 'the ethos, curriculum and pedagogy through the traditional sources of Islamic knowledge', while Muslim schools and colleges are those with no reconstruction of the 'educational philosophy or curriculum', providing a provision of learning with an Islamic perspective to the content, conducive to Islamic standards of 'dress, diet, and other religious observance' (Memon 2019: 6).

The debate around Islamic and Muslim educational providers in Britain and the roles played by secular institutions with them has been polarised (Scott-Baumann et al. 2020a: 194) and essentially circle around liberal values, individual choice and Muslim identity criteria. However, Muslims point to the potential in promoting 'diversity and tolerance' alongside their spiritual environment, but successive governments have viewed them with suspicion, and some have raised questions regarding the social impacts of 'segregating young people' (Ichijo 2014: 101). Nevertheless, Islamic educational institutions and their distinct curricula are viewed with a sense of 'an anomaly' within ethnic education (Reay and Mirza 1997: 478), and their 'traditional pedagogical methods and discipline' are often questioned (McLoughlin 2011: 605). The concern with regard to these institutions seems to be mainly based on the fact that they 'operate in the independent sector', and therefore are not subject to the same 'oversight' as publicly funded educational institutions (Cherti and Bradley 2011: 14). Others have argued that the failure to address ethnic diversity in primary, secondary and further education is the cause of 'a disproportionately high percentage' of students from ethnic minority backgrounds being allocated to lower streams (Gillborn and Gipps 1996: 80), thus increasing the popularity of these faith-based educational institutions which focus their provision on catering for the community. At the higher education level research has found that despite this image of university life being 'a haven of progressive thinking', their capacity to provide a welcome place for Muslims is called into question (Guest et al. 2020: 4). Also, the discourse of Islamic, cultural and linguistic identities has placed particular scrutiny on the role that such educational institutions could play in 'facilitating the radicalisation of young Muslims towards violent extremism' (Cherti et al. 2011: 1). Such claims increase 'the stigmatisation of Muslims as narrow-minded, culturally alien and prone to violence' (Guest et al. 2020: 4). Although the debate around radicalisation is not the focus of this research, issues like cultural homogeneity as a precondition for inclusion (Taras 2012: 319), or the targeting and stigmatising of Muslim communities (Bartlett et al. 2010: 8) are deeply inter-related. Islamic education attaches considerable importance to religious matters and ethical issues, but it also addresses everyday problems of life and living. Subsequently, it is fair to say that such institutions are not based on segregation between religious and secular education (Al-Fendi and Baloch 1980: 4), but on promoting an 'understanding of religious and cultural roots' (Halstead 2004: 526). Since Islamic educational institutes have responded to part of the spiritual, intellectual and cultural needs of the community, their activities have been directed towards the preservation of Muslim identities, helping students take pride in their religion, without giving serious thought to the nature of the distinctive education they provide or to the way they should deal with the philosophical and epistemological problems posed for Muslims by modern secular scientific knowledge (Halstead 2004: 520). As the Qur'an identifies the learning in religion with community interaction (Qur'an 9:122), there is a need to address this aspect within learner development strategies in order to address the expectations of the larger host community, European Muslims, and policymakers alike. One possible approach would be collaboration with secular academic institutes.

Programmes Delivery at the Islamic College

According to research on 'training and development of Muslim faith leaders' (Mukadam and Scott-Baumann 2010) there are around '40 independent colleges of an Islamic character', '30 of which are centres of Islamic religious training', while the rest combined traditional scholarship with modern secular thought (Scott-Baumann et al. 2020a: 75). This research will be based at one such institution that attempts deliver Islamic teaching within secular parameters. The Islamic College has an academic partnership with a secular university (Middlesex University), a unique feature that only a handful of Islamic institutions have successfully achieved. Established in 1998, the Islamic College attempts to have a non-sectarian approach and identifies itself as 'a fusion of the classic with the modern', 'to promote a new approach to the study of Islam and Muslims'. This integrated and interdisciplinary approach to Islamic studies is based on an 'insiders perspective to Islam' 'fostering a non-sectarian outlook' (Islamic College 2021). The Islamic College has developed a range of foundation, undergraduate and postgraduate programmes within its main campus offered to all applicants, all Muslims and non-Muslims alike. Additionally, the college offers a traditional *hawza* Shi'i leadership programme in an adjacent building. The pedagogical framework of the programmes offered at the college are geared towards those interested in acquiring a critical, constructive and comprehensive understanding of issues and topics related to Islam based on conjectures and refutations. This differs from the traditional Islamic educational approaches where the emphasis is often based on the transmission and memorisation of the Qur'an and traditions of the Holy Prophet. Additionally, the Islamic College is distinct in the delivery of its programmes by collaborating with Middlesex University, 'taking the lead' in forging a 'synergy between Islamic and Western approaches to education' (Geaves 2015: 67). In doing so, Middlesex University proclaim this to be 'working with enthusiastic and like-minded academics' to ensure that students access the 'very latest thinking and cutting-edge research' have made a commitment in ensuring that students studying partner institutions 'enjoy an equivalent student experience, and achieve appropriate standards' (Middlesex University 2021). This distinctive successful partnership arrangement is also based upon the positive approach of the community-based institutions such as the Islamic College to work collaboratively with the higher education institutions such as Middlesex University. This 'makes possible the important debate between secular and religious epistemic approaches' (Heap 2016: 131). The arrangement provides a platform for 'building criticality and self-critique into curriculum and pedagogy' and ensuring that 'quality assurance is constant and ongoing' (Scott-Baumann and Cheruvallil-Contractor 2015: 136). The Islamic College is commended by external examiners for its collaborative work, and the exchange of ideas and good practice in teaching and learning. The students have a distinctive opportunity within the British higher education system to learn, develop and further understand the challenges faced by the Muslim community in the West. They have the possibility of attaining additional knowledge and skills leading to higher education qualifications and better employment prospects. However, just as important to the community is the stated aim of the Islamic College to disseminate Islamic knowledge in an environment that accords with Islamic values and thus try to emulate Islamic norms and values in which that knowledge can mature, be nurtured and develop. The validated approach provides students the ability to critically read and evaluate Islamic texts, and to analyse clearly and critically a variety of Islamic views and schools of thought. Also, it allows students to think and judge independently, with a readiness to challenge and criticise accepted opinion, argue persuasively, coherently and with relevance on issues related to Islam, Muslim cultures both in history and in modern life. Nevertheless, the traditional approach provides the best opportunity for students who want a deeper understanding of Islam, its philosophy and law, in its right context and perspective. In recognition of this factor, and based on the Shi'i community formation of the college and the spiritual, intellectual and cultural needs of the community, a traditional theological *hawza* programme is also offered aimed at those seeking to become Shi'i community faith leaders in a confessional context.

The institution offers two sets of programmes, the academic programmes in Islamic studies and Islamic law covering the five Islamic schools of thought, providing an inclusive environment for both Muslims and non-Muslims from different cultures and backgrounds. The structure of such programmes is ideal for those wishing to undertake jobs in a range of positions such as education and teaching, training and development, translation and editing, culture and religious consultation, or want to get a broad insider understanding of Islam and many others. Additionally, it offers the *hawza* programme providing classical, authoritative knowledge about Shi'a Islam within a modern framework of study. This is coupled to a certificate of higher education in Qur'anic Arabic providing students with an in-depth knowledge of classical Arabic; the mastery of Arabic is regarded as a skill essential for understanding Arabic Qur'anic texts. In the past, the only way for young British Muslims to gain an in-depth leadership training was for them was to travel abroad to a traditional centre of learning such as Cairo, Egypt, Najaf, Iraq, Qum, Iran, or other places such as India or Pakistan to begin their theological studies. However, the training of British Muslim faith leaders in Britain has been gaining momentum. This provision dates back to 1975 (Scott-Baumann et al. 2020b: 134) with *darul ulooms* present throughout Britain provided by the Sunni neo-traditional and Deobandi institutions. The Islamic College is unique in providing the *hawza 'ilmiyya* programme of study for the Shi'i community, who are a minority in Britain, although the exact figure is not provided by the census (Census 2011). The *hawza* programme offers topics such as jurisprudential studies, Qur'anic studies, theology, philosophy, logic and mysticism, and is characterised by its considerable informality and the traditional styles of learning based on the independence of thought. The religious standards for the programme are set by lecturers and religious personalities who are familiar with the traditional *hawza* curriculum, and are accompanied by extracurricular activities through seminars, discussion groups and religious supervision, mentoring, and study circles. Graduates of this programme have moved on to become imams within Britain, religious teachers in Muslim schools, or have taken Muslim chaplaincy positions in prison and probation services and the National Health Service. Others have moved on to furthering their academic studies and have involved themselves with research on issues relating to Islamic culture and religious values. Some have also moved abroad to continue with their theological studies for in-depth understanding of the vast Islamic sciences to enable them to tackle contemporary issues and challenges faced by Muslims in the West.

A Critical Study Based on Six Critical Factors

This research investigated the motives behind the decision by many young Muslims to enter into theological studies programmes that offer a collaborative provision ultimately leading to certification by a secular academic institution. The study was carried out involving Muslim participants studying at the Islamic College. The exact figure for the Islamic College recruitment differs annually, but the intake for the academic programmes are around twenty new students per undergraduate programme and forty new students per postgraduate programme. The Qur'anic Arabic programme has an intake of around ten and the traditional *hawza* around fifty new students for the various traditional studies schemes the theological institution offers. Our study did not involve all students enrolled and was not based on new students; the study included students of different levels of undergraduate study. The participants were both Sunni and Shi'i students (male and female), as well as students enrolled on the faith leadership *hawza* programme who were all Shi'i (male and female). Non-Muslim students, who were predominately enrolled on the postgraduate programmes or distance education programmes, were not involved in this study. The forms were anonymous and completed online by 120 students with an equal ratio between the accredited and *hawza* programmes.

This research is aimed at identifying the reasons why students would opt to study their religion and theological learning to obtain a secular qualification and their interaction with the syllabus as well as the teaching environment. The methodology for this research revolves around situational logic, using philosopher Karl Popper's critical rationalist approach that knowledge can and should be rationally criticised. This method is taught at the Islamic College within their validated programmes as part of the research methodology sessions. The research is centred on the students' understanding and interaction with the programme and their modules, hence, situational logic helped to map those interactions having reconstructed the wider view of their situation (Popper 2014: 194). In doing so, it incorporated the tetradic schema that was introduced by Karl Popper (Keuth 2005: 307),[2] whereby the long juncture of the Prophetic mission to reach ultimate truth fits with the idea that knowledge is a process based on conjectures and refutations. Assuming that one begins the journey of knowledge with a problem, be it practical or theoretical, it proceeds by the formulation of a tentative solution to the problem, conjectural or hypothetical – a tentative theory, which is then submitted to critical discussions in light of the evidence available, and as a result, new theories will arise (Popper 2014: 141). The Islamic approach is that the basis of absolute knowledge is God, and obtaining True Knowledge is questionable as no one knows the hidden interpretation other than God (based on V3: A7), the source of certainty is only God (based on V13: A2). The call of Islam therefore concerns, above all 'the remembrance of a knowledge' embedded in 'the confirmation of knowledge' (Nasr 2009: 7), supporting the Prophets saying that 'Qur'an has many levels of meaning, the highest of which is known to God alone' (Nasr 2009: 26). Hence, the value of tentative understandings of the verse stems from its ability to withstand refutability, verifying the partial truth content of knowledge for those who seek and test that knowledge accordingly. The primary tool utilised to engage with the students was a questionnaire, since it allowed them to document their thoughts with open-ended questions. This was followed up with interviews in order to qualify any statements on their part. This was scheduled in with the routine college surveys instigated by Middlesex University and prompted within the timetable to elicit the student views on the quality of the programmes. All college survey reports are to be taken for discussion through the Islamic College Programme Voice Group. There were six factors that formed the basis of our research questions that this study aimed to address and were subsequently tested, the results of which are listed below:

1. When enrolling Muslim students to partake on the Islamic College's validated programmes, the question arises as to whether the course in question offered any new knowledge to the students that they may not already possess, as most are adherents of Islam. It was found that although both undergraduate programmes of study address the key fundamental beliefs, practices and historical events central to Islam, the depth of study and the approach taken in its delivery is of utmost importance. Regardless of the fundamental issues

---

[2] Tetradic schema attempt to show that the result of criticism, or error-elimination applied to a tentative theory, is the emergence of a new problem or several new problems, the decisive point is always how well does our theory solve its problems.

covered, in practice many students will not have a firm understanding of it or its basis. Subsequently, when lecturers are conveying their conjectures through formal lessons to the students, they act as educational authorities. Both sets of programmes, validated and traditional *hawza*, promote an Islamic environment and, except for a few lecturers on the collaborative programme, all lecturers are Muslims. One needs to see if lecturers would or would not encourage the students to take a critical stance towards the material presented to them, this determines whether they adapt or go against Popper's theory of knowledge. The theory advocates that it is only through a process of critical assessment that students can improve upon what they have been taught, since knowledge only grows through elimination of ignorance. When the students were asked about their motives behind enrolling for this programme, a minority of 5 per cent of those completing the forms said they were driven to do the programme seeking successful academic attainment, while the overwhelming majority replied that their decision was based either on an obligation to increase their Islamic knowledge or a desire to increase their level of faith for themselves. Islamic education gives importance to both 'knowledge and training' and regards both as 'indispensable to its objective' (Al-Fendi and Baloch 1980: 278). The research found that over 95 per cent of the students enrolled on the programmes in both categories found the curriculum to be appropriate to their belief system and that they had learned new aspects to their religion that they did not know before. The students of the validated programmes pointed out that they benefitted from the presence of Sunni and Shi'i students in the class because it enriched the discussions. Additionally, 72 per cent of students agreed that they would not have been able to sit the examinations and gain a reasonable grade without attending the lectures and tutorials offered. Students of the traditional *hawza* programme said that knowledge is linked to certainty which must come hand in hand with their practice of faith, since Islam considers knowledge and the purification of self as essential elements in its system of education (Shah 2015: 26). This indicates their preference of wholesome Islamic learning within a confessional context, and is in line with the understanding that Islam purports to be 'a total way of life' (Merry 2007: 48). However, it was not clear, nor was further explanation given, as to how the attaining of such purification could be identified within an educational environment.

2. Irrespective of one's own background knowledge, learned traditions or even prejudices, would the students of the programmes remain closed to criticism and insist dogmatically on their initial biases or background knowledge? It is this dogmatic attitude that is against the spirit of improving knowledge, and it is the Islamic College's stated approach to challenge dogmatic stances throughout its programmes. Such an approach encourages students

not to reach judgements 'without verifying the facts' because there is always the possibility of risk and error, and of being mistaken (Titmus 2014: 8). Therefore, is there a monologue style of teaching, consequently leading to indoctrination of belief? Although the Islamic College teaching team includes Muslims (Sunni and Shi'i) and a few non-Muslims, and both programmes share the same teaching resources, an extension to this line of query is that each lecturer will possibly adopt a teaching approach in favour of their own theological standing by presenting their own personal or religious bias. Would this be more prevalent in the traditional *hawza* programme than in the validated programmes that are open to all students irrespective of their personal belief? With regard to the way that the programmes are taught, and in order to establish whether students are able to interact and have dialogue with the lecturer, the programme is designed to introduce the students to go through a process of critically assessing what is presented to them, in order to analytically review previous-held knowledge or and present them with new knowledge. All participants from the Islamic College-validated programme acknowledged that they were able to take a critical stance with the lecturer and the material presented, with a number of students confirming without being prompted Popper's theory of knowledge when discussing help in solidifying their knowledge. However, 25 per cent of the traditional *hawza* programme students said that at times they were not able to take a critical stance with the lecturer, and of those who agreed, some admitted being able to do so only if they were given the information required to take the critical stance. This shows that the confessional approach to teaching could take hold and lead to 'indoctrination of students' in certain programmes (Tan 2012: 2), but it can be argued that this is the crucial point behind such programmes, to teach into rather than about religion. Nevertheless, students made it clear that they are continuously encouraged by the Islamic College to engage critically with the academic literature and move outside the confessional perspective, and as such rejected indoctrination in its negative sense. With regard to whether or not lecturers' bias was prevalent towards their own theological beliefs, the response by all students bar one in the two sets of programmes was that no bias was present in the teaching delivered at the Islamic College, providing a positive portrayal of knowledge gained. The one that did object stated that the lecturer concerned was more knowledgeable in one particular theological belief and therefore would represent it more passionately.

3. The philosophy of Islamic knowledge is that it should be internalised and reflected via one's actions, showing that there are practical consequences to knowledge as well as a personal responsibility. Unlike the secular approach, in an Islamic institution knowledge becomes infused with practice and

conduct. Consequently, students should practically benefit from their lessons that dealt with topics such as prayer or fasting in Muslim life, as well as use of the Qur'an in worship and everyday life. Does the study increase the level of one's spiritual understanding behind acts of worship? This underpins the root of this research, that students study their own faith for reasons other than just a secular qualification, they engage in these studies essentially to increase their religiousness. The issue with this theory is the term religiosity which is generally used to 'accentuate the subjective pole of religious experience' (Zaccaria 2010: 5). When testing this theory, the very fact that each individual holds a relative meaning of the term 'religiosity' could prove to be problematic, particularly if this understanding could also differ depending on their programme of study. But the challenge for this study is to try to assess whether or not one's religiousness has increased. Popper is of the impression that clarity is valuable, however, precision is not. He believes that there can be no point in trying to be more precise than the problem demands (Lami 2014: 67). However, a point raised within the traditional *hawza* programme is that Islam regards the knowledge linked to Allah through the Qur'an to be precise and unequivocal. Of importance is the engagement in 'the process of relating the rulings to their source', thus ascertaining its validity (Bhojani 2019: 1). What will subsequently be assessed is whether or not students feel that the quality of their worship has changed since embarking upon the programmes of study, allowing them to provide explanations of how. Having already confirmed the student's motivation regarding the attainment of knowledge, the curriculum offered should therefore address students' spiritual inclination in promoting an Islamic way of life, as opposed to addressing the pluralistic philosophy of merely imparting information. This point is agreed by all students involved, but was held more profoundly by students of the traditional *hawza* programme of study. The students were of the positive opinion that knowledge gained increased their religiousness. Sentiments that were expressed by both groups, indicating that the intrinsic value of knowledge lies in its implementation in daily life and the increase in one's inner inspirations. Although the link between knowledge and its implementation is complex and multilayered, the students embarking on the study felt that their education increased their sense of religious obligations and spirituality, guiding them to be more mindful of their duties and responsibilities. Students, particularly those on the validated programmes, responded that the critical aspect of the programme was beneficial just in acquiring new knowledge. This criticality helped in the acceptance of their faith and the Qur'an, each highlighting an improvement that they have felt personally. Consequently, it is fair to accept that the programmes at the Islamic College have increased the level of spiritual understanding by the students. This confirms that the Muslim students gain more than just a secular qualification; the programme is more than 'a mode of imparting information about religion' (Al-Fendi and Baloch 1980: 101), but an approach in improving 'mutual trust and confidence in modern Britain' (Mukadam and Scott-Baumann 2010: 63). The programme becomes a means of cultivating a religious attitude to life, inspiring dialogue in the 'sharing of an interdependent world' (Sahin 2018: 358). Nevertheless, its occurrence in their mind, heart and intellect is dependent on the students, who decide on the kind of knowledge they wish to integrate and into their life (Hasanah 219, 27). The students found the institution's focus on spiritual formation meant that their engagement with the Islamic College had increased their sense of religiousness without necessarily studying the traditional *hawza* programme. They also identified that other than academic excellence, scholarly discussions and the programmes' requirement for social development of students with the community helped with their religious focus.

4. One also needs to consider discussions around the British Muslim identities as a result of living in a civilisation that is said to promote morals and values not conducive to Islamic spiritual nourishment (Jawad 2011: 126). The question arises that as an outcome of studying the programmes, would students find themselves more grounded in their British Muslim identities. Whilst analysing the impact of religious practices taught on the student's practical application, it should be noted that Muslim students may not practise their faith but still advocate their Muslim identities. Would the programmes of study help students to internalise Islamic values towards British norms rather than simply appealing to mere symbols of Islam. Do they think they are compatible and promoting of dialogue? When students of the traditional *hawza* programme were asked whether or not they were able to distinguish the difference between the two forms of identity, one that was based on the practice of Islam and one that appealed to the mere symbols of Islam, 65 per cent said they were able to differentiate between the two, 30 per cent said they could not, whilst 5 per cent assumed both meant the same thing. For the students of the validated programmes, 91 per cent said they were able to differentiate between the two, 9 per cent said they were not. While expressing their thoughts, there was an overwhelming expression of compatibility between the two forms of identities. The students of the *hawza* programme identified the programme's Muslim identity as being self-representing and self-aware, and as being conscious of their belief, tradition and heritage. The students of the validated programme thought their programme's Muslim identity was about having an informed understanding of the tradition and belief formed on an outlook that is evolving and formed in addressing the needs and issues of the time in Britain. Consequently, we

see progressive movement in the identity-formation of most students towards a British Muslim identity perspective without necessarily having access to the secular standards of the validated programmes. For British Muslims have been confronted by two challenges, one of 'commonality, cohesion and integration', and the other of 'fluidity, multiplicity and hybridity' (Meer and Modood 2009: 490). Yet despite all the anxiety and phobias encountered, the students found the programme to be against self-segregation and disengagement from wider British society, but rather encouraging of tolerance, interaction and collaboration. This is further confirmed by the majority of the students again when they were asked to qualify the impact of the module upon them. They advocated an inner change from within their outlook, with 85 per cent agreeing that the programme has helped to mould their British Muslim identities, 10 per cent disagreeing and 5 per cent unsure. The students acknowledged that their programme was preparing them for connection with the particular needs of community and the wider society, and in being able to deal with key issues such as identity-formation.

5. By offering two distinct programmes, one that is traditional and the other that is validated by a secular institution, it is possible to see that there might be two different mind-sets to the role of the lecturer. One that requires them based on an Islamic viewpoint to be a role model to the students (Ashraf and Husain 1979: 104), and the other that incorporates Western philosophy in that the lecturer is relieved of such a responsibility. Are lecturers expected to be exemplars of Islam at the Islamic College? Should lecturers, as members of Muslim society, be role models to the students emulating the true Islamic philosophy of knowledge transforming it into practice? When students were posed this question, the majority of students in both set of programmes stated that they recognised the lecturers', particularly religious scholars', teaching to emulate Islam. They could be taken as role models but they realised a few modules are taught by non-Muslims on the validated programme. Although in the traditional *hawza* programme every student expressed this expectation, in the validated programmes, 82 per cent agreed whilst 18 per cent did not. No explanation was given by those who did not agree but extensive explanations were given by those who agreed. These were essentially based around the notion that lecturers are knowledgeable and respectful, people who practised Islam, pious and innovative scholars who upheld the customs and practices. Additionally, they expressed the belief that their lecturers should support them in how to approach certain issues that are raised with Islam, motivate them to study and help them in practising Islam.

6. It is often stated that pluralism is a 'necessary element' of the educational environment in a democracy in order to build tolerance of other value systems (Parker 1996: 104; Brown 2000: 473; Merry 2007: 3). This leaves those

students studying the traditional theological *hawza* programme at a disadvantage since they are included in secular democratic notions of pluralism, which often disregard religious diversity or religious articulations of identities. Consequently, if we agree with the concern, then they run the risk of living an insular life, socialising merely with people with the same religious beliefs, a phenomenon that is often identified as being a 'danger' of Muslim schools and colleges 'encouraging separatism' by the media and public figures (Sian et al. 2013: 59). However, once their education is completed they will be expected to work alongside mainstream society within their community with no appreciation of other value systems. Those students who attend the validated programmes, which are open to all within pluralistic social settings, supplement their Islamic identity formation through both intra- and inter-religious dialogue. Is the traditional *hawza* programme seen as creating a wedge between their true Islamic identities and that of the pluralistic ethos promoted in Britain? The issue of Muslimness in an educational context has recently emerged as the subject of intense suspicion and debate, and at times leading towards 'discrimination and racism' (Shah 2019: 341), but the *hawza* is the Muslim clerical leadership programme for the Shi'i community and as such its strategic positioning is different. Whilst negative indoctrination has already been shown to be untrue, there is yet a case to be made that there is a problem with 'indoctrination' in the confessional contexts. The debate was not about confessionalism versus pluralism, but rather about inclusion and isolation. The discussion was about the sharing of common values and challenging the ideology of othering. The students were asked whether their time at the Islamic College made them feel isolated from the rest of society: 94 per cent responded negatively, since they felt that they did socialise with the wider society particularly through dialogue with other faiths and cultures, including a number of religious institutions partnering Middlesex University. Also, there are many instances of involvement with students of other faith-based colleges through the collaborative partnerships. The other 6 per cent still acknowledged that there were no wedges or barriers involved. The students had a choice of university and decided to attend the programme because they wanted to study at an institution that promoted a Muslim ethos. For them, education was not about assimilation but an acceptance in a multi-faith society that allows Muslim youth to celebrate their own identity.

Conclusion

The validated programmes offered at the Islamic College through its collaboration arrangement with Middlesex University has arguably been one of the most successful examples of Islamic institution partnerships with a secular university. Such academic programmes play an important strategic role in promoting mutual respect and understanding in a multi-faith society. This approach has enabled the Islamic College to negotiate the boundaries of an inclusive, secularist and humanist society with proposals based on the Muslim community's identity concerns. Moreover, the validated programme of study offered is regarded as distinctive for successfully combining critical methods in Islamic studies with a faith-based perspective. This research has indicated that the validation of such programmes leads to a critical reflection of issues studied and offers an extensive critique of presented perspectives. As such, the academic programmes stimulate students' critical reflection on their tradition and their engagement with non-Islamic intellectual traditions in order to provide students with the skills to formulate balanced and informed views of their own tradition and identity. The students are taken on a journey of knowledge with tentative solutions that are submitted for critical discussions, and in light of the evidence presented by lecturers the students form their own deeper understandings. Thus, this study has shown the Islamic College to be effective in fulfilling the Popper's philosophy of the evolution of knowledge.

The diverse intake of the Islamic College was able to not only gain more knowledge about their faith, but also promote tolerance, interaction and collaboration; hence, the students were directed towards a better understanding of Islamic knowledge. As far as the awareness regarding the place of Muslims in Britain is concerned, this study found many students to have become more grounded within their identity as Muslims. They recognised that one is not required to assimilate to the major culture but required to contribute to the community at large. The students of the validated programme stated that they were able to benefit from the philosophy of secular education yet increase their spirituality and develop their identity within the British Muslim context. Yet this research has also shown the traditional Shiʻi *hawza* learning within the Islamic educational context to be successful in positively delivering authoritative Islamic knowledge within a modern framework of study. This was seen to be based on its delivery by Muslim lecturers with expertise from the theological centres and acquaintance with the traditional *hawza* curriculum, and their awareness of the challenges faced by Muslims in the West. Additionally, students on both sets of programmes highlighted the importance of the Islamic environment of the college, regarded this as having increased their religiousness. The programmes were successful not because of their qualifications, but because they took the learner nearer to an understanding of God, with some highlighting an improvement that they have felt personally, but such a link between knowledge and implementation is complex and often misunderstood. Even though a minority were not able to take a critical stance, this did not mean that the opportunity to have done so was not present. This appears to be a case for concern only when students themselves were not equipped with the information to take the opportunity available to them. As such, this research has indicated that fears regarding Islamic institutions promoting insular thinking not to be present, but rather such institutions promote a more cohesive society and can advance students and promote inclusion. Both students within validated programmes and traditional theological study were able to recognise that Islamic beliefs and practices can be maintained in a non-Islamic environment with the aid of education. At the same time, students within this study have pointed out that education delivered within an Islamic environment with an Islamic philosophy of addressing spiritual, emotional and intellectual needs is the key factor for their choice. Additionally, it was thought that despite validated programmes being designed to meet secular perspectives, their success remains in their ability to address fundamental foundations of Islam and their meaning, having a bearing upon the student's individual lives.

Despite the limitations of the data being confined to a single theological institution, the varied pool of the participants, the different styles of teaching arrangements, and the considerable amount of information gathered gives valuable insights into the mind-set of young British Muslims studying at Muslim theological colleges. This study is not only important in reviewing the importance of collaborative links between Muslim community and the higher education institutes, but also in enabling us to explore their impact on the personal and social development of Muslim youth in Britain of those studying at a theological college of education. In essence, we can conclude that the Muslim adherents are investing in academic qualifications in order to encapsulate the spirit of Islam within their daily lives, to change their daily practices and build on their knowledge base. With an aim of restoring clarity and conviction in an environment that is at times hostile, they pursue an educational endeavour involving criticality to achieve a calming sense of certainty for the beliefs they hold. They felt that there was a need to increase the spiritual understanding behind acts of worship, thereby increasing their religiousness. The academic programmes possibly provides an avenue to increase one's spirituality and religiousness outside a traditional theological programme, in turn helping adherents to develop their identity within the British Muslim context.

References

Abbas, T. (2007). 'Muslim Minorities in Britain: Integration, Multiculturalism and Radicalism in the Post-7/7 Period'. *Journal of Intercultural Studies.* 28 (3), pp. 287–300.

Al-Fendi, M. H. and N. A. Baloch (1980). *Curriculum and Teacher Education.* London: Hodder & Stoughton.

Ameli, S. R., A. Azam and A. Merali (2006). *Secular or Islamic?: What Schools do British Muslims Want for Their Children?* vol. 3. London: Islamic Human Rights Commission.

Ashraf, S. A. and S. S. Husain (1979). *Crisis in Muslim Education.* London: Hodder & Stoughton.

British Broadcasting Corporation (BBC) (2020). *France's Macron Asks Muslim Leaders to Back 'Republican Values' Charter*, available at: http://www.bbc.com/news/amp/world-europe-55001167, last accessed 30 July 2021.

Bhojani, A. R. (2019). 'Visions of Sharī'a: An Introduction', in A. R. Bhojani, L. de Rooij and M. Bohlander (eds), *Visions of Sharī'a.* Leiden: Brill, pp. 1–9.

Brown, M. C. (2000). *Organization and Governance in Higher Education.* London: Pearson.

Census (2011). *Religion in England and Wales 2011.* Office for National Statistics, available at: https://www.ons.gov.uk/peoplepopulationandcommunity/culturalidentity/religion/articles/religioninenglandandwales2011/2012-12-11, last accessed 5 November 2019.

Cherti, M. and L. Bradley (2011). *Inside Madrassas: Understanding and Engaging with British-Muslim Faith Supplementary Schools.* London: Institute for Public Policy Research, available at: https://www.ippr.org/files/images/media/files/publication/2011/11/inside-madrassas_Nov2011_8301.pdf, last accessed 10 June 2021.

Cherti, M., A. Glennie and L. Bradley, L. (2011). *Madrassas in the British Media.* London: Institute for Public Policy Research Briefing, available at: http://www.crescentsofbrisbane.org/00%20Files%20&%20Images/CCN330/Madrasas_in_the_media_Feb2011.pdf, last accessed 10 June 2021.

Bartlett, J., J. Birdwell and M. King (2010). *The Edge of Violence: A Radical Approach to Extremism*, Public Safety. Demos: London, available at: https://www.publicsafety.gc.ca/lbrr/archives/cn79051148-eng.pdf, last accessed 10 June 2021.

Douglass, S. L. and M. A. Shaikh (2004). 'Defining Islamic Education: Differentiation and Applications', *Current Issues in Comparative Education* 7(1): 5–18.

Elmi, M. J. (2012). 'Preface', in G. H. 'Adel, M. J. Elmi and H. Taromi-Rad (eds), *Hawza-yi 'ilmiyya, Shi'i Teaching Institution: An Entry from Encyclopaedia of the World of Islam.* London: Ewi Press, pp. i–x.

Geaves, R. (2015). 'An Exploration of the Viability of Partnership between Dar al-ulum and Higher Education Institutions in North West England Focusing upon Pedagogy and Relevance', *British Journal of Religious Education* 37(1): 64–82.

Gillborn, D. and C. V. Gipps (1996). *Recent Research on the Achievements of Ethnic Minority Pupils.* London: HM Stationery Office.

Gilliat-Ray, S. and R. Timol (2020). 'Introduction: Leadership, Authority and Representation in British Muslim Communities', in S. Gilliat-Ray and R. Timol (eds), *Leadership, Authority and Representation in British Muslim Communities.* Basel: MDPI, pp. 1–12.

Guest, M., A. Scott-Baumann, S. Cheruvallil-Contractor, S. Naguib, A. Phoenix, Y. Lee and T. Al-Baghal (2020). *Islam and Muslims on UK University Campuses: Perceptions and Challenges.* London: SOAS, available at: https://eprints.soas.ac.uk/33345/1/file148310.pdf, last accessed 10 June 2021.

Halstead, J. M. (2004). 'An Islamic Concept of Education', *Comparative Education* 40(4): 517–30.

Hashemi, N. (2009). *Islam, Secularism, and Liberal Democracy: Toward a Democratic Theory for Muslim Societies*. Oxford: Oxford University Press.

Heap, S. (2016). *The Universities We Need: Theological Perspectives*. London: Taylor & Francis.

Hirschkind, C. (2001). 'Civic Virtue and Religious Reason: An Islamic Counter Public', *Cultural Anthropology* 16(1): 3–34.

Ichijo, A. (2014). 'Religion in Education: The Faith Debates in Contemporary Britain', in M. Topić and S. Sremac (eds), *Europe as a Multiple Modernity: Multiplicity of Religious Identities and Belonging*. Newcastle-upon-Tyne: Cambridge Scholars Publishing, pp. 92–108.

Islamic College (2021). *About Us*. London: The Islamic College, see at: https://islamic-.ac.uk/about, last accessed 11 July 2021.

Jawad, H. (2011). *Towards Building a British Islam: New Muslims Perspectives*. London: Bloomsbury.

Kahani-Hopkins, V. and N. Hopkins (2002). '"Representing" British Muslims: The Strategic Dimension to Identity Construction', *Ethnic and Racial Studies* 25(2): 288–309.

Keuth, H. (2005). *The Philosophy of Karl Popper*. Cambridge: Cambridge University Press.

Lami, I. M. (2014). *Analytical Decision-making Methods for Evaluating Sustainable Transport in European Corridors*, vol. 11. New York: Springer.

Makdisi, G. (1981). *The Rise of Colleges: Institutions of Learning in Islam and the West*. Edinburgh: Edinburgh University Press.

McLoughlin, S. (1996). 'In the Name of the Umma: Globalisation, Race Relations and the Muslim Identity Politics in Bradford', in W. A. R. Shahid and P. S. Van Koningsvield (eds), *Political Participation and Identities of Muslims in non-Muslim States*. Kampen: Kok Pharos, pp. 206–28.

McLoughlin, S. (2011), 'United Kingdom', in J. Nielsen et al. (eds). *Yearbook of Muslims in Europe*, vol. 3. Leiden: Brill, pp. 595–618.

Middlesex University (2021). *Academic Partnerships*. London: Middlesex University, available at: https://www.mdx.ac.uk/business-and-partnerships/academic-partnerships, last accessed 11 July 2021.

Meer, N. and T. Modood (2009). 'The Multicultural State we're in: Muslims, "Multiculture" and the "Civic Re-balancing" of British Multiculturalism', *Political Studies* 57(3): 473–97.

Memon, N. A. (2019). *A History of Islamic Schooling in North America: Mapping Growth and Evolution*. London: Routledge.

Merry, M. S. (2007). *Culture, Identity, and Islamic Schooling*. London: Palgrave Macmillan.

Merry, M. S. (2018). 'Indoctrination, Islamic Schools, and the Broader Scope of Harm', *Theory and Research in Education* 16(2): 162–78.

Mesbahi, M. (2020). 'The Mosaic of Muslim Identity in Britain', in N. Khanfar (ed.), *Islam, Muslims in Britain: Radicalisation, Deradicalization, and Human Rights*. London: Centre for Arab Progress.

Modood, T. (2005). *Multicultural Politics: Racism, Ethnicity, and Muslims in Britain*. Edinburgh: Edinburgh University Press.

Modood, T. (2006). 'British Muslims and the Politics of Multiculturalism', in T. Modood, A. Triandafyllidou and R. Zapata-Barrero (eds), *Multiculturalism, Muslims and Citizenship*. London: Routledge.

Mukadam, M. and A. Scott-Baumann (2010). *The Training and Development of Muslim Faith Leaders: Current Practice and Future Possibilities*. London: Department of Communities and Local Government Publications, available at: http://www.communities.gov.uk/documents/communities/pdf/1734121.pdf, last accessed 10 June 2021.

Nasr, S. H. (2009). *The Heart of Islam: Enduring Values for Humanity*. Grand Rapids, MI: Zondervan.

Nielsen, J. (2004). *Muslims in Western Europe*, 3rd edn. Edinburgh: Edinburgh University Press.

Norton, A. (2020). *On the Muslim Question*. Princeton, NJ: Princeton University Press.

Panjwani, F. (2017). 'No Muslim is Just a Muslim: Implications for Education', *Oxford Review of Education* 43(5): 596–611.

Panjwani, F. and D. Moulin-Stożek (2017). 'Muslims, Schooling and the Limits of Religious Identity', *Oxford Review of Education* 43(5): 519–23.

Parker, W. (1996). 'Advanced Ideas about Democracy: Towards a Pluralist Conception of Citizenship Education', *Teachers College Record* 98(1): 104–25.

PEW Forum (2010). *Global Religious Futures*. PEW Research Center, available at: http://www.globalreligiousfutures.org/religions/muslims, last accessed 5 November 2019.

PEW Forum (2015). *Religious Composition by Country, 2010–2050*. PEW Research Center, available at: https://www.pewforum.org/2015/04/02/religious-projection-table, last accessed 5 November 2019.

PEW Forum (2017). *Europe's Growing Muslim Population*. PEW Research Center, available at: http://www.pewforum.org/2017/11/29/europes-growing-muslim-population, last accessed 5 Novemebr 2019.

Popper, K. (2014). *The Myth of the Framework: In Defence of Science and Rationality*. London: Routledge.

Reay, D. and H. S. Mirza (1997). 'Uncovering Genealogies of the Margins: Black Supplementary Schooling', *British Journal of Sociology of Education* 18(4): 477–99.

Ryan, L. (2014). 'Islam does not Change Young People Narrating Negotiations of Religion and Identity', *Journal of Youth Studies* 17(4): 446–60.

Sahin, A. (2018). 'Critical Issues in Islamic Education Studies: Rethinking Islamic and Western Liberal Secular Values of Education', *Religions* 9(11): 335–64.

Samad, Y. (2004). 'Muslim Youth in Britain: Ethnic to Religious Identity', paper presented at the international conference 'Muslim Youth in Europe: Typologies of Religious Belonging and Sociocultural Dynamics', Turin: Edoardo Agnelli Centre for Comparative Religious Studies, 11 June 2004, available at: http://www.cestim.it/argomenti/02islam/02islam_uk_sanad.pdf, last accessed 30 July 2021.

Scott-Baumann, A. and S. Cheruvallil-Contractor (2015). *Islamic Education in Britain: New Pluralist Paradigms*. London: Bloomsbury.

Scott-Baumann, A., M. Guest, S. Naguib, S. Cheruvallil-Contractor and A. Phoenix (2020a). *Islam on Campus: Contested Identities and the Cultures of Higher Education in Britain*. Oxford: Oxford University Press.

Scott-Baumann A., A. Ebbiry, A. D. M. Shams, S. Dhorat, S. Bagum, H. Pandor and J. Stolyar (2020b). 'Towards Contextualized Islamic Leadership', in S. Gilliat-Ray and R. Timol (eds), *Leadership, Authority and Representation in British Muslim Communities*. Basel: MDPI, pp. 133–48.

Sian, K., I. Law I. and S. Sayyid (2013). *Racism, Governance, and Public Policy: Beyond Human Rights*. London: Routledge.

Siddiqui, A. (2007). *Islam at Universities in England*. London: Department for Education and Skills, available at: http://www.dcsf.gov.uk/hegateway/uploads/DrSiddiquiReport.pdf, last accessed 10 June 2021.

Shah, S. (2015). *Education, Leadership and Islam: Theories, Discourses and Practices from an Islamic Perspective*. London: Routledge.

Shah, S. (2019). '"I Am a Muslim First . . ." Challenges of Muslimness and the UK State Schools', *Leadership and Policy in Schools* 18(3): 341–56.

Tan, C. (2012). *Islamic Education and Indoctrination: The Case in Indonesia*, vol. 58. London: Routledge.

Taras, R. (2012). *Challenging Multiculturalism: European Models of Diversity*. Edinburgh: Edinburgh University Press.

Titmus, C. J. (ed.) (2014). *Lifelong Education for Adults: An International Handbook*. Amsterdam: Elsevier.

Zaccaria, F. (2010). *Participation and Beliefs in Popular Religiosity: An Empirical–Theological Exploration among Italian Catholics*. Leiden: Brill.

Chapter 9

Navigating alongside the Limits of Mutual Interdependence: Flemish Islamic Religious Education

Naïma Lafrarchi

Introduction

In January and November 2015, Paris was shaken by a series of coordinated bombing attacks. In 2016, Brussels experienced a similar fate. In the aftermath of these terrible events, new collaborations and partnerships were forged. On 17 March 2015, the 'Paris Declaration' was launched: a call for action, at all levels, to strengthen the role of education in 'promoting citizenship and the common values of freedom, tolerance and non-discrimination, strengthening social cohesion, and helping young people become responsible, open-minded and active members of our diverse and inclusive society'.[1] In 2015, the Council of Europe described radicalisation as 'an individual or collective recruitment into violent extremism or terrorism'. In a similar vein, the Council of Europe also launched a new initiative titled 'Democratic Schools: Safe Spaces for All', which aims to assist education professionals and school communities as a whole.[2] The main idea of both initiatives is to contribute to an open, inclusive and safe environment in education across member states. In 2018, a Council of Europe report posed the following questions regarding education policy: do counter-terrorism policies give rise to contradictory demands on educators, asking them to build social cohesion and resilience while at the same time requiring them

---

[1] Informal Meeting of European Union Education Ministers (Paris, Tuesday, 17 March 2015); see also: European Commission (2016). *Promoting Citizenship and the Common Values of Freedom, Tolerance and Non-Discrimination through Education: Overview of Education Policy Developments in Europe following the Paris Declaration of 17 March 2015*. Luxembourg: Publications Office of the European Union.
[2] See at: https://rm.coe.int/leaflet-of-the-campaign-free-to-speak-safe-to-learn-democratic-schools/16 808e86b6; https://www.coe.int/en/web/education/free-to-speak-safe-to-learn-democratic-schools-for-all, last accessed 4 August 2021.

to employ a logic of suspicion in spotting potential radicals, i.e. towards their Muslim pupils? Could national policies designed to identify and prevent radicalisation inadvertently undermine the very social cohesion they aim to preserve (Ragazzi 2018)? Ragazzi reports that counter-radicalisation policies might come into conflict with some key principles promoted by the Council of Europe including: education is a transformative process; schools should be safe and free learning environments; education should be based on diversity; and teachers are seen as role models (Ragazzi 2018: 11).

In Belgium an Action Plan for the Prevention of Radicalisation Leading to Extremism and Terrorism (hereafter 'Action Plan Radicalisation') was launched on 3 April 2015 by the Flemish government (Vlaamse Regering (hereafter Vl. Reg.) 2015). This Action Plan Radicalisation set out a strategic framework which included eleven domains of action. The document did not include a definition of the concepts of radicalisation, extremism or terrorism. The main aim of the Action Plan Radicalisation was 'to detect as soon as possible [at an early stage] youth and young adults who are at risk of radicalising and keep them on board in our society . . .'. Furthermore, the government examined together with the Muslim Executive which joint actions could be put in place to prevent radicalisation (p. 2). Additionally, it stipulated: 'Finally, we also engage in the European policy' (p. 3). It explicitly refers to jihadism (p. 2) and Syrian foreign fighters (p. 3).[3] Thus, its main focus[4] is on violent Islamic religious extremism. However, it warns against a too narrow focus on religious radicalisation (p. 3). The first Action Plan Radicalisation was reviewed in 2017 and became known as 'The Action Plan for the Prevention of Violent Radicalisation and Polarisation' as social tensions shifted, and increasing polarisation was being felt (Colaert 2017: 168; Vlaams Parlement (hereafter Vl. Parl.) 2019; Vl. Reg. 2017b; Cops et al. 2020), also in the school context (Vl. Parl., 2019b). The increasing polarisation occurred parallel with and fuelled by the rise of a far-right political party, Vlaams Belang, and the spread of right-wing speeches on social media (VRT 2018). The term 'polarisation' in the title is justified as follows:

> polarisation affects personal relationships and undermines societal participation and stability. Radicalisation can lead to polarisation, but (inter)national development and events can also be a trigger [for polarisation]. Conversely, a polarised society can be a fruitful ground for intolerant radical ideologies.

---

[3] Belgium has the highest number of Syria foreign fighters per capita, see at: https://www.rferl.org/a/foreign-fighters-syria-iraq-is-isis-isil-infographic/26584940.html, last accessed 13 March 2021, see also Van Ostaeyen (2019).
[4] When reading the Action Plan Radicalisation together with other policy documents (Education Commission, Radicalisation Commission, Flemish Parliament, Flemish government) most, if not all, the interventions focus on Muslims, Islam, Islamic (religious) education, Islamic identity.

Therefore, the prevention of radicalisation and polarisation are jointly addressed (Vl. Reg., 2017a: 2). Its main aim remains unchanged: 'to detect as soon as possible signals of violent radicalisation and prevent people from radicalising' (p. 2). Reference to jihadism and Syrian fighters are no longer included. In contrast to its earlier version, the 2017 Action Plan Radicalisation does mention definitions of radicalism, (violent) radicalisation, extremism, terrorism and polarisation in its annex. Both Action Plans Radicalisation (Vl. Reg. 2015, 2017a) explicitly refer to stakeholders and partners that are expected to roll out and implement its strategic action points. Education is the most important stakeholder, as twenty of the forty (Vl. Reg. 2015) and thirty-eight of sixty-two (Vl. Reg. 2017a) of the action points refer to or involve education as a partner. In order to follow the progress and realisation of these action points, a 'Flemish Platform Radicalisation' has been installed comprising administrations in the following policy domains: healthcare, work, youth, job placement, integration, city policy and education, in conjunction with a radicalisation collaborator from the Flemish umbrella organisation Cities and Municipalities (Vereniging van Vlaamse Steden en Germeenten, VVSG), the Federal Officer of Home Affairs, and a representative of the Security and Prevention Service.

Regarding the de-radicalisation process and counter-discourse, both Action Plans Radicalisation explicitly mention Islamic religious education teachers and imams (mosques) as relevant and central partners. As a result, the representative bodies of Muslims in Belgium, namely, the Executive of Muslims of Belgium (EMB) and the Centrum voor Islamonderwijs (Centre for Islamic Education, CIO) were repeatedly called upon to collaborate closely and implement several action points (Action Plan Radicalisation 2015, 2017a; Action Plan Radicalisation Report 2020). In that matter, the Engagement Statement regarding 'interconvictional competences' was signed on 28 January 2016 by the Representative Bodies of the recognised religions and non-confessional belief systems, the Flemish Public Education representatives and the Flemish Minister of Education (Ministerie van Onderwijs en Vorming (Ministry of Education and Training) 2016b).[5] A second Mission Statement followed on 9 November 2016, signed by Flemish Minister of Education and the EMB/CIO (Ministry of Education 2016a). The Mission Statement includes the following action points: 1. reform of the CIO; 2. increase number and quality of Islamic religious education (hereafter IRE) teacher training in Flemish teacher training departments, and implementation of the IRE programmes for primary and secondary education; 3. strengthen the IRE inspection team and increase quality control of IRE lessons; and 4. develop a teaching (pedagogical) certificate for IRE. Action

---

[5] The Engagement Statement stipulates that from the school year 2016–2017 onwards, a minimum of six hours per year per grade has to be allocated to common interconvictional courses.

point 2 and 4 are of interest here (Ministry of Education and Training 2016a; Vl. Parl. 2016b, 2018, 2019). However, we need to make an important point: the legal representative body of Belgian Islam, the EMB/CIO, has delegated constitutional competences only with regard to 'Islam'-related courses within the Flemish teacher training programmes by determining the (minimum) qualifications of the IRE teachers as well as the appointment criteria for the selection.

This chapter sketches the relationship and the (legal) powers of the state to intervene, impose, formulate and outline the de-radicalisation and counter-discourse initiatives directed towards the EMB/CIO, more specifically towards the IRE teachers. In other words, what are the limits and boundaries of the separation of church/mosque and state based on the constitutional and legal framework? As Flemish cabinet negotiations and deliberations regarding the IRE teachers' training programme progressed, the following questions were raised[6]:

(a) To what extent can, and did, the state interfere with regard to prevention of radicalisation, counter-discourse towards the EMB/CIO taking to account the principle of separation of church and state in expecting to take an active role regarding this topics?
(b) In which way did the EMB/CIO translate and implement the formulated expectations in the Action Plans Radicalisation of 2015 and 2017?

In the following pages, I will give an overview of the Belgian constitutional relationship between church and state. Followed by a historical overview of the organisation of Islam since its recognition in 1974, the organisation of IRE and the IRE teacher training programmes up until the present. I will then sketch the main observations regarding the expectation towards IRE teachers and EMB/CIO, and their expected role as 'experts'. Before closing with the discussion and conclusion, a brief overview of academic findings regarding the concept de-radicalisation is given.

SEPARATION OF CHURCH AND STATE VS SHAPING THE RELATIONSHIP OF ISLAM AND STATE

Separation of Church and State

The first Belgian constitution in 1831 was the result of negotiations between Catholics and Liberals, a *modus vivendi* whereby an equilibrium was sought

---

[6] This chapter will not scrutinise this question. For a detailed analyses, see Lafrarchi 2021. But this question is of most importance as the Ministry of Education negotiate this issue and signed both official statements.

(Kamer van Volksvertegenwoordigers 1994; Torfs and Vrielink 2019). From the beginning, Belgium chose a type of regime built on the principle of separation of church and state, but combined with a system of state support for religion (Adams and Overbeeke 2008; Christians & Overbeeke, 2014). When looking more closely at this relationship, four Articles are of interest: Articles 19, 20, 21 and 181 of the Belgian Constitution. Articles 19 and 20 include the positive and negative freedom of religion, the right to choose one's own religion and the prohibition on imposing a belief/religion, respectively (Varin 2006). Article 21 forbids the state 'to intervene either in the appointment or in the installation of ministers of any religion [belief systems]'. The state pays the salaries and the pensions of the (recognised) ministers of religion (Article 181), and the religious education and non-confessional teachers appointed in public education. As a result, this relationship can be described as a mutual interdependence (Debeer et al. 2011; Van Den Berg 2018) or as a hybrid system (Sandberg and Doe 2007). However, support from the state can never be a justification for interference in 'religious' matters. For a proper understanding of the Belgian legal structure: Belgium is a federal parliamentary constitutional monarchy with three regions: the Brussels Capital region, the Walloon region and the Flemish region; and three communities, namely: the French, the Flemish and the German-speaking community. Education responsibilities have been allocated to the communities since 1988.

With regard to the constitutional right of religious education, Article 24 of the constitution is central. It stipulates that the state, that is, the three communities, must provide neutral public compulsory education, education that respects the philosophical, ideological or religious freedom of parents. Thus, based on Article 24, public schools must offer pupils and parents the choice to follow courses on one of the recognised confessional or non-confessional belief systems.[7] Based on the constitutional mutual interdependence, policymakers voiced explicit expectations towards the Islamic representative body, that is, EMB/CIO in the aftermath of the Paris attacks in November 2015 and January 2016. More specifically, IRE teachers and imams are expected to 'actively' contribute to the development of a counter-discourse and de-radicalisation process (Vl. Reg. 2015, 2017a, 2020; Commissie Onderwijs (Education Commission) 2016; Vl. Parl., 2016b, 2016c, 2016d, 2017a, 2019a). In order to do so, they expect a minimum teaching qualification, continuing professionalisation regarding de-radicalisation and counter-discourses, and mastering of Dutch (Education Commission 2016b, 2020). Recall, only the representative bodies have legal authority regarding the content and learning goals, organisation,

---

[7] Or to provide study material of their own in case they wish to venture outside the officially recognised belief systems.

IRE programmes, qualification and selection criteria for IRE teachers in public education, based on the principle of separation of church and state.

In the course of the last decades, government interference has been increasingly felt (Commissie Onderwijs en Vorming 2009; Commissie Onderwijs en Gelijke Kansen 2011b; Vl. Parl. 2011a, 2011c, 2012b, 2012c, 2013a, 2013b, 2016a, 2016b, 2016d, 2017a, 2017b, 2018; Commissie Onderwijs 2016, 2017; Vl. Reg. 2020). Under the flag of 'de-radicalisation' the government is venturing deeper and deeper into religious matters. Not coincidentally, this shift coincided with the emergence of Islam in Belgium (Kanmaz and El Battiui 2004; Kanmaz and Zemni 2008). The Muslim community and its representatives were seen as suspicious from the beginning. For example, the elected members of the EMB in 1998 were screened by the State Security Service (which happens up to this day, cf. fall of EMB-board members, 4 December 2020). The federal and Flemish government consider it their duty to engage with the – moderate Islamic – representation of Muslim communities and to establish a Flemish imam training. This position is reflected in the successive policy documents (Vl. Parl. 2004, 2005, 2009, 2014; Vl. Reg. 2004, 2009, 2014). The argumentations still lie in 'the will to stop the appointment of ministers/imams from abroad' and the ongoing 'security' discourse since the 1980s (Belgian Senate and Parliament 2002; Boender and Kanmaz 2002; Zemni 2011; Loobuyck et al. 2013; Federale Overheidsdienst 2018).

Shaping Islam, Shaping Islamic Religious Education, Shaping Islamic Religious Education Teachers

Shaping Islam

The position of Islamic religious education has always been an issue (Vl. Parl. 2003, 2011a, 2013b, 2016c, 2017b, 2018, 2019a; Commissie Onderwijs en Gelijke Kansen 2011b; Commissie Onderwijs 2017). It is marked by a long history that began with the arrival of Moroccan and Turkish guest workers and their families in the mid-1960s (Kamer van Volksvertegenwoordigers 1964). In 1974, Islam became a constitutionally recognised religion (Kamer van Volksvertegenwoordigers 1974; Foblets and Overbeeke 2004).[8] Since then, Islam-related policy has seen several shifts and foci. In the first period (1974–1989), the 'Islam' dossier was seen as part of foreign policy. During the second period (1989–1995), it was approached as a 'minority policy' issue.

---

[8] Belgium officially recognises and subsidises eight belief systems, including six religions, plus non-confessional humanism and Buddhism (since 1 October 2020). All are governed by a legally recognised body that acts as a representative body in negotiations with the government regarding its legal competences.

The third period (1995–2000) is characterised by a multifaceted approach towards Islam, reflecting the shifting attitudes of the government and the growing visibility of Muslims and upcoming Muslim voices. It was during this period that Muslims were asked to organise themselves by means of an institutionalisation of Islam (Manço and Renaerts 2000; Boender and Kanmaz 2002; Kanmaz 2002; Zemni 2003, 2011; Kanmaz and El Battiui 2004; Manço and Kanmaz 2004; Fadil et al. 2015). The idea was to have a representative body that could act as an interlocutor with the 'state' regarding religious matters (Panafit 1999; Husson 2012). As an official representative body, the Muslim Executive, which is of particular interest here, could have legal competences regarding Islamic religious education in public schools (Belgian Senate and Parliament 2002). The 9/11 event marked the beginning of a fourth period. New discourses, by state officials as well as in the (social) media, emerged. Discourses were about 'European/Belgian' Enlightenment values and norms, liberalism, as if Muslims do not adhere to the same values and norms. To cut a long story short, the question of 'What kind of Islam do the politicians and stakeholders want?' was raised. The current debates are not new as the Flemish political parties already preferred an 'integration' role, in addition to the role in the 'religious matters' for the Muslim Executive back in the 1990s (Zemni 2009). On the one hand, public authorities wanted to retain a certain amount of control over the organisation of Islam in Belgium. On the other hand, the community itself pointed to the fact that the state was meddling in religious affairs and accused it of infringing the institutional autonomy of the religion (Velaers and Foblets 2014). In sum, Belgian–Islamic relationships have known difficulties ever since the recognition of Islam in 1974 and are characterised by a relationship of mistrust and suspicion (Panafit 1999; Belgian Senate and Parliament 2002; Zemni 2003, 2011; Cesari 2009; Fadil et al. 2015; VRT 2020).

Shaping Islamic religious education

Belgium was one of the first European countries to recognise Islam as an official religion (Touag 2017). As a result, Islam enjoys the same status as the other recognised belief systems (Boender and Kanmaz 2002; Maréchal and Bousetta 2004). Back then the authorities entrusted the official Islamic temporal and religious practice mandate to the Islamic Cultural Centre (ICC) in Brussels (better known as the Central Mosque of Brussels). The ICC had important prerogatives, such as the organisation of IRE exams, IRE teacher training, the appointment of the IRE teachers, the content of the IRE courses and the IRE programme, and the training of imams. From 1999 onwards, the EMB – as the representative body – had inherited those prerogatives, as well as the IRE curriculum for primary and secondary education, the development of teaching materials, and ongoing professional development (Kanmaz and El Battiui 2004; Lafrarchi 2020, 2021).

Starting from 2008, the Centre for Islamic Education (*Centrum voor Islamonderwijs*, CIO), a mandated body of the EMB, has (till now) the delegated competences to organise exams, select and appoint IRE teachers, develop IRE programmes, collaborate with Flemish teacher training institutions, as well as a number of other responsibilities (Vl. Parl. 2011c). Over the last decade – and even more strongly since the attacks in Paris (2015) and Brussels (2016) – the lack of Dutch-language proficiency, the absence of the required degree and the lack of pedagogical and didactical competences of IRE teachers have been increasingly criticised by Flemish politicians (Vl. Parl. 2009, 2011c, 2012b, 2013b, 2012c; Commissie Onderwijs en Gelijke Kansen 2011c). In line with the de-radicalisation policy and the Engagement Statement of 28 January 2016, a new curriculum subject, 'interconvictional dialogue competences', including elements of the compulsory citizenship key competence, was developed by representatives of the CIO and the Public Education Umbrella GO!, which was launched in school year 2022–2023.

Shaping Islamic religious education teacher training

In 1996, the first negotiations between the EMB and the Erasmus University College Brussels (Erasmus Hogeschool Brussel, EhB) began, which in 1998 resulted in the first officially recognised IRE teacher training programme (VLHORA 2007). Its Professional Bachelor in IRE for secondary education was embedded in the regular three-year teacher training programme.[9] The IRE student-teachers attended – for the first time – *truncus communis* courses with other students in regular Flemish teacher training in a higher education institution. In this initial stage, and for almost ten years, the Erasmus University College Brussels had difficulties in finding qualified Dutch-speaking IRE lecturers for the Islamic courses.[10] To cater for the increased need for qualified IRE teachers the Centre for Adult Education (*Centrum voor Volwassenonderwijs*, CVO[11]), in collaboration with the EMB, established a one-year IRE teacher training at the graduate level.[12] A second three-year IRE teacher training programme was

---

[9] Students can only enrol with a Flemish secondary education level diploma or with a foreign recognised diploma.
[10] The first lecturer was a Dutch convert, the second a Flemish convert. After those two lecturers, several were appointed from the Netherlands and Flanders. Now, a first-generation Moroccan lecturer is teaching the Islam-related courses.
[11] One-year programme, not Professional Bachelor level, only three CVO offered the IRE programme, namely, in Brussels, Ghent and Hasselt.
[12] Equivalent of 60 ECTS. Still the IRE teachers had to be appointed by the IRE inspectors/EMB after an interview and oral exam. From 2019, the CVO was closed and merged into the regular university

launched at Group T (now University College Leuven-Limburg, UCLL) in 2007–2008. However, unlike the programme established at the EhB, this was not a government-led initiative, that is, it launched without any facilitating role or intervention by the Ministerie van Onderwijs en Vorming (Flemish Ministry of Education).[13] Another ten years after that (2017–2018), they launched another teacher training programme at Campus Diepenbeek.[14] Similar to the Erasmus University College Brussels, UCLL had a difficult time finding qualified Dutch-speaking IRE lecturers for their Islamic courses. In another development, the University of Antwerp – in collaboration with the EMB – started a Post-Academic Training (Post Academische Vorming, PAVO) in 2009–2010.[15] This PAVO was targeted mainly at IRE teachers. The University of Antwerp also experienced difficulties in finding and retaining qualified Dutch-speaking IRE teacher educators, as well as setbacks in the education of the students with regard to attendance levels, Dutch-language proficiency, study dropout, and (very) low graduation rates (Vl. Parl. 2011b; Piqueray et al. 2008, 2009). After an evaluation, the PAVO-programme ceased in 2011.

The 2012 resolution on the creation of a university programme in Islamic religious sciences provided insight into the difficulties in finding qualified Muslim lecturers and lists several reasons, such as the organisational instability of the EMB, the lack of qualified Dutch-speaking candidates, internal frictions and an unclear teaching format, which make it difficult to retain university college lecturers (Vl. Parl. 2011a, 2012a, 2012b, 2012c; Piqueray et al. 2008, 2009).

As Flemish society became more and more diverse, the need for university-educated, skilled Dutch-speaking Muslim intellectuals, as well as the high expectations placed on this demographic, kept on growing. In June 2013, the Ministry of Education installed a platform of prominent Muslims[16] to create a space for, first, exchange of ideas about the content of an Islamic programme, and, secondly, providing feedback on the content, education targets and labour outcomes of a one-year programme proposed by the Catholic University of Leuven (KU Leuven). The purpose was to create bridges between the expectations of the EMB, the Flemish Muslim communities, the Ministry

---

college training programmes with a limited number of hours internship (9 ECTS) in comparison with the regular three-year teacher training (24–30 ECTS).

[13] After the attacks in Paris in 2015 and in Brussels in 2016, the Ministry of Education played an active role in stimulating the deliberations and facilitating the encounter between the EMB and the teacher training departments of the Flemish University Colleges.

[14] Diepenbeek is a Flemish town with a large population of Turkish Muslims. The lecturer is Turkish and from that region as they expect this will motivate students to enrol in the IRE teacher training.

[15] See at: http://www.ucsia.org/main.aspx?c=*UCSIA2&n=89834&ct=81452, last accessed 25 March 2021.

[16] Political period 2009–2014 with Pascal Smet as Minister of Education. IRE inspectors, IRE teachers, prison counsellors, Muslim local politicians, and so on were invited. I was member of the platform as a researcher of the KU Leuven and Odisee Brussels.

of Education and, respectively, the Faculty of Theology and Religious Sciences (FTRS) and the Faculty of Arts (KU Leuven). Thus, the idea to create a Masters in Islamic theology and religious sciences was not an initiative of the EMB and was not conceptualised prior to collaboration with the EMB. The Masters was implemented in 2014–2015 as a one-year optional programme, integrated into the broader Masters in world religions which already existed at the FTRS and was open to both Muslims and non-Muslims.[17] In any case, since the academic year 2018–2019 a Masters degree is mandatory (cf. Mission Statement 2016) for IRE teachers teaching in higher secondary education.[18]

A turning point regarding the establishment of IRE teacher training can be observed since the Paris attacks on 7 January 2015, and even more since 13 November 2015. The association Thomas More Mechelen (TMM) launched a new IRE teacher training programme for secondary education in academic year 2015–2016, and a programme for primary education in 2016–2017. Additionally, TMM introduced a shorter study trajectory for IRE teachers at the Antwerp Campus in 2019–2020.[19] In the aftermath of the 2016 Brussels attacks, Artevelde University College launched an IRE teacher training programme for secondary education in 2016–2017,[20] and for primary education in 2018–2019.[21] In its turn, the Artesis Plantijn University College in the particularly diverse city of Antwerp started a Professional Bachelor for secondary education in 2017–2018, and for primary education three years later.[22] Finally, the last IRE teacher training programme was implemented in the academic year 2019–2020 at the Odisee University College in Brussels.[23] Karel de Grote University College did not implement an IRE teacher training programme despite being located in the very diverse city of Antwerp.

---

[17] A press release was issued on 23 March 2014 at the Catholic University of Leuven, available at: https://nieuws.kuleuven.be/nl/2014/ku-leuven-start-met-opleiding-islamitische-theologie-en-godsdie nstwetenschappen last accessed 25 March 2021; https://theo.kuleuven.be/islam-studeren/programma, last accessed 25 March 2021. One-third of the credits are allocated to the Islamic courses, while the *truncus communis* consists of Christianity-related courses.

[18] See at: http://www.standaard.be/cnt/dmf20170505_02868788, last accessed 4 August 2021.

[19] To achieve the IRE teacher training degree they only have to succeed regarding the Islam-related courses and specific IRE didactics.

[20] See at: https://www.arteveldehogeschool.be/opleidingen/bachelor/leraar-secundair-onderwijs/islamiti sche-godsdienst, last accessed 30 June 2021.

[21] Consulted on 29 January 2020, available at: https://www.arteveldehogeschool.be/opleidingen/bach elor/educatieve-bachelor-secundair-onderwijs/islamitische-godsdienst. The website states: 'These trainings are intended to cultivate an interest in Islam, an acknowledgment of the cultural heritage of mankind, and respect for differing thoughts, and to provide training in the proper use of religious concepts and problem-solving capacities.' As training they are envisioned to prepare students for life and participation in society, and to develop students' general talents and capacities. The programmes' vision is explicitly geared to recent developments in RE.

[22] See at: https://www.ap.be/artikel/lerarenopleiding-islam-meer-dan-religie; https://www.bruzz.be/same nleving/verplichte-master-voor-islamleerkrachten-2017-05-06; https://www.ap.be/opleiding/lager-on derwijs, last accessed 25 March 2021; https://www.ap.be/opleiding/secundair-onderwijs, last accessed 25 March 2021. The focus of this programme is on communication, collaboration, coaching and praxis.

[23] Approximatively 25 per cent of the Brussels population is of Muslims background, see at: http://www. npdata.be/BuG/286-Aantal-moslims/Aantal-moslims.htm, last accessed 7 February 2021.

One of the main reasons to implement those IRE programmes, which include a number of common courses for all students regardless of the chosen subject, i.e. *truncus communis*,[24] besides the increasing demand for IRE teachers, was to improve didactic–pedagogical teaching skills and to ensure the Dutch-language proficiency of the novice IRE teachers. Concretely, the IRE programmes include courses in, for example, class management, teachers' responsibilities, education and society, communication skills, internships, as well as specific IRE-related didactic–pedagogical courses.

Looking back, a significant number of the enrolled students did not obtain their degree or, through a longer pathway, did not acquire the expected level of Dutch-language proficiency and mostly had a technical or vocational secondary school degree before enrolling (VLHORA 2007). During the last years an improvement has been observed, though still the number of students obtaining their diploma is low (Commissie Onderwijs 2016, 2017; Vl. Parl. 2017a). Though, it has to be mentioned that women still have (more) difficulties in finding an internship in schools due to their head scarf. As the internship is a compulsory part of the curriculum this has hindered them in achieving their BA teachers' diploma which includes two compulsory school subjects.[25] Schools and school conglomerates still, with a few exceptions, do not allow Muslim women to teach another school subject wearing a head scarf (Verbeeck 2008; Vl. Parl 2021).[26]

As a consequence of the heated debates, since the academic year 2018–2019, every IRE teacher needs to obtain a recognised Flemish IRE teacher diploma in order to be allowed to teach IRE. We need to keep in mind that the content of Islamic courses falls under the constitutional responsibility of the EMB/CIO. The appointment of IRE teacher educators depends on the EMB/CIO in consultation with the teacher training department, as the latter is responsible for the *truncus communis* courses.

Navigating along the Boundaries

Belgian/Flemish Policy Navigating with Mutual Interdependence

On 2 November 2004, the murder of Dutch film producer, Theo van Gogh, shifted the general public's perception: whereas in the aftermath of 9/11, the

---

[24] The common courses for all students in the teacher training programme.
[25] Each student has to choose two school subjects to fulfil their BA degree. So, Muslim students choose Islam and another subject of choice. Hence, female students encounter difficulties in finding a school which allows them to wear their head scarf while teaching a subject other than Islam.
[26] Vlaams Parlement (2021). Verslag Plenaire Vergadering, 20 October 2021, available at: https://www.vlaamsparlement.be/nl/parlementair-werk/plenaire-vergaderingen/1561005/verslag/1565350, 1 (2021–2022); Verbeeck (2008).

'threat' seemed to come only from the 'outside' (cf. Twin Towers), now there seemed to be a 'threat' from the 'inside' as well (de Graaff et al. 2009). Since then that the concept of home-grown terrorism has appeared (Colaert 2017). A more recent dramatic event is the murder in France of history teacher Samuel Paty (18 October 2020), who was killed in response to a lesson he gave about 'freedom of speech' in which he used – among others – cartoons of the Prophet Muhammed. It is this so-called 'new' observation that put forward the 'new' persistent expectations regarding active preventive efforts by the IRE teachers (and imams) in the process of de-radicalisation and counter-discourse.

As mentioned above, the relation between church/mosque and state is regulated by the Belgian Constitution of 1831, a historic 'constitutional' compromise between Catholics and Liberals. Articles 19, 20, 21 and 181 of the Belgian Constitution are of interest here (cf. section 'Separation of Church and State vs. Shaping the Relationship of Islam and State', subsection 'Separation of Church and State', above). Article 21 prohibits the state from interfering in 'religious' matters, nominations . . . of any religion . . .' Article 181 includes the principle that salaries of religious leaders (chaplains, priests, imams, etc.) must be paid by the state. Teachers of religion and non-confessional belief systems are also paid on the account of the state (cf. Flemish Community). Based on this mutual interdependence, the Flemish government, policymakers and politicians imposed a minimum of qualitative requirements regarding IRE, including to at least 'examine' content which does not coincide with the 'European, Belgian, Flemish' values and norms (Vl. Parl. 2013a, 2013b, 2016b, 2016c, 2017a; Commissie Radicalisering 2015). IRE teachers are expected to be able 'to engage actively with societal issues, de-radicalisation process and counter-discourse' (Commissie Onderwijs en Gelijke Kansen 2011b; Commissie Onderwijs 2016, 2017; Vl. Reg. 2016, 2017a, 2020). However, based on Article 21, they do not have legal authority with regard to any aspect of the organisation of IRE courses. This legal prerogative belongs solely to the representative body, that is, EMB/CIO.

Worth mentioning here are the two turning points regarding IRE. First, the Engagement Statement signed on 28 January 2016 in the presence of the Flemish Minister of Education, which stipulates the minimum hours of 'common interconvictional courses' in compulsory education to be provided by all the representatives of the recognised belief systems. This Engagement Statement was a direct consequence of the dramatic events in Paris (7 January and 13 November 2015). Meanwhile, representatives of the CIO and the Public Education Umbrella GO! developed a compulsory learning framework 'interconvictional dialogue competences' with specific learning outcomes linked to the key competence 'citizenship'. Secondly, as a consequence of the Mission Statement signed on 9 November 2016 by the EMB/CIO and the Minister of Education, the appointed

IRE teachers have to hold a full Flemish teaching degree from the academic year 2018–2019 (Vl. Parl. 2017a, 2017b, 2018), and five new IRE teacher training courses were established at a breakneck speed to that end.

Islamic Religious Education Teachers' Navigation as 'Expected' Experts

The picture that emerges is far from positive with regard to IRE teachers and imams. Several issues have led to a polarisation of the public debate on Islam (Zemni 2011; Vl. Parl. 2016b, 2016c; *De Standaard* 2017; Commissie Onderwijs 2018a, 2018b; *Knack* 2020a, 2020b). Nevertheless, IRE teachers are asked to play an active role in the de-radicalisation process and counter-discourse, more precisely, to strengthen and foster social cohesion, and build resilience through trust, democratic education and critical thinking. The number of study days, seminars and workshops regarding de-radicalisation, controversial and sensitive topics is impressive (Vl. Reg. 2018, 2020).

Looking back, the first IRE teachers came from abroad or studied 'classical' Islamic theology abroad. Debates on the implementation of a Flemish IRE teacher and/or imam training started almost two decades ago (Husson 2007; Commissie Onderwijs 2009, 2011a; Vl. Parl. 2011a, 2012a, 2016a, 2016d). However, it was not until the academic year 2015–2016 that the implementation of IRE teacher training programmes in Flemish teacher training really came up to speed,[27] due to an increasing demand for qualified Dutch-speaking IRE teachers,[28] and policy views on the role of IRE teachers in de-radicalisation process and the dissemination of a counter-discourse (Vl. Reg. 2015, 2017b; Commissie Onderwijs 2016; Vl. Parl. 2016c, 2019a) in direct relation to public pressure following the Paris and Brussels terrorist attacks. Additionally, the observation that only a minority of the appointed IRE teachers had the adequate degree (Vl. Parl. 2016b, 2017a, 2018) urged policymakers to negotiate with the EMB/CIO and the Flemish teacher training institutions.[29] In this negotiation process, the Flemish Ministry of Education acted as a facilitator between the stakeholders (Ministerie van Onderwijs en Vorming 2016a, 2016b; Commissie Onderwijs 2017; Vl. Parl. 2017a, 2017b, 2018).

---

[27] See at: https://www.standaard.be/cnt/dmf20170505_02868788, https://www.vrt.be/vrtnws/nl/2018/04/11/vanaf-1-september-moeten-islamleerkrachten-een-opleiding-hoger-o, last accessed 25 February 2021.

[28] There are 65,000 Muslim pupils, with 39,000 in primary and 26,000 in secondary education; see at: https://www.tijd.be/politiek-economie/belgie/vlaanderen/aantal-leerlingen-in-islamlessen-in-10-jaar-verdubbeld/9847802.html;https://www.bruzz.be/onderwijs/aantal-moslimleerlingen-stijgt-fel-2018-05-23, last accessed 7 February 2021.

[29] The appointed teachers have to obtain the pedagogical certificate within the foreseeable future to be allowed to work as an IRE teacher; see at: https://www.n-va.be/persbericht/islamonderwijs-in-vlaanderen-enkel-met-juiste-diploma-voor-de-klas.

Regarding the formulated expectations in the successive Action Plans Radicalisation (2015, 2017a), the CIO made attempts to meet the expectations and action points regarding the IRE teachers by organising workshops on didactical material, use of ICT in IRE lessons; lectures dealing with sensitive subjects such as euthanasia, gender issues, sexual orientation, living peacefully together, religion and science, and moral education in IRE lessons; how to react and deal with radicalisation; lectures on secular topics; citizenship education; and interreligious dialogue (Vl. Reg. 2016, 2017a, 2020; Lafrarchi 2021). This aims to inform and equip IRE teachers with the tools to deal with polarised issues and to contribute to the expectations regarding de-radicalisation and counter-discourse.

The Network of Islam Experts is one of the initiatives established in October 2015 'to deliver a counter-discourse' as a direct consequence of the Paris attacks in January 2015. This network is embedded in, and legally falls under, the legal representative body, namely the EMB/CIO. The voluntary 'Islam experts' are IRE teachers with – at first – no in-depth experience or proficiency regarding de-radicalisation processes or academic research expertise.[30] The volunteers are deployed to inform school teams, teachers and pupils about Islamic (overall) topics in schools on demand. Additionally, they meet with Muslim pupils if they have specific Islam-related questions in response to an explicit demand from the school director. The network has no follow-up competences nor any judicial competence (e.g., reporting names of 'radicalised' pupils). As of late, they also organise mandatory workshops and seminars for the IRE teachers on demand and in collaboration with the CIO on de-radicalisation and secular topics. Nevertheless, it was, and still is, installed to enable and proclaim a 'moderate' voice of Islam in school context as seen by the politicians (Vl. Reg. 2015). The workshops or seminars are one-off events with no long-term trajectories, no follow up and no assessment of the results. This situation was prompted by the sense of urgency back in 2015. The 'urgent' situation did not call for a thorough approach or a step-by-step plan. The Flemish Peace Institute (FPI) published an overview of the existing de-radicalisation programmes, and counter-discourse did not seem to be significantly effective (Colaert 2017). In 2020, they published an evaluation of the implemented Flemish initiatives regarding effectiveness, and stated that such interventions – until now – have not proven to be significantly effective (Cops et al. 2020).[31]

---

[30] They had a few half-day training sessions with other professionals working, for example, in the social services (Vl. Reg. 2020).
[31] The FPI is an institution that has an advisory assignment for the Flemish government regarding peace education, historical commemoration and remembrance, and radicalisation. In 2017, they published a report titled '"Deradicalisation": Academic Insights Informing Flemish Policy', which addressed questions such as: what is the relationship between radical ideas and violent behaviour;, can one estimate the risk of extremist violence; what are 'de-radicalisation' processes; do counter-narratives make sense,

Moreover, the ministry of education has set up a mandatory meeting structure in which the EMB/CIO and those responsible for Flemish teacher training discuss IRE-related (secular) topics and content, mandatory workshops, teaching quality expectations, and follow-up of the established IRE teacher training included in the statements of 28 January and 9 November 2016 (Flemish Government 2020). Concretely, they are asked to 'spread an open and moderate Islam', 'to inform and educate the Muslim pupils regarding the liberal European values and norms', 'to teach about controversial topic as euthanasia, homosexuality, men/women relationships' (Vl. Reg. 2015, 2017a, 2020). A reminder, with respect to both signed statements, only the CIO, as the legal representative body of Flemish Islamic religious education, has delegated competences regarding 'Islamic' courses in Flemish teacher training programmes. However, there is definitely a tendency to negotiate the 'Islamic' content and expectations formulated by the politics and public.[32] Furthermore, in the case of IRE teacher training, the selection committee for the lecturer is composed of members of EMB/CIO and the Flemish teacher training department.

Navigating the Limits of Mutual Interdependence Based on a Fuzzy Concept

The emphasis on 'passing through' a 'moderate' Islam, Enlightenment values and norms, the implementation of and discussions about sensitive topics as freedom of speech, human rights, homosexuality, euthanasia, relationships between men/women, organ donation, evolution theory, abortion and so on, have come to the foreground in recent years. There is nothing new about this observation, but they have intensified. The many enumerated initiatives and collaborations in the evaluation reports are testimonies of the impact, influence and interference of the state within the organisation of IRE in compulsory education, and IRE teacher training (Vl. Reg. 2020). However the question remains: to what extent can the state interfere, impose content, professionalisation trajectories, mandatory de-radicalisation and counter-discourse workshops? IRE teachers are experiencing overdoses of 'de-radicalisation' seminars, as if they are the only target group which has 'to take responsibility' and 'solve the problem of Muslim youngsters'.[33] A clear connection between dramatic events occurring in the

---

and how do young people look at all this; and how can policymakers deal with Islam in a European context. A first evaluation report of both Flemish Action Plans Radicalisation was published by the FPI on 2 December 2020 (Cops et al. 2020). The main goal was to evaluate and map the effectivity of policy initiatives regarding de-radicalisation and inform policymakers.

[32] The meetings between the EMB/CIO and teaching departments take place behind closed doors. No public written reports are available of these meetings.

[33] The author has been present at many of those seminars and workshops. Feelings of frustration, stigma and despondency were spelled out by the IRE teachers. They felt that many other factors which could

public sphere and the heated debates on policy level can be observed. The radicalisation 'flag' seems to be the open door to pursue a certain policy regarding this topic. A number of questions arise regarding this observation.

First, the concept of radicalisation and de-radicalisation policy as such has raised many questions in the academic community (Coolsaet 2017), as it contradicts years of research in conflict studies (Franks 2006; Europol 2016; Backer et al. 2019; Coolsaet 2019; Fadil et al. 2019; Ravn et al. 2019; Cops et al. 2020). The radicalisation process is characterised by a complex multi-layered, intertwined and interfered action–reaction on the micro- (Tajfel and Turner 1979; Crenshaw 2000; Moghaddam 2006; Borum 2014; Feddes 2015; Doosje and Van Eerten 2017; Verkuyten 2018), meso- and macro-levels (Crenshaw 1981; Bakker 2006, 2015; Veldhuis and Staun 2009; Ponsaers et al. 2010; Borum 2011a, 2011b; Ponsaers 2011; Feddes et al. 2015; De Waele et al. 2017; Backer et al. 2019).[34] There is no linear causal predictable correlation between factors that lead to violent radicalisation of extremism acts (Colaert 2017). The social science literature and research in the pedagogical sciences also contest the grounds of indicators of radicalisation that are used by governments (Doosje et al. 2016; Macaluso 2016; Colaert 2017; Ragazzi 2017; Cops et al. 2020; Stephens and Sieckelinck 2020). Additionally, civil society groups voice similar concerns (van den Brandt, 2017). The report of the Flemish Peace Institute (Cops et al. 2020) states that radicalisation is a relatively new concept used since the attacks on the Twin Towers in New York. It is understood as 'a process whereby an individual slowly embraces radical ideas, is indoctrinated and recruited by foreign extremists, and finally turns to violent terrorist attacks' (p. 16).

In respect of radicalisation, counter-narrative projects are popular on European level, as well as in Flanders. However, there is no counter-discourse programme that has been shown to be irrefutably effective (Ferguson 2016; Doosje and Van Eerten 2017: 97; Gielen 2019: 11). The context, objectives, actors, theoretical approaches, top-down/bottom-up approach at least have to be taken into account before considering the effectivity of countering violent extremism (CVE) policy (Gielen 2019). These observations are in line with those reflected in international academia. In short, the first Flemish evaluation reports (Colpert 2017; Gielen 2017; Ragazzi 2017; Cops et al. 2020) show and reveal the difficulties in grasping the concept of radicalisation and the large spectrum of CVE programmes, and the complexity and importance of a multi-agency approach with experts from different scientific fields. Additionally, reports and the academic community underline the importance of the school as

---

lead to radicalisation were not taken to account, such as the headscarf ban in Flemish education, discrimination in school context and outside, racism and so on.

[34] See for reviews Schmid and Price (2011); Stephens et al. (2019).

a safe space and the teacher as educator in a school context. They caution us not to expect teachers to be the 'eyes and ears' of 'security intelligence'. This has proved to be counterproductive (Ragazzi 2018). In sum, the Flemish Peace Institute and the academic community all state clearly that 'investing only in security, without investing in a tight social fabric, will not lead to the expected results'.

In retrospect, the political discussions and public debates were an important incentive to motivate the Flemish teacher training institutes to implement IRE teacher training programmes in their regular curricula for the reasons and critics abovementioned (Vl. Reg. 2015, 2016, 2017b, 2018; Commissie Onderwijs 2016, 2017). This critical and pointed deficiency seems to open doors to 'transgress' the legal limits based on the mutual interdependence as defined in the constitution. Do Flemish policymakers cross the line of separation of church and state by expecting – putting pressure on – certain professionalisation trajectories, and organising workshops about specific topics, a certain specific 'content wise' IRE teacher training? What is the rationale behind this requirement? At least some policymakers have suggested that this requirement will eliminate – in the long run – some of the 'Islamic-related issues'.

Discussion and Conclusion

The aim of this chapter is to establish the current state with regard to the expectations of Islamic religious education in Flanders. The Belgian Constitution contains a number of provisions that regulate the mutual interdependence between church and state, which stipulate, among other things, that, in public schools, every child has the right to follow a course in an officially recognised belief system of his or her parents' choice paid by the state. Regarding Islamic religious education, every single aspect, that is, the IRE programme (content and didactical methods), qualification and professionalisation trajectories of the IRE teachers, and the appointment of IRE teachers fall under the legal responsibility of the representative body; in this case, the Executive of Muslims of Belgium (EMB) and the Centre for Islamic Education (CIO) based on the Belgian constitutional provisions (Articles 19, 20, 21, 24, 181). However, the relationship between the EMB/CIO and the state has been marked by mistrust and suspicion ever since the recognition of Islam in 1974, due to its alleged links with Saudi Arabia, internal issues and disagreements, and even more so since the election in 1998 of the EMB, when the federal state refused elected candidates based on information from State Security. On 4 December 2020, the EMB experienced a similar crisis, as the Ministry of Justice and Life Stances, based on information from the State Security, questioned the position of certain EMB council members.

In line with these observations, policymakers, politicians and public opinion frequently questioned, and still do, the content of IRE courses, the didactical–pedagogical tools used, the qualification of IRE teachers and their mastery of Dutch, the 'Islamic' approach and views circulated during IRE classes, their adherence to Belgian law, human rights, and the Enlightenment values and norms. Note that no qualitative or quantitative in-depth academic research has been conducted to scrutinise, map or evaluate the quality of IRE, to analyse systematically the didactical material or the language proficiency of the current IRE teachers. These critics, and the new phenomenon of home-grown perpetrators, strongly motivated the instalment of the three-year fully-fledged IRE teacher training at a breakneck speed after the dramatic events in Paris (2015) and Brussels (2016). The Islamic background of the perpetrators was an impetus to formulate expectations towards EMB/CIO, more specifically the IRE teachers (and imams). They were asked to 'actively' contribute to the de-radicalisation and counter-discourse. In that sense, the Action Plan Radicalisation (2015) explicitly refers to jihadism and Syrian foreign fighters. However, Islamic background is not 'the' only ultimate factor that leads to radicalisation, let alone to these terrible attacks.

Radicalisation is a non-linear, complex and multi-layered phenomenon triggered by a variety of factors. Using it uncritically is in direct contradiction with much of the empirical research in terrorism studies, conflict studies and the sociology of violence. So the academic community is sceptical towards the use of the concept of radicalisation understood as a process that can be spotted or anticipated. Like many other countries, Belgium/Flanders introduced a counter-discourse programme through a direct collaboration with the EMB/CIO. However, this method did not demonstrate an univocally irrefutable effectivity, as the root causes are complex and multi-layered.

The Action Plan Radicalisation and Polarisation reflects the shifted societal context wherein increasing right-wing extremist voices were heard in the public sphere and on social media. Still, the EMB/CIO is involved, and pointed out as an active partner in de-radicalisation and counter-discourse through mandatory workshops and lectures on secular topics, such as, for example, Belgian democracy, freedom of speech, human and women's rights, euthanasia, gender issues, sexual orientation, organ donation, abortion, religion and science, and interconvictional dialogue. To do so, two engagement statements were signed by the EMB/CIO in presence of the Minister of Education, on 28 January and 9 November 2016, respectively. A detailed registration of these numerous organised 'mandatory' events is reported to the Ministry of Education (Vl. Reg. 2020). By doing so, the Flemish government can follow up and keep track of whether the expected activities have been organised by the EMB/CIO. Furthermore, public and political debates formulate repeatedly explicit expectations towards the EMB/CIO and IRE teachers each time dramatic events occur. For instance, following the murder of Samuel Paty (18 October 2020) IRE teachers were asked to inform and teach the principle of freedom of speech. This is clearly motivated by the dramatic event, and directly linked to the 'Islamic' background of the perpetrator. This one-way communication is directed towards 'Islam', not to other recognised belief systems. Are the contradictory demands on IRE teachers being asked to build social cohesion, resilience and a 'safe space', on the one hand, and at the same time to be vigilant towards Muslim pupils not sending conflicting messages? Ragazzi (2018) warned of this contradictory message. The most important overall question is: is the whole school team not responsible for the resilience, social cohesion and 'safe space' in a school context?

These observations raise the following questions: did policymakers transgress in navigating along the legal limits of the separation of church and state principle applicable to all recognised belief systems? Is it really the central role of IRE teachers to focus on de-radicalisation and counter-discourse during their lessons? Based on the numerous actions, policy documents and political debates we can state that the legal competences were maximised and stretched regarding IRE in public education. This observation reflects an obvious willingness to interfere and impose expectations regarding IRE via the 'open' door, more specifically via the radicalisation 'flag' and 'security discourse', and Enlightenment values and norms as 'citizenship'. Moreover, as the second Action Plan Radicalisation explicitly points to the role of polarisation (cf. right-wing party and on social media), is it reasonable to expect only IRE teachers to work on democratic values, to build bridges and work on social cohesion, in other words, to contribute to a school as a 'safe space'? Nevertheless, education has the potential to play an important, positive role in the long-term perspective. While there are multiple roles for education, in general, the question is to what extent IRE teachers have to and could play a role in de-radicalisation processes and counter-discourse. The Belgian Constitution recognises the mutual interdependence between church and state, and this observation seems to have opened the door for policymakers to formulate explicit expectations towards EMB/CIO regarding de-radicalisation and counter-discourse.

For the three last established IRE teacher training programmes, it is obvious that they needed to be in line with the successive Action Plans (2015, 2017), the Mission Statement (2016) and Engagement Statement (2016) as policymakers formulated explicit expectations, and the representative bodies for IRE signed both statements in the presence of the Minister of Education. In that sense, they are clearly navigating the limits of the mutual interdependence regarding IRE. The 'open door' seems to be the radicalisation and security 'flag' to formulate expectations towards IRE teachers and the EMB/CIO. We notice that this attitude towards the other recognised belief system is not observed. However, due to the principle of separation of church and state, the minimum qualification is – legally – imposed on all the teachers in Flemish public education appointed by the recognised body of the belief systems as the constitution prohibits discrimination when applying the law regarding religious matters.

To conclude: based on the policy documents and the political debates, policymakers push and pull the limits of their discretionary legal powers, navigating to explore the boundaries and borders in order to maximise their political and legal powers regarding Islam in general, and Islamic religious education in particular.

REFERENCES

Adams, M. and A. J. Overbeeke (2008). 'The Constitutional Relationship between Law and Religion in the History of Ideas: A Contemporary European Perspective', *Global Jurist* 8(3). DOI: 10.2202/1934-2640.1277.

Backer, M. et al. (2019). 'Conrad: Constructive Analysis on the Attitudes, Policies and Programmes that Relate to "radicalisation"', Final Report. Brussels: Belgian Science Policy Office (BRAIN-be – BR/165/A4/CONRAD – Belgian Research Action through Interdisciplinary Networks).

Bakker, E. (2006). *Jihadi Terrorists in Europe: Their Characteristics and the Circumstances in Which They Joined the Jihad. An Exploratory Study*. The Hague: Netherlands Institute of International Relations Clingendael.

Bakker, E. (2015). 'EU Counter-radicalization Policies: A Comprehensive and Consistent Approach?' *Intelligence and National Security* 30(2/3): 281–305.

Belgian Senate and Parliament (2002). Session 2001–2002, 'Report on the Activities of the Permanent Committee of Supervision on the Intelligence and Security Services', 19 July 2002, DOC. 50 1851/001 (Parliament), 2–171/1 (Senate).

Boender, W. and M. Kanmaz (2002). 'Imams in the Netherlands and Islam Teachers in Flanders', in W. Shadid and P. Sj. van Koningsveld (eds), *Intercultural Relations and Religious Authorities: Muslims in the European Union*. Leuven: Peeters, pp. 169–80.

Borum, R. (2011a). 'Radicalization into Violent Extremism I', *Journal of Strategic Security* 4(4): 7–36.

Borum, R. (2011b). 'Radicalisation into Violent Extremism II: A Review of Conceptual Models and Empirical Research', *Journal of Strategic Security* 4(4): 37–62.

Borum, R. (2014). 'Psychological Vulnerabilities and Propensities for Involvement in Violent Extremism', *Behavioral Sciences & the Law* 32: 286–305.

Cesari, J. (2009). 'The Securisation of Islam in Europe', Challenge Research Papers, Research Paper No. 15, April 2009, available at http://www.ceps.eu.

Christians, L. L. and Overbeeke, A. J. (2014). 'The Place of Religious Rules and Principles in Belgian Law: An Overview', 19th International Congress of Comparative Law, 20–27 July 2014, Vienna, available at: http://hdl.handle.net/1871/52566.

Colaert, L. (2017). *'Deradicalisering'. Wetenschappelijke inzichten voor een Vlaams beleid*. Brussels: Vlaams Vredesinstituut.

Commissie Onderwijs en Vorming (2009). Commissievergadering vraag nr. 66, *Imaamopleiding – Stand van Zaken*, November 10.

Commissie Onderwijs en Gelijke Kansen (2011a). *Commissievergadering vraag 756 over de vooruitgang bij de organisatie van een volwaardig opleidingsaanbod voor islamkaders*, 13 January 2011.
Commissie voor onderwijs en Gelijke kansen (2011b). *Handelingen Commissievergadering. Vergadering C99 – OND11 (2010–2011), vraag 839 aangaande onderwijs intensiever te betrekken bij de strijd tegen het radicaliseren van jongeren en vraag 756 aangaande over de vooruitgang bij de organisatie van een volwaardig opleidingsaanbod voor islamkaders*, 13 January 2011.
Commissie Onderwijs en Gelijke Kansen (2011c). *Commissievergadering nr. C270-OND30 (2011–2012) over het tekort aan islamleerkrachten in het basis- en secundair onderwijs*, 9 June 2011.
Commissie Onderwijs (2015). *Vraag 1121 aangaande de imamopleiding*, Commissievergadering 19 March 2015.
Commissie Onderwijs (2016). *Vraag nr. 2098 over het actieplan van de Moslimexecutieve inzake het islamonderwijs*, Commissievergadering 19 May 2016.
Commissie Onderwijs (2017). *Vraag 1743 om uitleg over de islamopleidingen*, Commissievergadering 27 April 2017.
Commissie Onderwijs (2018b). *Vraag nr. 16 over de inhoud van de gebruikte handboeken islamitische godsdienst*, Commissievergadering 6 December 2018.
Commissie voor de bestrijding van gewelddadige radicalisering. (2015). *Vraag nr. 550 om uitleg over signalen van radicalisering binnen het Nederlandstalig onderwijs in Brussel*, Commissievergadering 15 December 2015.
Coolsaet, R. (2017). '(De)radicalisering tussen praktijk en ambiguïteit', *Cahiers Politiestudies* 42(1): 219–29.
Coolsaet, R. (2019). 'Radicalization: The Origins and Limits of a Contested Concept', in N. Fadil, Fr. Ragazzi and M. de Koning (eds), *Radicalization in Belgium and the Netherlands: Critical Perspectives on Violence and Security*. London: I. B. Tauris, pp, 29–51.
Cops, D., A. Pauwels and M. Van Alstein (eds) (2020). *Gewelddadige radicalisering & polarisering. Beleid & preventie in Vlaanderen: Evaluatie en uitdagingen*. Brussels: Vlaams Vredesinstituut.
Council of Europe (2015). *Action Plan on the Fight against Violent Extremism and Radicalisation leading to Terrorism*, Committee of Ministers, available at www.coe.int/cm.
Crenshaw, M. (1981). 'The Causes of Terrorism', *Comparative Politics* 13: 379–99.
Crenshaw, M. (2000). 'The Psychology of Terrorism: An Agenda for the 21st Century', *Political Psychology* 21(2): 405–20.
Debeer, J., P. Loobuyck and P. Meier (2011). *Imams en islamconsulenten in Vlaanderen: Hoe zijn ze georganiseerd?* Antwerp: Steunpunt Gelijkekansenbeleid.
de Graaff, B., C. de Poot and E. Kleemans (2009). 'Radicalisering en radicale groepen in vogelvlucht', *Tijdschrift voor Criminologie* 51(4): 331–44.
De Standaard (2017). *Islamleraren in de strijd tegen radicalisering*, 17 Mai 2017, available at: https://www.standaard.be/cnt/dmf20170517_02885987.
De Waele, M., H. Moors, A. Garssen and J. Noppe (eds) (2017). *Aanpak van gewelddadige radicalisering*. Antwerp: Maklu.
Doosje, B. et al. (2016). 'Terrorism, Radicalization and De-radicalization', *Current Opinion in Psychology* 11: 79–84.

Doosje, B. and Van Eerten, J. J. (2017). '"Counter-narratives" against Violent Extremism', in L. Colaert (ed.), *'Deradicalisation': Scientific Insights for Policy*. Brussels: Vlaams Vredesinstituut.
European Commission (2016). *Promoting Citizenship and the Common Values of Freedom, Tolerance and Non-Discrimination through Education: Overview of Education Policy Developments in Europe following the Paris Declaration of 17 March 2015*. Luxembourg: Publications Office of the European Union.
Europol (2016). *TE-SAT 2016*. The Hague: Europol.
Fadil, N., F. El Asri and S. Bracke (2015). 'Islam in Belgium: Mapping an Emerging Interdisciplinary Field of Study', in J. Cesari (ed.), *The Oxford Handbook of European Islam*. Oxford: Oxford University Press, 222–61.
Fadil, N., M. de Koning and F. Ragazzi (2019). *Radicalization in Belgium and the Netherlands: Critical Perspectives on Violence and Security*. London: I. B. Tauris.
Feddes, A. R. (2015). 'Socio-psychological Factors Involved in Measures of Disengagement and Deradicalization and Evaluation Challenges in Western Europe', available at: https://www.mei.edu/sites/default/files/Feddes.pdf.
Feddes, A. R., L. Nickolson and B. Doosje (2015). 'Triggerfactoren in het radicaliseringsproces', *Justitiële verkenningen* 42(2): 22–48.
Federale Overheidsdienst (2018). *Preventie van radicaliseringsprocessen die kunnen leiden tot geweld. Gids van lokale initiatieven en tools bestemd voor de actoren op het terrein*. Brussels: Federale Overheidsdienst Binnenlandse Zaken.
Ferguson, K. (2016). 'Countering Violent Extremism through Media and Communication Strategies: A Review of the Evidence', available at: http://www.paccsresearch.org.uk/wp-content/uploads/2016/03/Countering-Violent-Extremism-Through-Media-and-Communication-Strategies-.pdf, last accessed 20 December 2020.
Foblets, M.-Cl. and A. Overbeeke (2004). 'Islam in Belgium: The Search for a Legal Status of a New Religious Minority', in R. Potz and W. Wieshaider (eds), *Islam and the European Union*. Leuven: Peeters.
Franks, J. (2006). *Rethinking the Root Causes of Terrorism*. London: Palgrave Macmillan.
Gielen, A.-J. (2017). 'Evaluating Countering Violent Extremism', in L. Colaert (ed.), *'Deradicalisation': Scientific Insights for Policy*. Brussels: Vlaams Vredesinstituut.
Gielen, A.-J. (2019). 'Countering Violent Extremism: A Realist Review for Assessing What Works, for Whom, in What Circumstances, and How?' *Terrorism and Political Violence* 31(6): 1149–67.
Husson, J.-Fr. (2007). *Training Imams in Europe: The Current Status*. Brussels: King Baudouin Foundation.
Husson, J.-Fr. (2012). 'Le financement public de l'islam. Instrument d'une politique publique?' in Br. Maréchal and F. El Asri (eds), *Islam Belge au pluriel*. Louvain-la-Neuve: Presses Universitaires de Louvain, 241–58.
Kamer van Volksvertegenwoordigers (1964). 'Overeenkomst tussen België en Marokko betreffende de tewerkstelling van Marokkaanse werknemers in België, en bijlagen, ondertekend te Brussel op 17 februari 1964'. *Belgisch Staatsblad*, 17 June 1977.
Kamer van Volksvertegenwoordigers (1974). 'Wet van 19 juli 1974 tot erkenning van "de besturen belast met het beheer van de temporaliën van de islamitische eredienst". *Belgisch Staatsblad*, 3 May 1978.

Kamer van Volksvertegenwoordigers (1994). 'Gecoördineerde Grondwet van 17 Februari 1994'. *Belgisch Staatsblad*, February 27.
Kanmaz, M. (2002). 'The Recognition and Institutionalization of Islam in Belgium', *Muslim World* 92(1): 99–113.
Kanmaz, M. and M. El Battiui (2004). *Moskeeën, imams en islamleerkrachten in België, Stand van zaken en Uitdagingen*. Brussels: King Baudouin Foundation.
Kanmaz, M. and S. Zemni (2008). 'Moslims als inzet in religieuze, maatschappelijke en veiligheidsdiscours: de erkenning en institutionalisering van de islamitische eredienst in België', in E. Vanderwaeren and C. Timmerman (eds), *Diversiteit in islam. Over verschillende belevingen van het moslim zijn*, vol. 7. Leuven: Acco, pp. 109–56.
Knack (2020a). *Vier op de tien leerkrachten levensbeschouwing heeft juiste bekwaamheidsbewijs*, 4 February 2020.
Knack (2020b). *Het juiste antwoord is antwoord D: je bent een ongelovige*, 28 October 2020.
Lafrarchi, N. (2020). 'Assessing Islamic Religious Education Curriculum in Flemish Public Secondary School', *Religions* 11(3): 110.
Lafrarchi, N. (2021). 'Intra- and Interconvictional Dialogue in Flemish (Belgian) Secondary Education as a Tool to Prevent Radicalisation', *Religions* 12(6): 434.
Loobuyck, P., J. Debeer and P. Meier (2013). 'Church–State Regimes and their Impact on the Institutionalization of Islamic Organizations in Western Europe: A Comparative Analysis', *Journal of Muslim Minority Affairs* 33(1): 61–76.
Macaluso, A. (2016). *From Countering to Preventing Radicalization through Education: Limits and Opportunities*. The Hague: Hague Institute for Global Justice.
Manço, U. and M. Kanmaz (2004). 'Belgique. Intégration des musulmans et reconnaissance du culte islamique: un essai de bilan', in U. Manço (ed.), *Reconnaissance et discrimination. Présence de l'islam en Europe occidentale et en Amérique du Nord*. Paris: L'Harmattan, 85–115.
Manço, U. and M. Renaerts (2000). 'Lente institutionnalisation de l'islam et persistance d'inégalités face aux autres cultes reconnus', in U. Manço (ed.), *Voix et Voies Musulmanes en Belgique*. Brussels: Publications des Facultés universitaires Saint-Louis, pp. 83–106.
Maréchal, B. and H. Bousetta (2004). *Islam en moslims in België. Lokale uitdagingen & algemeen denkkader*. Brussels: King Baudouin Foundation.
Ministerie van Onderwijs en Vorming (2016a). *Engagementsverklaring voor een kwalitatief islamonderwijs van 9 november 2016*. Brussels: Ministry of Education and Training.
Ministerie van Onderwijs en Vorming (2016b). *Engagementsverklaring van de erkende instanties en verenigingen van de levensbeschouwelijke vakken en de onderwijskoepels van het officieel onderwijs en het GO! met het oog op een versterking van de interlevensbeschouwelijke dialoog op school van 28 januari 2016*. Brussels: Ministry of Education and Training.
Moghaddam, F. M. (2006). *From the Terrorists' Point of View: What They Experience and Why They Come to Destroy*. Westport, CT: Praeger.
Panafit, L. (1999). *Quand le droit écrit l'Islam. L'intégration juridique de l'Islam en Belgique*. Brussels: Bruylant.
Piqueray, E., W. Nonneman and C. Timmerman (2008). *Eindrapport. Haalbaarheidsstudie over een vormings aanbod voor islamkaders*. Antwerp: CeMIS – UA.

Piqueray, E., W. Nonneman and C. Timmerman (2009). *Rapport deel II. Project opleiding in 'Islamitische studies'*. Antwerp: CeMIS – UA.
Ponsaers, P. (2011). 'Het proces van radicalisering', in T. Spapens, M. Groenhuijsen and T. Kooijmans (eds), *Universalis. Liber Amicorum Cyrille Fijnaut*. Antwerp: Intersentia, pp. 975–88.
Ponsaers, P. et al. (2010). *Onderzoeksrapport polarisering en radicalisering: een integrale preventieve aanpak*. Brussels: FOD Binnenlandse Zaken, available at: http://besafe.jdbi.eu/kennisdatabank/polarisering-en-radicalisering.
Ragazzi, F. (2017). 'Countering Terrorism and Radicalization: Securitising Social Policy? *Critical Social Policy* 37(2): 163–79.
Ragazzi, F. (2018). *Students as Suspects? The Challenge of Counter-Radicalisation Policies in Education in the Council of Europe Member States*. Strasbourg: Council of Europe.
Ravn, S., R. Coolsaet and T. Sauer (2019). 'Rethinking Radicalization: Addressing the Lack of a Contextual Perspective in the Dominant Narratives on Radicalization', in N. Clycq, C. Timmerman, D. Vanheule, R. Van Caudenberg and S. Ravn (eds), *Radicalisation: A Marginal Phenomenon or a Mirror to Society?* Leuven: Leuven University Press, pp. 21–46.
Sandberg, R. and C. N. Doe (2007). 'Church–State Relations in Europe', *Religion Compass* 1(5): 561–78.
Schmid, A. P. and E. Price (2011). 'Selected Literature on Radicalization and De-radicalization of Terrorists: Monographs, Edited Volumes, Grey Literature and Prime Articles Published since the 1960s', *Crime, Law and Social Change* 55(4): 337–48.
Stephens, W., S. Sieckelinck and H. Boutellier (2019). 'Preventing Violent Extremism: A Review of the Literature', *Studies in Conflict and Terrorism*, DOI: 10.1080/1057610X.2018.1543144.
Stephens, W. and S. Sieckelinck (2020). 'Being Resilient to Radicalisation in PVE Policy: A Critical Examination', *Critical Studies on Terrorism* 13(1): 142–65.
Tajfel, H. and J. C. Turner (1979). 'An Integrative Theory of Intergroup Conflict', in W. G. Austin and S. Worchel (eds), *The Social Psychology of Intergroup Relations*. Monterey, CA: Brooks-Cole, pp. 33–47.
Torfs, R. and J. Vrielink (2019). 'State and Church in Belgium', in G. Robbers (ed.), *State and Church in the European Union*, 3rd edn. Baden-Baden: Nomos, pp. 11–50.
Touag, H. (2017). 'Un paradoxe belge', *Hommes & migrations* 1316. DOI: 10.4000/hommesmigrations.3793.
Van Den Berg, P. A. (2018). 'Liberalism, Modern Constitutionalism and Nation Building in the Belgian Constitution of 1831: Comparative Perspective', *Giornale di Storia Costituzionale* 35: 49–68.
van den Brandt, N. (2017). 'Public Renderings of Islam and the Jihadi Threat: Political, Social, and Religious Critique in Civil Society in Flanders, Belgium', in J. Mapril, R. Blanes, E. Giumbelli and E. Wilson (eds), *Secularisms in a Postsecular Age?* London: Palgrave Macmillan.
Van Ostaeyen, P. (2019). 'State of Terror: The Historical and Influence of the Belgian ISIS Contingent,. ECTC Advisory Network Conference, conference paper, The Hague, 9–10 April 2019.

Varin, C. (2006). *Education in a Federal System: A Case-study of Belgium*, CUREJ, available at: repository.upenn.edu/curej/24.

Velaers, J. and M.-C. Foblets (2010). 'Religion and the State in Belgian Law: National Report', in J. Martinez-Torron and C. Durham (eds), *Religion and the Secular State*. Provo: International Center for Law and Religion Studies, Brigham Young University, pp. 99–122.

Veldhuis, T. and J. Staun (2009). *Islamist Radicalisation: A Root Cause Model*. The Hague: Netherlands Institute of International Relations Clingendael, available at: https://www.diis.dk/files/media/publications/import/islamist_radicalisation.veldhuis_and_staun.pdf.

Verbeeck, B. (2008). 'Neutraal en toch divers. Een te moeilijke evenwichtsoefening voor het onderwijs in Vlaanderen?' *Ethiek & Maatschappij* 11(3): 13–25.

Verkuyten, M. (2018). 'Religious Fundamentalism and Radicalization among Muslim Minority Youth in Europe', *European Psychologist* 23(1): 21–31.

Vlaams Parlement (2003). *Voorstel van resolutie betreffende het islamonderricht in het onderwijs*. Stuk 1619 (2002–2003), Nr.1 Zitting 2002–2003, 18 March 2003, available at: https://docs.vlaamsparlement.be/pfile?id=1019329.

Vlaams Parlement (2005). *Beleidsnota. Onderwijs en Vorming 2004–2009*. Stuk 156 (2004–2005), nr. 1, 4 January 2005, available at: https://docs.vlaamsparlement.be/pfile?id=1026519.

Vlaams Parlement (2009). *Schriftelijke vraag nr. 66, Imamopleiding – Stand van Zaken*, 10 November 2009.

Vlaams Parlement (2010). *Vraag 54 van 20 oktober 2010*, available at: http://docs.vlaamsparlement.be/pfile?id=250479.

Vlaams Parlement (2011a). *Vraag nr. 1551 (2011–2012), nr. 5 Voorstel van resolutie betreffende de inrichting van een universitaire opleiding Islamitische Godsdienstwetenschappen Amendement voorgesteld na indiening van het verslag*, 26 June 2012, available at: https://docs.vlaamsparlement.be/pfile?id=1033664.

Vlaams Parlement (2011b). *Conceptnota voor nieuwe regelgeving een Vlaamse opleiding Islamitische Godsdienstwetenschappen*. Stuk 1227 (2010–2011), nr. 1 op 7 July 2011, available at: https://docs.vlaamsparlement.be/pfile?id=1034779.

Vlaams Parlement (2011c). *Vraag nr. 178 vzw Centrum Islamonderwijs – Samenwerking en subsidiëring*, 24 November 2011.

Vlaams Parlement (2012a). *Stuk 1227 (2010–2011), nr. 2 ingediend op 14 maart 2012 (2011–2012), Conceptnota voor nieuwe regelgeving over een Vlaamse opleiding Islamitische godsdienstwetenschappen*, available at: https://docs.vlaamsparlement.be/pfile?id=1033284.

Vlaams Parlement (2012b). *Vraag nr. 1551, 1 en 1551, 4 betreffende de inrichting van een universitaire opleiding Islamitische Godsdienstwetenschappen*, 21 June 2012.

Vlaams Parlement (2012c). *Stuk 1551 (2011–2012), nr. 2, Voorstel van resolutie betreffende de inrichting van een universitaire opleiding Islamitische Godsdienstwetenschappen*, 12 June 2012 (2011–2012), available at: https://docs.vlaamsparlement.be/docs/stukken/2011-2012/g1551-2.pdf.

Vlaams Parlement (2013a). *Schriftelijke vraag nr. 523, van 8 May 2013, Islamleerkrachten – Stand van zaken*.

Vlaams Parlement (2013b). *Vraag nr. 68 Leerkrachten islamitische godsdienst stand van zaken*, 18 October 2013.
Vlaams Parlement (2014). *Beleidsnota Onderwijs 2014–2019. Stuk 133 (2014–2015)*, nr. 1, 24 October 2015, available at: https://docs.vlaamsparlement.be/docs/stukken/20 14-2015/g133-1.pdf.
Vlaams Parlement (2015). *Beleidsbrief Onderwijs 2015–2016, 512 (2015–2016)*, nr. 1 16 October 2015.
Vlaams Parlement (2016a). *Schriftelijke vraag nr. 255 Federale aankondiging imamopleiding – Diplomavereisten*, 2 March 2016.
Vlaams Parlement (2016b). *Actuele vraag nr. 274 over de bekwaamheidsbewijzen voor islamleerkrachten*, 13 April 2016.
Vlaams Parlement (2016c). *Actuele vraag nr. 313 over het overleg met de Moslimexecutieve betreffende het islamonderwijs*, 27 April 2016.
Vlaams Parlement (2016d). *Schriftelijke vraag nr. 1 over Vlaamse imamopleiding – Stand van zaken*, 26 September 2016.
Vlaams Parlement (2017a). *Vraag 348 over het akkoord met de Moslimexecutieve betreffende de opleiding van islamleerkrachten. Plenaire Vergadering nr. 34*, 10 May 2017.
Vlaams Parlement (2017b). *Vraag nr. 313 over attest voor leerkrachten godsdienst, specifiek leerkrachten islam, in het Vlaams onderwijs, Plenaire Vergadering*, 18 April 2017.
Vlaams Parlement (2017c). *Beleidsbrief Onderwijs 2016–2017, 940 (2016–2017)*, nr. 1, 21 October 2016.
Vlaams Parlement (2018). *Vraag nr. 313 over attest voor leerkrachten godsdienst, specifiek leerkrachten islam, in het Vlaams onderwijs, Plenaire Vergadering*, 18 April 2018.
Vlaams Parlement (2019a). *Stuk 1806, nr. 1 (2018–2019) Verslag van de gedachtewisseling namens de Commissie voor de bestrijding van gewelddadige radicalisering over de derde voortgangsrapportage van het geactualiseerde actieplan van de Vlaamse Regering ter preventie van gewelddadige radicalisering en polarisering*, 15 January 2019.
Vlaams Parlement (2019b). *Plenaire Vergadering. Actuele vraag nr. 144 (2019–2020) over het toenemende rechts-extremisme op school*. 27 November 2019.
Vlaams Parlement (2021). *Verslag Plenaire Vergadering. Over het lerarentekort in Vlaanderen, Stuk 1 (2022–2023)*, 20 October 2021, available at: Retrieved 25 October 2021: https://www.vlaamsparlement.be/nl/parlementair-werk/plenaire-vergaderingen/1561005/verslag/1565350, last accessed 25 October 2021.
Vlaamse Regering (2004). *De Vlaamse Regering 2004–2009. Vertrouwen geven, verantwoordelijkheid nemen*, available at: https://www.vlaanderen.be/publicaties/de-vlaam se-regering-2004-2009-vertrouwen-geven-verantwoordelijkheid-nemen.
Vlaamse Regering (2009). *De Vlaamse Regeringsakkoord 2009–2014. Een daadkrachtig Vlaanderen in Beslissende tijden. Voor een vernieuwende, duurzame en warme samenleving*, available at: https://www.vlaanderen.be/publicaties/de-vlaamse-regering-2009-2014-een-daadkrachtig-vlaanderen-in-beslissende-tijden-voor-een-vernieuwende-duurzame-en-warme-samenleving.
Vlaamse Regering (2014). *De Vlaamse Regeringsakkoord 2014–2019. Vertrouwen, verbinden, vooruitgaan*, available at: https://overheid.vlaanderen.be/sites/default/fil es/media/documenten/organisatieontwikkeling/Het_regeerakkoord_Vlaamse_Regeri ng_2014_2019.pdf.

Vlaamse Regering (2015). *Actieplan ter preventie van radicaliseringsprocessen die kunnen leiden tot extremisme en terrorisme.* VR 2015 0304 DOC.0321/1BIS, 3 April 2015. Brussels: Vlaamse Regering.
Vlaamse Regering (2016). *Actieplan ter preventie van gewelddadige radicalisering en polarisering. Overzicht en maatregelen.* VR 2016 2904 MED.0158/2. Brussels: Vlaamse Regering.
Vlaamse Regering (2017a). *Actieplan ter preventie van gewelddadige radicalisering en polarisering. Overzicht en maatregelen.* VR 2017 0206 MED.0211/2TER. Brussels: Vlaamse Regering.
Vlaamse Regering (2017b). *Mededeling aan de Vlaamse Regering. Betreft Actualisering van het actieplan ter preventie van gewelddadige radicalisering en polarisering,* Brussels: Vlaamse Regering.
Vlaamse Regering (2018). *Actieplan ter preventie van gewelddadige radicalisering en polarisering Tussentijdse rapportage,* VR 2018 3011 MED.0446/2BIS, 10 December 2018.
Vlaamse Regering (2020). *Actieplan ter preventie van gewelddadige radicalisering en polarisering. Eindrapportage Mei 2020.* VR 2020 0506 MED.0175/2BIS, 15 May 2020, available at: https://onderwijs.vlaanderen.be/sites/default/files/atoms/files/Actieplan%20ter%20preventie%20van%20gewelddadige%20radicalisering%20en%20polarisering_eindrapportage_mei2020.pdf.
VLHORA (2007). *Onderwijsvisitatie. Onderwijs. Secundair onderwijs. Een onderzoek naar kwaliteit van de professioneel gerichte bacheloropleiding in het Onderwijs: Secundair onderwijs aan de Vlaamse hogescholen.* Brussels: VLHORA.
VRT (2018). '*Pano-Reportage: Wie is Schild & Vrienden Echt?*' available at: https://www.vrt.be/vrtnws/nl/2018/09/05/pano-wie-is-schild-vrienden-echt;https://www.vrt.be/vrtnws/nl/2018/08/31/pano-schild-vrienden.
VRT (2020). '*Negatief advies voor Grote Moskee: "Marokkaanse spionen in het bestuur, Moslimexecutieve moet orde op zaken stellen"*', available at: https://www.vrt.be/vrtnws/nl/2020/12/04/negatief-advies-voor-grote-moskee-drie-marokkaanse-spionnen-in.
Zemni, S. (2003). 'Islam en terrorisme: over enkele simpele amalgamen', in H. Bousetta (ed.), *Breek de stilte. Een burgerlijk standpunt van Belgische intellectuelen van Belgische intellectuelen van Maghrebijnse afkomst over de gebeurtenissen sinds 11 september.* Brussels: VUB Press, pp. 27–30.
Zemni, S. (2009). *Het islamdebat.* Berchem: EPO.
Zemni, S. (2011). 'The Shaping of Islam and Islamophobia in Belgium', *Race & Class* 53(1): 28–44.
Zemni, S. and Fadil, N. (2004). 'Religieuze zingeving in een seculiere maatschappij', in Chr. Timmerman, I. Lodewyckx, D. Vanheule and J. Wets (eds), *Wanneer wordt vreemd, vreemd? De vreemde in beeldvorming, registratie, beleid.* Leuven: Acco, pp. 203–22.

CHAPTER 10

The Need for Teaching against Islamophobia in a Culturally Homogeneous Context: The Case of Poland

Anna Piela, Katarzyna Górak-Sosnowska and Beata Abdallah-Krzepkowska

Introduction

The complexity of the task of teaching about Islam in Poland is exacerbated by the Polish socio-political context that comprises an ethnically and culturally homogeneous society, a right-wing government since 2015, the growing influence of far-right movements and the unmitigated dominance of the Roman Catholic Church (henceforth RCC) in the public sphere. All these factors not only create an environment in which Islamophobia thrives; they actively fuel it. For the purpose of this chapter, we ask: how can teaching against Islamophobia (involving transformation of attitudes and fact-checking) be delivered hand in hand with teaching about Islam in Polish educational contexts?

Given the lack of any religious education beyond Catholic instruction in 95 per cent of Polish schools (Balsamska et al. 2012), any sporadic references to Islam are made in the course of general education where it is framed in terms of conflict rather than dialogue between faiths (Górak-Sosnowska 2006). Post-secondary education is the first opportunity for Polish students to receive more detailed and systematic education about Islam and Muslims. Despite the hostile climate for Muslims (both indigenous and immigrant) and refugees, in Poland there is a marked interest in university humanities and social science courses and programmes that may have a partial focus on Islam, such as political science, sociology, anthropology and security studies. However, these disciplines (as taught in Poland) do not traditionally have a focus on the MENA region or south Asia (which might facilitate some familiarity with Islam as a cognate topic). In addition, post-colonial, ethnic, critical race or indigenous studies are fairly marginal in Poland in terms of theoretical influence.

This set of intersecting issues may prevent advisers from being able to successfully teach against Islamophobia in the classroom while advising on Islam-related projects.

While we recognise that 'Islamophobia' is a highly contested term (Cesari 2011), it is, nevertheless, useful in providing a coherent descriptor for 'experiences of discrimination, dehumanization, and misrepresentation of Muslims, those of Muslim heritage, and *a systemic miseducation about Islam itself*' (Kincheloe et al. 2010: x, emphasis added). There is a growing body of literature pertaining to Islamophobia recently exploring, notably, the process of racialisation of Islam as a part of the Islamophobic logic (Selod and Embrick 2013; Garner and Selod 2015; Selod 2015; Husain 2019). Thus, for the purpose of this chapter, we understand Islamophobia as a process existing in close synergy with anti-Islamism, anti-Muslimness and anti-Muslim prejudice as a part of a large ecosystem of systemic racism fuelled by White supremacy.

Importantly, Green (2019: 126) points out that 'ignorance of Islam does not fully account for the existence and persistence of Islamophobia'. Simply teaching the student population about Islam is not sufficient; they need to engage with the historical and political contexts of Islamophobia, as well as the complex modern-day Islamophobia networks that comprise funders, politicians, activists, media, celebrities and academics. Teaching against Islamophobia involves the study of non-Muslims and their attitudes, beliefs and actions related to Islam. These issues are outside the scope of introductory courses about Islam, but urgently require addressing. Yet there is a lacuna of pedagogical literature that would help educators tackle the problem of Islamophobic discourses and 'pseudo-knowledge' of Islam that find their way into the classroom (Green 2019). Some excellent practical approaches are made available on the Wabash Center website (2021), which offers access to syllabi, educators' reflections and pedagogical projects focused on teaching against Islamophobia. In the literature, scholars reflect on a variety of transformative anti-Islamophobic teaching strategies, including role-playing and engaging student voices (Housee 2012), critical reflection on intersecting inequalities (Martino and Rezai-Rashti 2008; Ahmadi and Cole 2020), and historical analyses (Elbih 2013).

However, we recognise the limitations of solutions that are embedded in different cultural contexts. For example, in the current socio-political climate in Poland (Piela 2020b), it would be unrealistic to hope for a state-funded, integrative, anti-discriminatory programme such as the Canadian 'Toward Understanding: Moving beyond Racism and Islamophobia', developed by the Muslim Educational Network, Training, and OutReach Service (MENTORS) and funded by the Ministry of Canadian Heritage Multiculturalism Program and the Canadian Race Relations Foundation (Zine 2012). Taking into account the difficulties related to teaching about a religious tradition actively vilified by the political elite and the media (Piela 2019, 2020a, 2020b) – in other words, teaching against Islamophobia – we suggest pedagogical approaches to supervising student research projects that address topics related to Islam and Muslims in the Polish context specifically. This may be especially relevant when Islam is addressed as an ancillary topic, and the need for anti-Islamophobia pedagogical training for both students and academic advisers is explicit.

Background: Religious Illiteracy in Poland at the Root of the Problem

In this section we provide a brief discussion of how primary and secondary level education may contribute to Islamophobic stereotyping by students at the tertiary level. We discuss the failure of religious instruction to provide religious literacy to Polish students as well as the unclear location of Islam as a social sciences topic in Polish academia.

The name of the only religion-related subject taught at Polish schools, *religia* ('religious instruction') might be misleading, as it means exclusively Catholic religious instruction. Prior to the transformation, religious instruction was delivered by local parishes; since 1990, religion is taught at schools. According to the treaty signed in 1993 with the Holy See, the Concordat, state preschools, primary and secondary schools provide the space for religious instruction, while the curriculum is designed by RCC authorities and delivered by RCC-licensed instructors. Its content covers almost exclusively confessional Catholicism. Available textbooks on religious instruction aim to inculcate Catholic belief and practice, rather than factual knowledge about a variety of religions (see Konferencja Episkopatu Polski 2010a).

Moreover, the core curriculum of religious instruction for all levels of education issued by the Episcopal Conference of Poland has hardly any space for religious traditions other than the Catholic one. In this 129-page document, other Christian denominations (Protestant, Orthodox) were each mentioned once, other monotheistic religions (Judaism, Islam) five times, and other religious traditions such as Buddhism or Hinduism, once only (see Konferencja Episkopatu Polski 2010b).[1] Religions other than Catholicism are also absent as a topic from the teaching curriculum (see Konferencja Episkopatu Polski 2010b). In other words, after sixteen years of elective religious instruction at school (at 2 hours per week), a Polish student becomes knowledgeable only in one particular denomination, that is, Catholic religion.

---

[1] The Polish Bishops' Conference is an official collective body that coordinates and supports the work of bishops across Poland.

The few mentions of Islam in the curriculum offer a very limited picture of this religion. Islam is simply listed together with other non-Christian religions and sects in the core curriculum. This point is under 'Introduction to mission', while the role of the teacher is to 'present the novelty of Christianity and warning against cult activity' (Konferencja Episkopatu Polski 2010b: 58). Further information about Islam (mostly the pillars of faith, symbols, early Arab conquests and mutual coexistence of Muslims and Christians in medieval Europe) are to be studied by students in other courses (history and civics), while the content of the religious instruction can only 'correlate' with these courses. This core curriculum provides a framework for the delivery of the teaching. Here the place of Islam is even more limited – it is only mentioned with regard to the Lord's Prayer in terms of monotheistic religions (with Judaism) and interreligious dialogue (Konferencja Episkopatu Polski 2010c: 94).

Students who do not wish to participate in religious instruction may, at least in theory, attend ethics classes at school once per week. In practice, ethics classes are difficult and often impossible to access; they are seen as ideological competitors of Catholic religious instruction. According to a study commissioned by the Polistrefa Foundation (Balsamska et al. 2016), 50 per cent of parents declared that ethics classes were simply unavailable in their children's schools. The ethics curriculum touches briefly upon Islamic moral foundations at the primary educational level. Interestingly, there has never been any other alternative to religious instruction than ethics, such as philosophy or religious studies (Zwierżdżyński 2017). The same report contends that students who attended ethics classes are often discriminated against and physically and verbally abused at school; Catholic rituals infuse school functions and spaces; crucifixes and Catholic imagery are ubiquitous in classrooms and hallways (Balsamska et al. 2016).

Current religious instruction in Polish schools offers very limited choices regarding religious literacy. Unlike in American or British schools where Islam may be discussed in social studies and religious education classes, respectively (Thobani 2006; Moore 2012), Polish students remain largely illiterate about Islam and other religious traditions, regardless of whether they embrace or resist confessional Catholic instruction at school (Mandes and Rogaczewska 2013). As Moore (2007) indicates, religious illiteracy can easily fuel culture wars and religious bigotry. It certainly affects attitudes to Islam and Muslims whose image is shaped predominantly by 'transplanted Islamophobia discourse' (Górak-Sosnowska 2016; Górak-Sosnowska and Pachocka 2019). The reference to a transplanted phenomenon signals that Poles have adopted external (Western) dominant narratives about Islam in a monocultural setting that is largely devoid of interactions with Muslims; their religious illiteracy, coupled with a lack of a strong Polish Muslim counter-narrative, has led to an essentialised understanding of Islam and Muslims which is prolific in the state media currently driven by right-wing political agendas.[2]

The problem with religious illiteracy is compounded by fragmentation of the body of knowledge about Islam in academia, and the lack of post-colonial studies in Poland. Poland's tumultuous history means that Poles, for a large swath of the period beginning at the end of the eighteenth century have been consumed by questions of Polish statehood and Poland's place in the changing geopolitical order. The partition period (1772–1918), followed by the two world wars with their grievous consequences and being subsumed into the Soviet bloc have all cemented the narrative of Polish victimisation (Renner 2016) which has become the foundation for a sense of national unity and solidarity. Historical encounters with Islam were fleeting and did not lead to sustained engagement with Muslim-majority states.

Post-colonial theory has been largely absent from East European intellectual currents. The central thrust of post-colonial studies, in particular how colonialism has profoundly impacted the indigenous peoples of Asia, Africa, Australia and the Americas in terms of power relations, economy and politics, has been missing from the Polish academic discourse.[3] The world history secondary education curriculum ends with the collapse of the Soviet Union (Wodowska 2019). Not only do many young Poles have no idea that Polish migrants and refugees were welcomed and supported by other nations, such as Iran and Mexico, in the past (Lukas 1977; Naeimi and Massoudi 2020), but also lack the intellectual tools to understand the religious and ethnic diversity of the contemporary world. As a result, diverse 'Others', including Muslims – are perceived and narrated as a homogenous, alien and threatening entity (Markowska-Manista 2016). The common trope in staff diversity training workshops at Polish HEIs – dressing up in ethnic costumes such as abayas or saris in order to understand the culture – is an indicator of the problem.

A further challenge is related to how discourses about Islam and Muslims are currently produced in Polish academia. First, the geographic scope of the study of Islam comprises mostly the Middle East and North Africa region. Secondly, in contrast to Polish academic departments studying Arabic language, literature and linguistics which have a relatively long history reaching back to the 1920s, departments studying politics, societies or international affairs of

---

[2] For example, reporting on Islam in Europe in the state-run TVP Info is centred on incidents in Poland's neighbour, Germany, portrayed as a country overrun by Muslim immigrants and refugees, unable to take control of its internal security. For a more detailed overview of such reporting, see Piela (2019, 2020a, 2020b).

[3] At the time of writing of this chapter, only four Polish public universities offered modules on colonial/post-colonial studies: the University of Warsaw, Jagiellonian University, the Adam Mickiewicz University in Poznań and the University of Wrocław.

Muslim-majority countries were only established as late as in the first decade of the twenty-first century. The first were those at the Department of Middle and Far East, Jagiellonian University, founded in 2000, and the Department of Middle East and North Africa, University of Łódź, founded in 2003. (Islamic studies did branch out of Arabic studies in the 1970s at the Arabic and Islamic Studies Department at the University of Warsaw, but it has lost its momentum. Currently, the department offers only degrees Arabic philology with a focus on language or literature.) As of 2021, there is not a single undergraduate or postgraduate 'Islamic studies' programme of study in Poland. Teaching about Islam in the form of discrete modules is mostly done under the auspices of Arab studies, Middle Eastern studies and security studies, as well as religious studies and theology at major Polish universities.

The loosely defined 'world of Islam' has never been of vital interest to Polish academia, as most attention has been devoted to countries and regions that are directly geopolitically significant to Poland (North America, Western Europe, Eastern Europe, Russia) or culturally similar (Eastern Europe). This has slowly begun to change in the early twenty-first century, marked by the 9/11 terror attacks and Huntington's notion of the clash of civilisations. The Polish public also wanted to have access to meaningful explanations and interpretation of these events. With a few notable exceptions, Polish Arabic-language specialists generally ceded the study of the new socio-political realities to other disciplines. Their linguistic and literary backgrounds would have been insufficient to effectively study political Islam in the contemporary world, the topic that attracts enormous attention at the moment. Soon, the new vacuum was occupied by political scientists and security studies experts who may have been unfamiliar with post-colonial studies literature, thus failing to provide a more nuanced perspective on Islam and Muslims. At the same time, the rise of interest in the Islamic world caused by international events such as 9/11 or the 'refugee crisis' in Europe have created demands for simple explanations of complex problems tailored specifically for Polish audiences. In academia, this translates into widely accepted stereotypical framing of research questions. In the following part of this chapter, we discuss our data which illustrates the general points made so far.

Unsurprisingly, a considerable number of the analysed student research projects in sociology, theology, anthropology, cultural studies and security studies focus on topics widely perceived as controversial, in particular the role of women in Islam, conversions to Islam or 'Islamist terrorism' (Moore 2012). This interest appears to correlate with Islam's increased profile in Polish media reporting and politics since Poland's military involvement in the invasions of Afghanistan and Iraq and throughout the moral panic of the 'refugee crisis' of 2015–2017. These topics are certainly common as points of departure for undergraduate students at

Western[4] HEIs. However, having previously taught, supervised and externally examined undergraduate dissertations in Islamic studies or sociology of Islam at several UK HEIs, we have noted that the academic instruction and supervision process allows for addressing narratives of anti-Muslim prejudice in student research. Supervisors who have integrated critical race theory (Crenshaw 1995), Islamophobia studies (Kumar 2012; Kundnani 2014), indigenous and post-colonial feminism (Spivak 1988; Mohanty 1991; Mojab 1998), and critical Islamic studies (Ali 2006; Wadud 2006; Hidayatullah 2014) into their teaching methodologies have at their disposal the intellectual apparatus of these disciplines that effectively deconstruct stereotypes stemming from racialisation of Islam (Galonnier 2015; Selod 2015), White and Christian right supremacy (Burlein 2002; Jones 2020), paternalistic feminism (Crosby 2014), and securitisation policies that target Muslims and other minorities (Kundnani 2014).

The dissertation abstracts that we have analysed inevitably show no such beneficial impact on student research. In our investigation, we do not aim to single out individuals; rather, we indicate areas in which academic instruction/supervision in Poland appears to lag behind in terms of providing students with cutting-edge intellectual tools that are likely to improve learning outcomes. We see the abstract as an important overview of an academic work that outlines the rationale, argument, structure, methodology and findings (Biggam 2015). An abstract that lacks these vital elements suggests that the main body of work may neglect these aspects too. In the final part of this chapter, we suggest practical recommendations for supervisors/mentors of student dissertations and explain why it is important to address the problem of inadequate provision in terms of supervision of Polish student dissertations that focus on Islam and Muslims.

The Study

This chapter is inspired, to a large degree, by abstracts downloaded by a research assistant from open-access Polish dissertation databases published online by twelve universities. Not all universities publish such data; some of them list only the dissertation title and the supervisor's name. The searches were made with

---

[4] The terms 'West' and 'Western' we use throughout this chapter are deployed with an awareness of the problematic and hierarchical vision of the world divided into 'East' and 'West', analysed famously by Said in his now classic work *Orientalism* (1978). Listing countries or regions that are considered to be a part of the West is not helpful without noting the problematic power dynamics of colonialism and neoliberalism. However, although much of contemporary social theory focuses on deconstructing 'the topic, the authority, and the assumed primacy of "the West"'(Young 1990: 19), it is difficult to disentangle oneself from the East–West dichotomy because it has infused public discourse globally, and this is reflected in the data we analysed. For Poland, the dichotomy East–West is troubling given its history of Soviet bloc membership and the 'borderland' fairly peripheral location.

the use of two key words: 'Islam' and 'Muslims'. The majority of the dissertations whose abstracts we read were written between 2009 and 2018.

The dissertations whose abstracts we reviewed were located within humanities and social science disciplines. This chapter does not intend to point fingers at specific faculty members or departments, but, rather, uses the abstracts as an indicator of a wider problem of how Islam and Muslims are addressed as a research topic in Polish academia. Therefore, we have decided against listing specific disciplines or departments, as some of them are easily recognisable, and we prefer to preserve their anonymity. We have also made a conscious decision to not quote the abstracts verbatim for the same reason.

In the first round of data-screening (Table 10.1), we identified N = 1,892 dissertations on the basis of keyword searches in the titles. They were grouped into fifteen broad categories. In the second round (Table 10.2), we downloaded all publicly accessible abstracts (N = 188) of the identified dissertations. Having coded independently 25 per cent of the final data corpus, we collaboratively developed a data coding schema that reflected the key themes emerging from the data. Due to institutional variations, the abstracts were not consistent in terms of content or structure: some of them included a brief mention of the literature, research questions, methods, findings and conclusions, but others consisted only of a general reflection on the topic.

The boundaries between topics were extremely porous; for example, the theme of 'Muslim women' ran through in 35 per cent of abstracts of dissertations whose main focus was 'terrorism', and in just under 75 per cent of dissertations whose main focus was conversion to Islam. The theme of media representations appeared in 90 per cent of abstracts of dissertations whose main focus was Islamophobia, and so forth. The distribution of topics in Tables 10.1 and 10.2 is different, as we did not have access to dissertation abstracts of all dissertations whose titles were published by respective HEIs. Given the space limitations, we have focused on the most popular paradigm, 'clash of civilisations', the two most common topics (terrorism and women in Islam), and ubiquitous semantic slippages as a symptom of racialisation of Islam in Poland.

Table 10.1 Phase 1: Distribution of Topics in the Topics-only Data Corpus

13	Refugees	110	Media, including social media
21	Religious practices in Islam	115	Islamic–Christian relations
29	Islamophobia	116	Islamic fundamentalism
37	Islamisation	118	Family, marriage in Islam
59	Conversion to Islam	173	Islam in the Polish context
67	Miscellaneous	357	Muslim women
81	Multiculturalism, integration, assimilation	532	Terrorism
85	Islamic state	1,892	Total

Table 10.2 Phase 2: Distribution of Topics in the Abstract Data Corpus

3	Refugees	12	Islam versus Christianity/Islamic–Christian relations
3	Entrepreneurship and finance	13	Islamic state
8	Islamophobia in Western Europe and Poland	13	Islam and Muslims in the media, including social media; representations
5	Islamic fundamentalism	14	Multiculturalism, integration, assimilation
6	'Islamisation' (including non-Western nations)	22	Miscellaneous
9	Women's conversion to Islam in Poland	25	Terrorism and jihad
10	Islam in the Polish context including Polish attitudes to Islam and Muslims	34	Women in Islam, veiling, Muslim feminism
11	Family, marriage in Islam, including interreligious marriage	188	Total

We made a collective decision to not use direct quotes from the abstracts, again, so as to preserve the anonymity of the authors and institutions.

CLASH OF CIVILISATIONS AND THE BINARIES OF THE SELF

The concept of the clash of civilisations is much older than Samuel Huntington's highly contested thesis (1993 and 1996). Although 9/11 is often considered as the 'beginning of the crisis' that is rooted in Islam, Arjana (2015) argues that 'Muslims are the monsters of the present, phantasms that result from an imaginary Islam that has been shaped over many centuries.' Bazian (2018) traces the origins of this discourse to the early Byzantine empire, when the leaders of the Church had to defend its place in a region being quickly dominated by Muslims.

At this point we want to focus on Bazian's claim that pertains to more recent history as it offers a possible viable rationale for the widespread use of Huntington's book as a theoretical framework for many dissertations on Islam in social science disciplines which constitute the majority of our corpus. Bazian (2018) claims that after the end of the Cold War, Huntington's thesis became one of the main contenders as new framework for understanding the global political order according to reified binaries of the self. Despite being refuted as simplistic and not based on evidence (see Said's article 'The Clash of Ignorance' (2001) and Ashford 2017), it also became an important foundation for the security agendas that followed 9/11 and security studies itself. Musgrove (2017) writes that 'the longevity of Huntington's thesis becomes more explicable when we treat it not as scholarship aimed at skeptics but as a sermon preached to the faithful'.

Although only three out of the 188 abstracts in our corpus mention Huntington's thesis (1996), the clash of civilisations paradigm forms, implicitly or explicitly, a conceptual backbone of some 53 per cent of the analysed abstracts. A foundation for the now classic Islamophobic argument, it was uncritically adopted chiefly in abstracts of dissertations focused on terrorism, media representations of Islam, multiculturalism, Islamist fundamentalism, Islamic state and 'Islamisation', as well as the majority of abstracts of the 'Women in Islam' category. Islam and Muslims are constructed as ubiquitously backward, regressive, traditional, uncivilized, violent and irrational, while the West was portrayed as modern, progressive, civilised, civilising, egalitarian, peaceful, scientific and rational. Most strikingly, the West is pictured as secular (despite frequent simultaneous claims of Europe's Christian heritage and commitment) and Muslims/the 'Muslim world' as automatically religious.

Here, the process of globalisation is often interpreted as somehow previously overlooked Muslim-majority countries to which they now have to adapt. 'Globalisation' is usually used as a loose synonym for 'modernisation', without the recognition that backlash against cultural homogenisation, a key feature of globalisation, occurs without regard to the imagined West–East divide, notably in places like Ireland, Catalonia and the Basque religion. Thus, narrowly defined globalisation is yet another plane on which the false dichotomy is deployed.

In the data corpus, Poles are considered a group separate from both Western Europeans and Muslims. All three, however, are reified, static and homogeneous. While the relationship between the first two groups is problematic in the writings of Polish students (which may reflect the discomfort of inhabiting the imagined borderland between the West and the East and the resultant power dynamics), it is clear that regardless of that, Muslims and Islam are the 'Other'. Rhetorical construction of Poland and Poles as non-Western is particularly useful for narratives, common in Poland, that cast Muslims and refugees as the 'problem that belongs to/of the West', as a fallout of colonialism (Hall and Mikulska-Jolles 2016).

Although Poland/Poles were not categorised as Western, they were definitely considered as European. The sentiment that Poland is the bulwark of Christian Europe was expressed frequently. However, Poles were portrayed in the abstracts as individualistic (a feature commonly ascribed to Western cultures), in contrast to 'intrinsically collectivistic' Muslims, neatly slotting both groups into 'modern' and 'pre-modern' categories (Kusserow 1999) (without any reference to the fact that a comparison between a national and a religious group necessarily involves a fundamental conflation of concepts; it would be much more difficult to argue this point using a comparison between Catholics and Muslims). It is then striking how the presence of Islam and Muslims seems to affect modalities of national identity: a boundary is drawn between Poland and the West as a strategy of avoidance (of taking responsibility for the real issues of tackling hate crime in Poland, or taking in refugees), but stereotypical aspects of Western-ness are keenly incorporated into the 'Polish–European' identity in the dubious clash of civilisations scenario. This leads us to the conclusion that ironically, Islam and Muslims function in the Polish imaginary as the 'Other' that is doubly constitutive of the Polish 'Self'(Hall 1992: 314).

'Islamic Terrorism'[5]

In the data, Islam and terrorism were considered to be overlapping entities and portrayed as the main security risk for Europe. The peaceful existence of European Muslims who have lived here for generations was largely dismissed or, in a few abstracts, framed as the 'fifth column' secretly supporting terrorism. Many abstracts in the data corpus enthusiastically embraced the official rationale for the 'War on Terror' (i.e., combatting global terrorist networks) and the subsequent presence of Allied troops in Afghanistan and Iraq as an antidote against terrorism, despite its questionable results in terms of civilian casualties and the limited capacity of this approach for defeating dispersed terrorist networks. 9/11 and the 'War on Terror' (nicknamed by some commentators (i.e., Daalder and Lindsay 2001) as the 'new Cold War') were perceived as a confirmation of Huntington's thesis which is dominant and accepted uncritically in the abstracts that pertain to terrorism. The kind of terrorism motivated by radical Islamist ideology seems to be a direct consequence of the implied divide between Islam and the West. The acts of terrorism carried out by fringe groups of Muslims are uncritically ascribed to Muslims or Islam. The clash of civilisations thesis is used widely to explain the acts of terrorism in cultural terms, without any acknowledgement as to the complex historical, political and socio-economic contexts of terrorism.

'Islamic' terrorism is treated as an object of study that is separate from its historical, political, social and economic contexts. None of the analysed abstracts referenced the impacts of colonialism, military conflicts incited, funded, armed and supported by Western powers in Muslim countries, plundering of natural resources, pitting local populations against each other, support for local dictatorships that impoverished populations. Right-wing, White supremacist terrorism (which often targets those who are racialised as the Other, including Muslims and people of Colour), a threat that is much more widespread, yet underestimated in the West (Wong 2011; Koehler 2016; Aaronson 2019; Bergengruen

---

[5] In the Polish language there is no word that would reflect the differences between 'Islamic' and 'Islamist'. We have decided to translate the Polish adjective 'islamski' as 'Islamic', since almost all the abstracts make a case for Islam being a scriptural source of terrorism.

and Hennigan 2019), was not mentioned in the context of global security risk. Not a single abstract addressed the fact that most terrorist attacks happen in Muslim-majority countries, and that Muslims make up by far most of the victims of terrorism (National Counter-terrorism Center 2011). This reflects the process of dehumanisation of victims who are cast as the 'Other', often fuelled by the media which focus on 'Muslim against non-Muslim' terrorism as a much more serious threat than 'domestic' terrorism, portrayed as enacted by troubled individuals (Powell 2011). This sort of messaging constructs victims like 'us', who evoke sympathy, and victims unlike 'us', 'collateral damage', whose demise is considered inconsequential and unworthy of attention. This is reflected (and also driven) by hateful narratives in Polish social media about refugees from the Middle East and Africa attempting to cross over to Europe by boat and drowning in the process (Guzek 2019).

On the one hand, Islamic terrorists are bombastically portrayed as a powerful, all-encompassing destructive force that threatens the West, in particular its political systems. Simultaneously, they are religiously motivated, fanatical and impossible to negotiate with. Here Islam is implied to be the ideology that feeds the movement (this is the second reason for why it is dangerous). They are variably presented as wanting to destroy political or belief systems, both of which are steeped in power and identity struggles (Margolis 2018). It is poignant how in this narrative Islam, as an entity, is often constructed as merely a 'problem' of the world that has to be addressed, rather than a part of the world itself.

Women in Islam

The topic of women in Islam is the focus of intense interest among Polish students writing about Islam; in addition to dissertations directly engaging the topic (thirty-four), some aspect of Muslim femininities was broached in all dissertations on family and marriage in Islam (eleven) and conversions (nine). The majority of analysed pieces reproduced the predictable stereotypes about Muslim women (referred to in a few abstracts as 'female Mahommedans'). They were described being oppressed by their families, in particular family members. The belief that Muslim women had to obey their husbands was deployed uncritically. The Islamic dress code was constructed as a particular dimension of this patriarchal oppression, with a widely held belief that Muslim women had to cover their faces, despite the niqab and the burka being worn by only a small minority (Piela 2021). This misconception may have its roots in a multifold increase of reporting, also in Poland, on women in Afghanistan after the US-led invasion invariably accompanied by photos of women wearing burkas. The burka was constructed in the political discourse as one of the key reasons why Afghani women had to be liberated, gaining geopolitical significance (Khiabany and Williamson 2011).

In one particularly poignant abstract, two imagined, singular subjectivities representative of all Polish and all Muslim women were constructed, with the author concluding that the Polish Christian woman has not only full agency, but also imagination and wealth, and does not bear any responsibility for her actions. This conviction is astounding given the very traditional gender roles (Duda-Mikulin 2015), as well as limitations on reproductive rights (Król and Pustułka 2018), the lack of legal protections for survivors of domestic violence, and a glaring gender-based pay gap in Poland (Bystydzienski 2005). 'The Muslim woman' produced in this and many other abstracts is completely devoid of agency. The deployed synecdoche resonates with 'Muslimwoman', defined by cooke (2008: 140) as 'the ascription of a label that reduces all diversity to a single image', one in which religion and gender are intertwined so tightly that they became one. The face veil is deployed here and in many other abstracts as a symbol of ubiquitous submission, in spite of the fact that only a small minority of Muslim women wear it. The veil or headscarf are often referred to as a straightforward requirement without recognition that many Muslim women do not cover their hair.

Misconceptions about Islam and its holy texts emerged particularly clearly in an abstract that discussed the concept of women's 'vocation for family life' (a Polish-Catholic turn of phrase) in Polish Muslims' (unspecified) publications, as well as in the Qur'an and legal Islamic texts. The irony of the argument that women's primary 'mission' to be a wife and a mother stems from 'Allah's edict' is highlighted by the immensely traditional gender role prescriptions in predominantly Catholic Poland (Graff 2001; Ryan et al. 2009). Although the debate about 'feminist edges' of Islam and the Qur'an continues (Hidayatullah 2014), there is largely a consensus that Muslim women and men's primary responsibility lies in the spiritual realm of believing in and obeying God (Badawi 2004). This supersedes any earthly duties and relationships, suggested by the abstract. The Polish-Catholic lens through which some students study and perceive Islam and cultural mores of Muslims (in particular, Polish Muslims who are inevitably enmeshed in both the 'Polish-Catholic' an 'Polish Muslim' ethical frameworks) may lead to conflation of these contexts. Furthermore, by treating all Muslims as naturally and automatically religious, students often tend to ascribe religious motivations for all their actions. Sedgwick (2013: 281) describes it as a 'classic methodological error to seek to explain everything that is done by a person or society that happens to be Muslim in terms of Islam'.

Another widely held belief regarding the role of women in Islam is related to paid employment; Muslim women are believed to not to be 'allowed' to work or study. Such generalisations are complicated by Muslim women's growing university enrolment numbers both in the West and Muslim-majority countries

(Ahmad 2001; Mir 2014; Winn 2016), as well as the existence of multiple barriers to employment, in particular, racist and anti-Muslim prejudice in the workplace (Open Society Institute 2004) that may prevent Muslim women from freely practising their religion, for example, wearing the headscarf or praying.

Some methodological aspects of the dissertations (where they are indicated in the abstract) often posed a problem for the authors. The 'role' or 'position' of women in *Islam* is often assessed using problematic types of data. One of the abstracts listed articles in a lifestyle magazine as data appropriate for assessing the 'role of religion in female Muslims' lives', rather than the media representations of this topic. It also considered unspecified 'statistics' from two Muslim-majority countries and described 'honour' crimes as affecting all Muslim-majority countries in a homogeneous manner. It is unclear how this medley of data types and foci may be helpful in answering the posed question, one that seems to call for insider perspectives, that is, narratives of Muslim women themselves. The difficulty with obtaining primary data such as qualitative interviews or ethnographic observations could be resolved by conducting secondary data analysis of data published in monographs and reports available online.

Using scriptural sources as the sole determinant of women's role in Islam, which we observed frequently in the data, leads to collapsing scriptural and 'lived' Islam. This in turn tends to erase the agency of believers who engage in active interpretation of texts, beliefs and practices. It also neglects the hierarchy of Islamic texts, historical and social contexts, and debates on hadith authenticity, vital to dynamic engagement with Islam (Armajani 2004). This reified conception of Islam (as an ideology, a structure or a heterogeneous collection of beliefs, practices and morals) portrayed in our data corpus be challenged with Asad's concept of Islam as a discursive tradition:

> A [discursive] tradition consists essentially of discourses that seek to instruct practitioners regarding the correct form and purpose of a given practice that, precisely because it is established, has a history. These discourses relate conceptually to a past (when the practice was instituted, and from which the knowledge of its point and proper performance has been transmitted) and a future (how the point of that practice can best be secured in the short or long term, or why it should be modified or abandoned), through a present (how it is linked to other practices, institutions, and social conditions). An Islamic discursive tradition is simply a tradition of Muslim discourse that addresses itself to conceptions of the Islamic past and future, with reference to a particular Islamic practice in the present ... Clearly, *not everything Muslims say and do belongs to an Islamic discursive tradition*. (Asad 2009: 21–2, emphasis added)

The topic of 'women's position in Islam' is further fraught by the lack of differentiation between Sunni, Shi'i and Sufi perspectives, as well as conservative, traditionalist, radical, revivalist, progressive and critical perspectives within Islam (the debate on the applicability of these terms notwithstanding) is a different example of slippage. For example, Saudi Arabia, where a largely conservative interpretation of Islam derived from the Hanbali school is the dominant one, was used twice as a representative example of women's position in Islam. Other abstracts that broached this topic framed it using concepts and understandings common in the loosely defined conservative family of interpretations of Islam. There were, however, two outliers in the data: abstracts that focused on the role of Muslim feminism. They referenced books by Amina Wadud, Asma Barlas and Leila Ahmed which have not, to our knowledge, been translated into Polish. Availability of key titles in this subfield (known as critical or feminist Islamic studies) to Polish students would offer alternative routes of exploration of this topic.

Semantic Slippages and Racialisation

In our analysis, we paid special attention to terminology. As many as twenty-nine of the abstracts contained what we called, borrowing from Fife (2004: 64), 'semantic slippages'[6]: the word 'Muslims' was used interchangeably with 'Arabs' (which obfuscates the existence of Arab Christians and non-Arab Muslims who incidentally make up the majority of Muslims worldwide). This conflation is fairly common among non-Muslims (Moghul 2010). However, the more surprising semantic slippage we encountered was that between Arabic and Turkish countries or cultures. In one of the abstracts, the author stated that Turkey was an excellent example of how 'global values' influenced Arabic countries. Such factual errors are not ideologically neutral: vital differences are passed over; identities are erased; and blanket ascription of negative qualities becomes possible. This apparent carelessness and resultant slippages are vital in the larger process of racialisation, defined by Garner and Selod as follows:

> The process of racialization entails ascribing sets of characteristics viewed as inherent to members of a group because of their physical or cultural traits. These are not limited to skin tone or pigmentation but include a myriad of attributes including *cultural traits such as language, clothing, and religious practices*. The characteristics thus emerge as 'racial' as an outcome of the

---

[6] The meaning of each of two or more words, objects or performances melds or slides, one into the other' (Fife 2004: 64).

process. Racialization provides the language needed to discuss newer forms of racism that are not only based on skin colour, as well as older forms. (Garner and Selod 2015: 12, emphasis added)

We have found evidence of racialisation of Muslims in the data. In fourteen of the abstracts, references to Muslim 'mentality', 'character', 'psyche' as aggressive, manipulative, greedy were made. Pseudo-psychosocial discourse that permeates this narrative is evocative of Bernard Lewis' article titled 'The Roots of Muslim Rage' (1990). It may also be traced to historical views of denizens of the Orient (Said 1978). Such stereotyping of Muslims by non-Muslims is frequent (see Fischer et al. 2007) and amplified by media which immediately draw connections to terrorism; it influences public opinion and, importantly, increases public support for policies targeting Muslims (Miles-Novelo and Anderson 2020) Although in Poland it may be compelling to dismiss these mechanisms as affecting mainly the West, it is worth noting the low tolerance for religious and cultural difference here (Sidorenko 2008), and the enthusiasm, in 2001–2002, for the Polish participation in the US-led occupation and plundering of Afghanistan and Iraq[7] (Lorenc 2008). In view of these social trends in Poland, student projects promoting anti-Muslim stereotypes such as those mentioned above have very troubling resonance.

Concluding Remarks

In December 2019, the Centre for Research on Public Opinion (CBOS) issued the results of the latest survey on Polish attitudes to Islam and Muslims (CBOS 2019). Forty-five per cent of the respondents declared a negative attitude to Islam, while only 17 per cent declared a positive attitude to this group. Only 14 per cent said they personally knew a Muslim. Ironically, 63 per cent of respondents see Muslims as intolerant towards other cultures and religions. These alarming attitudes translate into hate crime against Muslims, hostility towards refugees, and support for military operation against Muslim-majority countries that inevitably lead to mass civilian casualties. This context calls for a radical rethinking of how teaching about Islam and Muslims is approached and operationalised in Poland.

Our findings suggest that Polish students who write about Islam and Muslims do tend to form their reflections on the basis of stereotypes that underpin the

---

[7] Public support for the Polish involvement in the 'War on Terror' fluctuated between 77 per cent in September 2001, down to 43 per cent in January 2002, and up to 75 per cent in April 2002. In 2008, it plummeted to 21 per cent (Lorenc 2008).

'transplanted' global Islamophobic discourse, adapted and sometimes refracted by the local Polish-Catholic context. These frames of reference are reflected by assumptions, questions and conclusions offered in the abstracts. Based on the analysis, as well as our own teaching experiences, we have developed a checklist for educators to ensure that the projects being assessed do not perpetuate the most common stereotypes related to Islam and Muslims.

Successfully challenging misinformation and stereotypes about Islam and Muslims may be achievable through teaching a module 'against Islamophobia', rather than Islam itself, argues Green (2019). This option is more likely to be available in courses directly or indirectly referencing Islam, such as Islamic studies, global Muslim studies or Middle Eastern studies. Unfortunately, teaching 'against Islamophobia' is unlikely to be recognised as a priority in departments of political/security/cultural studies, where many of the investigated dissertations have been produced, at least for some time, given a sharp right turn in Polish politics, and, to some extent, in Polish higher education. However, the data analysed here may point to some modest ways of addressing Islamophobic bias we have observed.

Checklist for Student Dissertations

Avoid:

- Framing research problems by uncritically using the notion of a clash of civilisations and classic Orientalist tropes Islam (backward, regressive, traditional, uncivilised, violent, irrational) vs 'the West' (modern, progressive, civilised, peaceful, scientific, rational).
- Collapsing scriptural and 'lived' Islam (Qur'an and hadith vs practices of Muslims).
- Discussions of theological matters without placing them in historical, cultural and other contexts.
- Glossing over the interpretive diversity in Islam – especially omitting Shi'a and Sufi perspectives without explicitly stating that one focuses on the Sunni perspective, but also differences between progressive, conservative, radical Islam, etc.).
- Essentialising statements ('Islam is/Muslims are X').
- Semantic slippages and factual inconsistencies (fundamentalism vs terrorism; Arabs vs Muslims).
- Generalising the Polish perspective to wider groups.
- Discussing Islamist terrorism without any reference to its counterpart – White supremacist terrorism (such as the terrorist attacks in Christchurch, Norway, Hanau).

Practical Recommendations for Educators Who Teach about Islam and Muslims

- Decolonise the curriculum – go beyond the standard frames that show Islam exclusively in an antagonistic manner (the clash of civilisations paradigm); include scholars from regions and cultures under study; discuss colonialism and its impact on societies; use a variety of Muslim voices in teaching – interviews, books, social media content, invite Muslims for guest teaching.
- Where content is related to Islam and Muslims, make connections explicit – for example, instead of discussing natural resources in the Middle East out of context, broach the consequences of mining and trading for the populations living there, in the past and today.
- Discuss orientalist tropes in this genre. A lot of anti-Muslim stereotypes are distributed by popular culture. A translation of *Not Without My Daughter* (Mahmoody 1987) was the first remarkable example in that category, but the trope has been extensively reproduced in literature about 'harem insiders' (the 'Arab princess' trope).
- Discuss Islamophobic hate crime statistics, politicians' statements and media content (in the annual European Islamophobia Report and CAIR's Civil Rights Report).
- Avoid cultural appropriation through 'dressing up as Muslims' in the process of delivering teaching about Islam and Muslims (this is a popular practice in Poland).
- Expose assumptions about Muslims – we suggest the 'draw a typical Muslim' activity and discussion of results.

References

Aaronson, T. (2019). 'Terrorism's Double Standard: Violent Far-Right Extremists are Rarely Prosecuted as Terrorists', *The Intercept*, 23 March, available at: https://theintercept.com/2019/03/23/domestic-terrorism-fbi-prosecutions, last accessed 27 August 2020.

Ahmad, F. (2001). 'Modern Traditions? British Muslim Women and Academic Achievement', *Gender and Education* 13(2): 137–52.

Ahmadi, S. and D. Cole (eds) (2020). *Islamophobia in Higher Education: Combating Discrimination and Creating Understanding*. Sterling, VA: Stylus.

Ali, K. (2006). *Sexual Ethics and Islam: Feminist Reflections on Qur'an, Hadith, and Jurisprudence*. London: Oneworld.

Arjana, S. R. (2015). *Muslims in the Western Imagination*. Oxford: Oxford University Press.

Armajani, J. (2004). *Dynamic Islam: Liberal Muslim Perspectives in a Transnational Age*. Dallas, TX: University Press of America.

Asad, T. (2009). 'The Idea of Anthropology of Islam', *Qui Parle* 17(2): 1–30.

Ashford, E. (2017). 'What We Get Wrong about the Clash of Civilizations', *Cato Unbound* 6, February, available at: https://www.cato-unbound.org/2017/02/06/emma-ashford/what-we-get-wrong-about-clash-civilizations.

Badawi, L. (2004). 'Islam', in J. Holm and J. Bowker (eds), *Women in Religion*. London: Continuum, pp. 84–112.

Balsamska, J. et al. (2012). 'Pomiędzy tolerancją a dyskryminacją. Raport z badań' ('Between Tolerance and Discrimination. Research Report'). Fundacja na Rzecz Różnorodności Polistrefa, available at: http://laickie.pl/wp-content/uploads/2012/12/Raport-z-badan-do-internetu.pdf.

Balsamska, J. et al. (2016). 'Pomiędzy obowiązkiem a wyborem – etyka i religia w szkołach publicznych w Polsce. Raport z badań' ('Between Obligation and Choice: Ethics and Religious Education Classes in Polish State Schools. Research Report'). Fundacja na Rzecz Różnorodności Polistrefa, available at: https://polistrefa.pl/wp-content/uploads/2018/01/pomiedzy_obowiazkiem_a_wyborem.pdf.

Bazian, H. (2018). 'Islamophobia, "Clash of Civilizations", and Forging a Post-Cold War Order', *Religions* 9(9): 282–95.

Bergengruen, V. and W. J. Hennigan (2019). '"We are Being Eaten from Within". Why America is Losing the Battle against White Nationalist Terrorism', *Time*, 8 August, available at: https://time.com/564 7304/white nationalist-terrorism-united-states.

Biggam, J. (2015). *Succeeding with your Master's Dissertation*. Milton Keynes: Open University Press.

Burlein, A. (2002) *Lift High the Cross: Where White Supremacy and the Christian Right Converge*. Durham, NC: Duke University Press.

Bystydzienski, J. M. (2005). 'Negotiating the New Market: Women, Families, Women's Organizations and the Economic Transition in Poland', *Journal of Family and Economic Issues* 26(2): 239–65.

Centre for Research on Public Opinion (CBOS) (2019). 'Postawy wobec islamu i muzułmanów' ('Attitudes toward Islam and Muslims'), CBOS, December 2019, available at: https://www.cbos.pl/SPISKOM.POL/2019/K_148_19.PDF.

Cesari, J. (2011). 'Islamophobia in the West: A Comparison between the United States and Europe', in J. L. Esposito and Ibrahim Kalin (eds), *Islamophobia: The Challenge of Pluralism in the 21st Century*. New York: Oxford University Press, pp. 21–45.

cooke, m. (2008). 'Deploying the Muslimwoman', *Journal of Feminist Studies in Religion* 24(1): 91–9.

Crenshaw, K. W. (1995). 'Mapping the Margins: Intersectionality, Identity Politics, and Violence against Women of Color', in K. Crenshaw, N. Gotanda, G. Peller and K. Thomas (eds), *Critical Race Theory: The Key Writings That Formed the Movement*. New York: New Press, pp. 357–83.

Crosby, E. (2014). 'Faux Feminism: France's Veil Ban as Orientalism', *Journal of International Women's Studies* 15(2): 46–60.

Daalder, I. H. and J. M. Lindsay (2001). 'Nasty, Brutish and Long: America's War on Terrorism', Brookings Institution, 1 December, available at: https://www.brookings.edu/articles/nasty-brutish-and-long-americas-war-on-terrorism.

Duda-Mikulin, E. A. (2015). 'Gendered Migrations: An Exploration of the Influence of Migration on Polish Women's Perception of Gender Roles', PhD dissertation, University of Salford, available at: http://usir.salford.ac.uk/id/eprint/35634.

Elbih, R. N. (2013). 'Pedagogy of Post 9/11 United States: Muslim American Students' Experiences, Teachers' Pedagogies, and Textbook Analysis', PhD dissertation, University of New Mexico, available at: https://digitalrepository.unm.edu/cgi/viewcontent.cgi?article=1035&context=educ_llss_etds.
Fife, W. (2004). 'Semantic Slippage as a New Aspect of Authenticity: Viking Tourism on the Northern Peninsula of Newfoundland', *Journal of Folklore Research* 41(1): 61–84.
Fischer, P., T. Greitemeyer and A. Kastenmüller (2007). 'What Do We Think About Muslims? The Validity of Westerners' Implicit Theories about the Associations between Muslims' Religiosity, Religious Identity, Aggression Potential, and Attitudes toward Terrorism', *Group Processes & Intergroup Relations* 10(3): 373–82.
Galonnier, J. (2015). 'The Racialization of Muslims in France and the United States: Some Insights from White Converts to Islam', *Social Compass* 62(4): 570–83.
Garner, S. and S. Selod (2015). 'The Racialization of Muslims: Empirical Studies of Islamophobia', *Critical Sociology* 41(1): 9–19.
Górak-Sosnowska, K. (2006). 'Wizerunek islamu w Polsce na przykładzie podręczników szkolnych' ('The Image of Islam in Poland based on Representations in School Textbooks'), in K. Górak-Sosnowska, K. Pędziwiatr and P. Kubicki (eds), *Islam i obywatelskość w Europie*. Warszawa: Elipsa, pp. 237–51.
Górak-Sosnowska, K. (2016). 'Islamophobia without Muslims? The Case of Poland', *Journal of Muslims in Europe* 5(2): 190–204.
Górak-Sosnowska K. and M. Pachocka (2019). 'Inventing the Muslim Other in Poland (and Why Does it Differ from Western Europe)', in K. Górak-Sosnowska, J. Misiuna and M. Pachocka (eds), *Muslim Minorities and the Refugee Crisis in Europe*. Warszawa: SGH, pp. 223–34.
Graff, A. (2001). *Świat bez kobiet. Płeć w polskim życiu publicznym* (*The World without Women: Gender in Polish Public Life*). Warszawa: W.A.B.
Green, T. (2019). 'Teaching Islamophobia in the Age of ISIS', in C. Dorroll (ed.), *Teaching Islamic Studies in the Age of ISIS, Islamophobia, and the Internet*. Bloomington: Indiana University Press, pp. 125–44.
Guzek, D. (2019). 'Religious Memory on Facebook in Times of Refugee Crisis', *Social Compass* 66(1): 75–93.
Hall, D. and A. Mikulska-Jolles (2016). 'Uprzedzenia, strach, czy niewiedza? Młodzi Polacy o powodach niechęci do przyjmowania uchodźców' ('Prejudice, Fear, or Ignorance? Young Poles on the Reasons for Their Hostility towards Refugees in Poland'), Stowarzyszenie Interwencji Prawnej, available at: https://interwencjaprawna.pl/docs/ARE-116-uprzedzenia-mlodych-polakow.pdf.
Hall, S. (1992). 'The West and the Rest: Discourse and Power', in S. Hall and B. Gieben (eds), *Formations of Modernity*. Cambridge: Polity Press in association with Open University.
Housee, S. (2012). 'What's the Point? Anti-Racism and Students' Voices against Islamophobia', *Race, Ethnicity and Education* 15(1): 101–20.
Hidayatullah, A. (2014). *Feminist Edges of the Qur'an*. New York: Oxford University Press.
Huntington, S. (1993). The Clash of Civilizations? *Foreign Affairs* 72(3): 22–49.

Huntington, S. (1996). *The Clash of Civilizations and the Remaking of World Order.* New York: Simon & Schuster.

Husain, A. (2019). 'Moving Beyond (and Back to) the Black–White Binary: A Study of Black and White Muslims' Racial Positioning in the United States', *Ethnic and Racial Studies* 42(4): 589–606.

Jones, R. P. (2020). *White Too Long: The Legacy of White Supremacy in American Christianity.* New York: Simon & Schuster.

Khiabany, G. and M. Williamson (2011). 'Muslim Women and Veiled Threats: From Civilizing Mission to Clash of Civilizations', in J. Petley and R. Richardson (eds), *Pointing the Finger: Islam and Muslims in the British Media.* London: Oneworld, pp. 173–200.

Kincheloe, J. L., S. R. Steinberg and C. D. Stonebanks (2010). 'Foreword: Re-education against Miseducation', in J. L. Kincheloe, S. R. Steinberg and C. D. Stonebanks (eds), *Teaching Against Islamophobia.* New York: Peter Lang, pp. ix–xii.

Koehler, D. (2016). 'Right-Wing Extremism and Terrorism in Europe: Current Developments and Issues for the Future', *PRISM* 6(2): 85–104.

Konferencja Episkopatu Polski (2010a). 'Programy i podręczniki do nauczania religii obowiązujące w roku szkolnym 2019/20', Komisja Wychowania Katolickiego Konferencji Episkopatu Polski, 4 February 2019, available at: https://katecheza.episk opat.pl/kwk/programy-i-podreczniki.

Konferencja Episkopatu Polski (2010b). 'Podstawa programowa katechezy Kościoła Katolickiego w Polsce', Konferencja Episkopatu Polski. Kraków: WAM.

Konferencja Episkopatu Polski (2010c). 'Program nauczania religii rzymskokatolickiej w przedszkolach i szkołach', Komisja Wychowania Katolickiego Konferencji Episkopatu Polski. Kraków: WAM.

Król, A. and P. Pustułka (2018). 'Women on Strike: Mobilizing against Reproductive Injustice in Poland', *International Feminist Journal of Politics* 20(3): 366–84.

Kumar, D. (2012). *Islamophobia and the Politics of Empire.* Chicago, IL: Haymarket.

Kundnani (2014). *The Muslims are Coming! Islamophobia, Extremism, and the Domestic War on Terror.* London: Verso.

Kusserow, A. (1999). 'Crossing the Great Divide: Anthropological Theories of the Western Self', *Journal of Anthropological Research* 55(4): 541–62.

Lewis, B. (1990). 'The Roots of Muslim Rage', *The Atlantic* 266(3): 47–60.

Lorenc, M. (2008). 'Polska opinia publiczna wobec działań PKW w Afganistanie i Iraku' ('Polish Public Opinion of Polish Military Action in Afghanistan and Iraq'), *Środkowoeuropejskie Studia Polityczne* 2, available at: http://yadda.icm.edu. pl/yadda/element/bwmeta1.element.ojs-doi-10_14746_ssp_2008_2_13/c/9293- 9005.pdf.

Lukas, R. (1977). 'Polish Refugees in Mexico: An Historical Footnote', *Polish Review* 22(2): 73–5.

Mahmoody, B. (1987). *Not Without my Daughter.* New York: St Martin's Press.

Mandes, S. and M. Rogaczewska (2013). '"I don't Reject the Catholic Church – the Catholic Church Rejects Me": How Twenty- and Thirty-somethings in Poland Re-evaluate their Religion', *Journal of Contemporary Religion* 28(2): 259–76.

Margolis, M. F. (2018). *From Politics to the Pews: How Partisanship and the Political Environment Shape Religious Identity.* Chicago: University of Chicago Press.

Markowska-Manista, U. (2016). 'Walka ze stereotypami odmienności kulturowej – szkolne i pozaszkolne pola bitewne', in M. Dudzikowa and S. Jaskulska (eds), *Twierdza. Szkoła w metamorfozie militarnej. Co w zamian?* Warszawa: Wolters Kluwer, pp. 315–39.

Martino, W. and G. M. Rezai-Rashti (2008). 'The Politics of Veiling, Gender and the Muslim Subject: On the Limits and Possibilities of Anti-racist Education in the Aftermath of September 11', *Discourse: Studies in the Cultural Politics of Education* 29(3): 417–31.

Miles-Novelo, A. and C. A. Anderson (2020). 'The Effect of Media on Public Perception of Muslims in the United States', in A. W. Ata (ed.) *Muslim Minorities and Social Cohesion: Cultural Fragmentation in the West*. London: Routledge.

Mir, S. (2014). *Muslim American Women on Campus: Undergraduate Social Life and Identity*. Durham, NC: University of North Carolina Press.

Moghul, H. (2010). 'Why Arab and Muslim are Not Synonymous', *HuffPost*, 10 November, available at: https://www.huffpost.com/entry/even-the-new-york-times-d_b_766658.

Mohanty, C. T. (1991). 'Under Western Eyes: Feminist Scholarship and Colonial Discourses', in C. T. Mohanty, A. Russo and L. Torres (eds), *Third World Women and the Politics of Feminism*. Indianapolis: Indiana University Press, pp. 51–80.

Mojab, S. (1998). '"Muslim" Women and "Western" Feminists: The Debate on Particulars and Universals', *Monthly Review* 50(7): 19–30.

Moore, D. (2007). *Overcoming Religious Illiteracy: A Cultural Studies Approach to the Study of Religion in Secondary Education*. New York: Palgrave Macmillan.

Moore, J. R. (2012). 'A Challenge for Social Studies Educators: Teaching about Islam, Jihād, and Shari'ah Law', *Social Studies* 103(5): 179–87.

Musgrove, P. (2017). 'The Grim Fantasia of a Civilizational War', *Cato Unbound*, 8 February, available at: https://www.cato-unbound.org/2017/02/08/paul-musgrave/grim-fantasia-civilizational-war.

Naeimi, M. and A. Massoudi (2020). 'Materiality of a Forced Migration in World War II: Archaeology of Displacement of the Polish Exodus in Iran (from 1942)', in J. Symonds and P. Vařeka (eds), *Archaeologies of Totalitarianism, Authoritarianism, and Repression*, Palgrave Studies in Cultural Heritage and Conflict. Cham: Palgrave Macmillan, pp. 107–23.

National Counter-terrorism Center (2011). 'Report on Terrorism', Office of the Director of National Intelligence, Washington DC, available at: https://fas.org/irp/threat/nctc2011.pdf.

Open Society Institute (2004). 'Aspirations and Reality: British Muslims and the Labour Market'. Budapest: Open Society Institute, available at: https://www.opensocietyfoundations.org/uploads/7a81de84-e10e-492f-a5b5-1b012da82fef/british_muslims.pdf.

Piela, A. (2019). 'Islamophobia in Poland 2018', in E. Bayraklı and F. Hafez (eds), *Islamophobia in Europe Report 2018*. Istanbul: Seta Foundation for Political, Economic and Social Research.

Piela, A. (2020a), 'Islamophobia in Poland 2019', In E. Bayraklı and F. Hafez (eds), *Islamophobia in Europe Report 2019*. Istanbul: Seta Foundation for Political, Economic and Social Research.

Piela, A. (2020b). 'Reporting Islam and Muslims in Polish Media: The Case of the 2017 Independence March', in K. Radde-Antweiler and X. Zeiler (eds), *The Routledge Handbook of Religion and Journalism*. London: Routledge.

Piela, A. (2021). *Wearing the Niqab: Muslim Women in the UK and the US*. London: Bloomsbury.

Powell, K. (2011). 'Framing Islam: An Analysis of US Media Coverage of Terrorism since 9/11', *Journal of Communication Studies* 62(1): 90–112.

Renner, J. (2016). 'Poland–Germany: The Ritualisation of Apology', in C. Daase, S. Engert, M. Horelt, J. Renner and R. Strasser (eds), *Apology and Reconciliation in International Relations*. London: Routledge, pp. 71–86.

Ryan, L., R. Sales, M. Tilki and B. Siara (2009). 'Family Strategies and Transnational Migration: Recent Polish Migrants in London', *Journal of Ethnic and Migration Studies* 35(1): 61–77.

Said, E. (1978). *Orientalism*. London: Routledge & Kegan Paul.

Said, E. (2001). 'The Clash of Ignorance', *The Nation*, 4 October, available at: https://www.thenation.com/article/archive/clash-ignorance.

Sedgwick, M. (2013). 'Islam and Popular Culture', in J. T. Kenney and E. Moosa (eds), *Islam in the Modern World*. London: Routledge, pp. 279–98.

Selod, S. (2015). 'Citizenship Denied: The Racialization of Muslim American Men and Women post-9/11', *Critical Sociology* 41(1): 77–95.

Selod, S. and D. G. Embrick (2013). 'Racialization and Muslims: Situating the Muslim Experience in Race Scholarship', *Sociology Compass* 7(8): 644–55.

Sidorenko, E. (2008). 'Which Way to Poland? Re-emerging from Romantic Unity', in M. Myant and T. Cox (eds), *Reinventing Poland: Economic and Political Transformation and Evolving National Identity*. London: Routledge, pp. 100–16.

Spivak, G. C. (1988). 'Can the Subaltern Speak?' in C. Nelson and L. Grossberg (eds), *Marxism and the Interpretation of Culture*. Chicago: University of Illinois Press, pp. 271–313.

Thobani, S. (2006). *Islam in the School Curriculum: Symbolic Pedagogy and Cultural Claims*. London: Bloomsbury.

Wabash Center (2021). Website available at: https://www.wabashcenter.wabash.edu.

Wadud, A. (2006). *Inside the Gender Jihad: Women's Reform in Islam*. Oxford: Oneworld.

Winn, M. K. (2016). 'Women in Higher Education in Iran: How the Islamic Revolution Contributed to an Increase in Female Enrolment', *Global Tides* 10, available at: https://digitalcommons.pepperdine.edu/globaltides/vol10/iss1/10.

Wodowska, J. (2019). 'Bezdrożami historii. Program nauczania historii dla szkoły ponadpodstawowej'. Warszawa: Ośrodek Rozwoju Edukacji, available at: https://static.epodreczniki.pl/portal/f/res/RJANfQcf7hp8U/2/2WPZSwunsW5AUuy41hPJs5P9Q2eR3RCr.pdf.

Wong, F. D. (2011). *Christian Extremism as a Domestic Terror Threat*. Fort Leavenworth, KS: School of Advanced Military Studies, United States Army of Command and General Staff College.

Young, R. (1990). *White Mythologies and the West*. London: Routledge.

Zine, J. (2012). 'Anti-Islamophobia Education as Transformative Pedagogy: Reflections from the Educational Front Lines', *Aula Intercultural* 17 October, available at: https://

aulaintercultural.org/2012/10/17/anti-islamophobia-education-as-transformative-pe dagogy-reflections-from-the-educational-front-lines.

Zwierżdżyński, M. (2017). 'The Politics of Religious Education in Poland after 1990', in S. Ramet and I. Borowik (eds), *Religion, Politics, and Values in Poland*. New York: Palgrave Macmillan, pp. 137–59.

Chapter 11

Theology Faculties in Turkey: Between State, Religion and Politics

Abdurrahman Hendek

Introduction

Religion in education, from religious classes in primary and secondary schools to theology faculties in universities and even to religious symbols in classrooms, has always been a controversial issue in Turkey, a *laïc* (secular) state with a Muslim-majority population. This chapter seeks to map the development of theology faculties in Turkey. It argues that theology faculties have navigated between the confessional and the non-confessional since their establishment, and this has been closely related to the context of Turkish state policy, particularly the politics of religion. The development of the theology faculties will be explored through their history, their core purpose and curriculum, the employment areas to which their graduates progress and their distance-learning programmes. However, first, the religious landscape and politics of religion in Turkey will be provided as a background to the discussion, followed by a brief section on the key terms used in this discussion, namely, 'confessional' and 'non-confessional'.

The Politics of Religion in Turkey

A frequently cited estimate suggests that about 99 per cent of the Turkish population follows Islamic teachings (Minority Rights Group International 2018). Even though Islam, like any other religion, has different denominations, sects and interpretations, the majority of Muslims in Turkey are believed to observe Sunni Islam. There are also Alevis, who are recognised as followers of Islam, and it is estimated that between 10 and 15 per cent of the population follows Alevism (Minority Rights Group International 2018). It is estimated that non-Muslim religious minorities comprise less than 1 per cent of the population (Minority Rights Group International 2018). Moreover, Turkey has never experienced any significant waves of non-Muslim immigration, nor has it experienced a secularisation of society as some Western countries have. In other words, the vast majority of the population has historically remained Muslim. It is likely that because of this, theology faculties have historically been seen and imagined as Islam-centric institutions. However, the issue has always been a question of 'whose' or 'which' Islam, which has been inextricably linked with the politics of religion.

The collapse of the Ottoman Empire, which was considered to be an Islamic empire with a multi-religious and multi-ethnic society, has had a lasting impact on the Republic of Turkey's relationship with religion and ethnicity. The founders of the republic blamed the lack of unity among Ottoman citizens and an 'archaic' interpretation of Islam for the demise of the empire. In response, they sought to build a unified nation based on the concept of a single nationality and culture. A vital aspect of this culture was determined to be Islam, the religion of the vast majority of the population. Even though the founders of Turkey adopted French-inspired laïcism (secularism) and aimed to minimise the role of religion in the public and private sphere, they also regulated – and even promoted – a 'true' or 'rational' Islam, which was deemed compatible with the republican values, including nationalism, secularism and modernism, through state institutions (Berkes 1964; Shively 2008). In other words, through educational institutions, an authorised state version of Islam was, and is still, promoted and any divergence from this was considered archaic, radical, sometimes too soft, and often a threat to the national unity. Perhaps not surprisingly, many Muslim groups have challenged this understanding; some even completely disregarded and avoided the state institutions, which led to the survival of unrecognised and unregulated religious education institutions, such as *madrasas*. However, the politics of religion in Turkey have changed and evolved in accordance with socio-political developments, which transformed the critics into supporters and vice versa, especially following the introduction of the multi-party political system in 1946. These changes have had an impact on the evolution of theology faculties and their relations with *madrasas*, as will be discussed below.

Confessional and Non-confessional

It is important to define the terms 'confessional' and 'non-confessional' used in this chapter. This will be attempted here by reference principally to religious education (RE) literature in the United Kingdom. In RE literature, the terms 'confessional' and 'non-confessional' are often used to define RE approaches employed in state schools. The term 'confessional' often stands for a type of RE that encourages and aims at increasing the pupils' religious commitment; 'non-confessional' refers to educational (or secular) RE that concerns itself with objective and neutral religious study that is assumed to not seek to nurture pupils' faith in a particular belief system (Hendek 2020). At university level, Cush (2009) makes a distinction between theology and religious studies, which resonates with this distinction between 'confessional' and 'non-confessional'. According to Cush theology often implies

> confessionalism, theism, Christianity ... and perhaps more significantly, thinking about the questions raised by religions from one particular perspective, rather than trying to take account of as diverse a range of perspectives as possible. (Cush 2009: 27)

Cush claims, however, that religious studies require 'a *methodologically agnostic* approach' which aims at understanding religions, rather than endorsing or rejecting them (2009: 20–7, emphasis in original). Cush (2009) accepts that such a dichotomy has a degree of oversimplification, and that theology and religious studies, in the context of the United Kingdom, have evolved and have a lot of overlaps, but she maintains that they are still different in important ways. For example, she argues that religious studies, in its non-confessional approach, provides 'better preparation for becoming a teacher of Religious Education in state-funded community schools in England', which is recognised as a non-confessional and multi-faith subject (see also Smart 1988), while theology has vocational connections with Christian communities (Cush 2009: 19–22). Similarly, Smart (1988) makes a distinction between religious studies and theology, stressing the importance of having religious studies that deal with many traditions and where no one tradition has priority in the context of a 'pluralist' society, which has seen a transformation of RE towards the teaching of world religions in state schools. This shows that the debate over the distinction of theology and religious studies is closely related to the transformation of RE into a non-confessional and multi-faith subject in primary and secondary schools in the United Kingdom.

However, such a dichotomy between theology and religious studies is still open for debate. For example, D'Costa (1996) questions the possibility of confessional theology in secular universities. What D'Costa (1996) argues is that there is not a great dissimilarity between theology and religious studies in the United Kingdom:

> the increasing secularity of theology, both institutionally and methodologically, has produced a situation where many felt that actually what in practice

existed was the study of religion (not theology), and that the religion so selected for historical reasons was Christianity. (D'Costa 1996: 343)

Similarly, the British Academy's latest report (2019) makes no such distinction between religious studies and theology faculties. It states that:

> Today, Theology and Religious Studies is a diverse and interdisciplinary field covering many more religions from many different perspectives ... Our universities are not seminaries and are no longer inextricably linked to the Church or reliant upon its financial or political support. (British Academy 2019: 2)

So, this report did not make any distinction between theology and religious studies, but a distinction was made between religious seminaries and higher religious education institutions (theology and religious studies). In this case, religious seminaries are regarded as confessional educational settings, as opposed to non-confessional theology and religious studies in the universities. In the United Kingdom, there have for a long time been religious seminaries, some of which, particularly Christian seminaries, have links with the universities. Moreover, in recent years, there have been attempts to create such links for Muslim seminaries/*madrasas* (Geaves 2015; Scott-Baumann et al. 2019).

The discussion above shows that even though the term 'confessional' is often used for seminaries, it is also occasionally used for theology faculties to separate them from religious studies (e.g., Cush 2009), a view rejected by others (e.g., D'Costa 1996).

However, there are two problems here, beyond the question of which institution is confessional or not. The first concerns a fundamental issue: can there ever be a non-confessional approach to religion? Watson, for example, argues that every approach to religion is 'confessional' in the sense that it 'is founded on certain beliefs and has particular aims in mind' (Watson 2007: 3). In other words, there is no non-confessional approach to religion, but there are instead different 'confessionalities', some of which are religious and some of which are secular. Secondly, as Schreiner (2015: 149–50) argues, the terms 'confessional' and 'non-confessional' are abstract, and that, in practice, there are no clear-cut differences between them.

In essence, the terms 'confessional' and 'non-confessional' are not straightforward. They are used to define different institutions, and the dichotomy between them has been open to debate, while some have even questioned the very possibility of a non-confessional approach to the study of religion. With these debates in mind, the next section will explore the development of theology faculties in Turkey.

Theology Faculties in Turkey

Following a brief history, this section will explore the theology faculties in Turkey in terms of purpose and curriculum, employment areas and distance-learning programmes. The term 'theology faculty' is used here because *ilahiyat*, which is the name of the faculties in Turkey, is often translated to English as 'theology' (or sometimes as 'divinity'). Thus, the term 'theology' is not used to denote that these faculties are 'confessional' educational settings in Cush (2009) terms (see above). As will be seen, there has been much debate and confusion regarding the purpose and function of theology faculties in Turkey, ranging from non-confessional to confessional and even to seminaries.

A Brief History

In the Ottoman Empire, it was *madrasas* which historically provided secondary and higher education for Muslims, but in the nineteenth century, new modern schools were founded. The first modern theology faculty dates back to 1910, when the first modern university in the Muslim world, *Darülfünun* (the House of Sciences), was re-established in Istanbul, the capital of the Ottoman Empire, and one of its departments was *Ulûm-ı Âliye-i Diniye* (High Religious Sciences), but the department was later abolished and transferred back to *madrasas* (İhsanoğlu 2019: 62). This shows that there had already been some confusion regarding the place of higher religious education in terms of whether it belonged to *madrasas* or modern university prior to the establishment of the modern Turkish state.

The Republic of Turkey was established in 1923 and one of the first laws introduced focused on education. In 1924, the Unification of Education Act placed all education institutions, public and private alike, under the control of the Ministry of Education. Soon all *madrasas* were abolished, and a new theology faculty (*ilahiyat fakültesi*) was established in *Darülfünun* (Aşıkoğlu 2012). According to Berkes, the theology faculty was founded 'for the cultivation of the new religious outlook' (Berkes 1964: 484), which was a 'rational approach to the religion' (p. 490). The courses taught in the faculty were as follows:

History of *Kalam* (Islamic theology); History of *Hadith* (traditions/sayings of the Prophet Muhammad); History of *Tafsir* (Quranic exegesis); History of *Fiqh* (Islamic jurisprudence); History of Islam; Muslim Philosophy.

Ethnology of the Muslim Peoples; Contemporary Muslim Sects; Religious History of the Turks; *Tasawwuf* (Islamic mysticism).

History of Religions; Philosophy of Religion; History of Philosophy; Sociology of Religion; Psychology of Religion; Aesthetics and Islamic Art; Ethics. (categorisation as in original source) (Berkes 1964: 491; though Zengin,

2011: 156 argued that Pschology of Religion course did not exist at the faculty's programme at the time)

As can be seen, the faculty included courses related to Islam (especially the first group), as well as offering a broader range of courses, such as sociology and philosophy of religion. With this composition, the faculty was criticised for not giving enough time and importance to Islamic courses, and was found to be ill-equipped to raise religious functionaries (Ev 2017). Berkes (1964), however, criticised the faculty for diverging from its *raison d'être* which was 'the scientific study of religions'. Berkes (1964: 490–1) argued that originally it was decided that the courses related to Islam ought to be taught 'historically', and that other courses would employ a 'scientific approach' and be taught by 'men with no specialised Islamic education', but the practice was quite different, because 'the apologetic approach predominated' in the courses related to Islam, as they were taught by former *ulama* (religious scholars raised in the Ottoman *madrasas*).

It should be noted that the theology faculty was established in the same year as the Presidency of Religious Affairs, a state institution authorised to oversee all cases regarding the Islamic faith. In other words, even though the Republic of Turkey adopted French-inspired secularism to minimise the role of religion in the public and private sphere, it did not separate, or eliminate, religion from the state. Rather, it chose to regulate and control it. However, for Islam to be useful for the republic, it had to be, according to Berkes (1964: 484–5) 'reformed', 'enlightened' and 'humanised', and the theology faculty, along with the Presidency of Religious Affairs, was expected to contribute to this religious reform.

Indeed, in 1928, a religious reform proposal linked with the theology faculty was published in the press. The proposal endorsed the adoption of Turkish texts instead of Arabic texts in worship, the introduction of pews and musical instruments into mosques and even the abolition of the requirement to take off one's shoes before entering the mosque. However, the members of the faculty denied that they had prepared and ratified such a proposal. It is likely that one of the members of the faculty prepared the proposal and leaked it to the press without discussing it with his colleagues (Bein 2011: 126–9; Kara 2017: 130–6, 154–6). Eventually, the faculty was abolished in 1933. Even though the lack of student interest was often mentioned as a reason for the abolition (Aşıkoğlu 2012), according to Berkes (1964: 491), its members' disagreement over 'the question of a religious reform' was a significant contributory factor for its closure. In other words, those responsible for the secular establishment of the Republic did not see the faculty as capable of contributing to such a reform.[1]

---

[1] However, the state authorities did not give up the reform project: closure of Sufi orders and lodges, and the adoption of European headgear and dress in 1925, a change of the alphabet from Arabic to Latin and the removal of Islam from the constitution in 1928, and the change of *adhān* (call to prayer) from

Between 1933 and 1949, there was no theology faculty in Turkey, but the introduction of the multi-party system in 1946, which made religion in education a factor in the electoral calculations of political parties, made possible the re-establishment of theology faculties. In 1949, a new theology faculty (*ilahiyat fakültesi*) was established, this time, in Ankara University. According to Ok (2004), the purpose of the faculty was worded as follows:

> to make the study of religion possible on a solid and scientific ground; and to provide required conditions for the growth of intellectual religious scholars [*aydın din adamı*] with full professional knowledge and open minds. (Ok 2004: 203)

As can be seen, the purpose of the faculty resonated with a non-confessional approach. Moreover, the number of courses related to Islam were reduced. Probably because of this, the faculty attracted criticism from conservative circles. For example, Ali Fuat Başgil wrote that this faculty would produce 'religious critics, not religious scholars' (Başgil 2007: 276, first published in 1954).

Moreover, the then president of the Presidency of Religious Affairs, Ahmet Hamdi Akseki severely criticised the faculty, claiming that:

> ... today's Theology Faculty is not in a position to raise religious functionaries needed for the country. And this is not possible under these circumstances. However, we are not against to the existence of such a faculty within the university.
>
> [However, this faculty] is not what we want, [what we want is] a genuine religious institution that would raise distinguished Islamic scholars, tailored to the religious needs of the country in every field. And this, as in every part of the world, can only be achieved if it is managed by the Presidency of Religious Affairs. (reported in Cebeci 2005: 272)

As can be seen, Akseki saw the new faculty as ill-equipped to train religious functionaries and called for the establishment of a religious seminary under the control of the Presidency of Religious Affairs. However, this has never materialised, and the state has never allowed the Presidency of Religious Affairs to control a formal educational institution, except for the Qur'an courses which have been devised as adult educational institutions. The lack of an official Islamic seminary also explains why the theology faculties have often been linked to the

---

Arabic to Turkish in 1932 can be regarded as a part of this reform project. The latter reform especially caused much controversy, and it was abolished subsequent to the introduction of the multi-party political system.

training of religious functionaries, as there has been no other higher education institution, public or private, tasked with this function. Moreover, the theology faculties have been criticised for not providing a 'proper' Islamic education or for devoting too much time to courses such as philosophy. Even the name of the faculties, namely, *ilahiyat* has been subject to much criticism (Öztürk 2015).

Looking back to the 1950s, the government of the time established a different higher religious education institution. In 1959, the Higher Islamic Institute was established in Istanbul, and then counterparts were founded in other cities. These institutes were not part of universities; they were under the control of the Ministry of National Education. Moreover, a new faculty, the Faculty of Islamic Studies, was established in 1971 in Erzurum. As the name and programmes suggest (Islam appears in their names), these institutes and faculty were more inclined towards 'Islamic' higher education than the theology faculty in Ankara (Öztürk 2015: 33). However, according to Kara, even though there were differences between these institutes and faculties, their programmes and the areas of employment their graduates progressed to were similar and they were all aimed at raising 'intellectual [modern] religious scholars' (*aydın din adamı*) (2017: 375). Probably because of this, these faculties and institutes were transformed into theology faculties in 1982, making eight in total. Subsequently, the number of theology faculties rose from eight to twenty-four during the 1990s and their numbers further increased in the 2000s and 2010s under the governments of AK Parti (Justice and Development Party).

In Turkey, the politics of religion has evolved over time, partly because power has gradually transferred from a secular establishment to more conservative governments since the introduction of the multi-party political system in 1946. Over the last twenty years, the AK Parti, a conservative party, has governed the country. This transformation has had an impact on the theology faculties. For example, at the beginning of the 2010s, the Council of Higher Education started to name new faculties *İslami ilimler* (Islamic sciences) instead of *ilahiyat*. This created a diversity among the faculties in terms of name, if not in terms of programmes and purpose. However, in 2013, the Council of Higher Education proposed that all theology faculties would be named 'Islamic sciences' faculties and that courses related to philosophy would be reduced. This proposal can be seen as an attempt to make theology faculties more confessional both in name and content. However, the proposal was heavily criticised by the members of the theology faculties both because of its top-down imposition and because of the changes it proposed. Even the then-president of the Presidency of Religious Affairs, Mehmet Görmez, criticised the proposal arguing that no theology faculty can exist without 'philosophy courses' and that the name *ilahiyat* should not be changed in this way (Erturan 2013). Because of these criticisms, the Council of Higher Education abandoned the proposal, but the new faculties established since then have, for the most part, been named 'Islamic sciences faculties', and more courses related to Islam were added to both the programmes of theology and Islamic sciences faculties by the Council in 2015 (Nazıroğlu 2018: 186).

This brief history provides important clues to the development of the theology faculties in terms of their character as confessional and non-confessional. This will be discussed further below.

Purpose and Curriculum

İsmail Kara (2017: 337), a prominent religious scholar, asked the question as to 'whether theology faculties in Turkey are religious institutions or secular institutions' (*'Türkiye'de ilahiyat fakülteleri dini kurumlar mı, laik kurumlar mı?'*) and followed up with the assessment that there is, in fact, no easy answer to the question. However, Kara (2017: 390) noted that an analysis of the legislation and the intentions of the political elite would not be enough to fully understand these faculties. In particular, the official aims and purposes of these faculties may be in line with the non-confessional approach, but the teaching practice might be different. For example, the official mission statements of the faculties often include references to concepts such as 'knowledge, science, problem solving, critical thinking, interpretation, lifelong learning, tolerance, respect, virtue, openness to innovation and universality' (Nazıroğlu 2018: 183). According to Nazıroğlu, the theology faculties 'happily' adopt these concepts which are produced by 'the modern (Western) world' to justify their existence in a secular university, but he notes that 'it is very difficult to say that education and research activity [in these faculties] are carried out in the same direction' (2018: 183). This means even though theology faculties' mission statements often sound non-confessional, what is taught in practice might be much more confessional.

Moreover, with the establishment of Islamic sciences faculties, there is a tendency in official mission statements to highlight Islam and Islamic values (Osmanoğlu 2021: 25). For example, one faculty states that, among others, its aim is to raise a 'generation' that 'embraces, absorbs and lives Islamic consciousness and awareness at the personal level'.[2] This statement contains elements which might be considered as confessional, as the faculty aims at training students who 'embrace', 'absorb' and 'live' Islamic values.[3]

In other words, the official mission statements of theology and Islamic sciences faculties are now to some extent 'patchy' (Osmanoğlu 2021: 29). It is not clear whether the core function of these faculties is to raise pious Islamic

---

[2] See at: https://iif.aksaray.edu.tr/misyon—vizyon.
[3] It should be noted that the mission statement of the faculty also states that they aim to 'create an educational environment that is modern, democratic, respectful to human rights and freedom of belief', see at: https://iif.aksaray.edu.tr/misyon—vizyon.

functionaries who will absorb and live Islamic values or modern theologians who will carry out research on religions in an objective manner.

Theology and Islamic sciences offer almost identical programmes and courses, which means that, essentially, there is almost no practical difference between the two. One difference is that there are more courses on philosophy in theology faculties. The departments and the courses offered in today's theology faculties are as follows:

- Basic Islamic Sciences Department: *tafsir* (Qur'anic exegesis); hadith (traditions/sayings of the Prophet Muhammad); *Kalam* (Islamic theology); fiqh (Islamic jurisprudence); history of Islamic sects; *tasawwuf* (Islamic mysticism); Arabic language and rhetoric; Qur'an recitation.
- Philosophy and Religious Sciences Department: religious education; philosophy of religion; psychology of religion; sociology of religion; history of religions; history of philosophy; Islamic philosophy; logic.
- Islamic History and Arts Department: Islamic history; history of Turkish Islamic arts; Turkish-Islamic literature; Turkish religious music.

In a typical BA theology programme, the Basic Islamic Sciences Department courses constitute 55 per cent of the programme; 16 per cent of the programme comprises the Philosophy and the Religious Sciences Department courses, and 12 per cent of the programme comes from the Islamic History and Arts Department courses; the rest (17 per cent) is devoted to elective and other courses (Turan 2017: 72).

According to Turan (2017: 71), the theology and religious studies faculties teach 'the perspective of Islamic civilisation' through the Basic Islamic Sciences Department and Islamic History and Arts Department courses, while they make a connection with the 'West and its civilisation' through the Philosophy and the Religious Sciences Department courses.

As can be seen, these faculties include a wide range of courses, from those exclusively related to Islam, which constitute the majority of the programme, to courses related to other religions and philosophy, which teach the ancient philosophers as well as contemporary ones. Moreover, these faculties often include academics who have traditional views regarding religion, as well as those who hold modern views about Islam and other religions (Öztürk 2015: 34), which means the students are exposed to different approaches to religion.

Employment Areas

The development of the theology faculties should also be understood against the backdrop of their student demographics and the employment areas to which their graduates progress. According to Ok 'The students in divinity faculties in

Turkey are all Muslims', and this can be explained in relation to the religious landscape of the county as a whole, as Muslims comprise the overwhelming majority of the population (Ok 2004: 203).

Regarding gender, currently the majority of undergraduate students are female. According to 2021–2022 Council of Higher Education statistics, there are currently around 124,000 students enrolled in theology and Islamic sciences faculties' undergraduate programmes and 61 per cent of them are female. Considering that historically *madrasas* served only male students, the modern theology and Islamic sciences faculties' student demographics are radically different in Turkey, as there are now more female students than male students studying at theology and Islamic sciences undergraduate programmes. However, this ratio changes considerably in graduate programmes. Currently, 37 per cent graduate students are female. What is more, this ratio changes dramatically in academic posts, as only 23 per cent of academics are female (Yükseköğretim Kurulu 2022). This shows that even though most students are female in undergraduate programmes in theology and Islamic sciences faculties, there are somehow more male students in graduate programmes and more male academics, but this can change in the future.

Returning back to religious identity, according to one piece of research, a significant number of theology faculty students expect the ideal theology faculty student to have 'an Islamic identity and [Islamic] consciousness' (Osmanoğlu and Korkmaz 2018: 164). This means that not only do the students of the theology faculties have an 'Islamic identity', but they also expect the ideal theology faculty student to have an Islamic identity. According to Osmanoğlu and Korkmaz (2018), this shows that the expectation of Turkish society with regard to these faculties is different from the faculties' original intentions.

The expectation of Turkish society with regard to this faculty, however, is not without reason. If the employment areas these faculties feed into are considered, it can be seen that the vast majority of the graduates are employed as either religious functionaries, such as imams and Qur'an teachers under the auspices of the Presidency of Religious Affairs, or as RE teachers in state schools under the control of the Ministry of National Education. Some graduates stay in higher education for further study to become academics in the faculties. Therefore, these faculties cater for three distinct vocations: religious services, RE teaching and academia.

The graduates of theology faculties can work as imams and Qur'an teachers without any further qualification or the need to take further courses. This means that, in the eyes of the Presidency of Religious Affairs, the graduates of the theology and Islamic sciences already have the skills and qualifications to become religious functionaries. As the Presidency of Religious Affairs is one of the largest employers of the graduates of the theology faculties, this, in turn, forces the faculties to produce students who are well equipped to become religious functionaries. In other words, as Öztürk argues, 'the actual situation determines the objectives [of these faculties]' (2015: 48). In this sense, these faculties have been functioning as religious seminaries, because there has been no official religious seminary which provides higher religious education within or outside the state sector.[4] The call from conservatives for more Islamic-oriented teaching in the theology faculties, and the reforms that attempt to increase the number of the courses related to the Qur'an pursued by recent conservative governments, can be read against this backdrop. Moreover, it should be noted that the Presidency of Religious Affairs have recently established an academy to further train *ilahiyat* graduates. This is partly because of the understanding that the theology faculties' programmes are inadequate for raising religious functionaries.

Furthermore, the graduates of the theology faculties can become RE teachers without the requirement to take any further courses, as they receive teacher training during their studies at these faculties. There are two different RE teaching positions in Turkey. The first is the role of a specialist RE teacher at imam and preacher schools (*İmam Hatip Liseleri*), where the specialist RE teachers teach Islamic courses such as Qur'an and hadith. The second is the role of Religious Culture and Ethics Culture teacher. 'Religious Culture and Ethics Culture' is a compulsory course in primary and secondary schools and is officially characterised as a non-denominational and non-confessional subject (see Hendek 2019). In other words, the theology faculties should be producing graduates who can teach non-denominational and non-confessional RE as well as religious functionaries who are expected to absorb, live and teach Islamic values. This can be seen as paradoxical to some, and, as Cush (2009) would argue, non-confessional religious studies programmes are better equipped to produce RE teachers who would teach non-confessional RE in state schools.

Indeed, this is a serious challenge for these faculties and one of the factors that blurs their purpose and function. In the past, there were attempts to address the problem. For example, in 1997, the Council of Higher Education announced that the theology faculties would start to offer two distinct programmes: the first being a 'Theology Programme' (*İlahiyat Programı*) and the second being a 'Primary Religious Culture and Ethics Knowledge Teaching Programme' (*İlköğretim Din Kültürü ve Ahlak Bilgisi Öğretimi Programı*) (Yükseköğretim Kurulu Başkanlığı 1997).

---

[4] It should be noted there are also *İmam-Hatip Liseleri* (Imam and Preacher Schools). These are secondary schools under the control of the Ministry of National Education, which differ from other secondary schools in that more than 40 per cent of their curriculum is devoted to Islamic education courses such as Qur'anic exegesis and Islamic jurisprudence. They were established in 1924 to produce religious functionaries but abolished in 1930. They were re-established in 1951, and their rise and fall has been closely connected with the politics of religion in Turkey (Ozgur 2012; Aşlamacı and Kaymakcan 2017). Even though it has been these schools which have been tasked with producing religious functionaries, over the years, due to the rise in the number of their graduates, and a need for a graduate degree, a theology degree has gradually become an advantage and, in some cases, a requirement to occupy official religious functionary posts.

The Council of Higher Education explained the reason for this particular change thus:

> Some new arrangements have been made in order to provide religious services at a higher level, to better teach Islam to our young and to raise our young as individuals who are proud to be a member of the Turkish Nation and a citizen of the Turkish Republic, which is a laic, democratic and social state governed by rule of law, and are aware of the fact that *if you hear the call to prayer [adhan] sounds in this country and if our glorious Turkish flag is waving, we owe them to the Great Leader Atatürk, who founded the Republic, and his military and political friends.* (Yükseköğretim Kurulu Başkanlığı 1997: 63, original emphasis)

This short explanation very much summarises the complexity that the theology faculties face in Turkey. First, the Council referred to the provision of religious services. It was implied that the 'theology programme' would focus on educating students who could occupy the posts required by the Presidency of Religious Affairs, specifically to better provide religious services. If the graduates of this programme wanted to become teachers in the secondary schools or imam and preacher schools, then they needed to embark upon a one-and-a-half-year postgraduate teacher education programme. Secondly, the Council mentioned the teaching of Islam to the young. The Council is probably referring here to the Religious Culture and Ethics Knowledge course, and a new programme was proposed to train Religious Culture and Ethics Knowledge course teachers. The rest of the extract appears to be a declaration of the ultimate purpose of the theology faculties in the eyes of the secular establishment, which at the time had overthrown the Islamic-leaning Refah Parti through the '28th February post-modern coup.'

In 2006, the 'Primary Religious Culture and Ethics Knowledge Teaching Programme' was transferred to the education faculties, and this can be regarded as the full realisation of the non-confessional character of the Religious Culture and Ethics Knowledge course. However, in 2012, the Council transferred this programme back to the theology faculties and then subsequently abolished it altogether in 2014. Since then, the RE teachers, religious functionaries and future theologians have been graduates of the theology and Islamic sciences faculties via an almost identical programme, as had been the case before 1998.

The Opening of Distance Learning Programmes

As has been discussed, whether the theology faculties (and Islamic sciences faculties) are confessional or non-confessional institutions is open to debate, but what is certain is that some interested parties have never found these faculties confessional enough. This has, to some extent, resulted in the survival of unregulated and unrecognised places of Islamic education (Yüksel 2013).

Madrasas were officially abolished following the Unification of Education Act in 1924 and the legislation banned the founding of private religious schools (Gür 2019: 345). Therefore, currently, no madrasa can be opened in the state or private sectors in Turkey. Despite this, some madrasas have survived as unrecognised and unregulated places of Islamic education without a state licence. It is estimated that in the eastern part of Turkey alone, there are more than sixty madrasas (Yüksel 2013: 210). Even though their names, the age groups they cater for and their programmes differ due to the lack of a central organisation to regulate and organise these madrasas, a typical madrasa in the eastern part of Turkey offers between six and ten years of Islamic education and takes pupils who have completed primary education (ages 10–12). Moreover their curriculum almost exclusively focuses on Arabic and Islamic studies (Işıkdoğan 2012: 60-2).

These unregulated madrasas have been tolerated and sometimes even supported depending on the proclivities of the ruling government, but they have never been officially recognised as educational institutions by the state, which means that a madrasa diploma does not give access to any government job. This includes teaching and religious services as well as university education. Even though there have occasionally been attempts by politicians to appoint madrasa gradates as religious functionaries (Strateji Düşünce ve Analiz Merkezi 2016: 6), there has never been any concrete state policy to integrate madrasas and their gradates into the official system. In recent years, however, madrasas have come to the fore and there have been calls for their recognition and integration in one form or another.[5]

The core problem has been that madrasas are not recognised as educational institutions, and therefore their graduates must study for secondary and graduate degrees all over again in order to enter graduate or postgraduate level employment. However, constraints such as age and available time following years of madrasa education prevent most madrasa graduates from taking this route. One way of overcoming this difficulty, however, has been to enrol on official distance-learning programmes in order to obtain an official diploma, while at the same time studying at madrasas (Işıkdoğan 2012; Ataman et al. 2017).

Concerning university level distance-learning programmes, distance-learning theology education was first offered as a two-year associate degree (önlisans) in 1998 (Yükseköğretim Kurulu Başkanlığı 1997: 64). Moreover, in 2006, a distance-learning Degree Completion Programme in Theology (İlahiyat

---

[5] For example, there were two international symposiums (which were held in 2011 and 2012) which focused on the relation between theology faculties and madrasas, madrasa reform, and their integration and recognition (Işıkdoğan 2012; Narin 2013).

Lisans Tamalama Programı, İLİTAM) was offered so that the graduates of a two-year associate degree programme could obtain a BA in theology degree. Currently sixteen theology faculties across Turkey offer this programme and there are approximately 20,000 students studying on these programmes (Karateke 2020: 236). It should be noted that not all students studying on these distance-learning programmes are *madrasa* students/graduates, but a significant number of the students have *madrasa* connections (Altaş 2016). This means that these distance-learning programmes do provide an unofficial link between *madrasas* as traditional Islamic education institutions and the official theology faculties. Moreover, it seems that the current conservative government supports these programmes, as the number of theology faculties offering the İLİTAM programme and their quotas have increased significantly over the last ten years. Furthermore, there have also been discussions regarding establishing a distance-learning BA in theology programme,[6] which would make the current two-tier system simpler for those who want to receive an official theology diploma through distance-learning. However, this has not yet materialised.

Even though the distance-learning programmes link the theology faculties and *madrasas*, at least unofficially, there are still problems. Aside from the problem that there is no official linkage, the quality and validity of distance-learning degrees have been questioned (Kaymakcan et al. 2014), and that at a time when even the quality of the traditional face-to-face education of theology faculties is undergoing criticism (Ev 2017). There have even been calls for the abolition of distance-learning programmes altogether (Aşıkoğlu 2012). This would mean that alternative ways would have to be found for the recognition and integration of *madrasas*.

In addition to equal rights and the protection of the educational rights and religious requirements of those wanting to receive education in accordance with their religious and philosophical convictions (Parker-Jenkins et al. 2005), there might be also pedagogical arguments for the recognition of *madrasas*, as there might be skills and qualities that the *madrasas* and theology faculties can learn from each other (Narin 2013; Yüksel 2013; Strateji Düşünce ve Analiz Merkezi 2016). However, there are also inevitable challenges. Any official connection between theology faculties and *madrasas* will potentially complicate the function of the theology faculties and could result in them becoming more confessionally oriented. Moreover, some fear that any connection or recognition runs the risk of transforming the theology faculties themselves into *madrasas*, which, according to Çağrıcı (2017) are 'at the basis of the suffering and destruction of the Islamic world today'. This evokes the radicalisation trends in countries

---

[6] See at: https://www.memurlar.net/haber/786710/acikogretim-in-ilahiyat-lisans-egitimi-vermesi-icin-kdk-ya-basvuruldu.html.

that allow the continuation of *madrasa*s without reform. As some conservatives have never found Islamic education in the theology faculties to be meaningful enough, coupled with the recent efforts of the conservative government to add more courses related to Islam while removing courses related to philosophy (as discussed above), the fear here is that any official connection or recognition might be on *madrasa* terms. This, in practice, would result in a '*madrasa*-isation' of the theology faculties, rather than a transformation of madrasas on the terms of the theology faculties.

DISCUSSION

Nearly a hundred years of theology faculty experience in Turkey has shown that theology faculties (and their equivalents) have been closely related to the politics of religion in Turkey (Subaşı 2003). Their rise and demise, their programmes and even their names have been influenced by the politics of religion.

The first theology faculty was established in 1924 to educate modern religious scholars. Even though Berkes (1964: 490–1) argued that the faculty was established 'solely for the scientific study of religions', it seems very difficult to marry this aim with the expectation that the faculty would also contribute to the 'religious reform' project of Atatürk. It seems that there was no real intention to establish a 'non-confessional' faculty with a 'methodological agnosticism' (see Cush 2009), rather, the intention was to establish a faculty that would endorse the republican/secular version of Islam by contributing to the religious reform project of Atatürk. In essence, it was a 'confessional' faculty, but in a secular sense (Watson 2007). However, not only have some conservative Muslims criticised this endeavour, but the secular establishment has also doubted the capacity of the theology faculty to make such a contribution, which resulted in the closures of these faculties in the early years of the republic and their relatively low numbers up to the 1990s.

Moreover, even though the politics of religion has always been a prime factor in the fate of the theology faculties, these faculties have not always obeyed the political power. They did not give as much support to Atatürk's religious reforms that the secular establishment expected, and they resisted the more confessional-oriented reforms of recent conservative governments.

The history of the theology faculties in Turkey shows that they have oscillated between confessional and non-confessional characteristics, but overall, the secular confessionality, as a dominant approach, has given way to more religious confessionality over time, as some faculties today overtly express their confessional character. However, the actual teaching within the faculties has always been complex and to some extent more accommodative partly as a result of the influence of faculty members, who have different views regarding Islam and other religions, and partly due to different courses, which have ranged from Qur'anic exegesis to philosophy. It can be argued that the teaching in the theology faculties has probably included both religious and secular confessional and non-confessional approaches. Even though, in terms of the percentage of the courses, the pendulum has swung in favour of Islamic courses over the years with the increase in courses related to Islam, in terms of the approaches employed in courses, there has been a movement towards a non-confessional approach in certain courses.[7]

In addition to this, as these faculties have been producing religious functionaries, RE teachers and academics at the same time, this has further blurred the core function and purpose of the theology faculties (Hacınebioğlu 2004: 51). This has resulted in practical difficulties too. For example, whether these faculties can produce well-equipped graduates who will work in very different vocations has been questioned (Aydın 2005; Özsoy 2013; Öztürk 2015). Some have even argued that the lack of a uniform approach in these faculties has caused some students considerable stress in their religious thinking (Ok 2004).

However, this lack of a uniform approach can also be read positively: each theology faculty accommodates different approaches and offers different employment opportunities. This might be seen as an opportunity for students as they are exposed to different views and approaches to religions within the same institution. It means that even the students who want to become imams should study religions other than Islam, in addition to philosophy, sociology, arts, music and literature as these are all compulsory courses in these faculties.

Moreover, the distance-learning programmes currently connect the theology faculties to the *madrasa* students/graduates. As there may be skills and qualities that the *madrasas* and theology faculties can learn from each other, in addition to protection of the educational rights and religious requirements of those wanting to receive education in accordance with their religious and philosophical convictions, there might be a need for more concrete policies for integration and recognition. However, there is a risk that these connections could further complicate the function of these faculties.

Furthermore, even though Turkey is not as pluralist a county as some Western European countries, there is still, nevertheless, plurality within Turkish society, and the rights and religious requirements of religious minorities should also be taken into account when devising a higher religious education policy (Smart 1988). As the theology faculties have always been imagined as (secular or religious) 'Islamic' theology faculties ever since their establishment, this raises the

---

[7] This has been especially evident in courses related to other religions and philosophy. For example, Gündüz (2005) argued that the history of religions course has evolved 'from apology to phenomenology', while in the theology and philosophy of religion courses, 'non-exclusivist' approaches have been developed (Yaran 2005).

question of the educational rights of non-Muslims, as there is no official (or unofficial, for that matter) Christian or Jewish theology faculty or seminary in Turkey. Even though the number of Christians and Jews is tiny in Turkey, there should also be policies which take the rights and religious requirements of religious minorities into account. Moreover, even though the theology faculties in Turkey do not have any official denominational link or composition, they are sometimes 'accused' of training 'Sunni' RE teachers and religious functionaries by some Alevi groups,[8] and this means that there is also a likely need to reach non-Sunni populations who may wish to obtain graduate degrees in the field of religion.

However, it would be a serious challenge for these faculties to reach all these different groups and at the same time have a uniform approach to religion, such as that aspired to by a non-confessional approach. An alternative option, therefore, might be to divide the theology faculties into two or three different institutions (Kara 2013). *Madrasas* could also be legalised, and the Presidency of Religious Affairs and other religious groups could be allowed to establish religious seminaries which grant degrees. A non-confessional religious studies department could also be established to raise RE teachers (Smart 1988; Cush 2009). This option, however, would be a radically new idea for the Turkish Republic, which was characterised very early in its existence by one of its first acts of legislation, namely, the Unification of Education Law. This option, therefore, would require constitutional amendments as well as careful thought and planning.

Conclusion

Throughout the history of theology faculties in Turkey, there has been a relationship and tension between secular and religious confessional approaches, as these faculties have been tasked with training Islamic religious functionaries as well as the training of RE teachers and modern theologians. In terms of their composition, there are now more courses related to Islam, but at the same time, in some courses, there has been a movement towards non-confessional approaches.

Moreover, through distance-learning programmes, these faculties, to some extent, reach *madrasa* students who would normally not find the theology faculties Islamically confessional enough. With its rich list of courses and faculty members who have different views regarding Islam and other religions, from

---

[8] This issue was raised in European Court of Human Rights judgments on RE in Turkey, see *Hasan and Eylem Zengin v. Turkey* (Application no. 1448/04) and *Mansur Yalçın and Others v. Turkey* (Application no. 21163/11).

traditional to modern, these faculties offer a unique opportunity for students who want to study different aspects of Islam, other religions and philosophy from different perspectives, and then move on to work in different fields be they from religious services to non-confessional RE teaching. However, developing a core purpose while also fulfilling the remit of religious seminaries, non-confessional religious studies and denominational theology faculties, all present a serious challenge for these faculties. Furthermore, the question of how these faculties will reach non-Muslims and non-Sunnis also needs careful consideration and planning.

References

Altaş, N. (2016). 'Türkiye'de Dinî Yükseköğretim Alanında Uzaktan Eğitimle İlgili Algı Sorunları ve İLİTAM Uygulamaları', *Değerler Eğitimi Dergisi* 14(31): 7–42.

Aşıkoğlu, N. Y. (2012). 'Yüksek Öğretimde Din Eğitim ve Öğretimi', in R. Doğan and R. Ege (eds), *Din Eğitimi El Kitabı*. Ankara: Grafiker Yayınları, pp. 215–31.

Aşlamacı, İ. and R. Kaymakcan (2017). 'A Model for Islamic Education from Turkey: The Imam-Hatip Schools', *British Journal of Religious Education* 39(3): 279–92.

Ataman, K., V. Bilgin and F. Evrenk (2017). 'Modernization, Social Change, and the Persistence of Traditional Institutions of Religious Learning: The Case of Diyarbakir Madrasahs', *Uludağ Üniversitesi İlahiyat Fakültesi Dergisi* 26(2): 77–95.

Aydın, M. Ş. (2005). *Cumhuriyet Döneminde Din Eğitimi Öğretmeni Yetiştirme ve İstihdamı*, 2nd edn. İstanbul: Dem.

Başgil, A. F. (2007). *Din ve Laiklik*. Istanbul: Kubbealtı.

Bein, A. (2011). *Ottoman Ulema, Turkish Republic: Agents of Change and Guardians of Tradition*. Stanford, CA: Stanford University Press.

Berkes, N. (1964). *The Development of Secularism in Turkey*. Montreal: McGill University Press.

British Academy, The (2019). *Theology and Religious Studies Provision in UK Higher Education*. London: British Academy.

Çağrıcı, M. (2017). *Medrese Nostaljisi*, available at: https://www.karar.com/yazarlar/mustafa-cagrici/medrese-nostaljisi-3649.

Cebeci, S. (2005). *Din Eğitimi Bilimi ve Türkiye'de Din Eğitimi*. 2nd edn. Ankara: Akçağ.

Cush, D. (2009). 'Religious Studies versus Theology: Why I'm Still Glad that I Converted from Theology to Religious Studies', in D. L. Bird and S. G. Smith (eds), *Theology and Religious Studies in Higher Education: Global Perspectives*. London: Continuum, pp. 15–30.

D'Costa, G. (1996). 'The End of "Theology" and "Religious Studies"', *Theology* 99(791): 338–51.

Erturan, A. F. (2013). *Mehmet Görmez: İlahiyat Fakülteleri 'Felsefes'siz Olamaz*, available at: http://www.star.com.tr/politika/ilahiyat-fakulteleri-felsefesiz-olamaz-haber-789465, last accessed 27 June 2020.

Ev, H. (2017). 'Yükseköğretimde Din Eğitimi', in M. Köylü and N. Altaş (eds), *Din Eğitimi*, 8th edn. İstanbul: Ensar, pp. 268–306.

Geaves, R. (2015). 'An Exploration of the Viability of Partnership between Dar Al-Ulum and Higher Education Institutions in North West England Focusing upon Pedagogy and Relevance', *British Journal of Religious Education* 37(1): 64–82.

Gündüz, Ş. (2005). 'From Apology to Phenomenology: The Current State of the Studies of the History of Religions in Turkey', in Ş. Gündüz and C. S. Yaran (eds), *Change and Essence: Dialectical Relations Between Change and Continuity in the Turkish Intellectual Tradition*. Washington DC: Council for Research in Values and Philosophy, pp. 18–29.

Gür, B. S. (2019). 'Religious Education', in A. Özerdem and M. Whiting (eds), *The Routledge Handbook of Turkish Politics*. London: Routledge, pp. 339–48.

Hacınebioğlu, İ. L. (2004). 'Batıdaki İlahiyat ve Felsefe Eğitimindeki Bazı Yaklaşımların Türkiye'ye Dönük Uygulanabilirliği İle İlgili Bir Değerlendirme (İngiltere Tecrübesi)', in *Türkiye'de Yüksek Din Eğitiminin Sorunları, Yeniden Yapılanması ve Geleceği Sempozyumu, Isparta 16–17 Eylül 2003*. Isparta: Süleyman Demirel Üniversitesi İlahiyat Fakültesi, pp. 47–71.

Hendek, A. (2019). 'Country Report: Turkey', *British Journal of Religious Education* 41(1): 8–13.

Hendek, A. (2020). *Religious Education Policy in Turkey and England: A Comparative Perspective*. İstanbul: Dem.

İhsanoğlu, E. (2019). *The House of Sciences: The First Modern University in the Muslim World*. Oxford: Oxford University Press.

Işıkdoğan, D. (2012). 'Güneydoğu Medreselerinde Eğitim-Öğretim Faaliyetleri: Mardin Örneği', *Ankara Üniversitesi İlahiyat Fakültesi Dergisi* 53(2): 43–83.

Kara, İ. (2013). *İlahiyatların Çuvaldızı Kendilerine Batırmalarının Tam Zamanıdır*, available at: https://www.star.com.tr/acik-gorus/ilahiyatlarin-cuvaldizi-kendilerine-batirmalarinin-tam-zamanidir-haber-789311, last accessed 19 August 2020.

Kara, İ. (2017). *Cumhuriyet Türkiyesi'nde Bir Mesele Olarak İslâm 2*, 2nd edn. İstanbul: Dergah.

Karateke, T. (2020). 'İLİTAM Öğrencilerinin Bu Programı Seçme Nedenleri ve Karşılaştıkları Sorunlar: Fırat Üniversitesi Örneği', *Değerler Eğitimi Dergisi* 18(39): 233–60.

Kaymakcan, R., H. Meydan, A. Telli and K. Cevherli (2014). 'İlahiyat Lisans Tamamlama Programının Verimliliği Üzerine Olgusal Bir Araştırma', *Hitit Üniversitesi İlahiyat Fakültesi Dergisi* 13(26): 43–62.

Minority Rights Group International (2018). *Turkey*, available at: https://minorityrights.org/country/turkey, last accessed 9 February 2022.

Narin, İ. (2013). 'Bir Sempozyumun Ardından: Uluslararası Medrese ve İlahiyat Kavşağında İslâmî İlimler Sempzyumu', *Bingöl Üniversitesi İlahiyat Fakültesi Dergisi* (1): 159–83.

Nazıroğlu, B. (2018). 'İlahiyat Fakültelerinde Din Eğitimi ve Sorunları', in M. Köylü (ed.), *Türkiye'de Din Eğitimi ve Sorunları*. İstanbul: Dem, pp. 169–208.

Ok, Ü. (2004). 'Handling Doubt in Teaching Religion: A Turkish Case Study', *Teaching Theology and Religion* 7(4): 201–12.

Osmanoğlu, C. (2021). *Yüksek Din Öğretimi Kurumlarının Mezun Tasavvuru*. İstanbul: Dem.

Osmanoğlu, C. and M. Korkmaz (2018). 'Öğrencilerine Göre İdeal İlahiyat Fakültesi Öğrencisinin Nitelikleri ve Bunun İlahiyat Eğitimiyle İlişkisi', *Değerler Eğitimi Dergisi* 16(36): 119–78.

Ozgur, I. (2012). *Islamic Schools in Modern Turkey: Faith, Politics, and Education*. Cambridge: Cambridge University Press.

Özsoy, Ö. (2013). *İlahiyatın Meşruiyet Krize ve Üç Tarz-ı Tedrisat*, available at: https://www.star.com.tr/acik-gorus/ilahiyatin-mesruiyet-krizi-ve--uc-tarzi-tedrisat-haber-795344, last accessed 27 June 2020.

Öztürk, M. (2015). 'İlahiyat'ın Adı ve Amaçları', in S. Akyürek (ed.), *Bugünün İlahiyatı Nasıl Olmalıdır? -Sorunlar ve Çözümleri-*. İstanbul: Ensar, pp. 29–59.

Parker-Jenkins, M., D. Hartas and B. A. Irving (2005). *In Good Faith: Schools, Religion and Public Funding*. Aldershot: Ashgate.

Schreiner, P. (2015). 'Religious Education in the European Context', in J. Berglund, T. Lundén and P. Strandbrink (eds), *Crossings, Crosses: Borders, Educations, and Religions in the Northern Europe*. Berlin: De Gruyter, pp. 139–53.

Scott-Baumann, A., A. Ebbiary, S. Ad Duha Mohammad, S. Dhorat, S. Begum, H. Pandor and J. Stolyar (2019). 'Towards Contextualized Islamic Leadership: Paraguiding and the Universities and Muslim Seminaries Project (UMSEP)', *Religions* 10: 662

Shively, K. (2008). 'Taming Islam: Studying Religion in Secular Turkey', *Anthropological Quarterly* 81(3): 683–711.

Smart, N. (1988). 'Religious Studies in the UK', *Religion* 18(1): 1–9.

Strateji Düşünce ve Analiz Merkezi (2016). *Türkiye'de Medreseler ve Din Eğitimi*. İstanbul: Strateji Düşünce ve Analiz Merkezi.

Subaşı, N. (2003). '"İlahiyat" Nedir?' *Tezkire* 31–32: 65–74.

Turan, İ. (2017). 'Türkiye'de İlahiyat Eğitimi: İstihdam Alanı-Program İlişkisi Üzerine Bir Değerlendirme', *İstanbul Üniversitesi İlahiyat Fakültesi Dergisi* (37): 59–77.

Watson, B. (2007). 'Secularism, Schools and Religious Education', in M. C. Felderhof, P. Thompson and D. Torevell (eds), *Inspiring Faith in Schools: Studies in Religious Education*. Aldershot: Ashgate, pp. 3–15.

Yaran, C. S. (2005). 'Non-Exclusivist Attitudes towards Other Religions in Recent Turkish Theology and Philosophy of Religion', in Ş. Gündüz and C. S. Yaran (eds), *Change and Essence: Dialectical Relations Between Change and Continuity in the Turkish Intellectual Tradition*. Washington DC: Council for Research in Values and Philosophy, pp. 7–17.

Yükseköğretim Kurulu Başkanlığı (1997). *Türk Yükseköğretiminin Bugünkü Durumu*. Ankara: Yükseköğretim Kurulu Başkanlığı.

Yükseköğretim Kurulu (2022). *Yükseköğretim Bilgi Yönetim Sistemi*, available at: https://istatistik.yok.gov.tr, last accessed 9 February 2022.

Yüksel, M. (2013). 'Medresetu'z-Zehrâ Projesini Bugünden Okumak: Bölge/Kürt Medreselerini Din Eğitimi Merkezli Olarak Islah ve Geliştirme İmkânı ve Bunun Toplumsal Barışa Katkısı', in F. Gedikli (ed.), *Medrese Geleneği ve Modernleşme Sürecinde Medreseler II*. Muş: Muş Alparslan Üniversitesi, pp. 189–213.

Zengin, Z. S. (2011). *Medreseden Darülfünuna Türkiye'de Yüksek Din Eğitimi*. İstanbul: Çamlıca Yayınları.

CHAPTER 12

Closing Reflections: Going Beyond Secular–Religious and Confessional–Academic Dichotomies in European Islamic Studies

SARIYA CHERUVALLIL-CONTRACTOR

INTRODUCTION: POWER, INTERSECTIONAL IDENTITY
AND THE STUDY OF ISLAM[1]

This important volume explores the tensions and opportunities that emerge from the intellectual encounter in Europe between what are perceived as 'confessional' and 'academic' approaches to the study of Islam and Muslims. As indicated in a number of chapters in this volume, this dichotomy positions as 'confessional' the study of Islam by believing Muslims (e.g., Jones, Chapter 1; Johansen, Chapter 3; Gilliat-Ray, Chapter 4; Dreier, Chapter 6). Islamic studies as undertaken in European universities is usually positioned or labelled as 'academic'. A dichotomy on its own would be unproblematic. However, key to this dichotomy in approaches to the study of Islam is a power dynamic that, at least in Western intellectual contexts, posits 'academic approaches' to Islamic studies as more critical, more rigorous, more desirable and somehow as being superior to what are termed as 'confessional approaches'. This can be contrasted to preferences within diverse Muslim communities that continue to valorise traditional forms of Islamic learning, especially in relation to positions of religious authority and leadership within Muslim communities. However, as a young *alimah* (traditionally trained female Muslim scholar) stated to me in a discussion about Islamic scholars in Britain, 'Alims and *alimahs* need jobs and

---

[1] I would like to take the opportunity to thank editors Nielson and Jones for inviting me to engage with this volume and all the contributions within it. Perhaps due to my personal and professional proximity and vested interest in the subject matter being discussed, this has been a difficult piece to write with many false starts and a number of deleted drafts. Now that it has been written, I realise that I have enjoyed and have been challenged by this reflective writing journey.

for these we need university degrees'. And so even in Muslim contexts, traditional forms of Islamic studies are devalued in liberal and marketised contexts that privilege employability. It is these power dynamics that determine how we produce knowledge, and why and how new knowledge is disseminated and shared.

These power dynamics are gendered. In wider Western/European society female Muslim scholars suffer multiple penalties in relation to their minorityness (visible or not), Muslim-ness and their woman-ness. Enduring patriarchies in Muslim and wider Western contexts can devalue their scholarship and their societal authority. These power dynamics are also racialised and/or ethnicised with particular ethnic voices being allocated more authority (Nurein and Iqbal 2021). They are determined by intra-Muslim relations – for example, a Shia scholar who participated in the 'Islam on Campus' research project, underlined the criticality of the course he taught by emphasising the fact that he did not include books that were published in Saudi Arabia (Scott-Baumann et al. 2020). This comment was made to demonstrate how his course was meeting Western academic standards, yet as Saudi Arabia is largely a Sunni country, it may also emerge from Sunni–Shia tensions and a desire to portray one denominational stance as potentially more critical than the other. Such power dynamics are also underpinned by the excessive suspicion that Muslim communities in Europe must endure. Tensions that are historical (Kahf 1999; Malik 2013), as well as those that have emerged in relation to the so-called 'War on Terror' and the Preventing Violent Extremism agenda in various European contexts (Mythen et al. 2009; Morey and Yaqin 2011; Kundnani 2014).

Finally, these power hierarchies stem from a perception and a concern that Islam and Muslims are the most visible signifier of religiosity in increasingly more 'secular' Europe – the challengers to secular consensus (Schirin 2005). Particularly in urban contexts, Islamic religious and cultural practices can face – often pejorative – secular scrutiny as observed in recent hijab debates (Cheruvallil-Contractor 2018), in reaction to the building of new mosques (Allen 2017), and, indeed, as discussed in this volume in the study of Islam by Muslims in secular universities. In an all-encompassing secular–religious divide in Europe, Islam and Muslims become the different 'Other'.

Against this backdrop of intersectional marginalities, this chapter will build on the discussions in this edited volume to interrogate these power dynamics and to suggest an intellectual paradigm that moves away from hierarchical dynamics within Islamic studies, to paradigms that are co-produced, collaborative and more hopeful.

Closing Reflections

Writing from a Complex Positionality

Before I embark on my exploration, I present a short note on my positionality in writing this chapter and the methodologies that inform my writing. Recognising the power dynamics that determine Islamic studies, Gale and Hopkins (2009) suggest that researchers within the study of Islam must be transparent about their positionality in undertaking the research. As a feminist sociologist of religion, I further draw upon thinkers like Rose (1997) and Sultana (2007) to emphasise a need for Islamic studies academics to consider how they approach and transform the field, and how they in turn are transformed by it. My academic background in feminism insists on the inclusion of rarely heard voices in research, so that these voices can inform and shape how knowledge about them is produced (Cheruvallil-Contractor 2012). My feminism also insists on a commitment to challenge, interrogate and transform societal structures that marginalise particular groups within society (Purvis 1995). In the case of the discussions contained in this chapter, I am invested in exploring why Muslim approaches to the study of Islam are dismissed as confessional, whereas 'academic' Islamic studies was, at least historically, often unchallenged.

Finally, I am a practising Muslim, however, my scholarship is shaped not by the traditional religious study of Islam and Muslims. Instead, I am very much a product of Western academia and work within feminist and pragmatist epistemes. As a 'religious' woman in 'secular' academia, I experience the debates discussed in this volume on a daily basis. The eagle-eyed reader will have noticed the scare quotes around the identity characteristics in the previous sentence. I use them because, through my research on diverse non-religious identities, I realise that these two categories – religious and secular - are not a dichotomy but two sides of continuum (Cheruvallil-Contractor et al. 2021). How does my positionality as a researcher fit in the boundary-making discussions – both disciplinary and positional – set up by Jones (Chapter 1), Johansen (Chapter 3) and Gilliat-Ray (Chapter 4) in this volume? Do I, and other Muslim Islamic studies practitioners like me (or, e.g., Sidat Chapter 7 and Mesbahi, Chapter 8, this volume), transcend or flummox the confessional–academic dichotomy? Or do we advance Islamic studies paradigms by becoming veritable bridges between the two ends of the dichotomy? I will come back to this idea later on in this chapter.

A Note on Methodology

This chapter is not the outcome of a particular research project, it is more a reflective piece. Nevertheless, to satisfy the sociologist that I am, I need to include a short note on methodology. So, this chapter draws on insights from a decade of research on the study of Islam and Muslims, conducted within qualitative and collaborative research frameworks, as well as some personal reflections on the research that I have conducted. What I present here is a reflective ethnography that largely engages with British Muslims and their plural contexts. I will draw on the findings of various projects, including a UK government-funded project that sought to explore how Muslim faith leaders were training in the United Kingdom (Mukadam et al. 2010); a UK Economic and Social Research Council (ESRC)-funded project that explored collaborative partnerships between Muslim higher education institutions and UK universities (Scott-Baumann and Cheruvallil-Contractor 2015); and a UK Arts and Humanities Research Council (AHRC)-funded project that explored how Islam is lived, experienced, perceived and taught in various UK higher education settings (Scott-Baumann et al. 2020). Finally, as a sociologist, my work lays greater emphasis on lived 'everyday' experiences of religion than on theology and religious institutions. The everyday is messy and intertwines 'secular' and 'religious' considerations as coexisting aspects of individual identity. It entails the complex, untidy negotiations that take place in a person's life to construct a religious identity, which may at times differ from official doctrine (Ammerman 2010; Macguire 2014).

Contrasting and Bridging Epistemes: Studying Islam in Europe

From an historical perspective, scholarship on Islam has branched in two directions that are separated and identified by religious demarcations (Nanji 1997; König 2016). In this section, using the confessional–academic dichotomy as a point of departure, I reflect on the historical epistemological assumptions that underpin both ends of this dichotomy. History is important, as there are lessons to be learned from it for contemporary studies of Islam. In undertaking this brief yet purposive historical exploration, I build upon Johansen's contribution in this volume (Chapter 3) to explore disciplinary boundary work in the study of Islam in Europe.

The Study of Islam

The study of Islam dates back to the emergence of Islam over 1,400 years ago. A hadith narrative from Prophet Muhammad's (*pbuh*) lifetime cited in the hadith collection *Sahih Bukhari*, which is recognised by Sunni communities as authentic, refers to the establishment of spaces for religious education for women:

> Some women requested the Prophet to fix a day for them as the men were taking all his time. On that he promised them one day for religious lessons and commandments. (Sahih Bukhari vol 1, Bk 3, No. 101)

CLOSING REFLECTIONS

This is interesting – women in early Muslim communities felt marginalised from processes of knowledge acquisition, demanded access and were provided with opportunities to gain knowledge. The women gathered in a house and then Prophet Muhammad (*pbuh*), sent his companion Umar 'ibn al-Khattab to teach women the basis of Islam (Bewley 1999). There is an important gender dynamic in this narrative that highlights women's agency and also their centrality in historical Islamic intellectual traditions, which is somewhat lacking in contemporary contexts (Scott-Baumann and Cheruvallil-Contractor 2015).

This gender dynamic remains crucial to the study of Islam. So, to return to the narrative of the early study of Islam, there are multiple examples of informal schools for Muslims, male and female. As Islam grew and spread outside the Arabian Peninsula, these nascent spaces for the study of Islam were formalised and systemised as new and diverse Muslim communities sought to understand their faith. Inherent to the study of Islam developed in this early era is the lingual, cultural and geographic diversity of these early Muslim communities. New Muslim communities emerged in geographies that stretched from North Africa to Southeast Asia, not all of whom knew Arabic but who were keen to learn, understand and recite the Qur'an; who wanted to know the histories of earlier Muslim communities, and who wanted to intimately know the life history of the Prophet Muhammad (*pbuh*). Motivated by a desire to preserve consistency, accuracy and moral integrity of Islamic teachings in this phase of rapid growth, the study of Islam developed its own methodological, epistemic and pedagogical structures.

The methodological processes that underpinned the collation of hadith, or narratives from the Prophet Muhammad's (*pbuh*) lifetime, is an example of this systematisation and codification of Islamic intellectual traditions. A rigorous process of authentication and validation known as the sciences of hadith classification, or *Mustalah al-hadith*, emerged to ensure the trustworthiness and authenticity of each hadith that was recorded. Similar to contemporary academic settings (in any subject), disagreements about these methodologies existed and prevailed, shaped by early theological, demographic and socio-political contexts. Today, various collections of hadith exist but on the whole Sunni Muslims accept the authenticity of the *Sahih Sitta* or the six 'correct' books of hadith, of which the *Sahih al-Bukhari* and the *Sahih Muslim* are sometimes known as the 'two authentics' (Swarup 2002: 7). Shi'i Muslims have their own books, sometimes called the *Al-Kutub Al-Arb'ah* or 'the four books'. Hadith continue to be studied, debated and critiqued in seminaries and universities in diverse Muslim communities.

The systematisation of Islamic knowledge began in the first four centuries of Islam, which drew strongly on the pre-Islamic, quintessential Arab love of poetry (that is reflected in the melodious recitation of the Qur'an), grammar (to learn a new language), translations and hermeneutics, history (with particular emphasis on prophetic example and collating the Sunnah) and genealogy (Kennedy 2001). After this early systematisation, the diversification continued as new *madhhabs* (schools of thought), denominations, traditions were formed. According to Daftary (2001), by the tenth century the study of Islam had become enriched by the intellectual traditions of a diverse individuals, communities and cultures across the Muslim world. Other areas of study also emerged within these early Muslim traditions, for example, astrophysics and philosophy. Arab and Muslim thinkers in Spanish Andalusia learned, preserved and subsequently developed the thinking and writing of Greek and Roman philosophers and then transmitted this knowledge to European philosophers (Gutas 1998).

Today, the study of Islam has grown into a diverse intellectual tradition that is underpinned by its religious texts and the *urf* (customs) and *adat* (habits) of the various geographical contexts that it inhabits. It encompasses a number of what we today understand as modern academic disciplines, including poetry and literature studies, sociology and lived religion, philosophy and liberal critiques of dogmatic theology and also the physical sciences (Scott-Baumann and Cheruvallil-Contractor 2016). Emphasis within the Qur'an on 'reason' and 'understanding' meant that for the earliest Muslim communities – in Mecca and Medina in the prophetic era – learning and study was a significant aspect of religious life. Islamic intellectual traditions today retain 'a rich heritage of critical education' that it 'shares with Abrahamic faiths' and which comprises 'continuous self-examination, so that the faithful remain balanced in their religious observance', as also discussed by Sidat (Chapter 7) and Mesbahi (Chapter 8) in this volume.[2]

The study of Islam in contemporary seminaries and other Muslim institutions is not without critique. Scholars have written about their partial emphasis on rote learning (Geaves 2015), reduced value allocated to women's studies (Scott-Baumann and Cheruvallil-Contractor 2015), epistemological narrowness (Sidat, Chapter 7, this volume), curricula that do not always respond to contemporary challenges (Gilliat-Ray 2006) and so on. However there is significant good practice among other things around depth and breadth of the curricula, significant attention to language skills (Geaves 2015), and a commitment to inter-faith dialogue that often exceeds that in secular institutions (Scott-Baumann et al. 2020). To conclude this section, although rooted in pious belief and needing improvement on various fronts, there is also sufficient room within traditional Islamic studies for criticality, diversity of expression, intra-religious and inter-school debate.

---

[2] See at: http://www.theguardian.com/education/2016/jan/12/islam-education-extremism-schools-muslim-prevent?CMP=share_btn_tw, last accessed 27 January 2016.

Islamic Studies

In his contribution to this volume, Nielsen (Chapter 2) records the history of the study of Islam in Europe, noting that European responses to Islam are almost as old as Islam itself. This 'European Christian' or 'Western' intellectual engagement with Islam was underpinned by polemical ideas of the 'Other' (Hourani 1991; Nanji 1997; König 2016). These two religions, or indeed intellectual traditions (depending on how you view them), were separated by conflict (including violent conflict, the obvious example of which are the Crusades), but also linked in ways that may be described either as an 'Abrahamic' spiritual kinship (Hourani 1991). According to Hourani, Muslims and Christians:

> presented a religious and intellectual challenge to each other . . . With few exceptions, Christians in Europe who thought about Islam, during the first thousand or so years of the confrontation, did so in a state of ignorance. (Hourani 1991: 8)

As the first translations of the Qur'an into European languages became available in the twelfth century, there was more informed engagement with Islamic texts, at least the Qur'an, and there were a few European schools that rigorously engaged with Islam, although these remained exceptions (König 2016). There was extremely limited knowledge in European contexts of the systematised works of Islamic theology, law or spirituality (Hourani 1991) – the Islamic intellectual frameworks as developed by believers. This blind spot in historical European 'Islamic studies' that failed to recognise Islamic intellectual traditions still continues to pervade some aspects of contemporary Islamic studies and discourses around the academic and confessional study of Islam.

Building on this early European intellectual interest in Islam, Islamic studies emerged in the early modern period as a discipline of European origins and shaped by the polemical encounter between Christianity and Islam (Hourani 1991; Nanji 1997; König 2016). Early Islamic studies was motivated by a missionary zeal both towards Muslims as well as towards Christians living in the Middle East. In his exploration of the seventeenth-century scholar Johann Heinrich Hottinger's contributions to Arabic and Islamic studies (1620–1667), Loop asserts that Hottinger's approach was not historical in the 'modern sense of the word' (Loop 2013: 217). He regarded Islam as the 'arch-heresy' and his study of the history and theology of Islam was to uncover the activity of the Antichrist (Loop 2013: 217). So, rather than being the objective study of a subject, initial European 'Islamic studies' is underpinned by 'the historical marking of Islam as Europe's "other"' (Fadil 2019: 1).

In the twentieth century, this was followed by accusations that the discipline catered to the needs of a colonial and imperialist agenda, dehumanising individual Muslims and rendering invisible Muslim contributions to culture and civilisation. Most notable among these critiques is the seminal work of Edward Said, who criticises Orientalists and their 'othering' of the Orient as exotic, irrational and 'manifestly different' from the Occident (Said 1978: 328). Said's critique is by no means unopposed. Irwin criticises Said's 1978 book as a work of 'malignant charlatanry' (Irwin 2006: 2–3), and Rodinson accuses Said of ignoring the good work of many Orientalists (Rodinson 2002). Nevertheless, Said's critique remains influential. In her exploration of representations of the Orient by women, Reina Lewis concludes that European women travellers (in the Orient) also placed indigenous women either as other and inferior, cruelly repressed or promiscuous. Lewis asserts the need to effectively shift the discursive paradigms that structure our existence (Lewis 1996).

Chapters in this volume cite more recent late twentieth-century/early twenty-first-century developments in European Islamic studies. As noted by Lafrarchi (Chapter 9, this volume), across most European national contexts recent developments in Islamic studies (in particular where it has had governmental support) are underpinned by a policy need to limit radicalisation in Europe and beyond. In this 'new' Islamic studies there is a top-down emphasis on integrating migrant Muslim communities and training 'home-grown' imams or faith leaders. Piela et al. (Chapter 10, this volume), note how Islamic studies in Poland continue to view it through a stereotypical lens, and that the rightward shift in Polish politics makes this narrative difficult to challenge. So, while grounded in the European intellectual principles of post-enlightenment criticality, rigour and the 'secular-neutral university', both historical and contemporary 'Islamic studies' have faced critiques of the polemical otherisation of Islam, of pandering to European imperialist agendas and, most recently, of emphasising the study of Islam through a securitised lens. These critiques undermine ideas of the secular-neutral university and illustrate the epistemic injustice that sometimes pervades Islamic studies.

Beyond Dichotomies: Studying Islam and Islamic Studies

My historical ruminations are undertaken with a view to demonstrating that assumptions about criticality (or the lack of it), insider or outsider status and perception of value are by no means set in stone. Indeed, Dreier (Chapter 6, this volume), shows how the recent increase in Muslim heritage students joining university Islamic studies courses is blurring the boundaries between the confessional and the academic. A challenge that emerges is the distinction between religion and the religiosity of the Muslim scholar that can devalue or cause their scholarship to be excessively interrogated. Indeed, a senior scholar of Islamic studies told me how during their doctoral studies on an aspect of Islamic studies they were asked 'to leave their Islam at home'. Another Islamic feminist scholar spoke about hiding their conversion to Islam for fear of their intellectual output being dismissed by academia. Yet this challenge is also an opportunity to remake disciplinary and positional boundaries and to create spaces for research, teaching and knowledge-production in Islamic studies that bridges this dichotomy, as discussed by Mesbahi (Chapter 8) in this volume. Indeed, as an Islamic studies scholar of Muslim-heritage, my epistemological reliance on feminism (recognition of the hierarchies within knowledge) and pragmatism (foregrounding the significance of experience) has emerged from a need to underline the rigour and criticality of my work, while also giving me intellectual tools to justify my positionality within academic research.

This volume also brings to light the complex and highly localised nature of religion–secular debates in various European contexts, while also highlighting concerns, experiences, opportunities and challenges that are shared across all these contexts. For example, Agai and Engelhardt (Chapter 5, this volume) reflect on the impact of secular–religious debates on contemporary German Islamic studies provision. Hendek (Chapter 11, this volume) considers the Turkish experience of how Islamic studies has been influenced by its changing politics. When read together, these two chapters illustrate the moving goalposts and shifting boundaries between secularism and religiosity debates in Germany and Turkey, respectively. The moving–fluctuating debate brings challenges such as the need to evaluate existing approaches to Islamic studies and the loss of tradition. But the encounter between religious and secular approaches to Islamic studies, when considered sensitively, can also create opportunities to include fresh thinking, content and pedagogies, and inclusive spaces for the study of Islam, as shown by Mesbahi (Chapter 8, this volume).

Other challenges and opportunities emerging from this encounter involve the reshaping of classroom power dynamics. Berkson reflects on the challenges of being a non-Muslim teaching Islam, which can raise issues of authority and authenticity when there are Muslim students in the classroom (Berkson 2005). At the other end, Scott-Baumann et al. (2020) provide an ethnographic account of an Islamic studies class in a UK university to analyse the discursive dynamics at work in Islamic studies classrooms. Their reflections are as follows:

> Muslim sources are posited primarily as the 'object of enquiry', critically examined and their unreliability established. Modern Western scholarship on the Qur'an by historians of Islam is then introduced and validated. Their positivist historical approach is privileged as central to the study of religion. (Scott-Baumann et al. 2020: 170)

European Islamic studies is transcultural both in its primordial roots as well as in its contemporary experiences (König 2016). As more Islamic studies scholars emerge who may be of Muslim-heritage, but more crucially those of any background who are critically aware of the historical and contemporary hierarchies of knowledge, there is greater hope. These scholars can become interlocutors (Ebbiary 2021) between the various cultures – academic and societal – that inform Islamic studies (also Scott-Baumann et al. 2020; Sidat, Chapter 7, this volume). As we assert the politics and processes of Islamic studies we recognise that the boundaries between so-called 'academic' and 'confessional' approaches are fuzzy and permeable. I agree with Gilliat-Ray (Chapter 4, this volume) when she critiques the simplistic use of terms. I quote from her chapter, with a slight (yet important) modification:

> the simplistic use of the terms confessional and non-confessional seems to imply the holding of positions that place ~~individuals~~ disciplines at opposite ends of a spectrum, thus not allowing for the fact that one may adopt stronger or weaker positions in relation to all manner of doctrines or practices. (Gilliat-Ray, Chapter 4, p. 60, this volume)

Ataullah Siddiqui insists upon a need to move away from the study of Islam as something foreign. Instead, he suggests that Islam be studied as a subject that is integral to Britain and to the West (Siddiqui 2007). Scott-Baumann et al. (2020) recommend more dialogical forms of Islamic studies that are multidisciplinary, that recognise the intersectional identities of scholars and the complicated socio-political hierarchies within which we function. My student Hafza Iqbal's scholarship is an exemplar of this approach. She writes as a young woman, a Sufi and a traditionally trained Islamic studies scholar. She writes about Sufism and its changing nature within contemporary Britain, and in doing so draws upon both Western academic writings on Sufism as well as Islamic intellectual treatises on Sufism. More importantly, she draws upon her intimate personal knowledge of the everyday-ness of Sufi practice and the significant conviction that adherents have for their chosen spiritual path. Finally, she borrows methodologies from practical theology (from Christian contexts). Her thesis, successfully defended in December 2022, presents a robust analysis of what it means to be a Sufi in Britain today that is rooted both in Islamic texts and in ethnographic narratives from her fieldwork, effectively straddling the confessional–academic divide. Her research is illustrative of emerging forms of scholarship in the United Kingdom that bring 'confessional' motivations and training into 'academic' scholarship (Iqbal 2023).

Closing Reflections

Conclusion: Beyond Dichotomies in the Study of Islam in Europe

Writing this chapter has been an exercise in reflection: As I continue to reflect, I am reminded of the demographic changes that are afoot across all of Europe, the socio-cultural negotiations that follow, the societal hierarchies that underpin them, and the inevitable impact that these negotiations and societal hierarchies are having on higher education in general and on Islamic studies in particular. These negotiations and the social hierarchies that determine them are at the heart of the confessional–academic debates in Islamic studies in Europe, which are discussed in this volume. The same hierarchies that situate Islam as being foreign to Europe determine what kinds of study or indeed *whose* study is perceived as being confessional or academic. Women's studies and those of other minoritised groups might face further penalties.

To me, having reflected on this debate, there is a great and urgent need within Islamic studies to recognise the impact of these hierarchies. Islamic studies, or for that matter any study, is by no means a neutral endeavour in objective academic research. My feminist epistemology insists that objectivity in research and academic production is nigh impossible. Social hierarchies as articulated in political agendas often determine what is taught in Islamic studies courses, by whom and to whom. Perhaps one way to resolve this debate is to move away from it and instead interrogate the social hierarchies that underpin it. We, and by 'we' I mean academic leaders and thinkers, need to create courses with which all Europeans (Muslim or not) can engage, in ways that are beneficial to all of European society.

Epilogue

As I add finishing touches to this chapter, I am on holiday away from my home in Britain. I am in Belgium, a country that is not too far and in Europe, as well as being the focus of Lafrarchi's chapter in this volume (Chapter 9). Despite the geographical nearness, I am struck by the social, cultural and political differences between both countries. In Britain, despite being a first-generation, South Asian-heritage, unable to speak Arabic Muslim migrant, I feel at home – an insider on many fronts. In Belgium, I am a tourist, I am made welcome but I do not speak the language and use complicated hand gestures for simple questions such as, 'Where in the train station?' – incidentally, a question that is of existential significance to a lost tourist. Society in Belgium is different and I am somewhat of a linguistic aberration disturbing the flow of people, their words and their worlds. I encounter people in Belgium who are Muslim like me, but who, unlike me, are Belgian, who are fluent in French or German, who often also speak a dialect of Arabic and who are inherently at home in Belgium.

When I visit a mosque in Belgium, I am simultaneously an insider – on account of my visible Muslimness – and an outsider, who does not speak the congregation's language and who is culturally different. My difference is visible too and an elderly female congregant asks me where I am from, as the rest of the congregation leans forward, curious to know my answer.

As I continue my travels, I explore the historic streets of Ghent and pass by its university, established in 1817, when Ghent, Belgium and indeed Europe were very different places. Ghent University offers a well-received Bachelor degree in Oriental languages and cultures. On its website, the course title is followed by a description in parenthesis that says 'Arabic and Islamic Studies'.[3] So, at least linguistically, Islamic studies is signposted on a student-facing website as something that is foreign, and which comes from the Orient or the East.

As I continue to edit this chapter, I was reminded of the young French-speaking, Belgian Muslim woman, who showed me the way to the train station. She was bemused by my inability to speak either French or Arabic, and perhaps also by my hand gestures. I wonder what she would perceive of Ghent University's equation of her Belgian Islamic faith and her Arabic lingual heritage as things that are foreign, from far away and not from Belgium. I also wonder what she would make of the discussions in this volume. I cannot claim to speak for her, but I feel she would be bemused by our ruminations that are essentially about her identity, something that comes naturally to her as she fluidly slips between and negotiates the various aspects of her intersectional identity as a Belgian, a Muslim and a woman. Perhaps the future of Islamic studies will be determined by this dexterity of European youth, Muslim or not (some of whom will be the next generation of Islamic studies scholars), to navigate intellectual, personal and political positionalities.

References

Allen, C. (2017). 'Islamophobia and the Problematization of Mosques: A Critical Exploration of Hate Crimes and the Symbolic Function of "Old" and "New" Mosques in the United Kingdom', *Journal of Muslim Minority Affairs* 37(3): 294–308.

Ammerman, N. T. (2010). 'The Challenges of Pluralism: Locating Religion in a World of Diversity', *Social Compass* 57(2): 154–67.

Berkson, M. (2005). 'A Non-Muslim Teaching Islam: Pedagogical and Ethical Challenges. Teaching', *Theology & Religion* 8: 86–98.

Bewley, A. (1999). *Islam: The Empowering of Women*. London: Ta-Ha Publishers.

Cheruvallil-Contractor, S. (2012). *Muslim Women in Britain: Demystifying the Muslimah*. London: Routledge.

---

[3] See at: https://studiekiezer.ugent.be/bachelor-of-arts-in-oriental-languages-and-cultures-arabic-and-islamic-studies/2022.

Cheruvallil-Contractor, S. (2018). 'The Right to be Human: How do Muslim Women Talk about Human Rights and Religious Freedoms in Britain?' *Religion and Human Rights* 13: 49–75.

Cheruvallil-Contractor, S., P. Weller and K. Purdam (2021). 'Much More than a Negation of Religion: A Qualitative Exploration of the Diversity of Non-religious Identity in England and Wales', *Journal of Contemporary Religion* 36(2): 329–48.

Daftary, F. (2001). 'Preface', in F. Daftary (ed.), *Intellectual Traditions in Islam*. London: I. B. Tauris, pp. xi–xii.

Ebbiary, A. (2021). 'From Subjects to Interlocutors: Muslims in the Margins and the Academy', presented at the Religious Diversity and the Secular University, Cambridge, 8 July.

Fadil, N. (2019). 'The Anthropology of Islam in Europe: A Double Epistemological Impasse', *Annual Review of Anthropology* 48: 117–32.

Gale, R. and P. Hopkins (2009). 'Introduction: Muslims in Britain – Race, Place and the Spatiality of Identities', in P. Hopkins and R. Gale (eds), *Muslims in Britain: Race, Place and Identities*. Edinburgh: Edinburgh University Press.

Geaves, R. (2015). 'An Exploration of the Viability of Partnership between dar al-ulum and Higher Education Institutions in North West England Focusing upon Pedagogy and Relevance', *British Journal of Religious Education* 37(1): 64–82.

Gilliat-Ray, S. (2006). 'Educating the ʿUlama: Centres of Islamic Religious Training in Britain', *Islam and Christian–Muslim Relations* 17(1): 55–76.

Gutas, D. (1998). *Greek Thought, Arabic Culture: The Graeco-Arabic Translation Movement in Baghdad and Early 'Abbasaid Society (2nd–4th/5th–10th c.) (Arabic Thought and Culture)*. London: Routledge.

Hourani, A. (1991). *A History of the Arab Peoples*. London: Faber & Faber.

Iqbal, H. (2023). 'Sufi Hybrids: Audience, Evolution and Development of British Sufism', unpublished PhD dissertation, Coventry University.

Irwin, R. (2007). *For Lust of Knowing: The Orientalists and Their Enemies*. London: Penguin.

Kahf, M. (1999). *Western Representations of the Muslim Woman: From Termagant to Odalisque*. Texas: University of Texas Press.

Kennedy, H. (2001). 'Intellectual Life in the First Four Centuries of Islam', in F. Daftary (ed.), *Intellectual Traditions in Islam*. London: I. B. Tauris, pp. 17–30.

König, D. G. (2016). 'Islamic Studies: A Field of Research under Transcultural Crossfire', *Transcultural Studies* 2016(2): 101–35.

Kundnani, A. (2014). *The Muslims are Coming! Islamophobia, Extremism, and the Domestic War on Terror*. London: Verso.

Lewis, R. (1996). *Gendering Orientalism: Race, Femininity and Representation*. London: Routledge.

Loop, J. (2013). *Johann Heinrich Hottinger: Arabic and Islamic Studies in the Seventeenth Century*. Oxford: Oxford University Press.

Malik, M. (2013). *Anti-Muslim Prejudice: Past and Present*. London: Taylor & Francis.

Morey, P. and A. Yaqin (2011). *Framing Muslims: Stereotyping and Representation after 9/11*. Berlin: De Gruyter.

Mukadam, M., A. Scott-Baumann, S. Cheruvallil-Contractor and A. Chowdhury (2010). *Muslim Faith Leader Training: An Independent Review*. London: Department of Communities and Local Government, available at: https://assets.publishing.service.gov.uk/government/uploads/system/uploads/attachment_data/file/6155/1734121.pdf.

Mythen, G., S. Walklate and F. Khan (2009). 'I'm a Muslim, but I'm not a Terrorist': Victimization, Risky Identities and the Performance of Safety', *British Journal of Criminology* 49(6): 736–54.

Nanji, A. (1997). *Mapping Islamic Studies: Genealogy, Continuity, and Change*. Berlin: Mouton de Gruyter.

Nurein, S. and H. Iqbal (2021). 'Identifying a Space for Young Black Muslim Women in Contemporary Britain', *Ethnicities* 21(3): 433–53.

Purvis, J. (1995). 'From "Women Worthies" to Poststructuralism? Debate and Controversy in Women's History in Britain', in J. Purvis (ed.), *Women's History: Britain, 1850–1945: An Introduction*. London: Routledge, pp. 1–22.

Rodinson, M. (2002). *Europe and the Mystique of Islam*. London: I. B. Tauris.

Rose, G. (1997). 'Situating Knowledges: Positionality, Reflexivities and Other Tactics', *Progress in Human Geography* 21(3): 305–20.

Said, E. (1978). *Orientalism: Western Conceptions of the Orient*. New York: Pantheon.

Schirin, A. (2005). 'Muslim Challenges to the Secular Consensus: A German Case Study', *Journal of Contemporary European Studies* 13(3): 267–86.

Scott-Baumann, A. and S. Cheruvallil-Contractor (2015). *Islamic Education in Britain: New Pluralist Paradigms*. London: Continuum.

Scott-Baumann, A. and S. Cheruvallil-Contractor (2016). 'An Islamic Perspective', in S. Heap (ed.), *The Universities We Need: Theological Perspectives*. London: Routledge, pp. 124–42.

Scott-Baumann, A., M. Guest, S. Naguib, S. Cheruvallil-Contractor and A. Phoenix (2020). *Islam on Campus: Contested Identities and the Cultures of Higher Education*. Oxford: Oxford University Press.

Siddiqui, A. (2007). *Islam at Universities in England: Meeting the Needs and Investing in the Future*, available at: http://www.mihe.org.uk/the-siddiqui-report, last accessed 27 January 2016.

Sultana, F. (2007). 'Reflexivity, Positionality and Participatory Ethics: Negotiating Fieldwork Dilemmas in International Research', *ACME: An International Journal for Critical Geographies* 6(3): 374–85.

Swarup, R. (2002). *Understanding the Hadith: The Sacred Traditions of Islam*. New York: Prometheus.

Index

Note that universities are listed under their place names

Afghanistan, 183, 188, 189, 193
Alevi, 27, 97, 202, 219
Amsterdam, Free University of, 22–3
Ankara University, 208–9
Aoude, Safia, 39–40
Arabic, 15, 16–17, 24–5, 37, 62, 71, 81–2, 84, 99, 117, 119, 123, 136–7, 183, 192, 211, 215, 227, 229, 233–4
Atatürk, Kemal, 94, 214, 217
Austria, 20–1, 24, 27, 84, 93

Belgium, 20–1, 24, 151–70, 233–4
Blair, Tony, 19
Bosnia, 21, 71, 80, 92n, 93
Britain, 15–16, 18–20, 21, 25, 28–31, 55–6, 59, 110–24, 130–46, 223, 232, 233–4; *see also* United Kingdom
British Association of Islamic Studies, 7

Cambridge Muslim College, 95, 121
Cambridge University, 15, 16–17, 19
Cape Town University, 35, 43n
Cardiff University, 56, 62, 65
Catholic Church, 5, 8, 27, 29, 72, 74–5, 98, 154, 162, 178, 180–1, 187, 190, 194

Centre for the Advanced Study of the Arab World, 19
chaplaincy, 2, 62, 119, 122, 137, 162
Christian, 2, 4–5, 9, 22, 27–8, 37–9, 43, 55–6, 66, 71, 73–4, 80–2, 85–6, 100, 116–17, 129–30, 132, 180, 181, 184, 185–6, 190, 192, 204–5, 219, 229, 232
Collège de France, 15
Copenhagen University, 21–3, 36, 38, 40
counter-radicalisation, 6, 8, 38, 69, 153–6, 158, 162–6, 168–9
curriculum, 19, 32, 35, 40, 42, 43–6, 54–5, 67, 74, 86, 97, 115–16, 133, 135, 137, 139, 145, 157–8, 161, 167, 180–1, 182, 195, 202, 206, 210–11, 215, 228

Denmark, 4, 21–2, 37–8, 95
Deobandi, 7, 19, 111, 116, 136
distance learning, 66, 202, 206, 215–16, 218, 219
Diyanet İşlesi Başkanlığı, 24, 86; *see also* Presidency of Religious Affairs
Durham University, 17, 20

École des langues orientales vivantes, 15
Edinburgh University, 17, 19, 25

Index

Erzurum University, 209
Executive of Muslims in Belgium (EMB), 8, 154–65, 167–9
Exeter University, 20
extremism (Islamic), 1, 3, 65, 151–3, 166

Foreign and Commonwealth Office, 17
France, 5, 21, 25, 77, 93, 130, 162

Germany, 6, 7, 21, 23–4, 29, 41, 69–88, 92–105, 118, 231
Goldsmiths University, 43
Goldziher, Ignaz, 15

hadith, 28, 60, 81, 84–6, 115, 123, 191, 194, 206, 211, 213, 226–7
Huntington, Samuel, 183, 186–8
Hurgronje, Snouck, 15

imam training, 4, 5, 15, 20–4, 70, 79, 86, 93–5, 117, 137, 153, 157, 162–3, 168, 212–14, 218, 230
INHOLLAND University, 22–3
Institute for the Study of Islam in the Modern World (ISIM), 23
Islamophobia, 1, 8, 177, 179–81, 185–6, 194–5
Istanbul, 206, 209

Jagiellonian University, 183

Kalisch, Muhammad Sven, 27
Küng, Hans, 27

laicism *see* secularism
Leiden University, 15, 22, 25, 39–40
Łódź University, 183
Louvain, Université Catholique de, 21

madrasa, 8, 110–24, 133, 203, 205–7, 212, 215–19
Manchester University, 17
Middle East Centre for Arab Studies (MECAS), 17
Moroccan, 20, 156

Muhammad, Prophet, 27–8, 226, 227
Münster University, 23, 27, 41, 78, 82

Netherlands, 22, 24–5, 29, 39, 93, 95
North-Rhine Westphalia, 23

Osnabrück University, 77, 86, 94n
Ottoman Empire, 203, 206–7
Oxford Centre for Islamic Studies (OCIS), 20
Oxford University, 15, 16–17, 20, 35

Parker Report, 17
Persian, 12, 16, 25, 113
Poland, 8, 178–95, 230
Presidency of Religious Affairs, 207, 209, 212, 214, 219; *see also* Diyanet İşlesi Başkanlığı

Qur'an/Qur'anic, 24, 28, 62, 74, 81–2, 84, 86, 99, 100–1, 123, 132, 134–8, 141, 190, 194, 208, 211–13, 227–9, 231

radicalisation, 2, 7, 21, 26, 64, 81, 152–4, 168–9, 216, 230
Raza, Muhammad, 20
Reay Report, 16
Rotterdam, Islamic University of, 22–3

Sacy, Silvestre de, 15
Said, Edward, 164, 184n, 186
Saudi Arabia, 21, 167, 192, 224
Scarborough Report, 17
School of Oriental and African Studies (SOAS), 17, 20
secularism, 84, 130, 203, 207, 231
seminary, 2, 3, 5, 6–7, 10, 18, 28–9, 53–5, 61–7, 75, 84, 93, 110, 116, 117, 132, 205–6, 208, 213, 219–20, 227–8
Shia, 7, 83, 97, 224
Siddiqui, Ataullah, 18–20, 544, 131–2, 232
Sufi, 81, 113–14, 116, 192, 194, 232

Index

Sunni, 7, 27, 78, 83, 97, 114, 136, 137, 139–40, 192, 194, 202, 219, 224, 226–7
Sweden, 4, 21
Swiss, 22

ibn Talal, Walid, 19
terrorism, 2–3, 7–8, 17, 71, 118, 151–3, 162–3, 166, 168, 183, 185–7, 188–9, 193–4, 224
Tübingen University, 27, 77, 82
Turkey, 5, 8, 21, 25, 70, 80, 86, 192, 202–20, 231
Turkish/Turks, 8, 20, 23–5, 71, 78, 81, 156, 192, 202–20, 231

United Kingdom (UK), 3, 6, 7, 9–10, 16, 36, 45–6, 54, 65, 95, 118, 121, 131n, 184, 203–5, 226, 231–2
University College London (UCL), 35, 43n, 45
Urdu, 25, 112n, 117

Vienna University, 21

Warsaw University, 183
Watt, W. M., 25
women, 1, 3, 7, 8, 18, 28, 42, 44, 87, 97, 100, 101, 122, 165, 168, 183, 185–7, 190–2, 224–5, 226–7, 228, 230, 232–3, 234

EU representative:
Easy Access System Europe
Mustamäe tee 50, 10621 Tallinn, Estonia
Gpsr.requests@easproject.com

www.ingramcontent.com/pod-product-compliance
Lightning Source LLC
Chambersburg PA
CBHW070325240426
43671CB00013BA/2368